MW00343539

Social Creativity
Volume 1

Perspectives on Creativity
Mark A. Runco (ed.)

Social Creativity
Volume 1

edited by

Alfonso Montuori
California Institute of Integral Studies

Ronald E. Purser
San Francisco State University

HAMPTON PRESS, INC.
CRESSKILL, NEW JERSEY

Copyright © 1999 by Hampton Press, Inc.

All rights reserved. No part of this publication may be reproduced, stored in a retrieval system, or transmitted in any form or by any means, electronic, mechanical, photocopying, microfilming, recording, or otherwise, without permission of the publisher.

Printed in the United States of America

Library of Congress Cataloging-in-Publication Data

Social creativity / edited by Alfonso Montuori, Ronald E. Purser.
     p. cm. -- (Perspectives on creativity)
    Includes bibliographical references and indexes.
    ISBN 1-57273-128-1 (v. 1). -- ISBN 1-57273-129-X (v. 1 : pbk.). --
  ISBN 1-57273-130-3 (v. 2). -- ISBN 1-57273-131-1 (v. 2 : pbk.)
    1. Creative ability. 2. Creative ability--Social aspects.
  3. Creative ability in business. I. Montuori, Alfonso.
  II. Purser, Ronald E., 1958-   III. Series
  BF408.S55   1998
  153.3'5--dc21   98-35126
                                    CIP

Hampton Press, Inc.
23 Broadway
Cresskill, NJ 07626

Contents

Acknowledgments

Alfonso Montuori would like to thank Gianluca Bocchi, Mauro Ceruti, Allan Combs, Isabella Conti, Riane Eisler, Heinz von Foerster, Ervin Laszlo, David Loye, Edgar Morin, and Telmo Pievani.

About the Contributors

Alfonso Montuori. California Institute of Integral Studies, 1453 Mission Street, San Francisco, CA 94103

Ronald E. Purser. San Francisco State University, College of Business, 1600 Holloway Avenue, San Francisco, CA 94132

* * * * * * * * * *

Frank J. Barrett. Department of Management Systems, Naval Postgraduate School, Monterey, CA 93940

Frank Barron. University of California-Santa Cruz, 206 Florence Drive, Aptos, CA 95003

Morris Berman. 8015 Greenwood Avenue North 305, Seattle, WA 98103

Mary Catherine Bateson. Spelman College, Campus Box 293, 350 Spelman Lane, Atlanta, GA 30314

Vilmos Csányi. Department of Ethology, L. Eötvös University, H-2131 Göd, Jávorka S. u. 14, Hungary

Mihály Csikszentmihályi. University of Chicago, Department of Psychology, 5841 South Maryland Avenue, MC-2050, Chicago, IL 60637

Richard Kearney. University College Dublin, Department of Philosophy, Belfield, Dublin 4, Ireland

Ervin Laszlo. General Evolution Research Group, Vila Franatoni, 56040 Montescudaio (Pisa), Italy

Carol A. Mockros. Milken Family Foundation, 1250 Fourth Street, Second Floor, Santa Monica, CA 90401

James Ogilvy. Global Business Network, P.O. Box 8395, Emeryville, CA 94662

Mark A. Runco. California State University-Fullerton, EC 105, Fullerton, CA 92634

Dean Keith Simonton. University of California, Department of Psychology, Davis, CA 95616

Tony Stigliano. Saybrook Institute, 450 Pacific Street, Third Floor, San Francisco, CA 94133

Social Creativity:
Introduction*†

Alfonso Montuori
Ronald E. Purser

For the purposes of empirical research, Stein (1963) defined creativity as a "process which results in a novel work that is accepted as tenable or useful or satisfying by a group at some point in time" (p. 218). This definition has remained useful and current in creativity research, while capturing some crucial elements of the more popular understanding of creativity with such terms as process, novelty, and social acceptance. Over the years, however, the term creativity itself has become rather problematic: Torrance (1988) argued that "it defies precise definition" (p. 43) and Stein himself (1983) asked whether in some cases it has not become devoid of meaning altogether.

In recent years, criticisms of established forms of creativity research have surfaced in the literature (Conrad, 1990; Csikszentmihályi, 1990). Likewise, criticisms of the way creativity is conceptualized in our social and academic discourse have emerged as a result of the "postmodern debate," with a particular emphasis on the "deconstruction" of terms such as genius, originality, and progress (Attali, 1985; Barthes, 1977; Gablik,

*The authors wish to acknowledge Susan Hales and Tony Stigliano, of Saybrook Institute, for their ongoing dialogue on the social construction of the self and creativity, during which many of these ideas began to take shape. Our thanks to Charles Webel, also of Saybrook Institute, for his careful reading of the manuscript and his helpful suggestions.

†Footnotes followed by an asterisk (*) indicate extensive further discussions of systems theory's applications to creativity research.

1

1991; Kearney, 1988; Vattimo, 1985). Related criticisms that social science in general, and creativity research by implication, is ethnocentric and gender-biased have also gained prominence (Code, 1991; Sampson, 1993). (These criticisms will be explored extensively in the forthcoming volumes.) Postmodern sensibilities are visible not just in academia, but also in the practices of many artists (Gablik, 1984, 1991; Jencks, 1989; Norris & Benjamin, 1988). The implications of this problematization of the term creativity are far from clear, but certainly suggest a need to question and discuss our fundamental cultural and methodological assumptions about the phenomenon we call creativity.

We are approaching this problematization of creativity through an exploration of the context in which both the practices and discourse of creativity emerge. Our focus in this series has been shaped by several questions: (a) the importance of investigating group and social creativity as it manifests itself in collaborative creative activities in theater and musical performances, research and development laboratories, organizations, and communities; (b) the role of social, cultural, and historical factors in defining the discourse of creativity; (c) the way in which these factors have either inhibited or encouraged the practices that come under the heading of creativity; (d) how our understanding and definition of creativity and the creative process might change given a perspective that includes social factors; and (e) an exploration into the reasons why, until recently, social phenomena have largely been considered peripheral to the investigation of creativity, both in terms of methodology and larger cultural and intellectual traditions.

Volume 1 addresses general and interdisciplinary issues such as the social construction of creativity in history, the social construction of creative individuals, and the relevance of new philosophical and methodological approaches to creativity. Volume 2 focuses on creativity as a social phenomenon in organizations, with contributions from leading figures in the now extensive management literature. In Volumes 3 and 4, cultural and political factors and issues of social creativity in the arts and communities are addressed, with particular reference to issues of gender.

THE ORIGINS OF THIS PROJECT

This project was spawned by questions that initially arose largely out of the editors' personal experience, and out of our discussions with colleagues in the worlds of academia, business, and the arts. It reflects our need to understand problems that comprise a part of the everyday world of artists, academics, and businesspersons, along with our attempts to find ways of formulating those questions in an academic framework.

The senior editor has performed extensively as a professional musician, and is still actively performing and involved in the field. This experience provided the first impulse for an exploration of creativity as a social phenomenon, particularly because an overview of the creativity literature showed a dearth of research on the social dimensions of creativity such as creative groups in the performing arts, and a strong emphasis on individuals of genius working in relative isolation.

Musical performance in a band can be an enormously rewarding experience: One realizes that it is possible to do far more together than alone, because the music is an emergent property of the relationships in the group. The organic nature of musical groups can ideally create a situation where the collaboration is enormously enriching, and the music emerges out of the constant interplay of musicians rehearsing, performing, and recording.[1] The kind of sensitivity required for chamber music is one of many further possible examples, and jazz in particular illustrates the collaborative nature of this process, both in terms of the interplay during performance and in the way the characteristics of individual musicians contribute to the whole sound of the band (Gioia, 1988; Leonard, 1987).

In order for a working musician to perform with others, whether live or on a recording, there are numerous steps that involve collaboration and potentially conflict with others. One's relationship to one's fellow musicians, the level of rapport, compatibility, skills, and the ensuing interpersonal dynamics can make all the difference between a good and a bad performance. Working with others can be the source of much joy and creativity. We have probably all had the experience of finding a colleague or a group of people with whom we feel we somehow resonate, where dialogue seems enriching and creativity blossoms: Ideas are thrown back and forth, conversations spark new lines of thought, with each person adding his or her own perspective and area of expertise.[2] Interpersonal relations, however, can also doom many creative projects, and indeed it was the senior editor's experience of seeing his own band torn apart at the height of its success by bickering and squabbles that led him to study both the "positive" and "negative" aspects of the social dimensions of creativity.

Intragroup relations are not the only social factors affecting a career in the music world. The relationship between musicians and critics, the recording industry, and the public is a crucial factor of not only one's success or lack of it, but also of the quality and nature of the creative process. The resources available, ranging from venues where one can perform to the availability of recording studios to opportunities for distribution of product to the level of financial backing and independence one enjoys, and the role of market forces (discussed by Stigliano in this volume) are constantly on the mind of the performers. They do not determine, but certainly affect the creative person, process, and product. These factors produce certain constraints and possibilities that profoundly affect the creative process, if the latter is defined more broadly to include social interactions, a position on which there is no consensus in the literature.

Many creative activities today involve social and collaborative processes, from artists and technicians working together in theater groups and movie productions to scientists working in laboratories. Both artists and scientists work within the context of larger forces that include the world of business, and also esthetic, social, economic, and political trends that profoundly affect the direction of their creativity. It seems to us that these social processes need to be understood, because this is surely relevant to the experience of creative persons.[3]

Returning to the example of musical performance, a lack of available performance spaces can obviously severely constrain a musician's ability to work. If there are no venues, one must either create them, encourage others to do so, or move to a location where they are available. If there are no venues in a particular city, young people will not be exposed to live music, and will find little outlet should they decide to form a band.

The senior editor's experience in London during the late 1970s and early 1980s (Montuori, 1993) dramatically showed how social and economic conditions have a profound impact on musical creativity (cf. Hebdige, 1979). In the early and mid-1970s, large corporate record companies such as EMI had control over the popular music industry, defining who would and would not get a recording contract. A typical catch-22 situation inhibited the growth of new potential: In order to get a recording contract, one had to be seen performing live, and in order to perform live club owners insisted on showcasing only bands with recording contracts.

Partly in a reaction against the monopoly of corporate record companies, the "punk" revolution of 1976 led to the emergence of numerous independent record companies and distributors, which ensured that more bands could make themselves heard. A host of small and cheap recording studios sprouted all over London to meet the demand for low-budget demo tapes and other recording projects. New clubs and other venues appeared, willing to showcase unknown bands. Musicians from all over England traveled down to London, or started up their own scene in other cities. Independent distribution networks where set up to ensure the new recordings where available in record stores. A direct result of this was the "second British invasion" of America, with bands such as the Sex Pistols and the Clash, and later Elvis Costello and Joe Jackson. Despite the fact that the large corporate record companies eventually reestablished their dominance by absorbing the independents, this period has influenced popular music very strongly well into the 1990s not merely in terms of musical performance, but also by providing a model for the reemergence of independent record companies and distribution systems.

London was, and still is, a powerful attractor for musicians all over the world. Clearly most people would be hard-pressed to compare this episode to Florence in the Renaissance, Periclean Athens, or Vienna at the turn of the century, but undoubtedly something was going on that might be called a brief "creative outburst." This episode also points to the fact that there are certain historical periods and places which seem to be associated with creativity. It suggests to us the need to develop an understanding of how social environments can promote or inhibit creativity, and, of course, how our definition of creativity determines our selection of exemplars.

Much research has focused on finding and encouraging creative individuals, but considerably less has looked at how social factors can promote creativity for all (Barron & Harrington, 1981; Montuori & Purser, 1995; Stein, 1983). This question has great relevance for education, organizations, and collaborative creative processes in general, ranging from colossal movie productions to the fostering of creativity in families and communities. It also affects those whose creative work is typically performed alone, such as writers: if there is no "market," and there are no traditions, no mentors, no publishers willing to invest in new talent, no experiences to draw on, the conditions will simply not be right for creative writers to blossom. The social and economic climate may indeed be limiting or encouraging the potential for individuals to become creative, again if we assume that creativity is not simply a function of innate ability and/or purely intrapsychic processes but is also the product of interactions that can both inhibit and foster creativity.

Our own experience consulting with large corporations has shown that despite a strong interest in the cognitive aspects of the creative process, most people working in organizations are confronted with very complex bureaucratic worlds, and it is not enough for them to simply generate new ideas for products or processes. A lot of other "messy" variables come into play, having to do with bureaucratic obstacles, the nature of the organizational culture, power dynamics, the economic climate, and so forth. We have repeatedly heard from individuals, including top industrial researchers (Purser & Montuori, 1995), whose problem was not generating creative ideas, but being allowed to do something with them. If organizations are not set up to encourage creativity and innovation, individuals arguably suffer—as do the organizations, eventually (see Volume 2, this series).

Putting creativity to work means dealing with the constraints and possibilities of the larger social systems in which we live. In order for creative individuals and groups to thrive these social factors need to be considered. The creative process, we would argue, also extends beyond intrapsychic processes to issues of resources, political and organizational constraints, and all the other factors that come into play when we try to make our visions a reality.

Academics are also subject to the vagaries of intellectual and economic fads and funding agencies, which can considerably affect both the direction of creative work and the opportunities available. If the intellectual climate, funding agencies, university departments, and academic publishers do not encourage certain research avenues, some researchers will find there is simply no room for their work.

Another significant example of the way social forces affect creativity (and discourages collaborative creative efforts) is the way coauthored papers are generally not viewed as examples of the ability of the authors to collaborate, but at times actively penalized as indications that the authors somehow could not manage on their own. In a culture that orients primarily to individual achievement, with reward systems in place that recognize individual but not team efforts (a fact of life in the academy, industry, science, and even architecture and the fashion industry), there will be little encouragement for people to learn how to work together cooperatively or, for that matter, explore the nature of cooperative enterprises.

Should these social factors be included in discussions of the creative process? This question is the subject of an emerging debate in the literature (e.g., Csikszentmihályi, 1988, 1990; Montuori & Purser, 1995; Stigliano, this volume; Runco, this volume). "Social" issues clearly affect, and are in turn influenced by, the psychology of individuals. Some researchers even take the position that a clear differentiation between the psychological or intrapsychic sphere and the social and cultural sphere is simply not possible, given the "social construction of the self" (e.g., Gergen, 1985, 1991; Hales, 1986; Sampson, 1993; Spiro, 1951). Systems theory, social constructionism, hermeneutics, and other approaches hint at the possibilities of exploring the social dimensions of creativity while raising important issues of a philosophical and methodological nature concerning the relationship between self and society, the nature of cognition, and the legitimacy of the very categories we use to describe and differentiate self and society, raising the question, Are disciplinary categories (e.g., psychology, sociology) blinding us to the realities of our experience (Csikszentmhalyi, 1988; Stein, 1963)? What has fallen between the cracks? How might we best study complex phenomena in a contextual perspective without becoming victims to a tendency for overgeneralized abstractions, misplaced encyclopedism, and an inability to translate our thought into research programs?

We would argue that interpersonal, social, and economic questions are not only of great relevance to our *understanding* of creativity as a larger, social and historical phenomenon, but can have direct influence on the *potential* of individuals to be creative, on the *reception* of works, and on the *direction* of their creative efforts. It follows that we should begin to focus also on the nature of environments that foster creativity. Perhaps we can speak of a *plurality of creative processes*, depending on our scope, our system definition.[4] Creativity can be viewed in terms of genetics, brain functions, personality factors, interpersonal relations, cultural forces, and so forth. A contextual view, drawing on new methodological approaches outlined by some of the contributors to this series, would recognize the interaction of all (or at least some) of these factors without attempting to be exhaustive or totalizing, but avoiding the pitfalls of reductionism (Luhmann, 1990; Morin, 1983, 1992).

In this series we are therefore interested in individuals, groups, and communities operating in their social, political, and economic contexts, along with the larger philosophical, methodological, and theoretical problem of the differentiation between social and personal, external and internal, what is necessary and unnecessary to our understanding of creativity, and the whole issue of the role of environments in fostering or suppressing creativity.

CREATIVITY RESEARCH

The initial thrust of creativity research focused on identifying the personality traits and cognitive styles of creative people and on developing tools for stimulating individual creativity (Barron & Harrington, 1981; Woodman & Schoenfeldt, 1990). Surveying the field, Mockros and Csikszentmihályi (this volume) wrote:

> Researchers who study creativity often concede that cultural norms and practices influence the development and expression of creativity. Nevertheless, the magnitude of the impact of such forces have on expression of ability and creativity is generally underestimated. For the most part, attention is focused on how cognitive factors, or other individual characteristics such as personality, values, problem-finding orientation, and motivation, contribute to the appearance of creativity and eminence. Such an orientation only peripherally addresses issues related

to how historical, social, and cultural environments impact various life
experiences and expressions of creativity. (p. 179)

However, new perspectives and research voices in psychology and the
human sciences are beginning to emerge with direct relevance to effecting
changes in our view of creativity. It should be remembered that these efforts
themselves do not appear *ex nihilo*, and have illustrious antecedents in the
earlier creativity literature.

As early as 1955, Barron wrote:

> The psychological conditions which make a society or an epoch
> consistently creative have been little studied, but it seems that social
> conditions analogous to those seen in individual creativity are important.
> Freedom of expression and movement, lack of fear of dissent and
> contradiction, a willingness to break with custom, a spirit of play as well
> as of dedication to work, purpose on a grand scale; these are some of the
> attributes which a creative entity, whether vast or tiny, can be expected to
> have. (p. 485)

In 1963, Stein stated:

> Creativity is the resultant of *processes of social transaction*. Individuals
> affect and are affect by the environments in which they live. They do not
> interact with their environments without changes occurring in both
> directions. The early childhood family environment transaction
> predisposes the individual to creativity or sets up intrapsychic barriers to
> creativity. Later, adult environment transactions similarly encourage or
> inhibit creativity. (p. 218)

Stein (1953) had already pointed out the mutually causal nature of
interactions between persons and their environment, whereby changes
occur in both, rather than simply going one way.[5] His statement also
suggested the need to study interactions throughout the lifespan.

Barnett (1953) also tackled the issue of the relationship between
individual and society in the creative process, arguing for a
sociopsychological approach not unlike Stein's. He wrote:

> Every innovation is a combination of ideas. The only bonds between its
> parts in a cultural setting are mental connections; they are instituted with
> the first individual mind to envisage them, and they dissolve with the last
> individual mind to retain a recollection of them. The mental content is
> socially defined; its substance is, in major part, dictated by tradition. But
> the manner of treating this content, of grasping it, altering it, and
> reordering it, is inevitably dictated by the potentialities and the liabilities
> of the machine which does the manipulating; namely, the individual mind.
> (p. 16)

Barnett's work focused specifically on innovation as the basis for cultural change, which he described as:

> at once a psychical and cultural phenomenon, because the content of a thought predisposes the part it will play with respect to others. Its custom-determined substance will determine just which one of the possible mental reaction patterns it will provoke. Understood in this way, there can be no legitimate distinction between the psychological and the cultural approaches to the problem of cultural change. (p. 16)

Barnett's work is relevant also because his emphasis on the larger social and cultural implications of creativity and innovation allows us to see the creative process from a broader perspective, embedded in a mutually casual relationship in which numerous forces, both psychological and cultural, are at work. Despite this early interest, and the extensive work of researchers such as Barron and Stein, it was only in the late 1980s that interest in the social dimensions of creativity really took hold.

In order to place the concept of social creativity in its sociohistorical context, we summarize a selection of the relevant research. The first researcher to study genius systematically, Francis Galton (1869), was already severely criticized by Charles Horton Cooley, William James (1927), and the philosopher John Robertson (1937), all of whom felt that Galton was not taking the social and economic environment into consideration. For them, genius did not appear regardless of circumstance, as Galton stated. Robertson stressed that "genius is conditioned economically, morally, and socially" (p. 654), and went on to write that individualistic societies, so often credited with creating conditions favoring the survival of the fittest in the intellectual as well as in the physical life, are seen rather to have fixed conditions that theoretically are perhaps the least favorable to a maximum development of potential mental faculties.

Robertson (1937) pointed out that a predominant number of creative individuals arose either from the leisure classes or were in some other way economically privileged, and an enormous waste of creative talent in the lower classes was being perpetuated by the belief that genius would emerge no matter what the conditions. The political implications of this issue are, of course, considerable. If one assumes that genius emerges no matter what, little if any attention has to be paid to creating a supportive environment, and education or social welfare really make no difference. The argument that poor people are not as creative or successful because of "character deficiencies" such as laziness, stupidity (low I.Q.), genetic "inferiority," and so forth follows rather too easily from the position that creativity is a god-given or genetic talent, which emerges no matter what the social conditions. It also justifies providing superior educational experiences for the rich and gifted, because they are "fit" to benefit from them, and inferior ones to the poor, because presumably they are determined to stay poor and unimaginative anyway (cf. Stein, 1983). And if perchance they are really brilliant, they will surmount all obstacles. This debate is no mere historical curiosity, because it resurfaced quite prominently in the *New York Times Magazine*'s October 9, 1994 cover story profiling Charles Murray, a conservative social scientist who wants to abolish welfare on the basis of research on I.Q., genetics, and economics.

So this initial debate between some giants of American and English intellectual history squarely sets the tone for the discussion of social creativity by addressing not simply methodological or theoretical issue, but also its moral, political, social, and economic implications. Psychologists have therefore not entirely neglected the social aspects of creativity, as we have already stated. The 1963 volume *Scientific Creativity*, for example, edited by psychologists Calvin Taylor and Frank Barron, contains extensive discussions of environments that foster creativity, with specific reference to scientific research and R&D laboratories, including a chapter by the philosopher of science Thomas Kuhn on the role of tradition and innovation in science. Stein's (1963) chapter, which outlined a transactional approach to creativity, recognized the disciplinary split between psychologists and sociologists as a source for the apparent dichotomy between research on individual and social factors in creativity.

Arieti (1976) devoted a considerable part of his study of creativity to social and cultural factors affecting creativity. He drew on the work of the anthropologists A. Kroeber and C.E. Gray, and the sociologist L.A. White, on historical periods that seemed particularly creative, such as the Renaissance. Interestingly, he found that there is a paradoxical or at least ambiguous premise in Kroeber's (1944) and Gray's (1961) work. Although they seem to consider great men as the makers of clusters of high civilization, they see them as having been shaped *exclusively* by economic, social, and political factors. However, Arieti asked, can we really see people only as "inevitable mechanisms or measures of cultural expression"? (p. 299). In other words, the anthropologists take a view diametrically opposed to the one typically associated with psychologists, giving primacy to the social and excluding the psychological.[6] This question of disciplinary and methodological "slants" is addressed later and by Simonton's important chapter in this volume.

The paradoxical premise of the two anthropologists is rooted in the same problem that Stein (1963) identified earlier, and led psychologists to focus mainly on the individual: disciplinary fragmentation. Anthropologists study cultures, sociologists study societies, psychologists study individuals, and their method and scope of inquiry reflects their disciplinary background, and the major problem seems to be that there is little if any communication between them. Indeed, as Wilshire (1989) has suggested, in the socialization of intellectuals in the academy some considerable efforts are made to maintain disciplinary "purity," and eliminate polluting influences from other disciplines.[7] Our concern is the need to address real problems and issues which seem to fall between the disciplinary cracks.

Addressing the issue of disciplinary boundaries, Csikszentmihályi (1988) felt forced to defend his use of systems inquiry, with its inevitable interdisciplinary implications, from the charge that he was engaged in "a betrayal of psychology in favor of historical or sociological approaches" (p. 336). He rightly justified his position by stating that creativity is a complex problem, and that "we need to abandon the Ptolemaic view of creativity, in which the person is at the center of everything, for a more Copernican model in which the person is part of a system of mutual influences and information" (p. 336).

In 1972 Barron published *Towards an Ecology of Consciousness*, in which he attempted to lay out a program of ecological research into consciousness and creativity that would take a broader perspective. Pointing to the complexity of the phenomenon of creativity, which he has always studied in a systemic manner (Montuori, 1993), Barron wrote that "the psychology of creativity has been in my own mind a forerunner of an ecological perspective on consciousness" (pp. 107-108). Discussing the ecology of consciousness, Barron (1972) stated:

> Ecology as a branch of biology deals with the interrelationships between plants and animals and their complete environments. Consciousness refers to the mysterious fact that this primarily material universe somehow evolved the capacity to be aware of itself, and even to be aware of its own awareness, the peculiarly human distinction. The ecology of consciousness, then, must deal with the complete environment that Man experiences and with the interrelationship between structure and process in it that condition consciousness. (p. 96)

He went on to say that "the way in which both individual and collective consciousness relate to another and to the physical and biotic environment is the subject matter of the ecology of consciousness" (p. 97). This essay was a precursor to the present interests in ecological and systemic perspectives on consciousness and creativity, and was expanded in Barron's (1979, 1988, 1995) more recent work.

More recently, Harrington (1990) attempted to develop a theory which links the the creative process, person, and environment in an ecology of creativity. Harrington, like Barron, used biological metaphors and focused on *social creativity* as opposed to private creativity—acts that are novel and have value to or substantial impact on people far removed from those who initiate them. Describing the "distributed" nature of social creativity, Harrington (1990) wrote that creativity "does not 'reside' in any *single* cognitive or personality process, does not 'occur' at any *single* point in time, does not 'happen' at any *particular* place, and is not the product of a *single* individual" (p. 149). This approach also addresses the major, but often hidden, role that relationships and valuing processes play in creative social systems. The ecological approach is an extremely promising one, for it elevates the importance of the habitat and conditions necessary for fostering the growth and maintenance of creative social systems.

Arieti (1976) proposed a systems model of the interaction between culture and individual whereby (a) "the individual offers or exposes his biological potentialities to the culture," and (b) there follows "the acquisition, on the part of the individual, of things already present in culture" (p. 305). This acquisition is mediated by interpersonal relationships, and Arieti cited such precursors of social constructionism as George Herbert Mead, Dewey, Fromm, and Sullivan, whose work has emphasized the importance of socialization. A dynamic, circular process between culture and individual follows, as the cultural influences are absorbed by the individual and transmitted again after interpretation.

Arieti attempted, therefore, through the use of a systems model, to reconcile culture and individual in terms of a mutually causal process (cf. Caley & Sawada, 1994; Laszlo, 1972; Macy, 1991; Maruyama, 1963, 1976; Morin, 1983, 1992). Arieti stressed the importance of the environment for creativity, and listed nine sociocultural factors that foster creativity: availability of cultural means; openness to cultural stimuli; stress on becoming and not just on being; free access to cultural media for all citizens, without discrimination; freedom, or even the retention of moderate discrimination, after severe oppression or absolute exclusion; exposure to different and even contrasting cultural stimuli; tolerance for diverging views; interaction of significant persons; and promotion of incentives and awards.

Parmeter and Garber (1971) asked creative scientists to rate creativity factors. The most important environmental factors were freedom to work on areas of greatest interest, recognition and appreciation, broad contacts with stimulating colleagues, encouragement to take risks, and toleration of nonconformity. Amabile's recent work (Volume 2, this series) also supports these findings. Gruber (1988) also stressed the importance of rich and complex interactions with the external milieu, citing the influence of Malthus on Darwin.

Amabile's (1983) extensive study of the social psychology of creativity contradicted Arieti's assertion that promotion of incentives and awards foster creativity. She defined the intrinsic motivation principle of creativity as follows: "People will be most creative when they feel motivated primarily by interest, enjoyment, satisfaction, and challenge of the work itself—not by external pressures" (Hennessey & Amabile, 1989, p. 11). Most importantly, Hennessey and Amabile wisely emphasized the need to follow two lines of inquiry, namely the already considerable work on personality characteristics of creative people, and an examination of social environmental factors. They asserted that "what we must now develop are research paradigms acknowledging that neither class of factors, by itself, can carry the day" (p. 34).

Like Arieti, Csikszentmihályi (1988) has used a systems approach to study creativity. The nature of this approach led him to study the creative explosion in Florence in the 15th century. Some of his findings seem to contradict Amabile's discussion of intrinsic motivation, and raise questions regarding the role of "fit" between intrinsic motivation and market demands and rewards that deserve further study:

> [In] the art of the early Renaissance . . . the starting point of production is to be found mostly not in the creative urge, the subjective self expression and spontaneous inspiration of the artist, but in the task set by the customer. (Hauser in Csikszentmihályi, 1988, p. 336)

According to Csikszentmihályi, creativity cannot be studied by isolating individuals and their practices from their social and historical milieu, but is instead the product of these three shaping forces, the individual, the social system, and the domain. He found that little if any attention has been paid to the social system, and his own work is particularly important in showing how social influences shaped and fostered the development of a creative social period in Florence. As Mockros and Csikszentmihályi (this volume) state:

> According to systems theory, creativity should be viewed as a part of a complex dynamic system of feedback in which novel ideas and acts may result in creativity only in the context of an interaction with a symbolic system inherited from previous generations, and with a social system qualified to evaluate and accept novelty. (p. 180)

Csikszentmihályi's (1990) essay summarizes two points of his systemic approach to creativity:

> First, that it is impossible to define creativity independently of a judgment based on criteria that change from domain to domain across time. And, secondly, that creativity is not an attribute of individuals but of social systems making judgments about individuals. (p. 198)

As an example, he writes:

> Rembrandt's creativity was constructed after his death by art historians
> who placed his work in the full context of the development of European
> painting and who pointed out novelties and differences between his work
> and that of his predecessors . . . without the comparative evaluation of art
> historians, Rembrandt's creativity would not exist. (p. 199)

As we shall see, particularly in Runco's contribution to this volume, this is
a controversial position because it stresses the role of social systems,
judgment, and the reception of art. A more social approach to creativity is
bound to raise considerable methodological and philosophical questions,
which we feel may be very useful in opening up considerable lively debate
by questioning the fundamental assumptions of creativity research.

Using an interactionist perspective, Woodman and Schoenfeldt
(1990) also maintained that social and contextual influences must be
accounted for in any explanations of creative behavior. In his encyclopedic
and voluminous research on social factors and creativity, Simonton (e.g.,
1984, 1988, this volume) showed that such social factors as war intensity,
social reinforcements, competition, and internal disturbances (e.g.,
revolutions, riots), have influenced the lives of eminent artists and scientists.
He views creativity as a form of leadership, inasmuch as the creative person
influences others, highlighting the interpersonal nature of creativity.

Anthropologist Donald Brenneis (1990) asked why we focus so
much on individual creativity, and used examples of musical creation from
different cultures to illustrate some very different conceptions of music
making. His research gives us glimpses of the social and cultural
dimensions of creativity, thus revealing how ethnocentric our conception of
creativity is, both in space and time. A cross-cultural approach has also
been used by Lubart (1990) and Ludwig (1992), in a further attempt to
broaden our understanding to include the many different ways in which the
phenomenon of creativity is conceptualized throughout the world, and its
relation to different practices.

Helson's (1990) ongoing work on the creativity of women provides
an alternative and much needed perspective that has only recently begun to
make inroads into the research. In an essay that summarizes much of her
pioneering research of creativity in women, she concluded with the following
statement, which suggests that an understanding of women's creativity
requires precisely the kind of contextual approach we have been suggesting:

> we think the understanding of creativity in women requires attention to
> the social world, to individual differences in motivation and early object
> relations, and to changes in society and the individual over time. In fact,

we believe that the study of creativity in general needs all of these directions of attention. (p. 57)

The importance of gender in discussions of creativity will assume considerable importance in the near future, and the implications will extend beyond methodology to include social and moral issues. They are addressed at some length in upcoming volumes of this series.

SOCIAL CREATIVITY: THE CHALLENGE OF COMPLEXITY

Individualism

Despite the not insubstantial attention placed on the social dimensions of creativity in the literature, it does not, until recently, seem to have spawned a larger stream of ongoing substantive creativity research and debate. This is perhaps not surprising given the fact that the majority of the literature surveyed originates in the United States, a culture that orients strongly to individualism, and whose method of study has historically largely been reductionistic (Sampson, 1983, 1993). The focus of both social recognition and research has therefore been on creative individuals at the expense of the social environment and interaction.

On the basis of crosscultural comparisons, Stewart and Bennett (1991) made some broad generalizations about North American cultural patterns (cf. Hampden-Turner & Trompenaars, 1993; Marsella, DeVos, & Hsu, 1985). They argued (a) that North Americans view the self as the "cultural quantum in society" (p.134); (b) that "in the American self, there is a remarkable absence of community, tradition, and shared meaning which impinge upon perception and give shape to behavior" (p. 130); (c) that North Americans reject "sociological and philosophical principles" (p. 135) and replace them with psychological theories; (d) that the nature of North Americans' self-concept prevents them from understanding the enormous cross-cultural variations in self-concepts; and (e) that despite the emphasis on freedom of choice and autonomy, North Americans are subject to subtle but pervasive pressures to conform, to be *free like everybody else* (cf. Slater, 1991).

We believe these cultural factors have played a considerable role in shaping the North American understanding of, and research into, creativity (cf. Stein, 1992, on the sociohistorical context of creativity programs). From points (a) and (b) it would follow that because North Americans view the self as the cultural quantum of society, and mostly do not view themselves in a historical and social context to the extent that, for instance, the Germans and the Japanese do, historical and social considerations have generally been omitted from discussions of creativity, with greater emphasis placed on synchronic studies of the individual (Barron & Harrington, 1981; Csikszentmihályi, 1988, 1990).

Consequently, as point (c) suggests, psychological theories of creativity have until recently been preeminent over sociological or philosophical approaches (Montuori & Purser, 1995; Stein, 1963). Following from point (d), little emphasis has been placed on cultural differences in the study of creativity (Lubart, 1990), and differences in self-concept have been left out of considerations of the creative person, process, and product.

Finally, point (e) suggests that despite the emphasis on the individual, little attention has been paid on the societal pressures on creative individuals, and on creativity researchers themselves, to conform to certain socially sanctioned historical attitudes, behaviors, and research programs. In other words, we have generally been unwilling to explore the extent to which we are shaped by our culture, and in the case of the encouragement and promotion of creativity, we have focused on individual factors rather than attempts to change social circumstances.[8]

Stewart and Bennett (1991) wrote that "when confronted with people who do not locate the self within the individual, most Americans are bewildered. That the self can be centered in a role or in a group is to them a culturally preposterous idea" (p. 132). It should also be pointed out that conversely, according to anthropologist Clifford Geertz (1973), the North American concept of the self strikes most of the world's population as very peculiar. The first part of Stewart and Bennett's statement points to the tendency for *projective similarity* found in North American laypersons and intellectuals, or the assumption that people are everywhere the same, and therefore that they can be categorized and judged by North American standards (cf. Hampden-Turner & Trompenaars, 1993). The second part of the statement is indicative of the strong resistance found in North Americans for collaborative or group enterprises, which they view as inevitably leading to dependence and a subsequent loss of autonomy (Slater, 1991).[9]

With this individualist focus, collaborative creative processes are not valued as highly as individual efforts. This, however, is not to say that there are no cooperative creative enterprises in the United States: a country that is known for its movie industry and has spawned such highly interactive, collaborative art forms as jazz must surely know *something* about collaboration (Becker, 1982; Loye, Volume 2, this series), but it certainly does not seem to be a subject of major academic interest, as, for instance, the lives of individuals of great genius (Gardner, 1993). Again we have to ask to what extent disciplinary categories and cultural biases have obscured our understanding and appreciation of creative processes.

It is also interesting to note that the focus in research on group creativity has largely been on brainstorming (see Runco, this volume), an artificial procedure, rather than on natural everyday interaction, as if brainstorming sessions where the only time people grudgingly get together to "generate ideas." The assumption is that time has to be set aside to collaborate creatively in a structured manner, because apparently this does not happen spontaneously. From a North American individualist perspective interactions are viewed as either neutral or a hindrance to the individual (Sampson, 1993) and hence to creativity, but rarely as "creativogenic."[10*]

In contrast to what is found in North America, Tatsuno's (1990) research on creativity in Japan showed that teamwork and a sense of harmony are quite as integral to Japanese creativity as the individual struggling against the environment is in the West. In Japan, Tatsuno argued, one might almost say that *all* creativity is group creativity. North Americans can undoubtedly be creative in groups: As we already pointed out, perhaps the most interactively group-oriented creative art form, jazz, is a product of North American soil, at its best reconciling both great individuality and great cooperation and team membership.[11] Jazz may in fact provide a powerful metaphor for organization and collaboration (Montuori, 1989; Purser & Montuori, 1994). However, the concept of creative interaction still seems largely alien, and will continue to do so if the individualist myth of the lone hero versus the many remains the only formulation between self and other.[12]

An awareness of the social and historical factors affecting creativity researchers may lead us to study—and indeed celebrate—the social creativity of creativity research and discourse—and the social creativity of the peculiar practices that fall under the heading of creativity in our society. This is clearly not intended as an *attack* on North American values or on North American creativity researchers, particularly because the latter represent the very tradition that stimulated the editors to do this work. However, we do hope that it will point to the existence of certain "blind spots" in much discourse and many practices, which become all the more clear when viewed from a crosscultural perspective.

Reductionism

Methodological reductionism is another factor in the lack of attention paid to creativity as a social phenomenon. In explicit imitation of the scientific method, this methodological slant may have led to a focus on what was perceived to be the smallest identifiable variable, such as the individual (methodological individualism), with the exclusion of "external" factors such as the social environment (Sampson, 1977, 1978, 1981, 1983, 1993).

Whatever creativity is—and as we have seen, Torrance (1988) argued that "it defies precise definition" (p. 43)—it seems to be a complex, multifaceted phenomenon. In much of the existing psychological creativity research, boundaries have been drawn tightly around the self, with the individual as privileged locus of inquiry. Research on individuals at the exclusion of their sociohistorical context has allowed researchers to reduce complexity and engage in manageable research. In answer to this challenge of complexity, one of the more significant trends in creativity research over the past 10 years has been the use of systems approaches along with a renewed interest in the social dimensions of creativity. Systems theory, or the science of complexity,[13*] argues that we must understand any system in the context of its environment, in its relation with time, and finally in its relationship with the observer (Emery, 1969; Morin, 1983, 1992), and provides a way of thinking about complexity which tends to be avoided by traditional methods.

Systems approaches suggest that it is possible to extend the boundaries of our inquiry to include other, previously omitted, phenomena, which can give us new and important perspectives on creativity. Csikszentmihályi's (1988) question "*where* creativity" is useful here, because it points our attention, among others, to the struggles of creative individuals and groups in their social, economic, and political contexts, and, on a more abstract level, to creativity as a phenomenon occurring in space and time.

As Runco (this volume) stated, the systems approach has come to be associated with a focus on the social dimensions of creativity. However, there is nothing intrinsic to systems approaches that requires they be concerned with "social" systems or society *as opposed* to individuals, a danger that both Runco and Simonton rightly address in their contributions to this volume. A systems approach is equally amenable to personality research. In fact, Schwartz (1987) went as far as stating that "the concept of personality and the concept of a system are one and the same" (p. 218) and several other personality-oriented psychologists influenced by systems theories have chosen to view the person as a system *embedded in a larger social system* (Allport, 1968; Gray, Fidler, & Battista, 1982; Gruber, 1988; Guidano, 1987; Krippner, Ruttenber, Engelman, & Granger, 1985; Macy, 1991; Stein, Volume 2, this series; Wilden, 1980). Systems theories can challenge the traditional distinction between "social" and "individual"

(Emery, 1982; Laszlo, 1972), and draw our attention to mutually causal, recursive processes (Maruyama, 1963, 1976; Morin, 1992) without obliterating the individual.[14]

The methodological problem, from the perspective of systems theory, would not be studying creativity by focusing on individual intrapsychic processes, or cerebral lateralization, or, for that matter, groups (every discipline to some extent having its own "elementary unit"). The problem is not even attempting to focus the level of explanation on smaller and smaller units, which may indeed produce useful and valid information (e.g., genetic factors, mental processes, the role of cerebral hemispheres, etc.), but rather to *reduce the explanation to just one level.*

Personality or cognitive approaches to creativity are not reductionistic per se. However, if creativity is viewed as *nothing but* a factor of personality, or *nothing but* a factor of cognitive or genetic forces, or, for that matter, *nothing but* the product of historical forces, then we are falling victims to a kind of reductionism (whether genetic, psychological, or sociological) that severely restricts and impoverishes our understanding of creativity. A systemic or contextual approach stresses the importance of considering the relationships *between* "focal settings," and the process of, and criteria for, the *system definition* whereby we outline our subject of inquiry.

Our belief is that by studying the creative process at various focal settings, which include all the concentric circles from genetics to group processes to the historical zeitgeist, and the interactions between them, we can obtain a richer picture of the process that can be of great relevance in putting creativity to work. Our purpose is not to downplay any of the research focal settings, but to encourage further research and discussion into and *between* focal settings and disciplinary perspectives, particularly the ones which have thus far been given less attention.

From a systemic perspective, the question of whether creativity is an individual or a social process, occurring either "inside" or "outside" the individual, can be approached by sidestepping the formulation of the question in terms of either/or, and moving toward a mutually causal approach that sees creativity as an interactional process occurring in the relationship between system and environment, individual and society, inside *and* outside (Barnett, 1953; Caley & Sawada, 1994; Ceruti, 1986; Goerner, 1994; Harrington, 1990; Laszlo, 1972; Maruyama, 1963; Mead, 1934; Montuori, 1989; Morin, 1992; Stein, 1963). Creative products, processes, and persons emerge therefore as the process of the *interactions* between an individual or a group and the environment.

Further Considerations

A broadening of our scope occurs when we see creativity as a phenomenon in time and space, occurring in different eras and different cultures, and taking on quite different forms from the ones to which we are accustomed in 20th century, Western discourse. As several chapters in this series will show, there are substantial historical and cultural differences in the way people have thought about creativity, and consequently in their creative processes and products.

There already exist a multiplicity of methodological perspectives on the phenomenon of creativity (Rosner & Abt, 1974; Runco & Albert, 1990). A brief overview of the wealth of important work going on in psychology is enough to point to the use of numerous approaches ranging from psychometrics to psychohistory, from social constructionism to cognitive psychology, from systems theory to phenomenology.[15] Numerous anthropological (e.g., G. Bateson, 1972; M. Bateson, 1990; Geertz, 1973; Kroeber, 1944), sociological (e.g., Becker, 1982; Wolff, 1984; Zolberg, 1990) and historical (e.g., Boorstein, 1993; Kearney, 1988; Mokyr, 1990; Simonton, 1988) studies also deserve attention.

All these efforts bring numerous, often contrasting and at times seemingly incompatible, perspectives to bear on a complex question. We believe this proliferation of perspectives is a potentially very valuable source of new understandings and new conceptualizations of creativity. Rickards and De Cock (Volume 2, this series), have attempted to outline a "multiparadigmatic" approach to creativity research. One of our major interests as editors of this series is to develop dialogues among disparate researchers, pointing out areas that have not been addressed, and areas of substantial overlap. Every methodological slant inevitably leaves something out of its inquiry, something that it considers *noise*. This very noise, however, can be the source of new learnings as it opens up new avenues of inquiry that create not just more questions but different kinds of questions, questions that may well not have been addressed previously (Ceruti, 1986).[16*]

A reductionist formulation would argue that social or personality phenomena are *unnecessary* for our understanding of creativity, and yet it is interesting that what is considered unnecessary varies from discipline to discipline, as for instance with sociological reductionism (e.g., Kroeber, 1944), which argues that an understanding of individual persons and their mental processes is largely unnecessary, or the more familiar form of psychological reductionism (cf. Zolberg, 1990). All methodological slants and boundaries of system definition open up certain possibilities and create constraints that limit other avenues of inquiry. The notion of system definition itself allows us to understand the constructive process that guides our inquiry, the creation *by an observer* of a system/environment definition (Ceruti, 1986; Luhmann, 1990) and its consequent implications for what is necessary/unnecessary for our understanding of the phenomenon.

The existence of alternative approaches and questions can provide an extremely useful form of self-knowledge, as we see ourselves and our assumptions questioned by the existence of different approaches. New positions and methods often arise as reactions to existing ones, and in so doing often define themselves in opposition to what they are criticizing (Wilden, 1980). The issue of where social approaches to creativity stand in relation to existing psychologically oriented research is addressed in a number of different chapters in this volume.

This proliferation of approaches to creativity, with a concomitant plurality of understandings of creativity, suggests the need to explore the *discourse* of creativity. Not just what we are finding out about creativity, but the whole process in which we find out about it, define creativity, study it, and talk about it. Investigations of "folk psychology" or popular discourse about creativity and creative persons would also be very useful here. We need to understand the history and evolution of the concept of creativity (see Kearney, 1988, 1991, this volume) and of creativity *research* and *practices* as we know them today (see Stein, 1992, for an important step in this direction). This is particularly relevant in an age when we speak of both creative genius and creative accounting, when the word creativity is used in discussions of advertising, finance, art, science.

If, as Stein (1983) suggested, the meaning of creativity in everyday use (and even in academia, given the postmodern debate) is becoming far from clear, we must also recognize that thus far his own definition of creativity, with which we began this introduction, or one very much like it, can still be considered the standard against which both critics (postmodern or otherwise) and laypersons apply themselves. Melucci (1994) avoided a precise definition of creativity and argued that it does not exist as a univocal object. He therefore chose to investigate the cultural discourse of creativity and the discourse and practices of those persons who describe themselves as creative, or are defined as such by others. This may become *one* fruitful strand of a plurality of investigations of the phenomena we call creativity.

As we begin to address the discourse of creativity and its history, we inevitably come across such issues as methodological choices and their history in social science as it is practiced in the United States, Europe, Asia, and the rest of the world. How do historical, intellectual and cultural traditions affect not just the discourse but the practice of creativity? These questions have been addressed by Kroeber (1944), Kearney (1988), Simonton's extensive research reviewed in his contribution to this volume, and Stein (1992). As we explore these historical and social issues we also find ourselves inevitably confronted with issues of power and domination, raising questions such as: Who, if anyone, sets the agenda for creativity, shaping trends in the arts and sciences, determining who shall be considered creative or not in the public mind (Stigliano, this volume; Zolberg, 1990)? And who, if anyone, sets the agenda in creativity research?

These kinds of broader questions of intellectual history are addressed far more often in other countries, where they are considered eminently relevant to our understanding of creativity—in Europe, for instance, where historical and sociological traditions and the German tradition of Frankfurt school critical theory are much more strongly embedded in the culture, and consequently in the discourse of creativity, but also in more historically conscious Italy (Adorno, 1976, 1981; Attali, 1985; Melucci, 1994; Trombetta, 1989; Vattimo, 1988). These questions and more need to be addressed from a plurality of perspectives. They presently fall somewhat awkwardly between a number of different disciplines, sometimes being generally ignored for lack of an appropriate category or methodology, or with discussions in one discipline often appearing without any reference to the work done in other disciplines.

We believe therefore that creativity research ought to address the recent critiques of individualism (e.g., Bellah et al., 1985; Sampson, 1993) and reductionism (e.g., Laszlo, 1972; Montuori, 1989; Morin, 1983, 1992), arising in a variety of disciplines, and that the subject of creativity may in fact be a very fertile area in which to study the implications of these critiques. Bellah and his associates have suggested that these North American individualistic cultural patterns may be changing toward a greater awareness of interdependence. If this is indeed so, then we should see this reflected in creative persons, processes, and products (Bateson, 1972; Gablik, 1991; Montuori & Purser, 1995; Sampson, 1989), and, as the emergence of a social focus on creativity already attests, in creativity research.

Finally, the problematization of creativity brings us face to face with the issue of values. What do we value about creativity, and why? Why is it important for us to be creative, and why do we value some creative individuals and some creative products? If the ability to create a new product or new processes is not intrinsically valued because of its novelty or originality—if, in other words, we are moving away from a privileging of the new simply for the sake of the new (a "modernist" tendency)—then what values determine our judgements about creativity? If new is not necessarily better, if "don't stand in the way of progress" is an untenable phrase because we are not sure what progress really is and we are dissatisfied with previous formulations of the concept, where does creativity fit in? And what of the role of "conservatism"? Is it possible to be both creative *and* conservative?[17]

As we have already stated, our main purpose in this series on social creativity is to broaden the discourse on creativity. We believe the emphasis on the social dimensions of creativity represents an important trend that touches on many crucial issues in psychology, the social sciences, and philosophy. The study of creativity in its social and historical context addresses many existing conceptual polarizations between self and society, sociology and psychology, individualism and collectivism, isolation and community, reductionism and systemic approaches, change and stability, and even good and evil (cf. Hampden-Turner & Trompenaars, 1993; Wilden, 1980). It suggests the need for an approach that is interdisciplinary, historical, ecological, systemic, critical, and aware of cultural and gender differences (Barron, 1972; Helson, 1990; Runco & Albert, 1990).

INTRODUCTION TO THE CHAPTERS

The chapters in this first volume cover a broad range of topics and serve as an introduction to some of the many possible ways in which "social creativity" can be approached. Creativity occurs in space and time, and is informed and shaped by our knowledge. When we speak about creativity, how far does our thinking extend in time and space? Where is the creativity we speak of, spatially and temporally? What is the knowledge and theory base we use to discuss it? The contributors to this volume take us far and wide afield, exploring many different creative spaces and times, and using many different forms of knowledge and knowledge creation to illuminate this complex phenomenon for us.

Roots of Creativity

Creativity in its broadest sense leads us to Creation itself, the beginning of universe before space and time—or, rather, the stories we tell ourselves about our origins. How do those stories of cosmic Creation influence our view of human creation? Do they provide a root metaphor for our understanding of the creative process? The chapter by Frank Barron, a pioneering creativity researcher, begins, appropriately enough, with a discussion of Genesis, taking us back to the beginning of world.

Barron leads us back to the root metaphor of what he calls "monotheism and the seven days," the Judeo-Christian story of a single male creator. This metaphor traces our concept of creativity and creation squarely in Western culture and history, and opens up the possibility of many other generative metaphors for creation—the creation of creation. Proposing as an alternative the metaphor of sexual co-creation, Barron wrote, that viewed from this perspective, all creation is a collaboration.

Barron's opening chapter points to several of the themes found throughout this series. They include a move away from the image of the lone genius to a more collaborative and socially embedded notion of creativity; the importance of biological metaphors, and metaphors in general, as they both illuminate and occlude our understanding of phenomena; the vital role of a gender-holistic approach to creativity, which includes both male and female halves of humanity, both intrapsychically in terms of psychological integration of the contrasexual element, and in the social and political sphere; the need for a historical approach which traces the development of our concept of creativity and creation; and finally, the heritage of existing creativity research, and the notion of the creative person.

From the moment of Creation to the history it sets in motion: Richard Kearney's chapter traces the historical development of the concept of imagination in Hebrew, Greek, Modern, and Post-Modern thought, providing us with the historical context necessary to understand how our concept of creativity and imagination has changed in Western history leading up to the "wake of imagination" of postmodernity (Kearney, 1988).

The widely influential postmodern debate has opened a Pandora's box with its "deconstruction" of established categories. Most importantly perhaps for discussions of creativity, the critiques of modernist conceptions of the self, originality, progress, and "the author," have raised questions that have permeated the art world and had quite a substantial effect on its practices and discourse. The influential French semiotician Roland Barthes (1977) has described the "death of the author," and stated:

> Succeeding the Author, the scriptor no longer bears within him passions, humours, feelings, impressions, but rather this immense dictionary from which he draws a writing that can know no halt: life never does more than imitate the book, and the book itself is only a tissue of signs, an imitation that is lost, infinitely deferred. (p. 147)

Some eminent novelists, such as John Barth (1984) and Milan Kundera (1988), have argued that the novel is exhausted, that there's nothing left to say. The idea of the novel as "quest" is finished, and the idea of a movement from A to B is replaced in the fiction of Thomas Pynchon,

Umberto Eco, Italo Calvino, Robert Anton Wilson, and others as a baffling, never-ending trip through a labyrinth of signs, novels about novels, shifting—and by no means omniscient—authorial voices, and so on (Kearney, 1988). Creativity research must begin to take these discussions into account if it is to remain relevant to the concerns of artists and creative individuals in general.

Discussing the implications of postmodernism for the social sciences, Rosenau (1992) wrote:

> On the most obvious level the post-modern "death of the author" largely eliminates one form of academic inquiry. The absence of the author erodes the legitimacy of historians, sociologists, psychologists and other social scientists who seek to analyze the life experiences of a single individual, be it Aristotle, Keynes, Freud, Marx, or Mother Teresa. (p. 32)

This statement clearly has profound implications for creativity researchers and is likely to cause substantial debate. The individual subject is disappearing in postmodern discourse. However, is this perhaps a peculiar form of what might be called "semiotic determinism," replacing the view of the self-contained individual with a network of socially constructed "signifiers without signifieds"?

Using a hermeneutic approach, Kearney critiqued the "postmodern abandon" of established categories in a historically constructive fashion, stressing the need to develop a narrative and ethical imagination that plays a role both in linking us to our history and showing us possibilities for the future; what he has termed the ethical demand to imagine *otherwise*. Rather than a disconnected play of signifiers (Baudrillard, 1983), Kearney's (1991) hermeneutic imagination "is recognized as a mode of discourse where *someone actually says something to somebody about something*" (p. 177). Kearney's work is important because it takes seriously the postmodern critique of modernity, but refuses to let go of the twin concepts of imagination and ethics, in fact arguing for an "ethical imagination," a term with considerable implications for our understanding of social creativity.

CREATIVITY AND MODERNITY

As Kearney's chapter indicates, our prevailing view of creativity was shaped by modernity, and the next two chapters explore some of the ways modernity has "created" creativity, from both psychological and sociological perspectives. Cultural historian Morris Berman examines creativity from both cross-cultural and historical perspectives, extending our reach in space to include Asia, and focusing in time on the period after the Renaissance in the West. His chapter cogently illustrates how forms of creative expression between the East and the West have profoundly different psychodynamic orientations and psychic costs, mainly because they are products of different cultural milieus. As a cultural historian and astute social critic, Berman argued that Western creativity is schismogenic in nature. This term, derived from the work of Gregory Bateson, indicates a "vicious circle" of positive feedback gone out of control. According to Berman, Western creativity is seen as an eruption from the Freudian unconscious, has a strong addictive component, is obsessed with "self-expression," and resembles a form of exorcism as the individual attempts to heal a psychic split, where creative work becomes all-consuming. Berman then goes on to suggest that different psychodynamic patterns of creativity are possible. Using dramatically different examples from artistic production in the East, premodern societies, and minimalist music, Berman illustrates how creative expression varies in different social, cultural, and historical contexts, and how we can indeed use such a perspective to imagine creativity otherwise.

As we proceed, we begin to focus in on more specific conceptions of creativity as they arise through the interaction of time, space, and knowledge. In his study of the interplay of artistic, social, and economic developments in the 19th century, philosopher Anthony Stigliano introduces us to the rise of Romanticism and Consumerism, which, he argues, has led to the concept that we now call "creativity." Stigliano's chapter puts the development of a certain concept of creativity in its historical context, and most importantly highlights the interaction between Romanticism, in the arts as in philosophy, and economic forces on the verge of mass production.

Creativity, as we see, was by no means isolated from market forces, but very much influenced by it. Art, after all, is also a profession. Stigliano points out how this interaction was dissimulated with the ever increasing Romantic focus on individuality and autonomy, leading to an ever greater economic interdependence accompanied by ever greater claims for the isolation and uniqueness of the artist.

Whereas in premodern times craftsmen were clearly employed by noblemen and others to perform a certain function, with the Renaissance the birth of the artist lead to the emergence of the romantic concept of the genius, who distanced himself from, and at times vigorously rejected, the market place. Stigliano's chapter, which draws extensively from critical esthetic theories, ends with a call for further research into the political and economic dimensions of art, artists, and the art world, and the need for an assessment of their impact on psychological theories.

LANGUAGE AND THE REDISCOVERY OF THE ORDINARY

New ways of knowing present new perspectives on creativity. Recent developments in philosophy and the social sciences point to different ways of conceptualizing the what, where, and how of creativity. In response to the view of the person as a self-contained, possessive individual, an increasing number of theorists now argue that that even if we choose to view the person with boundaries tightly drawn around the skin, the "inside" is not somehow separate from the social world: Cognition itself is social, and a self is always already social.

Social psychologist and organizational theorist Frank Barrett presents a challenge to the modernist view of creativity by drawing on a variety of philosophical perspectives, namely hermeneutic theory, ordinary language philosophy, speech act theory, and the work of Vygotsky and Bakhtin. Central to Barrett's argument is the primacy of language and the creative power of discourse. Barrett critiques foundationalist or "naive realist" epistemologies, writing that "there is no direct access to reality unmediated by language and preconceptions" (p. 135). Given this premise, he then inquires into the way language, knowledge, and creativity are constructed in a dialogical process. Following Wittgenstein's discussion of "language games" and his view of language and thinking as a contextual, rather than "private," process, Barrett points to the way action is shaped by language and language is shaped by action in an ongoing, recursive process. Finally he offers a recent example of how a change in a community's discourse rules made possible the creation of new action alternatives.

The constitutive role of language in experience is further explored by anthropologist Mary Catherine Bateson's discussion of "ordinary creativity" in contemporary society, highlighting the role of discovery and improvisation as modalities of learning individuals use to compose their lives in the face of rapid change and discontinuity. Viewing life itself as a work of art, as she did so successfully in her 1990 work *Composing a Life*, Bateson maintains that ordinary creativity involves a process of discovery whereby people improvise ways of adapting to discontinuities and circumstances where the competencies and assumptions of the participants—in terms of class, culture, social status, and so on—are quite dissimilar. By presenting and interpreting several short cases of ordinary creativity, in spaces where one would perhaps not normally look for creativity, Bateson shows how individuals who do not share the same linguistic or cultural codes use sequences of improvised behaviors as a means of sustaining joint performances. For Bateson, it is clear that creativity often goes unrecognized, and does not occur in isolation.

Bateson's work is particularly important in drawing our attention to the phenomenon of improvisation, which is deserving of much wider study and may open up considerable new avenues for creativity research (Purser & Montuori, 1994).

CREATIVITY AT WORK

Creative persons grow and work in the context of their environment. The next two chapters address the development of creative persons from infancy to maturity. The first chapter discusses the experiences of a wide number of eminently successful individuals, and the second is a more detailed autobiographical account of the life of a single scholar.

Mockros and Csikszentmihályi examine the role of social influences on the development of eminent individuals and their careers in the arts, sciences and business. Based on interviews with Nobel laureates, Pulitzer Prize winners, and innovative CEOs, their study reveals just how influential and instrumental social support systems such as mentors, collaboration with colleagues, and encouragement from spouses are to the development of talent, achievement, motivation and success in different fields. Their findings demonstrate how social influences, social norms, and the social context interact with the development of the creative person by providing opportunities, transmitting values, encouraging interests, affirming self-confidence, and developing competency. In the professional and adult development of eminent individuals, Mockros and Csikszentmihályi also examine the differential availability and qualitative differences of such social influences with regards to gender. Their chapter shows that creative women typically face cultural barriers which diminish their access to supportive social systems conducive to the development of eminence.

Philosopher, futurist, and consultant to business, James Ogilvy, brings a plurality of perspectives to bear on the question of social creativity. While drawing on postmodern philosophy, and its decoupling "of the concept of creativity from the individual ego" (p. 226), Ogilvy also brings in a cross-cultural perspective to show how in Japan, for instance, creativity is conceived in a much more social, collaborative way. After discussing the theoretical destabilization of the commonly accepted notion of creativity in the West, Ogilvy approaches the actual practice of social creativity in his own consulting work with the Global Business Network. Ogilvy does not regard the postmodern destabilization and deconstruction of creativity (discussed also in Kearney's chapter) as a cause for despair, but rather as an opportunity to "open up the possibility that some of our ideas about the ontology of individuality might be wrong, and the delights and benefits of creativity we previously ascribed to individual persons alone might also be practiced by groups to great advantage" (p. 236).

CULTURE AND PERSONALITY

Despite the excitement about the possibility of integrating crossdisciplinary and social approaches to creativity, we must remain aware that with any new development in our research there are also potential problems. Historically there has been a tendency for academia and intellectual thought to fall victim to trends and fads like everyone else, and hail the new while rejecting the old. Particularly problematic is the tendency to define the new in *opposition* to the old. Might something like this happen with the "social turn" of creativity research? In this section, Mark Runco and Dean Keith Simonton, appropriately the editors of two leading academic journals devoted to creativity research (respectively, *Creativity Research Journal* and *The Journal of Creative Behavior*) tackle this important issue.

Mark Runco's chapter provides us with some thoughtful insights into the potential perils of a social approach to creativity. Runco's primary concern is the role given to the social judgment of creative products, and recent attempts to define the word creative too narrowly. If we can only speak of a creative product—and therefore call the person who produced it creative—when there is a social consensus on the matter, creativity will be considered only in unambiguous cases, such as Picasso or Einstein, as in the provocative but problematic statement by Gardner (1993) that "no person or work can be considered creative unless it is so deemed by relevant social institutions," and that "if they are not ultimately accepted, then they may be bizarre or anomalous but not creative" (p. 33). Who, though, is to judge—or, for that matter, select—the judges of "unambiguous" creativity? The potential for an extremely elitist conception of creativity arises, with judgment in the hands of a select few. In an age of increasing cultural diversity, there may be enormous disagreement about what is, and what is not, creative, and unambiguous choices may be either extremely hard to find, or force us to go over and over the usual time-tested exemplars of genius, who may themselves be due for reappraisal as they are exposed to critiques from dissenting voices.

A further question raised by Runco, with implications that go far beyond creativity research, is where does this position leave the the ambiguous? Perhaps creativity researchers need tolerance for ambiguity to remain creative. But most importantly, Runco states, where does this allow room for the study of creative potential, particularly in children, and the emerging concept of "everyday" creativity (addressed by Bateson and Barrett in this volume, and Eisler and Montuori and Richards in forthcoming volumes), which may not be public enough or "grand" enough to even attract any form of judgment, let alone consensus?

It seems impossible to escape the fact that calling a person, process, or product creative is in fact a judgment. The very use of the word creativity as opposed to something else—whether by art critics, Nobel or Pulitzer Prize committees, or even creativity researchers—attests to that. The important question is what the criteria are for such judgments. Runco's warning therefore is timely and important. It reminds us that the use of the term *creative*, whether by a lonely individual to describe her or himself, or by a social system making a judgment, is distinctly problematic.

Although not so critical of social approaches to creativity as Runco, Simonton points out that attempts to redress "psychological reductionism" must not flip-flop into a "sociological determinism." Beginning with an overview of sociological and anthropological theories of creativity, Simonton asks what the role of psychologists is given the new awareness of the importance of social factors. Himself one of the leading figures in the research of social factors in creativity, Simonton is not at all convinced that creativity researchers should now become sociologists or anthropologists. Psychologists still have a lot to contribute, in his opinion, and the importance of individual persons must not be downplayed.

EVOLUTIONARY PERSPECTIVES ON CREATIVITY

If we broaden our view of creativity in space and time again, using a different knowledge base, we can look at the phenomenon of creativity in nature. Evolutionary theorist Vilmos Csányi takes this broad view of the creative process in living systems, starting with the cell and working his way to social structures, focusing in particular on the recent upheavals in Eastern Europe. Csányi tackles the concept of creativity in the context of evolutionary processes, and presents a definition of creativity at the biological level using an evolutionary systems perspective. Csányi uses the multilevel lens of systems science to account for the creativity in different component systems, from the emergence of new molecules to sweeping transformations and social changes in societies. Given the emerging interest in the biological and evolutionary perspective in the creativity literature, Csányi's chapter makes an important contribution.

We began this book with creation and the beginning of space and time, and end with speculations concerning creativity and the transcendence of space and time. The final chapter in this volume takes us into uncharted territory, as the eminent systems philosopher Ervin Laszlo explores the question of why so many important innovations seem to have occurred at the same time by people who were unaware of each other. Providing a radically new and controversial perspective on the "genius versus zeitgeist" debate discussed by Simonton, Laszlo proposes that acts of genius may involve the utilization of the human mind in ways as yet unrecognized. Laszlo offers that the creative mind is able to deeply concentrate on the problem it is working on, creating an altered state of consciousness. Drawing extensively from research in quantum physics, Laszlo argues that the power of such focused attention and one-pointedness results in an altered state of consciousness, which opens the mind to a nonlocalized or "psi" field (articulated in depth in his 1993 volume *The Creative Cosmos*), thereby connecting to other like-minded individuals who are simultaneously engaged in similar types of problems. Laszlo draws on research in Italy which has found that the brain waves of two test subjects in deep meditation become doubly synchronized: Not only do the left and right cerebral hemispheres become synchronized within each subject, but brain wave synchronization also occurs between the two subjects. The simultaneous development of creative products, Laszlo speculates, may be the result of the patterned interaction between minds which actually transcends ordinary boundaries of space and time.

CONCLUSION

As we have attempted to show in this collection of essays, the implications of social approaches to creativity are very broad. At the very least, they remind us that in their explorations of creativity, inquirers always select a certain scope of inquiry in their definition of the system to be studied; that a creativity system has subsystems and exists within a larger system; that there are continuous interactions between all systems; that any system operates within time and space; that these interactions between system and environment can be viewed by the inquirer as complementary, antagonistic, concurrent, or simply irrelevant, as in the case of nonsystemic inquirers; and that there are a number of different methodological slants which determine our subject of inquiry, and the results of our inquiry. Creativity can therefore be viewed systemically as a phenomenon that takes place in a *network of mutually interactive and causal relationships*, extending from the genetic to the global.

A vital question that we hope will receive much more attention is the importance of understanding and creating the "conditions for creativity." This issue has extremely broad implications, ranging from education to politics to R&D laboratories. In volume 2 of this series we explore this question specifically in the context of organizations, where considerable research is already being done.

Many important methodological and philosophical questions remain open, and of course it has been the intention of the editors to bring out these questions and open the dialogue rather than attempt to close it. Our hope is that this heterogeneous collection will stimulate interdisciplinary discussion and debate, and prompt new research in areas that have yet to receive much attention. We are particularly eager to see the development of *collaborative, interdisciplinary research projects*, in which scholars with different backgrounds and perspectives join together to work on the issue of (social) creativity. We might envision for instance a psychologist and a sociologist, a historian and a philosopher, an anthropologist and an economist collaborating on research in to the social dimensions of creativity. The results might be exciting and controversial: The collaboration between Runco, a psychologist, and Rubenson, an economist, on the "psychoeconomic approach to creativity" points in this direction (Rubenson & Runco, 1992). Another complementary approach might involve open-ended discussions with individuals and groups involved in creative enterprises in an attempt to address some of the issues most relevant to them. Again, a plurality of disciplinary perspectives can be brought to these kinds of discussions.

Creativity as a concept may be broad enough and rich enough to stimulate important social research, as indeed in our opinion it already has. It allows us an important entree into the nature and relationship of the self and society, and the concepts of the good, the true, and the beautiful. Creativity is intimately connected to our vision of progress and the good, our understanding and concept of human capabilities and potentials, the moral implications of change and human action, and even to the stories we tell ourselves about cosmic creation. It is consequently conceptualized differently in different times and places (Kearney, 1988; Lubart, 1990): It is an evolving, historical concept.

NOTES

1. The issue of creative group performance has not been widely discussed. One of the reasons for this may be the methodological difficulties psychologists have faced in addressing this issue. Boyd (1992) provided a series of accounts from contemporary musicians in which collaboration is discussed among many other topics. The anecdotal accounts she offers albeit from

leading musicians, are for a general public. Nevertheless, they provide some interesting insights that should not be overlooked by psychologists and other researchers who may be put off by the popular nature of the book. Many books on jazz, including autobiographies of leading players, also provide useful anecdotal information.

2. In an important paper Maruyama (1974) argued that in order to develop creativity in children they must develop the ability and skills to amplify each other's ideas, and suggested the use of exercises involving nonhierachical interaction in groups. He called for an educational philosophy based on cooperative, mutual amplification. Maruyama's concept of mutual amplification can be extended beyond the education of children to apply to any interaction (see Caley & Sawada's 1994 edited volume of papers by Maruyama applying this concept to a variety of disciplines).

3. See, among others, Attali (1985), Blacking (1987), Stockhausen (1989) and Zolberg (1990) for a critical discussion of the connection between art, culture, and commerce.

4. The notion of system definition and other methodological issues are addressed later.

5. Maruyama's (1974) aforementioned discussion of creativity in terms of mutual causality is also extremely relevant here.

6. A similar dichotomy between individual and society has been found in a discussion of the arts of Zolberg (1990), who distinguished between two opposing camps, the "individualists" and the "sociologists," with consequences parallel to the "cultural determinism" versus "psychological reductionism" debate found in Simonton and Arieti. For instance, Zolberg criticizes the work of Becker (1982), which stresses the social and collaborative aspect of the production of art. She argued that despite the important corrective element in Becker's work, which deflates the romantic view of the lone genius, he ends up by espousing a view of creativity that omits the individual almost entirely.

7. This process of purification can at times be seen as a function of defending "intellectual turf." As the work of Kuhn (1970) also suggests, researchers invest entire professional careers in one research question and one methodological approach, and may thus feel threatened at more than merely an intellectual level by attempts to create "paradigm shifts." Their very livelihood may be at stake, particularly if a shift moves research funding and status away from their chosen field and/or approach.

8. Slater (1991) also argued that the "Individual-versus-society myth" is deeply embedded in North American culture. This myth is closely related to the "lone genius myth" (Montuori & Purser, 1995), which also sees culture and society—other people, in other words—as an obstacle to the self-realization and self-expression of individuals. But Slater (1991), like Stewart and Bennett, pointed out that "the very wish to escape our culture is itself a product of cultural conditioning" (p. 154), and therefore manifests itself in clearly pre-established roles that have taken on mythical status in North

American culture, from the Lone Ranger to James Dean to Einstein (cf. Bellah, Madsen, Sullivan, Swidler, & Tipton, 1985).

9. The enormous recent interest in "teamwork" in the management literature attests to the urgent need to redress this problem in industry. Efforts to import team-based Japanese management methods without taking cultural differences into account are bound to fail, particularly since for the Japanese dependence is a virtue and for Americans it is considered a fate almost worse than death (Slater, 1991). Viewing management practices of other cultures as "tools" that can be borrowed in a decontextualized manner is highly problematic and reflects the North American tendency to discount culture and historicity (Hampden-Turner & Trompenaars, 1993).

10. The individualist view described above is diametrically opposed to the systems view that "the whole is more than the sum of its parts." In fact it emphasizes the equally valid corollary, that a system is also less than the sum of its parts, because any system imposes certain constraints on its parts (Morin, 1983, 1992; Wilden, 1980). These constraints inhibit the part, and allow it only limited expression of its full capacities. Societies impose constraints on individuals, as do groups and any form of social organization, including marriage and family. Individuals also impose constraints on their own "parts" in choosing careers, spouses, and in making other decisions that may inhibit some of their potentials, while opening up others (cf. Ceruti, 1986; Morin, 1992).

Much of our thinking about creativity has stressed these constraints imposed on creative individuals and the creative process by society and relationships in general rather than the potential for creativity in cooperation and collaboration. We speak derisively of decisions made by committees, and stress the need creative individuals have for isolation and freedom from distractions, of the independence of creative individuals from their environment. According to systems theory, however, a system is both more and less than the sum of its parts (Morin, 1983). Focusing on one half of that statement (i.e., either less or more), does violence to the complexity of the system.

Along with imposing certain constraints, interactions among individuals in a larger system can also trigger emergent properties which could not be predicted through knowledge of the single individuals. The whole is more than just the sum of its parts, it is more than the global unity, because of the appearance of emergent properties. Systems can open up possibilities for parts which the parts in and of themselves might not be able to have. Being part of a research group, a musical or theater group, or a community opens up possibilities while creating constraints.

11. It should be noted that jazz is the product of a minority, and may therefore represent different cultural values from mainstream North American culture. The African roots of jazz have probably given it the crucial basis in collaborative social creative processes.

12. A more critical and political question might address the possibility that the lack of emphasis on social creativity in organizations might be part of a

policy of "divide and rule," designed to prevent creative and potentially destabilizing collaborations among workers.

13. The main focus of traditional scientific methods has been on simplicity, on reducing phenomena to their single elementary units, and on finding the general laws which govern these units. Emerging mainly through the successes of physics in controlling systems through the manipulation of these elements, traditional reductionist approaches were eagerly embraced by social scientists in an effort to put their own disciplines on the same level of scientific status as the natural sciences. Although reductionist approaches have historically been very successful, there are some problematic aspects to it. Morin (1983) argued that, "Simplification isolates and therefore hides the relational nature consubstantial to the system (relations not only with the environment, but with other systems, with time, with the observer and conceptualizer)" (p. 186, translation by AM).

Recent developments in science have led to what has been called the challenge of complexity (Bocchi & Ceruti, 1985). We are becoming aware of the irreducible complexity of phenomena ranging from atoms to star systems, from cognitive systems to human societies, and this complexity is mostly not amenable to reductionistic approaches. Science is beginning to view complexity as a basic fact of existence and not as an exogenous, chaotic element interfering with the "purification" of a single variable to be manipulated. *Our understanding of complexity emerges out of the inclusion of relationships as a constitutive part of the phenomena we want to understand.*

The term *complexity* is generally defined as the length of the minimal program required to compute a number (Pagels, 1988). But, as Pagels pointed out, this is an algorithmic definition, and another definition might be "a measure of how hard it is to put something together starting from elementary parts" (p. 67). Morin (1992) described complexity as a recognition of complex causality, or "more specifically an eco-auto-causality, where auto causality means recursive causality in which the organizing process elaborates the products, actions, and effects necessary for its creation or regeneration, and where autocausality needs causality from outside" (pp. 130-131). In other words complexity entails a shift in our description of phenomena, which at minimum recognizes mutual, recursive, and circular causality. For excellent and accessible discussions of complexity and chaos theory applied to the social science, see Goerner (1994) and Laszlo (1991). Maruyama (1963) is the classic original reference for mutual causality.

As Morin (1983) noted, recently scientific inquiry has begun to move away from thinking about objects and essences to systems and relationships. The atom itself, the synecdoche of reductionist thought because of what was thought to be its indivisible, irreducible nature as an elementary unit, is now seen as a system of reciprocally interacting particles. And even particles themselves are not the irreducible, indivisible elementary unit to which everything can "ultimately" be reduced, because, as Morin pointed out, they seem to suffer from an identity crisis, being at times waves and at others particles. By analogy, this same 'identity crisis' may be said to afflict our understanding of human beings, viewed both as single actors, and as parts of larger social entities, depending on the perspective and methodology of the investigator (Valle, 1981).

Angyal (1941) argued that what is needed is a shift from elementary single units to systems viewed as a *unitas multiplex*, or complex unity. The Latin root of the word complex, complexus, means different elements interlaced together to form a single fabric. In fact, on of the characteristics of complexity is its unity in diversity. "Complexity emerges at the center of the One as, at the same time, relativity, relationality, diversity, alterity, duplicity, ambiguity, uncertainty, antagonism, and the union of these notions which are complementary, competitive, antagonistic" (Morin, 1983, p. 190, translation by AM). Whatever we choose to call the One (the observing system's process of system definition), Morin argued, whether atom, brain, self, group, or society, we will always find ambiguity, and diversity in the complexity that is inherent in any unity. A system is an interrelation of elements and a global unit constituted by those elements in interrelation. A system is both unity and diversity, in fact, it is a unity in diversity.

14. Early systems theories have been criticized for being a form of totalizing, coercive sociological determinism (e.g., Lyotard, 1979), but recent work, particularly that of Laszlo (1972, 1991), Maruyama (1976), Caley & Sawada (1994), French sociologist Edgar Morin (1983), and the German philosopher Niklas Luhmann (1990), the latter two largely not translated in English, have squarely rejected this criticism and developed extremely sophisticated philosophical and methodological contributions.

15. Kearney's (1991) work provides an excellent introduction to philosophical approaches to the imagination and creativity, from Husserl to Lyotard. Conrad (1990) developed a critique of creativity research from a phenomenological perspective.

16. Systems theory, and specifically the so-called *second cybernetics* (Von Foerster, 1983), has argued for the reintegration of the observer into scientific inquiry. A system does not exist as an ontological entity *out there*, ready-made, in the world. Von Bertalanffy's (1975) systems view of the world was what he called a *philosophy of positions* (cf. Pepper, 1942), influenced by the philosopher Hans Vailhinger. Discussing the latter's philosophy as "As-If," he wrote:

> Each interpretation of reality is an audacious adventure of reason, to use Kant's expression. There is only the alternative: Either we renounce any interpretation of the "essence" of things—which is the well-founded opinion of science—or, if we venture upon such an interpretation which is only possible if patterned after ourselves, we must remain conscious of its merely metaphorical character. For we have not the faintest proof that the "real" world is of the same nature as the minute corner given to us in our

own international experience. Such an interpretation, therefore, can have no other value than that of an analogy, an As-If according to Vailhinger. (pp. 70-71)

Any observed system is always described by an observing system. The observing system makes certain choices about what to define as system and environment. It is almost as if a circle were drawn around our subject of inquiry defines what Montuori (1989) has referred to as the "scope" of inquiry. When studying human behavior, do we draw the circle around the human brain, or our genes, or the immediate space around our bodies, or our families? What is left outside of this circle is generally considered an epiphenomenon by reductionist researchers. The argument is that *ultimately* what lies outside the circle is of no significance—which leads to statements that describe A as *nothing* but a function B. Ceruti (1986) wrote:

The observer's operations and decisions intervene on several levels in the process of system construction. They trace, first of all, the boundary between system and environment, and establish the relationship between system and subsystem, between global dynamics and components. A system is always, at the same time, a subsystem and a suprasystem, and its dynamic is regulated by the constraints of the dynamics in which it participates, and in turn imposes constraints on the dynamics of the various components. (p. 107, translation by AM)

A systemic approach sees this proliferation of scopes as a reflection of the plurality of perspectives generated in the study of a phenomenon, and the polysystemic nature of systems. A systems approach therefore *problematizes* our understanding of phenomena by emphasizing their complexity, which becomes apparent when we observe the variety of relationships and interrelationships any system entails.

Ceruti (1986) explained the historical nature of this shift in our conception of knowledge and knowing from a systems/cybernetic perspective by pointing out that it involves a rejection of the ideal of a fundamental, objective vantage point, the result of science's neutralization of the observer's values and perspectives (with the inquirer as objective "bystander"). He argued that no neutral language is possible or even desirable, and the observer cannot be considered as somehow standing outside of the events that are observed (cf. Code, 1991).

The challenge to the bystander perspective is addressed very clearly by Ceruti, who stated that in our century we have moved from a view of knowledge as a cumulatively built edifice to one of context. This eliminates the possibility of the knower as outsider, or bystander, and reflects an awareness of how knowledge stands not outside our world, but is in it, and in us, and all knowledge passes through problem formulations, categories, and disciplines.

Ceruti (1986) wrote that, consequently, knowledge is now beginning to study its own origins. Drawing on Von Foerster's (1983) development of the cybernetics of cybernetics, we are studying not just *observed* systems, but the *observing* system, a shift from acquired knowledge to the roots and matrices of that knowledge in history, biology, anthropology, politics, and so forth (Luhmann, 1990; Morin, 1983). In other words, every statements is made by somebody, and nobody has a "God's eye view from nowhere" that is completely purified of historical, social, political, economic, and methodological context (cf. Code, 1991; Sampson, 1993).

17.   A recent issue of the excellent *Creativity Research Journal* (1993, *6*, 1-2) was devoted to moral creativity, providing further evidence that the social impact of creativity, as well as the impact of society on creativity, is taking on considerable importance.

REFERENCES

Adorno, T. W. (1976). *Introduction to the sociology of music*. New York: Continuum.

Adorno, T. W. (1981). *Prisms*. Cambridge: MIT Press.

Allport, G. (1968). The open system in personality theory. In W. Buckley (Ed.), *Modern systems research for the behavioral sciences* (pp. 343-350). Chicago: Aldine.

Amabile, T. (1983). *The social psychology of creativity*. New York: Springer.

Angyal, A. (1941). *Foundations for a science of personality*. Cambridge, MA: Harvard University Press.

Arieti, S. (1976). *Creativity: The magic synthesis*. New York: Basic Books.

Attali, J. (1985). *Noise: The political economy of music*. Minneapolis: University of Minnesota Press.

Barnett, H. G. (1953). *Innovation: the basis of cultural change*. New York: McGraw-Hill.

Barron, F. (1955). The disposition towards originality. *Journal of Abnormal and Social Psychology, 3*, 478-485.

Barron, F. (1963). The needs for order and disorder as motives in creative action. In C. W. Taylor & F. Barron (Eds.), *Scientific creativity: Its recognition and development* (pp. 139-152). New York: Wiley.

Barron, F. (1972). Towards an ecology of consciousness. *Inquiry, 15*, 95-113.

Barron, F. (1979). *The shaping of personality*. New York: Harper & Row.

Barron, F. (1988). Putting creativity to work. In R. Sternberg (Ed.), *The nature of creativity* (pp. 76-98). Cambridge: Cambridge University Press.

Barron, F. (1995). *No rootless flower: An ecology of creativity*. Cresskill, NJ: Hampton Press.

Barron F., & Harrington, D. (1981). Creativity, intelligence, and personality. In M. Rosenzweig & L. Porter (Eds.), *Annual review of psychology* (Vol. 32, pp. 439-476). Palo Alto, CA: Annual Reviews.

Barth, J. (1984). *The friday book.* New York: Putnam.

Barthes, R. (1977). *Image-music-text.* London: Fontana.

Bateson, G. (1972). *Steps to an ecology of mind.* New York: Ballantine.

Bateson, M. C. (1990). *Composing a life.* New York: Plume.

Baudrillard, J. (1983). *Simulations.* New York: Semiotext(e).

Becker, H. S. (1982). *Art worlds.* Berkeley: University of California Press.

Bellah, R., Madsen, R., Sullivan, W., Swidler, A., & Tipton, S. (1985). *Habits of the heart.* Berkeley: University of California Press.

Blacking, J. (1987). *A commonsense view of all music.* Cambridge: Cambridge University Press.

Bocchi, G., & Ceruti, M. (Eds.). (1985). *La sfida della complessità* [The challenge of complexity]. Milano: Feltrinelli.

Boorstein, D. (1993). *The creators.* New York: Vintage.

Boyd, J. (1992). *Musicians in tune. Seventy-five contemporary musicians discuss the creative process.* New York: Simon & Schuster.

Brenneis, D. (1990). Musical imaginations: Comparative perspectives on musical creativity. In M. A. Runco & R. S. Albert (Eds.), *Theories of creativity* (pp. 170-189). Newbury Park, CA: Sage.

Caley, M. T., & Sawada, D. (Eds.). (1994). *Mindscapes. The epistemology of Magoroh Maruyama.* New York: Gordon & Breach.

Ceruti, M. (1986). *Il vincolo e la possibilità.* [Constraint and possibility]. Milano: Feltrinelli. (Eng. trans., 1994, *Constraints and possibilities: The evolution of knowledge and knowledge of evolution.* (A. Montuori, trans.). New York: Gordon & Breach.)

Code, L. (1991). *What can she know? Feminist theory and the construction of knowledge.* Ithaca, NY: Cornell University Press.

Conrad, S. D. (1990). Toward a phenomenological analysis of artistic creativity. *Journal of Phenomenological Psychology, 21,* 103-120.

Csikszentmihályi, M. (1988). Society, culture and person: A systems view of creativity. In R. Sternberg (Ed.), *The nature of creativity* (pp. 325-339). Cambridge: Cambridge University Press.

Csikszentmihályi, M. (1990). The domain of creativity. In M. Runco & R. Albert (Eds.), *Theories of creativity* (pp. 190-212). Newbury Park, CA: Sage.

Eisler, R., & Montuori, A. (forthcoming). Creativity, gender, and society: Ungendering, contextualizing, and reintegrating. In A. Montuori & R. E. Purser (Eds.), *Social creativity, Volume 3: Cultures and communities.* Cresskill, NJ: Hampton Press.

Emery, F. E. (Ed.). (1969). *Systems thinking: Selected readings.* London: Penguin.

Emery, M. (1982). *Searching: In new ways, for new directions, in new times.* Canberra: Australian National University Press.

Gablik, S. (1984). *Has modernism failed?* New York: Thames and Hudson.

Gablik, S. (1991). *The reenchantment of art.* New York: Thames and Hudson.

Galton, F. (1869). *Hereditary genius: An inquiry into its laws and consequences.* London: Macmillan.

Gardner, H. (1993). Seven creators of the modern era. In J. Brockman (Ed.), *Creativity* (pp. 28-47). New York: Simon & Schuster.

Geertz, C. (1973). *The interpretation of cultures.* New York: Basic Books.

Gergen, K. (1985). The social constructionist movement in modern psychology. *American Psychologist, 40,* 266-275.

Gergen, K. (1991). *The saturated self. Dilemmas of identity in contemporary life.* New York: Basic Books.

Gioia, T. (1988). *The imperfect art. Reflections on jazz and modern culture.* New York: Oxford University Press.

Goerner, S. M. (1994). *Chaos and the evolving ecological universe.* New York: Gordon & Breach.

Gray, E. G. (1961). An epicyclical model for Western civilization. *American Anthropologist, 63,* 1014-1037.

Gray, W., Fidler, J., & Battista, J. (Eds.). (1982). *General systems theory and the psychological sciences. An edited compendium on the state of the art organized around the human knowledge process* (Vols. 1 & 2). Salinas, CA: Intersystems Publications.

Gruber, H. (1988). Inching our way up Mount Olympus: The evolving systems approach to creative thinking. In R. Sternberg (Ed.), *The nature of creativity* (pp. 243-270). Cambridge: Cambridge University Press.

Guidano, V. (1987). *Complexity of the self: A developmental approach to psychopathology and therapy.* New York: Guilford.

Hales, S. (1986). Rethinking the business of psychology. *Journal for the Theory of Social Behaviour, 16*(1), 57-76.

Hampden-Turner, C., & Trompenaars, A. (1993). *The seven cultures of capitalism.* New York: Doubleday.

Harrington, D. (1990). The ecology of human creativity: A psychological perspective. In M. Runco & R. Albert (Eds.), *Theories of creativity* (pp. 143-169). Newbury Park, CA: Sage.

Hebdige, D. (1979). *Subculture. The meaning of style.* New York: Methuen.

Helson, R. (1990). Creativity in women: Inner and outer views over time. In M. Runco & R. Albert (Eds.), *Theories of creativity* (pp. 46-58) Newbury Park, CA: Sage.

Hennessey, B., & Amabile, T. (1989). The conditions of creativity. In R. Sternberg (Ed.), *The nature of creativity* (pp. 11-38). Cambridge: Cambridge University Press.

James, W. (1927). *The will to believe and other essays in popular philosophy*. New York: Longmans, Green and Co.

Jencks, C. (1989). *What is post-modernism?* New York: Academy Editions/St. Martin's Press.

Kearney, R. (1991). *Poetics of imagining. From Husserl to Lyotard*. London: Harper Collins.

Kearney, R. (1988). *The wake of imagination: Toward a postmodern culture*. Minneapolis: University of Minnesota Press.

Krippner, S., Ruttenber, A. J., Engelman, S. R., & Granger, D. L. (1985). Towards the application of general systems theory in humanistic psychology. *Systems Research, 2*, 105-115.

Kroeber, A. (1944). *Configurations of culture growth*. Berkeley: University of California Press.

Kuhn, T. (1970). *The structure of scientific revolutions*. Chicago: The University of Chicago Press.

Kundera, M. (1988). *The art of the novel*. New York: Perennial.

Laszlo, E. (1972). *Introduction to systems philosophy. Toward a new paradigm of contemporary thought*. San Francisco: Harper.

Laszlo, E. (1991). *The age of bifurcation. Understanding our changing world*. New York: Gordon & Breach.

Laszlo, E. (1993). *The creative cosmos. A unified science of matter, life, and mind*. Edinburgh: Floris Books.

Leonard, N. (1987). *Jazz: Myth and religion*. New York: Oxford University Press.

Lubart, T. (1990). Creativity and cross-cultural variation. *International Journal of Psychology, 25*, 39-59.

Ludwig, A. M. (1992). Culture and creativity. *American Journal of Psychotherapy, 46*(3), 455-469.

Luhmann, N. (1990). *Sistemi sociali. Fondamenti di una teoria generale* [Social systems. Foundations of a general theory.] Bologna: Il Mulino.

Lyotard, J-F. (1979). *The postmodern condition: A report on knowledge*. Minneapolis: University of Minnesota Press.

Macy, J. (1991). *Mutual causality in Buddhism and general systems theory*. Albany: State University of New York Press.

Marsella, A. J., DeVos, G., & Hsu, F. L. K. (Eds.). (1985). *Culture and self.* New York: Tavistock.

Maruyama, M. (1963). The second cybernetics: Deviation amplifying mutual causal processes. *American Scientist, 51*(2), 164-179.

Maruyama, M. (1974). Paradigmatology and its applications to cross-disciplinary, cross-professional and cross-cultural communication. *Dialectica, 28,* 135-196.

Maruyama, M. (1976). Toward cultural symbiosis. In E. Jantsch & C. H. Waddington, (Eds.), *Evolution and consciousness: Human systems in transition* (pp. 198-213). Reading, MA: Addison-Wesley.

Mead, G. H. (1934). *Mind, self, and society.* Chicago: The University of Chicago Press.

Melucci, A. (1994). *Creatività: Miti, discorsi, processi* [Creativity: Myths, discourses, processes.] Milano: Feltrinelli.

Mokyr, J. (1990). *The lever of riches. Technological creativity and economic progress.* New York: Oxford University Press.

Montuori, A. (1989). *Evolutionary competence.* Amsterdam: Gieben.

Montuori, A. (1993). The social future of creativity. *Komotion International, 6,* 3-12.

Montuori, A. (1996). Frank Barron's ecological vision. In A. Montuori (Ed.), *Unusual associates: Essays in honor of Frank Barron.* Cresskill, NJ: Hampton Press.

Montuori, A., & Purser, R. (1995). Deconstructing the lone genius myth: A contextual view of creativity. *Journal of Humanistic Psychology, 35*(3), 69-112.

Morin, E. (1983). *Il Metodo. Ordine disordine organizzazione* [Method. Order disorder organization.] Milano: Feltrinelli. (Eng. trans., 1992, *Method. The nature of nature.* (R. Belanger, trans.). New York: Peter Lang.)

Morin, E. (1992). The concept of system and the paradigm of complexity. In M. Maruyama (Ed.), *Context and complexity. Cultivating contextual understanding* (pp.125-136). New York: Springer-Verlag.

Norris, C., & Benjamin, A. (1988). *What is deconstruction?* New York: Academy Editions/St. Martin's Press.

Pagels, H. (1988). *Dreams of reason. The computer and the rise of the sciences of complexity.* New York: Simon & Schuster.

Parmerter, S., & Garber, J. (1971). *Creative scientists rate creativity factors.* Research Management, *14,* 65-70.

Pepper, S. C. (1942). *World hypotheses.* Berkeley: University of California Press.

Purser, R., & Montuori, A. (1994). Miles Davis in the classroom: Using the jazz ensemble metaphor for enhancing team learning. *Journal of Management Education, 18*(1), 21-31.

Purser, R., & Montuori, A. (1995). Knowledge development and epistemologies of practice: A systems theoretic analysis. In M. Beyerlein (Ed.), *Advances in interdisciplinary studies of work teams* (pp. 117-162). Greenwich, CT: JAI Press.

Robertson, J. (1937). The economics of genius. In V. F. Calverton (Ed.), *The making of society* (pp. 624-660) New York: Random House.

Rosenau, P. M. (1992). *Post-modernism and the social sciences. Insights, inroads, and intrusions.* Princeton, NJ: Princeton University Press.

Rosner, S., & Abt, L. E. (Eds.). (1974). *Essays in creativity.* Croton-on-Hudson, NY: North River Press.

Rubenson, D. L., & Runco, M. A. (1992). The psychoeconomic approach to creativity. *New Ideas in Psychology, 10*(2), 131-147.

Runco, M., & Albert, R. (Eds.). (1990). *Theories of creativity.* Newbury Park, CA: Sage.

Sampson, E. (1977). Psychology and the American ideal. *Journal of Personality and Social Psychology, 35,* 767-782.

Sampson, E. (1978). Scientific paradigms and social values: Wanted—A new scientific revolution. *Journal of Personality and Social Psychology, 36,* 1332-1343.

Sampson, E. (1981). Cognitive psychology as ideology. *American Psychologist, 36,* 730-743.

Sampson, E. (1983). *Justice and the critique of pure psychology.* New York: Plenum.

Sampson, E. (1989). The challenge of social change for psychology: Globalization and psychology's theory of the person. *American Psychologist, 44*(6), 914-921.

Sampson, E. (1993). *Celebrating the Other. A dialogic account of human nature.* Boulder: Westview Press.

Schwartz, G. E. (1987). Personality and the unification of psychology and modern physics: A systems approach. In J. Aronoff, A. I. Rubin, & R. A. Zucker (Eds.), *The emergence of personality* (pp. 217-254). New York: Springer.

Simonton, D. K. (1984). *Genius, creativity and leadership.* Cambridge, MA: Harvard University Press.

Simonton, D. K. (1988). Creativity, leadership and chance. In R. Sternberg (Ed.), *The nature of creativity* (pp. 43-75). Cambridge: Cambridge University Press.

Slater, P. (1991). *A dream deferred. America's discontent and the search for a new democratic ideal.* Boston: Beacon.

Spiro, M. (1951). Culture and personality. The natural history of a false dichotomy. *Psychiatry, 14,* 19-46.

Stein, M. (1953). Creativity and culture. *Journal of Psychology, 36,* 311-322.

Stein, M. (1963). A transactional approach to creativity. In C. W. Taylor & F. Barron (Eds.), *Scientific creativity. Its recognition and development* (pp. 217-227). New York: Wiley.

Stein, M. (1983). Creativity in *Genesis. Journal of Creative Behavior, 17,* 1-8.

Stein, M. (1992). Creativity programs in sociohistorical context. In S. Parnes (Ed.), *Source book for creative problem solving* (pp. 85-88). Buffalo, NY: Creative Education Foundation Press.

Stewart, E. C., & Bennett, M. J. (1991). *American cultural patterns: A cross-cultural perspective* (rev. ed.). Yarmouth, ME: Intercultural Press.

Stockhausen, K. (1989). *Towards a cosmic music.* Longmead: Element Books.

Tatsuno, S. (1990). *Created in Japan. From imitators to world-class innovators.* New York: Harper Business.

Torrance, E. P. (1988). The nature of creativity as manifest in its testing. In R. Sternberg (Ed.), *The nature of creativity* (pp. 43-75). Cambridge: Cambridge University Press.

Trombetta, C. (1989). *La creatività. Un utopia contemporaneà* [Creativity. A contemporary utopia]. Milano: Bompiani.

Valle, R. (1981). Relativistic quantum psychology: A reconceptualization of what we knew. In R. S. Valle & R. von Eckartsberg (Eds.), *The metaphors of consciousness* (pp. 419-436). New York: Plenum.

Vattimo, G. (1985). *La fine della modernità. Nichilismo ed ermeneutica nella cultura post-moderna* [The end of modernity. Nihilism and hermeneutics in post-modern culture]. Milano: Garzanti.

Von Bertalanffy, L. (1975). *Perspectives on general systems theory.* New York: Braziller.

Von Foerster, H. (1983). *Observing systems.* Seaside, CA: Intersystems Publications.

Wilden, A. (1980). *System and structure: Essays in communication and exchange.* London: Tavistock.

Wilshire, B. (1989). *The moral collapse of the university.* Albany: University of New York Press.

Wolff, J. (1984). *The social production of art.* New York: New York University Press.

Woodman, R., & Schoenfeldt, L. (1990). An interactionist model of creative behavior. *Journal of Creative Behavior,* 24(1), 10–20.

Zolberg, V. L. (1990). *Constructing a sociology of the arts.* New York: Cambridge University Press.

PART ONE

ROOTS OF CREATIVITY

1

All Creation is
a Collaboration*

Frank Barron

Creativity as we have seen has been written about quite extensively during the past 100 years especially, and a model of the creative process on which most observers agree has emerged. One well-known statement of it is that of the psychologist Graham Wallas, who summarized many observations and condensed the multifarious events attending creativity into four simple stages. These stages are: preparation, incubation, illumination, and verification (Wallas, 1926). Add to this model of process the Biblical picture of Genesis, and we have "monotheism and the seven days," a metaphor for what might also be called "the hero creator and the stages of the creative process." More simply, let us call it the theory of *The Single Creator.*

This is the standard to which I shall offer an alternative image after describing it in the terms popularized by Wallas in his theory of process and explicated by recent research on the characteristics of persons who achieve reputations for their individual creativity. The basic alternative I shall consider is: co-creation and mutuality, or simply, collaboration.

---

*This chapter is reprinted from Frank Barron, *No Rootless Flower: An Ecology of Creativity*, 1995, © Hampton Press, Inc.

THE SINGLE CREATOR

Let us begin with a metaphor for the "great mystery" of creation. Genesis tells us of the beginning of the world and its taking shape through the purposive action of God. The story is told in images for which there are clear analogues in mental life. Creation arises out of the void, and its materials as they begin to assemble are in chaos. The primary chaos acquires depths and degrees of form. Earth takes shape, and waters cover the earth. Days pass, primeval darkness gives way to light, Adam is formed from the dust. God looks on His works and finds them good.

The trouble has just begun, of course. In the arid wasteland God has made a garden in which to place those made in His likeness. First there is Adam, a creature of dust made enthusiastic by the breath of God. The Creator has blown the breath of life into dead matter. Eve seems to come as an afterthought, but certainly a great convenience, for God entrusts her with at least half the work of generation. The question of this or that is now out of Divine hands. The creatures will go forth into the world to live their own lives. Being born, they are free.

This image of God the creator as male, and the first creature as a man rather than a woman, is with us still. It is one of those "universal ideas" or "archetypes," resident for ages in the human psyche. Yet, if God is evolving through His creatures, as some modern views maintain, the Judaic imagery is in the process of changing—however slowly, oh so slowly! And, of course, there are other archetypes, in the great world outside the Judaic-Christian tradition. It remains, however, one of the hidden assumptions in most Western theories of human creativity. Bringing that assumption to light so that it may be challenged has been one of the achievements of the psychology of creativity in the past two decades or so.

So much for the "great mystery" as metaphor. From the great mystery to the small mystery seems a big step downward, until we remember that it is the small mystery—human creativity—which has given us this account. Out of the small the great has arisen. The psychic case (i.e., the human being in introspection on the creative process) generates the account of the cosmic case. This is the starting point of the ancient theory of correspondences, the replication in the microcosm of the cosmic process.

Modern statements of the creative process in human creativity have emphasized the serial nature of creation in a single psyche. Henri Poincaré's famous essay on the process of discovery in mathematics, based on his own intellectual history and his own specific discoveries, is as good a place as any to start. In the following passage, Poincaré tells of his discovery of certain mathematical functions:

Ideas rose in crowds; I felt them collide until pairs interlocked, so to speak, making a stable combination . . .

Then I turned my attention to the study of some arithmetical questions apparently without much success and without a suspicion of any connection . . . Disgusted with my failure, I went to spend a few days at the seaside, and thought of something else. One morning, walking on the bluff, the idea came to me, with just the same characteristics of brevity, suddenness, and immediate certainty. (Poincaré, 1915, cited in Ghiselin, 1950, pp. 25-26)

Recall that Poincaré, in 1904, in his address as president of the European Physical Society, had called for a special theory of relativity, and Einstein as we all know was to produce one obligingly within the year. Einstein's personal modesty is well known, but so are some of the statements attributed to him that would at least place him on a conversational first-name level with the Deity (e.g., "God does not play dice with the universe"). One of the sentences in a popular psychiatric diagnostic inventory is, "I am a special agent of God," which if answered True earns you a point for Paranoia. But many a famous human creator has come perilously close to an affirmation of God's agency in his own humble person. Nietzsche spoke of the writing of *Thus Spake Zarathustra* (words taken from his last work, tellingly titled "Ecce Homo"):

One can hardly reject completely the idea that one is the mere incarnation, or mouthpiece, or medium of some almighty power. The notion of revelation describes the condition quite simply; by which I mean that something profoundly convulsive and disturbing suddenly becomes visible and audible with indescribable definiteness and exactness. One hears—one does not seek; one does not ask who gives: a thought flashes out like lightning without hesitation . . . there is an ecstasy . . . a feeling that one is utterly out of hand . . . shuddering thrills pass through one . . . a profound happiness. (cited in Ghiselin, 1950, pp. 209-210)

Dozens of examples might be adduced from science, art, commerce, invention, architecture, jurisprudence, religion, war, even peace. Max Ernst wrote of his "discovery" of frottage, written apparently in ignorance of the notebooks of Leonardo or the poetry of Michelangelo:

It all started on August 10, 1925, by my recalling an incident of my childhood when the sight of an imitation mahogany panel opposite my bed had induced one of those dreams between sleeping and waking. And happening to be at a seaside inn in wet weather I was struck by the way the floor, its grain accentuated by many scrubbings, obsessed my nervously excited gaze. So I decided to explore the symbolism of the obsession, and to encourage my powers of meditation and hallucination. I took a series of drawings from the floorboards by dropping pieces of paper on them at random and then rubbing the paper with blacklead. As I looked carefully at the drawings that I got in this way—some dark, others smudgily dim—I was surprised by the sudden heightening of my visionary powers, and by the dreamlike succession of contradictory images that came one on top of another with the persistence and rapidity peculiar to memories of love. . . .

Now my curiosity was roused and excited, and I began an impartial exploration, making use of every kind of material that happened to come into my field of vision: leaves and their veins, frayed edges of sacking, brushstrokes. (Ernst, 1937, cited in Ghiselin, 1950, p. 58)

Arthur Koestler, in *The Act of Creation* (1964), brought together a multitude of examples which support the earlier synthesis of such accounts by Wallas. Wallas simplified (in fact, oversimplified) these accounts into his well-known 4-stage theory. His concise statement of the stages is easy to remember, and it falls in nicely with the idea of a single heroic creator.

Stage 1. Preparation.

Intense study, immersion in a problem or an experience, involvement in it with curiosity, interest, attention, fascination, love, or what have you—engagement, an existentialist might say—these are the characteristics of the stage of preparation. It is a "getting ready" through a sort of growing *up to* or growing *in to* a condition which makes further creative work possible. The materials are there and are assembled so that action may begin. The process is developmental, with stages similar to those of personal and social growth in childhood: trust, initiative, industry. A phase of latency leads on to conception and incubation when fascination reaches a certain point. Poincaré emphasized the importance of conscious work on a problem; Helmholtz spoke of "investigation of the problem in all directions." Conscious direction, discipline, hard work, and attention, accompanied by perplexity in the face of an apparently unsimplifiable but challenging complexity are the hallmarks of *preparation*.

Stage 2. Incubation.

This stage is marked by an almost autonomous process of bringing together and coalescing the elements discerned or given in the stage of preparation. At the beginning of this stage the seed must reach its goal or be received into the nurturing egg. Max Ernst, again, in a phrase quite innocent of any suggestion of the metaphor of sexual procreation, spoke of collage as "the exploitation of the chance meeting on a non-suitable plane of two mutually distant realities" (cited in Ghiselin, 1950, p. 66). Andre Breton earlier (1920, p. 60) wrote of the process of collage: "It is the marvelous capacity to grasp two mutually distant realities without going beyond the field of our experience and to draw a spark from their mutual juxtaposition." Koestler (1964) spoke of "the perceiving of a situation or idea in two self-consistent but habitually incompatible frames of reference." He later calls this "the bisociation of independent matrices" or "the juxtaposition of matrices," implying by the term matrix a complex gestalt and suggesting their interpenetration to create a new, higher-order gestalt. Poincaré, as we have noted, talked about "the atoms which rose in crowds; I felt them collide until pairs interlocked . . . making a stable combination." (cited in Ghiselin, 1950, p. 30).

Stage 3. Illumination.

Wallas (1926), again, innocently of any sexual connotation, spoke of "the appearance of the 'happy idea.'" It is "the culmination of a successful train of association, which may have lasted an appreciable time." The terms *flash* and *click* are used to describe the moment when dark gives way to light, and the "happy idea" is born. It is commonplace that men speak of their ideas as "my children." Fathers, of course, give credit where credit is due, including cases in which they would rather disclaim any share in the parentage of the idea, by saying, "Well, it's your baby." Illumination, then, is the moment of birth.

Stage 4. Verification.

To continue the metaphor, this is the stage of owning up, justifying, and "bringing up baby." More exactly, it is the stage when the product of preparation, incubation, and illumination is tested by the light of day, namely, by critical, reasonable inspection, measurement, proof, and validation by social consensus as to the fact that it works. (Picture the conscientious obstetrician checking out the neonate!) The idea now, said Poincaré, must "be reduced to an exact form." No more dreams, fantastic speculations, unsubstantiated expectations. The "happy idea" must go out into the world, to live and grow, or to die or be cast aside.

To sum up the standard description, the days or stages describe a process initiated by a single creator, occurring basically in the mind of the creator, and ending with a clear assignment of responsibility to one creative being.

This psychological account of the creative process cannot be coordinated perfectly to the process of cosmogenesis. Yet, there are strong parallels or analogies.

Modern theories of the genesis of the solar system (such as those of Kant and Laplace) posit a limitless waste of chaotic primordial matter as the raw material for the formation of our sun and its planets. They accept gravity as the agency for bringing particles into relationship with one another. The collision of the primeval atoms generated heat, and in Kant's mistaken view, initiated rotation as well. Laplace took rotation for a given and imagined that it was simply increased in speed in the sun, so that as the primordial gases and liquids spun faster and faster they were thrown off from the sun as one might picture splashes of mud from a bicycle wheel. These were held in orbit, themselves continuing to rotate to produce nearly perfect spheres (although bulging a bit at the equator and somewhat flattened at the poles, as our own beloved oblate spheroid Earth is).

The collocation of materials from a chaotic primordial mass can be likened to the stage of preparation, swarms of seemingly unrelated facts grown denser through study (i.e., gravity). Add a bit of turbulence, the twin principle of gravity, to give excitement, and you have the condition of incitement which leads to conception and incubation. For incubation to occur in this model of physical cosmogenesis, a satellite endowed with water and an ozone blanket must first be formed and then fertilized. The analogy to the Biblical narrative, even in the simple form of the female given separate being first as the rib of the male (a portion of sun taking form as a satellite), is striking.

The elements in physical cosmogenesis, then, are in brief: (a) primordial matter, or preconfigurative materials (gaseous, liquid, solid, dust); (b) conditions leading to the collisions of strangers, and their sticking together, or drawing together; (c) heat; (d) a rotating or encircling tendency, perhaps itself primordial; and (e) time and space for events to shape new bodies.

For life to occur, additional conditions are necessary—water and just the right amount of sun shield for the satellite sphere. In a contemporary psychological theory such as Jung's, water is understood to be a symbol for the collective unconscious, and the sphere is the self; its shell or shield is the ego. Perhaps these are far-fetched analogies, but how else is one to understand the small mystery in terms of the great?

So much for the main, or main-line, model of the creative process which has prevailed both in the general imagination and among gifted observers for the past century. What then of the creative person?

Research on the creative person in a wide variety of callings has proceeded apace since 1950. I was privileged to take part in some 15 years of such research, utilizing the so-called holistic method of personality assessment, which featured intensive interviews centered on the creation of specific works, as well as interviews as to one's personal history and one's philosophy of life. In our research at Berkeley we studied more than 300 persons of international reputation as the outstanding creative individuals in their fields. A common core of characteristics appeared consistently across fields:

1. *Independence of judgment,* defined operationally as the ability to resist a group consensus shown to be false.

2. *A preference for complexity,* apparent contradictions, the incomplete and imperfect, challenging puzzles (as opposed to the superficially simple); however, the search for simplicity within complexity remained the key. We formulated this perceptually as a strong drive for closure combined with a resistance to premature closure.

3. *A strong desire to create* and to place oneself in a situation favorable to the expression of one's creative (as opposed to various other) abilities.

4. *A deep motivation* or drive that I have dubbed *the cosmological motive.* It is the desire to create one's own universe of meaning, very personally defined. A culture the size of a county suffices for some; or the world in a grain of sand; or the death of the heart when first love fails. Faber found enough insect life in his backyard to formulate organic laws for a multitude of ecologies; Einstein took the universe itself for his place to be. Watson and Crick found a double helix in DNA and thereby a universally important structure. The apple has proved to be quite a sufficient form for the exploration of some of the most profound problems of modern art.

5. *Lots of personal troubles,* linked to an intense sensibility; but evidence of conventional psychopathology are coupled with unusually high ego strength and sense of reality. I formulated this perhaps unfortunately in the phrase "occasionally crazier, but adamantly saner" than the more average person. The basic point is that creative people may in fact have less stability (be more subject to mood swings, to intense depressions as well as euphoria, and to schizotypic thought processes) on the basis of inherited mental disorders, but they capitalize on these afflictions

in their creative work. Or, alternatively, they may simply be more aware of the crud and the cruelties as well as the blessings and glory of life.

6. *A strongly intuitive nature,* an ability to see in the as-yet preconfigurative a potential form—and this irrespective of the dimension of time and the realization of the form by another space and time; for what is intuited (i.e., looked deeply into) may remain unexplored and not brought into being.

7. *Patience.* This is perhaps best understood in the ancient sense of the term, "suffering the pain to occur," but its manifestations take the form of homely traits such as persistence, endurance, faith in oneself, and basic optimism in the face of difficulties. It may show itself in a continuing attention to detail, even when no reward for painstaking work appears in sight. It speaks for the sort of excellence praised in the Longfellow poem, "Gradatim": one fashions "with greatest care/Each minute and unseen part/For the gods see everywhere."

CO-CREATION AND MUTUALITY

This I think is the stage we as a species currently are in. It began most dramatically with the making of the atomic bomb, that awesome, brilliant, yet dark triumph of collective intellect in response to a collective bestiality that was darker still. It requires a recognition of the other, not in a blind coupling nor even in a comforting awareness that someone else is traveling the same path, but in objective relationship and in voluntary, responsible cooperation. It is happening in small and important ways all around us today. It is the task put to us by history in the relationship among nations. Most dramatically, of course, and most momentously, it is the relationship between the U.S. and what had until recently been the U.S.S.R. The question basically is whether or not an unprecedented cooperation is possible in the face of the threat of an unprecedented catastrophe.

The cosmic metaphor is based on an evolved clockwork order, a design of incredible finesse, mutuality refined to the ounce and the inch. Newton's world may have given way to Einstein's in scientific theory, but to the poet in each of us that macroscopic order, the furnishing of the firmament in shining orbs and spirals, is eternal and imaginative. Its creation, of fire and ice, air, earth, and the flowing waters, is understood in the human imagination in sexual terms.

The Sun as phallus and Earth as the female vessel is perhaps the oldest of the nature myths of creation. The key point in this metaphor of sexual differentiation in the cosmic orbs is that each is necessary to the other. Earth cannot conceive, bear, and flower without the Sun; and the Sun would burn itself out fruitlessly without Earth. Given heat, Earth provides the materials for creation. Of these, soil and water are the two most important ingredients. Add to these the wind, which blows the seed of life hither and yon, and pitch, or menstrual blood, to enfold and feed the seed, and you have the elements of the most primitive, animistic religions, as alive today in our collective psyches as they were in the souls of the ancients. (We must not forget the moon, of course, the third hand of the great clock from whose positions we measure the days, the months, and the years. The moon in its phases is fickle and moody, "crazed with much childbearing," as the poet W. B. Yeats put it.)

An uncanny phenomenon of human biology comes to provide another great simplification. That phenomenon is *twinning,* the birth of two infants rather than one. The genetics of twinning, of course, was not known until fairly recently, and so the mystery could include both male and female twins as coming from the seeding of a single egg. The swan (Jove) thus begets, and Leda bears; the fertilized egg of the world yields up Castor and Pollux, Helen and Clytemnestra; or in other accounts, Apollo and Diana, Adam and Eve, Eve and Lilith. Myths of the twins as the creative principles occur all over the world, in all times; and even today they are believed as articles of faith among many primitive peoples. The idea of twin creators remains compelling to as many people on Earth in the 20th century as does the idea of one God.

Biological gender, or sexual differentiation, is the source of variety, and through sexual selection gives the reproductive advantage so important to organic evolution. But does biological co-creation by male and female add anything to our view of the essential ingredients in the creative process psychologically? This is a question that must be raised in psychological theories of creation. (I have used the term *co-creation* to replace the usual term *procreation* because I think it gives a clearer image of the symmetry of the contribution from the male and female sides of the equation. I should add that in the biological context I distinguish male and female in the sense of biological gender, but that when we move to the psychological context, I refer to masculine or feminine *modes of consciousness,* either or both of which may be present in either the male or female biological individual.)

What, then, are the distinctive features of biological sexual reproduction so far as the coupling parents' contribution to the characteristics of the offspring is concerned?

First, the basic biological story. Each of us begins in the union of two cells—a sperm from our father and an egg from our mother. The fertilized egg is the bridge between two generations, parents and offspring, and contains an equal contribution from the male and female parent in the form of chromosomes (bearing genes, which carry messages in which much of the story to unfold is already written). This is co-creation.

The well-known details of meiosis and of crossing over (the selective exchange of equivalent parts between the two members of each chromosome pair) need not concern us here. The main point is that fertilization accomplishes the relatively random union of two parental cells, each containing a haploid number of chromosomes that carry new and unique combinations of the preexistent genes. The numbers, of course, are vast, as unimaginable as the number of stars in a galaxy. Each potential human parent (each co-creator) is capable of producing 19 million million (19,000,000,000,000) genetically different kinds of sperm or eggs. What then does it mean to be "an individual"—to be like all others, like our parents in many particulars, yet unexampled? No wonder it is hard to "become ourselves." Think what it must feel like to be a *new idea* in the world! Good luck, new ideas, hope you can *realize* yourselves!

So, what are the key ingredients in this process of biological co-creation in the human case? And to what are they analogous in the creative process described psychologically?

I am happy to say that the psychology of co-creation needs further study!

Joking aside, the dialectics of co-authorship, creative collaboration, the creativeness of groups (large and small), the resolution of antagonisms, the management of collisions, the forging of new agreements, and the encouragement and facilitation of creative change—these are the problems on the frontiers of research and theory in the social sciences. The psychology of creativity is in my view the link among all the sciences as well as the arts, and our task is to be alert to metaphors and to proceed rationally in advancing these matters. We needn't fear that this will lead to some finished system of knowledge. The extension of consciousness, or the raising of the level of consciousness, does not imply the elimination of conflict, but rather the joining of opposite principles in new relationship to one another. Not unlike marriage, no doubt, and not unlike a play or a ballet or an opera either, for all three, if they are successful, show us conflicts resolved at a higher level.

In the biological analogy, then, two almost unimaginably unique constellations of genes are brought together from afar (*remote* association!). To a gene on a chromosome of a sperm, a human male parent must seem an extraordinarily vast enclosure out of which to be thrust on an incredibly long journey through darkness to an unexpected, unimaginable, incredibly receptive landing place. If it gets there. Max Ernst's lovely surrealistic "antagonistic planes" and Arthur Koestler's "bisociation of matrices" seem pallid against the background of this reality. From afar the seed and the egg come together to generate the totally new. Just as in physical cosmogenesis, it takes two to make this a meeting, a co-creation, a collaboration. It takes attraction, collision, heat, gravity, and turbulence, often more than a bit of rotation, the spinning-off of parts, fecundation, nurturance, harvesting, replanting.

In brief, once again, it takes more than one. The lone creator is an insufficient metaphor. All creation is a collaboration.

REFERENCES

Breton, A. (1920). Preface to Max Ernst exhibition. New York.

Ghiselin, B. (Ed.). (1950). *The creative process.* Berkeley: University of California Press.

Koestler, A. (1963). *The act of creation.* New York: Macmillan.

Poincaré, H. (1915). *Mathematical creation: The foundations of science.* Lancaster, PA: Science Press.

Wallas, G. (1926). *The act of thought.* London: Watts.

2

The Narrative Imagination

Richard Kearney

Does the narrative power of imagination still have a role to play in our contemporary Western society? In an age where traditional practices of story telling are being increasingly replaced by technologies of information and simulation, can we sustain the notion of a human imagination that is both creative and responsible? Is there an ethical vocation for narrative imagination in our present Civilization of the Pseudo-Image?[1] These are some of the questions I wish to address in this chapter. I begin with a genealogy of some Western stories of imagination before moving on, in the second part, to a discussion of the ethical implications of narrative imagination in our so-called "postmodern" society.

ANCIENT STORIES OF IMAGINATION

From the outset of Western civilization, the notion of creative imagination was treated with both fascination and suspicion. This was as true of the Judeo-Christian tradition as it was of the Greek. Both the biblical account of Adam's fall and the Greek myth of Prometheus' fire prefigure the ancient belief that imagination is a faculty which enables mortals to emulate the divine power of making. As soon as humans came into possession of imagination they threatened to set themselves up as equals of the gods. This was a recurring motif of most cosmogenies.

Several biblical and Talmudic commentators identified the creative power of imagination (*yetser*) with an inclination to supplement the work of the divine creator (*yotser*). It was to this end, they even suggested, that God left the Seventh Day of Creation (*yetsirah*) uncompleted (see Kearney, 1988).[2] Some Talmudists, it is true, denounced imagination as an "evil impulse" (*yetser hara*) bent on subverting the sovereignty of Yahweh. Rabbi Jannai, for instance, declared that one who "obeys his yetser practices idolatry"; Jochanan Nuri claimed that "the evil yetser is the strange god within man" warned of in Psalm 81; yet another Talmudic text reads, "Repentance arose in my heart, says God, that I created in him the *yetser hara*, for if I had not done this he would not have been able to rebel against me". If imagination was roundly condemned by one body of Talmudic and theological interpretation, however, there were others which held that Adam's transgression be viewed as a "happy fall." *Happy* in so far as it permitted humanity to enter history and serve as cocreator with God in the completion of the world, transfiguring "evil" imagination into "good" (*yetzer hatov*). This was doubly happy for Christian theology in that the Fall made possible the subsequent historical Incarnation of the Divine Word as flesh.

Although acknowledging the caveat concerning "graven images," this more benign reading tended to affirm the creative power of imagination as the "image and likeness" of God. It is noteworthy that although Yahweh encourages some of his servants to practice the art of making by deciphering the alphabet of the Book of Creation (*Sefer Yetsirah*), He invariably insists that they work together in *community* to achieve this end rather than setting themselves up as god-like individuals who lord it over their fellows. This ethical scruple is fundamental to the Talmudic accounts of the Book of Creation. As the famous exegete Judah Ben Barzilaii stated, the making of a new history is never the result of a single human imagination (the error of Enosh the idolater) but requires humans to work together in social cooperation under the guidance of the Torah. In support of his contention, he cited this "old recension" of the *Sefer Yetsirah*:

> Abraham sat alone and meditated on the Book of Creation, but could understand nothing until a heavenly voice went forth and said to him: 'Are you trying to set yourself up as my equal? I am one and created the Book Yetsirah and studied it: but you by yourself cannot understand it. Therefore take a companion, and meditate on it together, and you will understand it'. Thereupon Abraham went to his teacher Shem, son of Noah, and sat with him for three years, and they meditated on it until they knew how to create a world. (cited in Scholem, 1952, p. 176)

In biblical tradition, in short, the poetical question of imagination was intimately bound up with ethical questions of community. The same might be said, albeit with a distinct inflection, of the ancient Greek accounts of creative imagination. On the face of it, the Platonic critique of imagination (as *phantasia* and *eikasia*) in books 7 and 10 of the *Republic* would seem to have inaugurated a long tradition of moral disapproval, extending to the Middle Ages and beyond. Mortals, according to Plato, have no right to "imitate" the Gods by means of their imaginations because the divine is perfect, immutable, and timeless, whereas human images are no more than contingent and changeable "copies" of material appearances.

Plato defined imagination as a "poor child of poor parents." At three removes from the original transcendental model of truth, images are merely imitations of imitations. The tree painted by the artist, for instance, is an "imitation" of the material tree as it exists in nature, which in turn is but an "imitation" of the ideal pattern of tree existing in the world of the Forms. To emulate the divine is blasphemy. Only the divine demiurge, spoken of in the *Timaeus*, has the right to shape the material world according to the suprasensible Forms. Denouncing the works of Homer, Hesiod and the poets, Plato went on to declare that because the "state of God is perfect and the least liable to be changed into different shapes" (*Republic*, 381), it is inconceivable that he would create or communicate by means of imagination (*kata phantasias*, *Republic*, 282). However, curiously and paradoxically, it is this very power of the divine to communicate through mystical images which Plato himself celebrates in certain passages of the *Timaeus* and *Phraedrus*.[3] In these so-called "mystical" passages Plato speaks of a "divine madness" (*mania, manteia, enthousiasmos*) that comes to possess imagination enabling it to apprehend and intuit forms inaccessible to both sensible and intelligible experience. No longer serving as imitation of second-hand appearances, *phantasia* now becomes the mirror image, so to speak, of the transcendental Sun itself.

Plato, it seems, is radically contradicting himself. Imagination, denounced in the *Republic* as the lowest of all faculties, is now being hailed as the highest power of vision!

One finds some hint of a solution to this paradox, I believe, in Plato's account of the Prometheus story in the *Protagoras* (321-322). Here Plato appeared to celebrate the power of making (*techné demiourgiké*) bestowed on mortals by Prometheus in the form of a divine fire stolen from Mount Olympus. This act of transgression and generosity liberated humans from the servile order of nature into the creative order of culture where, as Plato put it, they were now free for the first time to cultivate the earth, make clothes and dwellings for themselves, invent speech and "erect images of the gods." It was by virtue of this "creative art" that mortals were said to "have a share (*methexis*) in the portion of the gods." This "divine kinship" of creativity, however, led to violent conflict, for each mortal now wished to set himself up as a god and was unable to live in community with fellow mortals. Thus Zeus sent down Hermes to supplement the art of creation (*demiourgiké techné*) with the "art of politics" (*techné politiké*). It was this second art of social cooperation that enabled humanity to use creative imagination in an ethically responsible fashion. In addition to the power to transform the world, mortals now acquired "the quality of respect for others and a sense of justice, so as to bring order into our cities and create a bond of friendship and union" (*Protagoras*, 322c).

The second great founding tradition of Greek culture—the Aristotelian—also acknowledged a central role for *phantasia* in the ethical life of the *polis*. The *De Anima* (III, 3, 427-428, 431-432) accords imagination a fundamental mediating role between corporeal sensation (*aisthesis*) and intellectual thought (*noesis*). Human deliberation with regard to moral action requires to be mediated and enlivened by images. Indeed without this mediational role of *phantasia*, said Aristotle, the human soul would not be *motivated* to take action in the world, pursuing certain desirable forms of "imagined" behavior and avoiding undesirable ones. It is by recalling images of the results of past actions and projecting images of possible future outcomes that moral agents are moved to adopt this or that course of behavior. Aristotle almost went so far as to suggest that without the mediational role of imagination, humans would be unable to act ethically at all. However, like most Greek thinkers, he is also aware of the dangers of phantasia; hence his insistence that *phantasia* be limited to a "middle" status between sensation and reason and not be left unguided lest in fever, lust, or sleep it lead to degenerate behavior (*De Anima*, 429).

Whereas Philostratus and several neo-Platonists tended to stress the positive mediations of imagination, many of the later medieval thinkers offered a more hostile account of its penchant for idolatry, lies, and demonic possession. However, it is probably fair to say that most leading figures of the "Christian synthesis" of biblical and Greek legacies carried on the paradoxical heritage. Thus, for example, Augustine could denounce the proclivities of corporeal imagination and praise the resurrectional properties of "spiritual" imagination (*De Gen.*, XII). Aquinas, for his part, was able to corroborate Bonaventure's warnings against the demonic potential of imagination and, at the same time, commend its powers (a) to receive prophetic visions from God (*Sec. Secondae*, 171-173), and (b) to deliberate about future ends by "dividing, composing and forming different images even of things not received through the senses" (*Summa Th.*, I, 84, 6).

Thus we find the medieval *imaginatio* developing the function of mediator between the "lower" order of corporeal impulses, passions and drives (*appetitus/sensus*) and the "higher" order of spiritual thought (*ratio/contemplatio*). The controversies over the use of religious images in the Middle Ages exemplify this ambivalent status of imagination in telling fashion. Many Church edicts on iconography were deeply wary of the idolatrous tendencies of imaging, with the Byzantine Church actually outlawing religious art in 745; however, several notable authorities did promote a "pedagogical" use of images for instructing the faithful in the great mysteries of religion. Thus Gregory the Great argued in the sixth century that "painting can do for the illiterate what writing can do for those who read." Holy paintings and icons of the Passion and Deposition, this reasoning went, could move onlookers to contemplate more keenly the narratives of Sacred Scripture. Because the divine had made itself historically manifest through Christ, the Madonna, and the Saints, these could provide us with suitable figures for imitation. However, the very holiness and uniqueness of these persons meant that the icon maker or religious portraitist could not simply produce life like representations of people or follow his own creative fancy. The religious image was there not to express the originality of the artist or the reality of human nature. It was neither a construction nor a description but a representational mediation of sacrosanct types ordained by an age-old Tradition. "A medieval artist of Western Europe," as E. H. Gombrich (1972) noted, would not have understood "why he should invent new ways of planning a church, of designing a chalice or of representing the sacred story where the old ones served their purpose so well" (p. 119). For medieval iconographers or builders of basilicas, modern notions of "originality" were quite unthinkable.

The central lesson medieval teaching took from its Greek and biblical traditions was that imagination could serve a "good" function as mediator of transcendent reality (via religious *imagos*), but became "evil" as soon as it mistook itself as origin or end in itself. The great crime of imagination, as both Adam and Prometheus illustrated, was the hubris of *immediacy*; that is, the temptation to supplant the divine and set oneself up as a "little god" lording it over the universe. The great virtue of imagination, by contrast, was to serve as indispensable agency of *mediation* between the transcendent and the immanent, the divine and the human, the spiritual and the sensible, providing mortals with narrative images which make present what is absent and thereby motivate the human soul to remember the past, anticipate the future, and, above all, act in the present.

MODERN STORIES OF IMAGINATION

This was to change. In the modern era, imagination ceased to be thought of as a medium of imitation and representation and was hailed instead as a power of production in its own right. No longer seen as a mirror that reflects and reproduces copies, imagination gradually assumed the status of a creative origin of vision projecting new worlds out of itself. Whereas Descartes hailed the *cogito* as master and possessor of nature, Kant went a step further proclaiming *transcendental imagination* was the common source of both our sensible and intelligible experience—an "indispensable faculty of the human soul without which no knowledge whatsoever would be possible." This rise of modern imagination represented a triumph of subjectivity.

The mutation from *mimetic* to *productive* paradigms of imagining coincided with a number of "Copernican revolutions." In science it corresponded, obviously, to the discovery by Copernicus and Galileo that the earth is no longer centre of the divinely orchestrated universe, as Ptolemy had taught, but one planet amongst others whose cosmic rotations are determined by laws knowable to the human mind. In social history, it corresponded to the dismantling of the medieval hierarchies and feudal monarchies (the displacement of the King as divinely elected head of society) and their replacement by new bourgeois or workers' republics. In religion, it corresponded to the breakup of medieval Christendom and the emergence of alternative Protestant and "dissenting" religions (not to mention secular atheisms) that defied the orthodox authority of the Pope and affirmed the spiritual primacy of individual believers. In art, it found echoes in the triumph of Renaissance and Romantic humanisms whose emphasis on the "originality" of human expression represented a mutiny against the traditional aesthetic of subservient mimesis.

What was true for modern authors of art was equally true for its spectators. The introduction of one-point perspective with Renaissance painting made "a god of the spectator who becomes the person on whom the whole world converges, the Unmoved Onlooker. Perspective gathers the visual facts and makes them a unified field" (Hughes, 1980, p. 17). Finally, in the realm of the philosophy of imagination that directly concerns us, it was in Kant's famous claims for the primacy of transcendental imagination made in the first edition of *The Critique of Pure Reason* (1781), and subsequently developed by German Idealists like Fichte and Schelling, that the "Copernican Revolution" reached its conceptual apex.

What I call the modern paradigm of imagination was epitomized by the persuasion that the productive human self was henceforth to be celebrated as centerpiece of the universe. Transcendental imagination was hailed accordingly as the darling of modern romanticism—receiving such enthusiastic accolades as "the divine spark in man" (Keats), "another name for absolute power" (Wordsworth), "the spiritual fountainhead divine" (Blake), "the unconscious poetry of being" (Schelling), "prime agent of all human perception" (Coleridge), "the very possibility of our consciousness, our life and our being" (Fichte).

The claims of romantic idealism were refined somewhat by later existentialist and phenomenological thinkers. Nietzsche developed the modern primacy of imagination into a theory that all truth is but a mask of art, all value but an invention of self. Whereas Husserl, the founding father of phenomenology, redefined imagination as an intentional act of consciousness capable of bringing us into immediate intuitive contact with the "essences" of things. He declared "fiction to be the source of all eternal truths"; and his disciple, Sartre, went further still in affirming imagination to be the transcendental precondition of human freedom. We are free to the extent that we deploy our creative power of imagination to negate (*néantir*) the world as given and project new possibilities of existing. "Man is what he makes of himself," Sartre's formula ran, precisely because imagination posits each individual subject as the *immediate* source of the creation of meaning. A similar point is made by Bachelard (1957) in *Poetics of Space* when he argued that a phenomenology of imagination "must do away with all *intermediaries* . . . it is not a question of observing but of experiencing being in its *immediacy*."[4]

This paradigm shift from traditional to modern theories of imagination is exemplified in the mutation of the "solar" metaphor. Although imagination was conceived in the Greek, biblical, and Medieval cultures as a "mirror" reflecting the light of a transcendent sun, modern culture redescribes it as a sun in its own right—a "lamp" creating and projecting light from within itself onto the surrounding world. This dramatic shift from self-as-mirror to self-as-sun, however, was already anticipated by other poets. Standing on the threshold between old and new worlds, Shakespeare dramatized the "overreaching" powers of imagination as it threatened to topple the sun from its place in the natural order and plunge the world into darkness. Accounts of this solar reversal often came in response to the murder of divinely elected Kings such as Hamlet's father or Duncan in *Macbeth*. It is no doubt, however, in the apocalyptic speech of Ulysses in *Troilus and Cressida* that Shakespeare most strikingly articulated the implications of transgression against the solar hierarchy:

> The heavens themselves, the planets, and this centre,
> observe degree, priority and place,

insisture, course, proportion, season, form,
office, and custom, in all line of order:
and therefore is the glorious planet Sol
in noble eminence enthroned and sphered
amidst the other: whose med'cinable eye
corrects the ill aspects of planets evil,
and posts, like the commandment of a king,
sans check to good and bad . . .
O' when degree is shaken,
which is the ladder of all high designs,
the enterprise is sick . . .
Take but degree away, untune that string,
and, hark! what discord follows . . .

Once the transcendent Reign of Sol collapses, the corresponding authorities of God, King, Father, and Reason fall into question—the result is that the human self which set itself up as Lord of the universe finally destroys itself from excess of its own ambitions:

And the rude son should strike his father dead:
force should be right: or rather, right and wrong,
between whose endless jar justice resides,
should lose their names, and so should justice too.
Then everything includes itself in power,
power into will, will into appetite:
and appetite, an universal wolf,
so doubly seconded with will and power,
must make perforce a universal prey,
and last eat up itself. (Act I, Scene 3)

Although Shakespeare's metaphors of the solar shift display a mind tormentingly suspended between tradition and modernity, the more fully-fledged advocates of modern humanism who followed him had no such reservations. Kant, as we saw, expressed his version of the Copernican Revolution in terms of the centrality of imagination and the affirmation of "solar" will as sovereign legislator. Hegel endorsed the subjectivist character of modern aesthetics as an expression of the fact that the creative mind is "properly satisfied only when it has penetrated with its thought all the products of its own activity" (1975). On the other hand, representing the more materialist side of the solar dialectic, Karl Marx argued in 1843 that we would remain incapable of the modern discovery that "man is the highest being for man," until such time as we dispelled religious belief in a transcendent deity: "Religion is the illusory sun about which man revolves so long as he does not revolve about himself." Traditional alienation, he argued, stemmed from the erroneous belief that "I owe to another not only the continuance of my life but also its *creation*, its source." Independence and liberty only come when self acknowledges itself as creative origin of power. We thus witness a crucial mutation from the premodern view that the alienated self is one who does not believe in God as "solar" center of the world, to the modern view that she or he is one who *does* believe in such a God. For modernity, the human self is free when it is its own master and is its own master when it "owes its existence to itself"!

It was undoubtedly the romantic poets, however, who most emphatically altered the Shakespearean ambivalence. Baudelaire (1971) made the metaphor of solar revolution his own when he hailed imagination as "queen of the faculties" "illuminating things with (its) spirit and projecting its reflection onto other spirits": and goes on to affirm that imagination "is positively related to the infinite," being "fit to govern the world since it has created it" (pp. 26-27). It is undoubtedly Shelley, however, who offered the most extravagant paean to imagination as sovereign Sun of the universe when he wrote in *Epipsychidion*, "Your light, Imagination! which, from earth and sky and the depth of human fantasy, like a myriad of prisms . . . fills the universe with its luminous rays and slays error, that worm, with more than one solar arrow of its sounding thunder."

This cursory review of the paradigm shift in the solar metaphor of creativity suggests how modernity is epitomized by the reign of productive imagination. All the aforementioned examples testify to the condition of a modern subject that finds itself homeless in a world bereft of traditional mediations and resolves to build a new house for itself in imagination. The transcendental imagination—under whatever pseudonym—purports to fill the spiritual desert with its own creations, to become its own promised land.

Some would argue that the modern cult of imagination became so inflated that it eventually foundered, ran out of wind, degenerated into a terminal crisis of self-parody commonly known as *postmodernity*. By this reading, the productive paradigm degenerates into a parodic paradigm where imagination circulates aimlessly in an endless play of simulation. Images are no longer seen as "authentic" expressions of a creative human self but as imitations of imitations of imitations—without "origin" and without "end." Thus one might say that the premodern metaphor of the *mirror* and the modern metaphor of the *lamp* both give way to a postmodern metaphor of a circle of looking glasses, reflecting surface images in a game of infinite multiplication. Or, to put this genealogy of paradigms in a Joycean formula, the traditional figure of the *artificer* (mimesis) is surpassed by the modern figure of the *penman* (self-expression) and eventually by the postmodern figure of the *postman* (anonymous communications system).

Elsewhere, I have tried to show how this postmodern picture of self-multiplying images without depth or interiority is a dominant preoccupation of not only postmodern theorists but also many contemporary authors, artists and film makers.[5] My purpose in this study, however, is not to rehearse such arguments but to show how the genealogical story of imagination running from ancient cosmogony to contemporary crisis provides us with some useful pointers to a discussion of the ethical importance of imagination today. Whereas traditional accounts—biblical and Greek—prescribed a political or communal function for human creativity, modernity celebrates a more subjective and solipsistic approach, while postmodernity appears to declare the entire project of social creativity redundant. It is against this genealogical backdrop that I now explore some of the ethical consequences of imagination for contemporary society. These I will treat under two main headings: (a) Imagination as Historical Narrative, and (b) Imagination as Narrative Identity.

Thus we move from our preliminary exposé of narratives of imagination to a brief analysis of the narrative imagination itself—that without which, one might say, there would never have been a story of imagination in the first place.

IMAGINATION AS HISTORICAL NARRATIVE

One of the key functions of imagination discussed by contemporary hermeneutics is its ability to "provide ourselves with a figure of something"(Ricoeur, 1988, p. 184). Thus imagination can serve the role of rendering what is absent present, or quasi-present. Translated into the idiom of historical time, this means liberating us from the blind amnesia of a limitless present by projecting us towards a future or retrieving a forgotten past. Projection is the "utopian" function of imagination, retrieval the "testimonial" function.

In *Time and Narrative*, Ricoeur (1988) analyzed the testimonial role of imagination in relation to historical narrative. A contemporary poetics of narrative, he argued, must include a sense of ethical responsibility to "the debt we owe the dead" (p. 184). We would not be able to respond to the summons of the historical past were it not for the mediating/schematizing function of imagination that provides us with "figures" for things that happened but are forgotten or suppressed from memory. The responsibility here is a double one. On the one hand, narrative imagination provides us with figural reconstructions of the past that enable us to see and hear things long since gone; on the other, it is committed to "standing for" these things as events that actually happened. Here we encounter the complex ethical right of the past as it once was to incite and rectify our narrative retellings of history. We recall our debt to those who have lived, suffered, and died. We remind ourselves, for example, that gas ovens and gulags did exist, that Nagasaki and Cambodia *were* bombed, that political crimes and injustices *have been* inflicted on innocent people over the centuries.

The ostensible paradox here of course is that it should be *imagination* that responds to the ethical summons to respect the "reality of the past." It is poetics that comes to the service of ethics as a means of recalling our debt to those who acted, suffered, and died. The service is by no means a simple one. In addition to narrative reenactment— reappropriating the past as present under the category of the Same— historical imagination also has a duty to the *otherness* of the past by way of expressing the past precisely as *past*; that is, *as* something that is no more. "It is always through some transfer from Same to Other, in empathy and imagination, that the Other that is foreign is brought closer" (Ricoeur, 1988, p. 184). It is this hermeneutic *transfer by analogy* that enables us to transport ourselves into alien or eclipsed moments, refiguring them as *similar* to our present experience (failing which we would not be able to recognize them) while acknowledging their *dissimilarity* as historically different and distant. In short, the narrative reappropriation of the past operates according to a double fidelity (a) to the past as present and (b) to the past as past.

To the extent that it remains ethically responsible to historical memory, imagination refuses to allow reconstruction to become a reduction of the other to the self, of difference to sameness (Lyotard, 1991). Thus when we talk of narrative imagination providing us with "analogies" of the past as-it-actually-was, we should appreciate that the analogous "as" is a two-way trope of *absence-in-presence*.

The narrative refiguration of the past comprises a complex interweaving of fiction and history. Once we recognize that historical narrative involves a *refiguring* of the past we can admit that the writing and telling of history deploys strategies of literary practice—plot, composition, character, point of view. That is why the same text can be a great work of history *and* a great work of fiction. It can tell us about the way things actually happened in the past at the same time as it makes us see, feel, and live it *as if* we were there. Moreover, this "fiction effect" of history can often enhance, rather than diminish, the task of standing-for. One thinks, for example, of Michelet's version of the French Revolution, a historical narrative whose literary qualities are almost comparable to Tolstoy's *War and Peace*. Fiction can serve history, and this service includes an ethical as well as a poetical dimension.

The deployment of novelistic techniques by historians to place vividly before the reader's mind some long past event or personage was already recognized by Aristotle in the *Rhetoric*, under the title of *lexis* or "locution"—a manner of making things visible as if they were present. The danger is, of course, that the figural "as if" might collapse into a literal belief, so that we would no longer merely "see-as" but make the mistake of "believing" we are actually seeing. This danger of the "hallucination of presence" (easily leading to dogmatism or fundamentalism) is resisted by the ethical vigilance of historians who sustain a proper dialectical balance between engagement and disbelief.

However, critical freedom from naive illusion is not the only ethical responsibility of narrative imagination. Equally important is the responsibility to refigure certain events of deep ethical intensity that conventional historiographical methods might be tempted to overlook in favor of a so-called "objective" explanation of things. In a case like Auschwitz, for instance, it would seem that the practice of "neutralization" is quite inappropriate. The biblical watchword *Zakhor*, "*Remember!*" is more ethically fitting in such circumstances. This is something Primo Levi (1987), a survivor of the camps, made hauntingly plain in his resolve to tell the story as it happened in the most vivid fashion imaginable. The recourse to narrative tropes and devices to achieve this impact is motivated throughout by an ethical imperative: *people must never be allowed to forget lest it happen again.* Or, as Levi himself put it in his conclusion to *Si c'est un Homme?*: "The need to recount to 'others,' to make the 'others' participate, acquired in us before and after our liberation the vehemence of an immediate impulse . . . and it was in response to such a need that I wrote my book".

In such cases, rememoration takes on an ethical character of testimony quite distinct from the triumphalist commemoration of history's Great and Powerful. And if the latter often tends to legitimate ideologies of domination and conquest, the former moves in the opposite direction—that is, toward a *felt* reliving of past suffering, injustice or horror *as if* we (readers/listeners/spectators) were actually there. The distinction is important. The cause of the *tremendum horrendum* needs narrative imagination to plead its case lest it slip irrevocably into oblivion.

Horror attaches to events that must never be forgotten. It constitutes the ultimate ethical motivation for the history of victims. The victims of

Auschwitz are, par excellence, the representatives in our memory of all history's victims. Victimization is the other side of history that no cunning or reason can ever justify and that, instead, reveals the scandal of every theodicy of history. (Ricoeur, 1988, p. 187)

In such instances, the refigurative powers of narrative imagination prevent abstract historiography from neutralizing injustice or, quite simply, explaining things away. This ethical task of retrieving the specificity of historical sufferings from sanitizing homogenization applies not only to the positivist reductionism of certain historical scientists but also to the speculative systematizing of Hegel's Ruse of Reason and the mystical musings of Heidegger's Destiny of Techné (which put gas chambers and combine harvesters into the same category) (Wolin, 1992).

The ethical role of imagination in remembering the horrible is tied to a specific function of *individuation* in our historical consciousness; namely, the need to respect the *uniquely unique* character of events such as the Holocaust, Hiroshima, or the Gulag. It is precisely this function that appears to be increasingly threatened by our contemporary culture of simulation where the role of imagination is reduced more and more to a play of surface imitation and repetition devoid of reference to historical reality. Jameson (1985) decried this eclipse of the historically real or unique as a postmodern cult of the depthless present. However, other commentators of contemporary culture, such as Baudrillard and Lyotard, seem at times to celebrate this absence of reference. Lyotard claimed that the forms and figures of imagination fall short of presenting the "irrepresentable" nature of the postmodern sublime, whereas Baudrillard hailed the postmodern condition of "irreference" where even the historical reality of war is reduced to a game of spectacle and simulation (see Baudrillard, 1983). We can no longer distinguish between what is real and unreal in contemporary representations of things, and one is tempted to conclude that it is a short step indeed from Baudrillard's kind of thinking here to the claims of pseudohistorians like Faurrison or Irving that the gas chambers never existed. In any case, what the postmodern cult of irrepresentability and irreference disputes is the power of historical imagination to singularize and retrieve certain incomparable events for ethical consideration.

The more narrative imagination individuates and singularizes historical memories the more we strive to understand them, and the more we understand them the better able we should be, in the long run, to scientifically explain them. It is less a question, therefore, of simplistically opposing "subjective" imagination to "objective" explanation than of appreciating that explanation without imagination is ultimately inhuman.

The refigurative act of *standing-for* the past provides us with a "figure" to see and to think about, to imagine and to respond to. "Fiction gives eyes to the horrified narrator. Eyes to see and to weep. The present state of literature on the Holocaust provides ample proof of this. Either one counts the cadavers or one *tells the story* of the victims" (Ricoeur, 1988, p. 188).

Moreover, the interweaving of fiction and history reminds us of the fact that both narrative modes share a common origin in *epic*. A particular characteristic of epic is that it preserves the memory of suffering (or glory in other contexts) on the *collective* scale of societies. Placed in the service of the unforgettable, narrative permits us to live up to the task of social memory. For history-telling to forfeit this testimonial vocation is to risk becoming an idle game of exotica or a positivism of dead facts. Neither option is ethical. "There are crimes that must not be forgotten, victims whose suffering cries less for vengeance than for narration," as Ricoeur reminded us. "The will not to forget alone can prevent these crimes from ever occurring again" (p. 189). Here the ethical debt to social memory joins forces with the poetical power to narrate.

IMAGINATION AS NARRATIVE IDENTITY

The second function of contemporary imagination I wish to mention here is *narrative identity*. Once again we find that the very notion of human identity—social and individual—is increasingly threatened in a postmodern civilization where human subjects are defined as "desiring machines" (Deleuze) or "effects of signifiers" (Derrida). The best response to this contemporary crisis of identity is not, I suggest, to seek to revive some substantialist notion of the person as essence, cogito, or ego, but rather to look once again to the resources of narrative imagination.

The most fitting response to the question "Who is the author or agent?" is to tell the story of a life. The perduring identity of a person, presupposed by the designation of a proper name, is provided by the narrative conviction that it is the same subject who perdures through its diverse acts and words between birth and death. The story told tells about the action of the "who," and the identity of this "who" is a narrative identity.

The narrative self, be it individual or collective, involves an ongoing process of self-constancy and self-rectification that requires imagination to synthesize the different horizons of past, present, and future. (Something recognized by Heidegger in his hermeneutic rereading of Kant's theory of transcendental imagination) (see Kearney, 1988, pp. 189-

195). The narrative concept of self thus offers a dynamic notion of identity that includes mutability and change within what Dilthey called the cohesion of one lifetime (*Zusammenhang des Lebens*). This means, for example, that the identity of social subjects is recognized as a constant task of reinterpretation in the light of new and old stories we tell about ourselves and others. The social subject becomes, to borrow a Proustian formula, both the reader and writer of its own life. No less than the story of an individual life, the story of a society is perpetually refigured by all the real or fictive stories it tells about itself. A society's self-image is a "cloth woven of stories told" (Ricoeur, 1988, p. 246).

The narrative model of self-identity has been developed by a number of contemporary thinkers, from Ricoeur and MacIntyre to Taylor and Benhabib. They argue the rudimentary point that the Enlightenment view of the disembodied cogito, no less than the empiricist illusion of a substance-like self, fail to appreciate the fundamental processes of *socialization* through which a person or community acquires a self-identity capable of projecting a narrative into the world of which it is both an author and an actor (see Benhabib, 1992, p. 5f). The narrative model of identity suggests that the age-old virtue of self-knowledge, first promoted by Socrates and Seneca, involves not some self-regarding ego but an examined life freed from archaisms and dogmatisms. The ethical subject of collective or individual self-knowledge is one clarified by the cathartic effects of historical/fictional narratives conveyed by its culture. Self-constancy is therefore a property of a subject instructed by the figures of a culture it has critically and creatively applied to itself (Ricoeur, 1988).

At the level of personal identity, this narrative clarification occurs when the individual commits itself to working the bits and pieces of unintelligible, suppressed or forgotten experience into some coherent narrative in which it can acknowledge a self-constancy in and through change. However, this model of analytic working-through (*Durcharbeitung*) equally applies to the collective stories of communities recounted by historians. Just as psychoanalysis can show how the story of a life comes to be composed through a series of rectifications applied to preceding narratives, so too the history of a society proceeds from the series of corrections and clarifications new historians bring to their predecessors' accounts (mythical and historiographical).

A community comes to imagine and to know itself in the stories it tells about itself. To take the classic case of biblical Israel, it is precisely in the telling and retelling of its own foundational narratives that the historical community bearing its name was formed. Exemplifying the hermeneutic circle of narrative identity, it draws its self-image from the reinterpretation of those texts it has itself created. For both collective and personal identity, stories proceed from stories.

If narrative identity is to be ethically responsible, however, it must always bear in mind that its roots in narrative imagination ensure that its self-constancy is always permeated with self-questioning. There is a fundamental fluidity and openness built into models of narrative identity by virtue of the recognition that it is always something made and remade. A society which acknowledges that it reconstitutes itself through an ongoing process of narrative is as incapable of self-righteousness as it is of fundamentalism. Any temptation to collective solipsism is resisted by the imaginative tendency of narrative to freely vary worlds foreign to ourselves, And it is this same propulsion of narrative imagination beyond itself towards otherness that entails an ethical movement towards social action and commitment.

Citing the well-known example of a subject's capacity to keep its promises over time and history, Ricoeur (1988) affirmed that narrative identity is only equivalent to "true self-constancy" in the moment of decision which makes "ethical responsibility the highest factor in self-constancy" (p. 249). Thus, to return to our example of Israel, we might say that it is the Jewish community's ability to reimagine itself through its own narratives which provides it with not only the coherent identity of an historical people but also the ethical resource to imagine the narratives of others (e.g., the Palestinians) to whom they appear implacably opposed. The ethical moment of decision might thus be seen as an expression of the Jewish imagination's constancy of narrative memory which recalls the age-old moral demand to liberate the imprisoned, to care for "the famished, the widowed and the orphaned."

The idea that narrative identity is somehow ethically neutral or empty is further belied by the obvious evaluative and prescriptive dimension of narrative *persuasion*. Every imaginative narrative challenges its reader/recipient with the basic Rilkean summons: Change your life!

CONCLUSION

I would like to address, finally, a certain claim of postmodern theory—running from Foucault and Lyotard to Deleuze and Derrida—that poetics has priority over ethics. This sometimes expresses itself in an aesthetic of "deliberate irresponsibility" as has been said of Foucault, or in one of indecisive "indifference" as has been suggested of Derrida (see Kearney, 1987; Miller, 1992). Whatever about the accuracy of such claims, however, they do betray a legitimate anxiety that postmodern poetics, left to itself, can be a dangerous game.

What I have been arguing is that narrative imagination provides us with both a poetics *and* an ethics of responsibility in that it propels us beyond self-reference to a relation of analogy/apperception/empathy with others. This extension of the circle of self involves an "enlarged mentality" capable of imagining oneself in the place of the other; a mentality that Arendt (1977) considered essential to genuine ethical judgment. "The power of judgment rests on a potential agreement with others," she wrote:

> and the thinking process which is active in judging something is not, like the thought process or pure reasoning, a dialogue between me and myself, but finds itself always and primarily, even if I am quite alone in making up my mind, in an anticipated communication with others with whom I know I must finally come to some agreement. From this potential agreement judgment derives its specific validity. . . . It needs the special presence or others "in whose place" it must think, whose perspectives it must take into consideration, and without whom it never has the opportunity to operate at all. (pp. 220-221; see also Isaac, 1992)

This "representative" mode of ethical imagination is a liberation from one's own private interests without being a liquidation of one's basic identity. "The more people's standpoints I have present in my mind while I am pondering a given issue, and the better I can imagine how I would think and feel if I were in their place, the stronger will be my capacity for representative thinking" (Arendt, 1977, pp. 220-221). Ethical judgment, it appears, solicits a basic act of altruism or kenosis wherein the self flows from itself towards the other through the free variation of imagination. Opening us to foreign worlds, and enabling us to tell and listen to other stories, narrative imagination serves as precondition for the representative. It is this ethical act of imagination, in the final analysis, that transfigures the self-same self into a self-for-another.

What I would say in conclusion is that, in spite of current pronouncements on the demise of creative imagination, our contemporary society of spectacle and simulation has more need than ever of its narrative powers. These powers are necessary, as I hope to have shown, both to refigure historical memory and to transform our understanding of identity into an ethical model of selfhood—individual and social. Imagination is not, needless to say, always on the side or the angels. However, as our genealogical and ethical analyses have indicated there is in imagination, and especially its narrative functions, a profound moral commitment to a dimension of otherness beyond the self, a commitment that in the moment of ultimate decision enables the self to imagine itself as another and to imagine the other as another self. Without such imagining it is difficult to see how any ethics—ancient, modern, or postmodern—could properly exist.

NOTES

1. Roland Barthes described our contemporary mass-media society as a "Civilization of the image," whereas Daniel Boorstin spoke of America becoming a culture of "pseudoevents." See my discussion of these notions in *The Wake of Imagination*, 1988, especially the Introduction and Part III entitled "Postmodern Narratives."
2. See my chapter in *The Wake of Imagination*, 1988, on "The Hebraic Imagination," pp. 37-78.
3. See *The Wake of Imagination*, pp. 103-105.
4. I attempt a more developed treatment of these phenomenological theories of Husserl, Sartre and Bachelard in the opening chapters of my *Poetics of Imagining*.
5. For a development of this argument see *The Wake of Imagination*, pp. 251-398 and *Poetics of Imagining*, pp. 170-232.

REFERENCES

Arendt, H. (1977). The crisis in culture. In *Between past and future* (pp. 220-221). Middlesex, England: Penguin.

Bachelard, G. (1957). *Poetics of space*. Boston: Beacon Press.

Baudelaire, C.-P. (1971). Salon de 1857. In *sur l'art 2* (pp. 26-27). Paris: Gallimard.

Baudrillard, J. (1983). *Simulations*. New York: Semiotexte.

Benhabib, S. (1992). *Situating the self*. New York: Routledge.

Gombrich, E.H. (1972). *The story of art*. London: Phaidon.

Hegel, F. (1975). *Aesthetics* (J.M. Knox, trans.). Oxford, England: Claredon.

Hughes, R. (1980). *The shock of the new*. London: BBC Publications.

Isaac, J. (1992). *Arendt, Camus and modern rebellion*. New Haven, CT: Yale University Press.

Jameson, F. (1985). Postmodernism and consumer society. In H. Foster (Ed.), *Postmodern culture* (pp. 111-126). London: Pluto Press.

Kant, E. (1981). *The critique of pure reason* (N.K. Smith, trans.). New York: St. Martins Press.

Kearney, R. (1987). *Dialogues with contemporary continental thinkers*. Manchester, England: Manchester University Press.

Kearney, R. (1988). *The wake of imagination*. London: Hutchinson.

Kearney, R. (1991) *Poetics of imagining*. London: Routledge.

Levi, P. (1987). *Si c'est un homme?* Paris: Julliard.

Lyotard, J.F. (1991). *The inhuman*. Stanford, CA: Stanford University Press.

Marx, K. (1963). *Karl Marx—Early writings* (T. Bottomore, ed.). London: Watts

Miller, J. (1992). *The passion of Michel Foucault*. New York: Simon and Schuster.

Ricoeur, P. (1988). *Time and narrative* (Vol. 3). Chicago: University of Chicago Press.

Scholem, G. (1952). *On the Kabbalah and its symbolism*. New York: Schocken.

Wolin, R. (1992). *The Heidegger controversy*. Cambridge, MA: MIT Press.

PART TWO

CREATIVITY AND MODERNITY

3

*The Two Faces of Creativity**

Morris Berman

There is one aspect of Western creativity that has been commented on by sociologists and cultural historians alike, and that is its peculiar tendency to burn out or destroy the artist, often at a relatively young age. Why this should be so remains unclear, but the "tortured artist syndrome," represented by figures as diverse as James Dean and John Keats, does seem to be a persistent feature of modern Western life. Thus Elliott Jaques (1970), some years ago, provided ample statistics to show a recurrent pattern of midlife crisis, frequently leading to death, among creative people, whereas Katinka Matson (1980), in *Short Lives*, gave the reader a series of extremely interesting vignettes that reveal artistic self-destructive tendencies all too clearly. In a similar vein, A. Alvarez (1973), in his study of suicide, argued that modern creativity is "provisional, dissatisfied, restless". All of this, as the cultural anthropologist Gregory Bateson (1958, 1973) would have said, comes under the heading of *schismogenesis*—the tendency to move toward climax or breakdown; and in this sense, modern Western creativity is a reflection of the culture in which it is embedded. There are exceptions, of course, but the cliché of the driven (and, frequently, alcoholic) artist is not only common, but actually a kind of cultural ideal—a "good thing," as it were; or at least, something we have come to expect.

*This is a slightly edited version of a chapter from Morris Berman, *Coming to Our Senses*, New York: Simon & Schuster, 1995.

That creativity has to be self-destructive or schismogenic is, accordingly, taken as a given. Genius continues to be regarded as akin to madness, and creative individuals are somehow seen as members of a separate species, inhabiting worlds that most of us will never see or even understand. The problem with this way of viewing human creativity is that it is ahistorical. It assumes that the mainsprings of the creative impulse are somehow archetypal, true for all time; that in effect, there is only one way to "do it." As a result, we have thousands of histories of art, music, science, architecture, and so on, but apparently nothing on the history of creativity itself. Of course, if the creative act is fixed for all time, then there is nothing to write. But suppose this were not so? Suppose the creative process itself has evolved over the centuries, or millennia? This would mean that there is more than one way to do it, and that future creativity might be a very different animal from the one it is now. My guess is that the creative process can be understood both historically and psychodynamically, in terms of a typology, and that such a typology can lay bare not only the nature(s) of creativity itself, but also of the wider culture(s) of which it is a part. Both in art and in society, schismogenesis leading to breakdown might not be the only option we have. What follows is thus an investigation into the varieties of creative experience as well as an attempt to explore what the alternatives to the schismogenic model are or might be.

One of the best treatments of the subject occurs, surprisingly enough, in an extraordinarily bad piece of historical writing published by Sigmund Freud (1964) in 1910; namely, his study of the life and work of Leonardo da Vinci. As a historical argument, the essay is a complete failure, a mass of unsubstantiated conjecture and speculation. Yet in a few short pages, Freud generates a typology of the creative process that strikes me as being immensely suggestive, and it is one that stayed in my mind long after I forgot the discussion of Leonardo, per se. Freud's typology is too stark, and it is also incomplete; however, given the available alternatives, it is not a bad place to start. Freud was specifically interested in intellectual activity, and its relationship to sexuality; but I believe that if we are willing to broaden this and talk in terms of sensual experience of the world in general—an experience that includes curiosity and exploration as major components—his analysis can be extended to all forms of creative work. Let me, therefore, take a bit of poetic license with Freud's exposition, modifying it in certain ways, and see whether it can be helpful to the inquiry at hand.

Freud began his discussion by noting that there is a certain type of person who pursues creative activity "with the same passionate devotion that another would give to his love" (p. 27). The crucial event, says Freud, is the fate of what he calls the "period of infantile sexual researches" (p.

29), or, more generally, the pleasure the child takes in the sensual exploration of its surroundings. This may include curiosity about the birth process, but the larger expression is a tactile-erotic one, and this total lack of inhibition tends to make the parents nervous. Unconsciously, they are stirred to remember when they, too, were like this, and how this openness toward the world got quashed. Disturbed by this unconscious awareness, they do the same thing to their own children. The impulse then gets thwarted and repressed, and this, said Freud, has three possible outcomes. In the first and overwhelmingly typical case, the child's curiosity gets shut down. The child learns that such openness, such creative expression, is risky business. The result, says Freud, is that creative expression "may be limited for the whole of the subject's lifetime" (p. 29). In the second case, the child's development is sufficiently strong to resist the repression to some degree. The repressed sensuality then returns from the unconscious "in the form of compulsive brooding, naturally in a distorted and unfree form, but sufficiently powerful to sexualize thinking itself and to color [creative or artistic] operations with the pleasure and anxiety that belong to the sexual processes proper" (p. 30). The brooding never ends; eros is transferred to the creative activity and the latter becomes a substitute for it. In the third case, said Freud, "the libido evades the fate of repression by being sublimated from the very beginning" (p. 30). The transition is smooth, the quality of neurosis absent; the instinct operates freely in the service of creative activity.

In general, Freud's schema (modified) might look something like this:

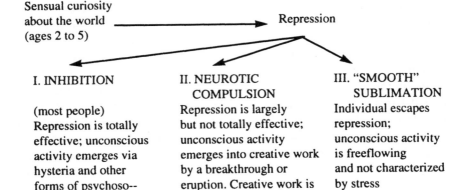

Sensual curiosity about the world (ages 2 to 5) ⟶ Repression

I. INHIBITION	II. NEUROTIC COMPULSION	III. "SMOOTH" SUBLIMATION
(most people) Repression is totally effective; unconscious activity emerges via hysteria and other forms of psychoso--matic illness. Posture toward life is one of (usually unconscious) fear and hatred.	Repression is largely but not totally effective; unconscious activity emerges into creative work by a breakthrough or eruption. Creative work is the substitute lover.	Individual escapes repression; unconscious activity is freeflowing and not characterized by stress

There is not much to say about Type I creativity, because it is the counterexample, the decision to give up on creativity (and really on life) altogether. The repression is so effective that all creative expression is blocked forever. Most people mask this early defeat with substitute activity, but it shows up somatically, or psychosomatically, when they are caught off guard. Type II, the neurotic model, was—as far as Freud was concerned—typical of most creative work. As we have said, in this case the person fights back, for the spirit is not completely extinguished. However, the result of this partial repression is a situation soaking in ambivalent emotions. The creative work has an obsessive quality to it; one is "married" to one's work, as the saying goes. Tension and passion are the characteristic modes of expression here.

Type III is the least familiar case. The repression is very slight, and the translation of sensual energy or exploring spirit into creative work is carried out with a minimum of trauma. Such work has a relaxed, spontaneous feeling. In the early pages of the da Vinci biography, Freud put Leonardo into this category; by the end of the book, however, he is forced to conclude, based on his own evidence, that the Italian master was a Type II. As a result, Creativity III emerges as an empty category. It is an intriguing possibility, and Freud's insight here is intuitively brilliant, but it would seem to be a category without content, hanging in the middle of nowhere.

One possible candidate for Creativity III might be children's art. I saw such artwork myself many years ago when I worked in a Montessori nursery for 3-year-olds, who had not as yet been hit by too much repression. As aides or counselors, we were instructed never to put the children on the spot by asking them what it was they were painting or constructing, and indeed, they exhibited virtually no performance anxiety whatsoever. It was a pleasure to watch their glee as they immersed themselves in their "work." Looking back, I wouldn't call it great art, but it certainly was not compulsive or conflict-ridden. For better or worse, there were no van Goghs in that nursery. The problem is that if that is all that can be put in this category, then it is not very interesting. What I wish to argue is that Creativity III constitutes a mode of expression that includes most medieval art, the art of non-Western cultures, and the art of traditional societies. It approximates what we call craft, as opposed to art as such. As a result, it throws the creativity of the Western, post-Renaissance world into sharp relief, for it involves a psychodynamic entirely different from that of Creativity II. Modern creativity, or Creativity II, should be seen for what it is: a local and, in fact, fairly recent phenomenon that organizes bodily energy in a particular way. In doing so, it produces a mode of expression that is very powerful and focused, but extremely draining, both for the individual and for the culture at large. In its most extreme and perhaps most talented form, it tends to have the effect we have already mentioned—that of taking the lives of its representatives at a fairly early age.

When I first began thinking about this subject, and specifically about how creativity manifested itself in my own life, there was no avoiding the fact that I fell into the second category. I conformed very well to the popular image of the writer who stayed up all night fueling himself with coffee and tobacco, pacing the floor in frustration as ideas refused to come, and sitting down and writing things out in white heat when they finally surfaced. The pattern was clearly addictive-obsessive; neurotic, in short.

Yet as I thought about it more, I began to see that these were the surface manifestations of a deeper drama. The most creative work I had done resulted from a psychic crisis that ran very deep, and which, once triggered, I was powerless to control. The French psychiatrist Jacques Lacan said that we state our problems on the symbolic level before proceeding to solve them, and something like this had happened to me. It began with the speculation that if worldviews were artifacts, the magical worldview that antedated modern science must have real validity. The more I began to follow that train of thought, the more archaic consciousness began to take me over. Finally, I was in deep trouble. How does the line from *Faust* go? "Two souls reside within my breast." I was both a modern and an ancient, a scientist and an alchemist, and neither side would release its grip. It was a rocky ride, but I had no choice except to live out those contradictions. Once the traditional/modern gap opened up within my psyche, my fate was sealed: I had to heal that split or die. And this, I believe, is the number one characteristic of Creativity II: It is a contemporary form of exorcism. (I am not talking here about *productivity*, which has *no* psychic energy behind it, and that merely involves turning out work in a mechanical fashion.) In Creativity II, you are possessed by an internal conflict, and the work is undertaken to resolve it. You create from pain; or, as John Fowles put it in one of his novels, you create from what you lack, not from what you have. It is this that gives modern poetry, for example, what Robert Bly has called a "leaping" structure. Chaucer, by way of contrast, derives his power from the beautifully crafted language of the narrative. *The Canterbury Tales* are not soaking in unconscious power; they do not "leap," as do, say, many of Bly's own poems.[1]

The second characteristic follows from this: You create yourself out of your work; the work is characterized by "self-expression." In the modern period, art and self-expression (something Chaucer was not after) have practically become synonymous. Creative work must bear a personal signature or style, whereas in the Middle Ages it tended to be anonymous.

Medieval artists typically did not sign their work. Cennino Cennini's essay of 1400, *Il Libro dell' Arte*, announced the artist's intention to break with this tradition, and the book is usually regarded as a turning point, marking the end of the craft tradition and the call for modern artistic creativity. Once again, Fowles (1969) is relevant here. "Romantic and post-Romantic art," he wrote, "is all pervaded by . . . the flight of the individual from whatever threatens his individuality" (pp. 52-53). Modern creativity, he essentially argued, is heavily fueled by the desire to prove that one exists.

A third characteristic, which tends to follow from the first two, is that the creative insight is seen to break through, or erupt from, the unconscious. It is this eruption that generates the psychic split that demands to be healed, and that alters the personality structure so that the work of integration becomes self-expression. Traditional creativity would have to be different, because traditional societies tend, in varying degrees, to be swimming in the unconscious already. Hence, there is nothing, or at least much less, to erupt.

Fourth, modern creative work has a strong addictive or compulsive component; the artist is expected to outdo him- or herself with each succeeding product. ("I work as my father drank," George Bernard Shaw once remarked, quoted in Erikson, 1962, p. 45). It is here that we see the schismogenic character of modern creativity most clearly. The structure is one of "upping the ante;" in other words, work is often "unfinished" because it is done in the pursuit of an inaccessible ideal. It must depart from tradition, must create a new genre, and it grows difficult to keep on doing this. As a result, modern creativity tends to have high psychic costs. The examples of an intense, sustained burst of creative work followed by suicide are legion: Vincent van Gogh, Dylan Thomas (suicide by alcohol), Janis Joplin (possible suicide by drug overdose), Sylvia Plath, Anne Sexton, and on and on. The work ineluctably moves toward breakdown. It is for this reason that so many creative people stop doing what they are doing in their late thirties: They know where it is all leading.[2]

This also explains, in part, why the public loses interest in writers such as Norman Mailer. Mailer's first work, *The Naked and the Dead*, remains his best. From the standpoint of modern creativity, the artist is expected to set up and leap over increasingly higher hurdles. This is the structure of an ever-expanding economy; it is not steady-state. Mailer's career was over almost before it began. The modern Western public is trained to expect novelty from its creative sector; it quickly loses interest in artists who have nothing "new" to offer.

Finally, modern creativity often involves, as Freud said, the sexualization, or at least eroticization, of the activity. One's work becomes one's lover—one's central, and obsessive, relationship. All the dramas that are typically played out in such a relationship get played out here: the initial romantic rush, the subsequent tapering off, jealousy and possessiveness, and finally disillusion and the search for a new love. There is a heavy overlap of Oedipal energy here: Male artists are notorious mama's boys; "heroes" winning battles for the mother. And they do this precisely by innovating, by rupturing tradition—that is, by slaying the father.[3]

We have, in the West, many images that glorify the notion of creativity as being a triumph over adversity. We speak of "the shit that fertilizes roses," or the grain of sand in the oyster that leads to the generation of a pearl. This is the stuff of *Reader's Digest* stories and Ann Landers columns, and these images do capture a truth although they mask a larger one. The truth they capture is that creative work can and often does emerge out of conflict; the truth they mask is that other psychodynamic patterns of the creative process are possible, and that, historically, the conflict model may actually represent an aberration. My goal in this chapter, however, is not to condemn modern Western creativity as "bad" and to enshrine Eastern or premodern creativity as "good." It is, rather, to argue that there are different somatic or energetic processes involved in each case. There is a way, given my own upbringing, that no Indian raga will ever move me as much as Mozart, no Japanese landscape painting resonate for me as deeply as Cézanne's evocative scenes of the Midi. In fact, modern Western art has a brilliance that no medieval icon or Eastern painting can ever approximate, in my view. My point here however, is that it takes a particular energetic configuration to create such an effect, and if Freud is right about Creativity II it actually requires early somatic damage that leads to a distrust of the body and a corresponding shunting of that bodily energy upward, toward the head. The center of gravity is too high, so to speak; there is a way in which the very brilliance of Western creativity depends on its instability, its extremely high level of tension and stress.

Yet the conflict model of creativity, as Freud realized (although he wasn't able to prove it), does not exhaust the entire subject. Psychologists from Otto Rank to Rollo May have insisted on the necessity of stress or tension for the creative act, without realizing that this is a formula for only one type of creative expression.[4] In *Caliban Reborn*, Mellers (1967) addressed himself to the issue of conflict and self-expression, and emphasized how specific it is in time and place:

> While this conception of art is our birthright and has gone to make the world we live in, we have to realize that in the context of history the notion is both newfangled and restricted. It is relevant to only about the last five hundred years of Europe's history. (p. 2)

The difference between music as magic (traditional music) and music as expression, he said, is that the former lacks the element of harmonic tension. Such music, he added, has a strong corporeal component: "In the music of primitive cultures . . . the rhythm is usually corporeal and the music is never self-expression but rather a communal act of work or play which may have magic(al)as well as social significance" (p. 4). Mellers went on to say that "the compositional principles inherent in European music before the Renaissance are not radically distinct from those of Oriental music" (p. 9). In both Gregorian chant and the Indian raga, rhythms such as breath or heartbeat constitute the creative source. The invention of harmony—something of which traditional and Oriental cultures were aware, but which (said Mellers) they never chose to emphasize—ruptured this pattern. That is, it shifted music from a Creativity III to a Creativity II structure.

Many years ago, living near New York City, I used to play a kind of game, experimenting with the shift between Creativity III and Creativity II energy patterns, without really knowing what I was doing or why. In upper Manhattan, I would go to the Cloisters, which houses the medieval collection of the Metropolitan Museum of Art in a Romanesque and Gothic setting, and then, having spent several hours there, would go directly to midtown and to the Museum of Modern Art. I would recommend this experiment to anybody. If you stay tuned to your physical reactions, the effect is quite remarkable. The immersion in a "craft" environment, complete with tapestries, carved wooden doors, stained glass, and illuminated manuscripts, creates a very soothing sensation. The body lets go, as it were, and time seems to stand still. The sensation of silence and tranquility is particularly striking. To follow this up with an immersion in 20th-century art is to give yourself a real shock. The sensation here is one of excitement and anxiety; the dreamy and magnetic sense of wholeness, or union, is replaced by a chaos and dramatic brilliance that explodes on the canvas, or from the sculptures. As in the case of van Gogh (see later discussion), it is as if the breakdown of the psyche resulted in the breakthrough of art. Two hours in such a place as this leaves one both exhilarated and emotionally spent. This simple experiment conveys only a fraction (I suspect) of what it means to live in one culture as opposed to the other, and how very different the psychic and emotional pattern that lies at the root of Creativity II is from that which underlies Creativity III.

In December 1986 I unintentionally repeated this experiment, but in reverse. The Metropolitan Museum had mounted an exhibit of van Gogh's last 18 months—"Van Gogh at Saint-Rémy and Auvers"—and I took the opportunity to see it. I had originally planned to stay several hours;

as it turned out, I was totally exhausted in 90 minutes by the intensity of color and emotion that escalated in van Gogh's painting in direct proportion to his increasing madness. Whether it was accidental or deliberately planned by the exhibition's organizers, I do not know, but the show exited onto a very different sort of exhibition, entitled "Individuality and Tradition in 17th-Century Chinese Art." The impact was enormous; I felt a sudden "whoosh" as all of my energy returned to ground level. As I sat and looked at the lovely, relaxed prints of mountains and landscapes, a great feeling of peace came over me. I felt a bodily sense of centering, coming home. I realized that I loved van Gogh, but that I couldn't live with him hanging on my living room walls. The intensity was simply too great; and his creative pattern—which is very typical of Type II creativity—reflected this. In the final 70 days of his life, living under the care of Dr. Gachet at Auvers-sur-Oise, van Gogh turned out no fewer than 40 paintings. By contrast, Kung Hsian, one of the 17th-century Chinese painters displayed at the Met, turned out comparatively few; his comments on this are all of a piece with the Creativity III style. "Little by little is better than more and more," wrote Kung Hsian; "this is the advanced stage of a painter." He wrote: "When you are afraid of producing too much painting, you will make a good painting" and explained that, "Being clever is not as good as being dull. The uses of cleverness can be grasped at a glance, while apparent dullness may embody limitless flavor." These are sentiments that would never have occurred to van Gogh; nor do they occur to most of us.[5]

My goal here, again, is not to make a judgment, but rather to point out a very significant cultural contrast. The first four elements I identified as being characteristic of Creativity II—healing a split, self-expression, eruption from the unconscious, and an addictive (escalating) pattern—all add up to the schismogenic structure discussed earlier. Add to this the fifth factor of sexual and Oedipal or erotic tension, and you have a situation that cannot help but be as brittle as it is brilliant, as neurotic as it is rich. It is thus not that Creativity II is "wrong," but that in the late 20th century this mode of expression has been pushed to the breaking point. In an evolutionary sense, it cannot extend its trajectory any further. As a result, what we are witnessing in a whole variety of fields is not merely the creation of yet another style or genre, but the transformation of the creative act itself into something else. If creativity has a past, it also has a future, although it is not easy to predict at this stage what it will be. I shall return to this question later on; for now, it might be valuable to try to obtain a deeper understanding of the psychological basis of schismogenic creativity.

The schismogenic nature of Western creativity was first (indirectly) recognized by the Jungian writer Erich Neumann (1949/1979) in *The Origins and History of Consciousness.* The essential argument of the book is that the consciousness of the individual passes through the same stages as that of the human race at large, and that mythology is the map of that evolution. The first myths, said Neumann, are creation myths: The earth is submerged, or nonexistent, and is precipitated out of a watery chaos. This is certainly the drama described, for example, in the opening chapter of Genesis.

The second set are hero myths, and these record the *process of differentiation.* The symbols of the first category are water, or the egg, or the ourobouros, reflecting a unitary consciousness or the absence of consciousness: no tension, no opposites, no differentiation. The symbols of the second category are the sun—the entry of light into darkness—and also journeys and conquests. The Odyssey, for example, can be read as a psychic journey involving the hero's differentiation from the unconscious, and, in general, from the archetype of the Great Mother. It is the drama of ego versus unconscious, light versus dark, male energy versus female energy, that makes the archetypal journey so fascinating, even to the modern reader. Again and again, Odysseus experiences the enormous pull of that great, unconscious, undifferentiated female power, the desire to melt or merge back into it, to go unconscious, as he once was as a very young infant or a fetus. What makes him a hero, however, is that he refuses this option. He is not interested in the dark energy of the unconscious, and his "victory" over this is symbolized by the blinding of the cyclops, whose eye is the "third eye" of intuitive understanding.[6]

With the birth of the hero, which is really the birth of the ego (or, perhaps, of a certain type of ego), the world becomes ambivalent. It is split into masculine and feminine, black and white, left and right, God and the devil, ego and unconscious, and this becomes the great drama that all cultures have to deal with, at root. In the Far East, the solution has been characterized as Taoistic—that is, "both/and"; yin and yang are seen as transformable, interpenetrating, and, as I shall discuss shortly, this has given Eastern creativity a particular style. In the West, and especially since the Renaissance, the solution has been Manichaean—that is, "either/or"; the two poles are mortal enemies, locked in combat to the death. And in the West or Near East, in particular, this has given rise to a third type of myth that tends to combine the first two: the myth of Set and Osiris, or the twin brothers. In this myth, two brothers emerge from the Void (Primal Unity), or the womb, or the Great Mother; namely, the Hero and the Great Mother Representative. The Hero urges separation from the Great Mother; the Representative wants to merge back into her. Thus there is a tension that is never resolved.[7]

This is, of course, a mythological struggle, played out in the Western psyche. The twin brothers' conflict is intermediate between hero and creation myths. A defiant ego has emerged, but it is fearful of complete separation. Set and Osiris, or Cain and Abel, are really two parts of the same person. We hear these conflicting voices particularly at those moments when we are about to give in to an addiction: taking a cigarette, smoking a joint, drinking a martini, eating a slab of cheesecake. The body wants merger; the mind says: Resist (or is it the reverse?). This is, in fact, the theme of *Dr. Jekyll and Mr. Hyde*, which is nothing less than a twin brothers' war. Robert Louis Stevenson (1886/1981) wrote:

> I thus drew steadily nearer to that truth, by whose partial discovery I have been doomed to such a dreadful shipwreck: that man is not truly one, but truly two. . . . I saw that, of the two natures that contended in the field of my consciousness, even if I could rightly be said to be either, it was only because I was radically both; and from an early date, even before the course of my scientific discoveries had begun to suggest the most naked possibility of such a miracle, I had learned to dwell with pleasure, as a beloved daydream, on the thought of the separation of these elements. If each, I told myself, could be housed in separate identities, life would be relieved of all that was unbearable. . . . It was the curse of mankind that these incongruous faggots were thus bound together—that in the agonized womb of consciousness, these polar twins should be continuously struggling. (pp. 79-80)

What does all this have to do with creativity? The point is that creativity—or at least Creativity II—is the *product* of this internal tension. As Neumann (1949/1979) put it, "{This} tension is what we call culture"; and in this I think he may have been mistaken. Being a Jungian, he saw this dynamic as universal and archetypal, and perhaps to varying degrees, it is; however, different cultures express it differently and deal with it differently, and this may be the crucial point. Nevertheless, Neumann's formulation of twin brothers arguing over the Abyss is an especially important clue as to what goes on in modern creativity. The "game" is to let the whole drama play itself out on the terrain of the psyche, and channel the resulting energy into art, poetry, or whatever. It is precisely here that we find the mechanism which underlies the brilliance of modern Western creativity, giving it its keen edge and also its tragic aspect. For in order for his or her work to be increasingly brilliant, the artist has to generate greater and greater twin-brother splits, or encounters with the Void, from which to recover. Finally, as in the case of Dylan Thomas or Janis Joplin or so many others, the gap becomes too great. The chasm widens beyond their heroic powers, and they cannot manage to get back. Modern creativity is a battlefield of psychic, and often physical, corpses.

A good study of this turbulent or tormented phenomenon in modern art occurs in a work by James Lord (1965) called *A Giacometti*

Portrait, which is a study of the great sculptor, Alberto Giacometti, at work. It very clearly embodies the first four themes of modern creativity that I have noted. Giacometti is never satisfied with his work; it is never, in his eyes, really finished; he sees his Self totally on the line every time he sits down before an easel or a piece of clay, and so on. Lord wrote how he once found Giacometti at a nearby café on a coffee break, his hollow eyes gazing into nowhere, "staring into a void from which no solace could come" (p. 38; see also Lord, 1985). Any healing that is engendered tends to be short-lived. You are constantly challenged to create yourself, and this process never ends. "I work in a state of passion and compulsion," said the artist Joan Miró in 1959: "When I begin a canvas, I obey a physical impulse, a need to act. . . . It's a struggle between me and what I am doing, between me and the canvas, between me and my distress."[8]

The problem with this struggle is that it often ends in death or madness.

There are numerous examples of Western creativity one can take as illustrations of Type II and, as I indicated earlier, much of this is well documented. The classic example of the tortured-genius syndrome, and one that has been worked over in great detail is that of Vincent van Gogh, whose art was so clearly "a cry of anguish," an attempt to merge with life, a substitute for intimacy. "The more I am spent, ill, a broken pitcher," he wrote, "by so much more am I an artist—a creative artist" (quoted in Lubin, 1972, pp. 3, 16; see also Matson, 1980). This is one of the paradoxes of modern creativity—that the search for self-expression actually winds up depleting the Self. The artist of the Type II category is like a broken doll, an *imitatio Christi*, exhausting himself or herself for art's sake, which is "all." In this case, however, you are the agent of your own crucifixion: You make something greater than yourself, seek the unattainable, become a flawed vessel, ultimately emptied or destroyed. For van Gogh and many others, acute depression is somehow welcome, a source of creative drama and energy.

A more complex and interesting example of the Creativity II pattern is Wolfgang Amadeus Mozart, about whom so much has been written in recent years. Exactly what happened in Mozart's infancy we shall never know, but there is evidence to suggest the presence of repressed antagonism toward his father, Leopold, for nearly 25 years (see Haldane, 1960 and Hildesheimer, 1983). Very early on, Leopold Mozart, himself a musician, realized he had a prodigy on his hands, and proceeded to take on the role of impresario, abandoning his own career and dedicating his life to that of his son. He made Wolfgang totally dependent on him, stage managing virtually every step of Mozart's rise to fame. As a child,

Wolfgang was fond of saying, "Next to God comes Papa"; and if antagonism was present, it must have been very deeply buried. Mozart's letters home during this period—about 20 years—were filled with an ostensible love and appreciation of Leopold, and his music during this time was childlike, exuberant, spontaneous. Operas and concerti literally poured from his pen. There is simply no evidence of conflict here, and the style of work reflects this.

All of this gradually began to change in the late 1770s. Wolfgang began to realize that his father had effectively kept him a child all his life, and that Leopold still, after all of his (Wolfgang's) achievements, was disappointed with him. He began to realize also that he feared and resented Leopold, and by 1781 the resulting anger began to surface in some of their correspondence. There was only so much Mozart could say, however, for Leopold was by now an old man, and Mozart did not want to hurt him. But the conflict that had been so deeply buried finally surfaced, with even more needing to come out; and all of this got channeled into his work. Hildesheimer (1983), one of Mozart's more recent biographers, noted that the 4 years from 1784 to the end of 1787 were Wolfgang's most prolific and creative ones, and that this was also the period of his greatest experimentation and discovery. Mozart's interest in destroying old genres and creating new ones was at its height during this time. As Hildesheimer wrote, "the revolutionary Mozart is the Mozart of his last eight years" (p. 138). Repressed Oedipal rebellion surfaces in his two most brilliant operas. In *The Marriage of Figaro* (1786), which was based on a play by Beaumarchais that had long been banned in Vienna, Figaro, the servant of a member of the nobility, Count Almaviva, thwarts the latter in an amorous adventure and emerges the victor. As Hildesheimer tells us, Mozart:

> knew {that} Figaro was no fairy tale. His theme yielded a model for his own behavior; an unconscious drive, probably long latent, came to the surface and tempted him to stop living according to the rules imposed on him from outside. He began to "let himself go." (p. 184)

It was this opera that so antagonized precisely the class that Leopold had toadied to, so as to grease the wheels of his son's career, that marked the beginning of the career: the descent into poverty and, by the end, relative obscurity.

The theme of the upper-class Don Juan character, whose sexual conflicts are so great as to drive him to seduce virtually every woman he meets and who comes off rather badly for it, is repeated and greatly magnified in Mozart's opera *Don Giovanni*, which appeared the very next year in 1787, only 5 years after Leopold's death. It is surely one of the greatest operas of all time, and it is interesting to note that Freud once remarked that it was the only opera that interested him. We need hardly wonder why: One of Mozart's own addictions to the libretto was the reappearance of the slain father as an accusing ghost (the statue). Critics said he stole the theme from Hamlet, but they hardly had to look that far afield. What we find in Mozart's work from this point on, with its obvious attack on the aristocracy, its Oedipal themes, and its smashing of traditional genres, is the working out of powerful internal conflicts through the creative act itself. Mozart was not necessarily suffering here; indeed, Hildesheimer claimed he was getting high off of all this conflict. But my point is that the later Mozart is a classic Type II, and that the energy was coming from a place of anger and frustration. This energy—and it had 25 years of repression behind it—was clearly phenomenal. Between *Figaro* and *Don Giovanni* (18 months), Mozart wrote 35 separate works; between *Don Giovanni* and *Così fan tutte* (13 months), 63 more compositions. These were followed, in 1791, by a mass of chamber music, cantatas, and court dances, plus two more operas, one of which was *The Magic Flute*; here, the Oedipal conflict is revealed as finally resolved: Sarastro, the obvious father figure, is the priest of universal love. As Peter Shaffer (1980) has Mozart's arch-rival, Antonio Salieri, say in the play *Amadeus* when Salieri attended the premiere of the opera and saw the silhouette of Sarastro against the sun: "And in this sun—behold—I saw his *father*! No more an accusing figure but forgiving!—the highest priest of the Order—his hand extended to the world in love! Wolfgang feared Leopold no longer: A final legend had been made!" (p. 83).

The catharsis was apparently successful. As Hildesheimer (1983) noted, the spontaneous, childlike effect of Mozart's earlier years, absent since 1778, reappears now in the music for the first time in 13 years; significantly, *The Magic Flute* would seem to lack the power and brilliance of *Figaro* and *Don Giovanni*. It was, in any event, too late. Believing that someone had poisoned him, Mozart began, in 1791, to write his own requiem, the "Requiem Mass," which was never completed. He died at age 35, for reasons that remain obscure to this day.[9]

I wish to return, finally, to what I have called traditional creativity, or Creativity III. There are endless examples of this, of course, and I could easily furnish at this point texts of Japanese haiku, photographs of ancient Greek or Egyptian vases, or Hopi or Celtic designs, in addition to the 17th-century Chinese landscape painting mentioned earlier. Let me, however, refer to only one classic painting, which is, because of its immense popularity, probably familiar to many readers—namely, the famous ink drawing of six persimmons attributed to Mu ch'i, an artist who lived in

Szechuan province (central China) in the late 13th and early 14th centuries. The drawing has been reproduced in many art books and histories of art, and it shows six persimmons; two white, two gray, and two that are black. The simplicity and elegance of the drawing make it one of the most beautiful works of Eastern art ever to have appeared. Here is the commentary of one modern student of Chinese art, Chang Chung-yuan (1970):

> This picture of six persimmons is one of the best works ever produced by Chinese artists. Before Mu ch'i picked up his brush, his mind was in a state of no-thought. Thus, we have in this painting a manifestation of the primary indeterminacy of the uncarved block. What his mind reflected at that moment his brush would put down. First two deep black contours and then to their left two gray contours. To the extreme left and right he placed two plain white contours. The ink wash of the two first contours is pitch black without any shading at all, and the two contours at the left are all gray with only a light touch. The two outside contours are pure white. The shades of the ink wash from dark to gray and from gray to white correspond to the inner process going on in the painter. When he was still in the depth of the preconscious, the density of his creative night found expression in two dark contours. With the awakening of his consciousness, the inner darkness loses its density and manifests in two gray contours. As he awakens fully, his creative innocence is entirely unveiled. So the white contours are its expression. What is expressed in the picture corresponds to what happened in his mind. Through his brush-work, the various states of his mind can be traced from the primary indeterminacy of the uncarved block to transparency.[10]

The first thing that strikes me about this work and, indeed, about the whole Creativity III genre, is the absence of what might be called a "Freudian layer." There is seemingly no pent-up sensual or sexual struggle in this material. Eros and internal conflict do not play much of a role. What Chang described is a fairly smooth descent *into* the unconscious, not an eruption from it. Hence, it is clear that the dark persimmons would come first, in a state of meditative trance, and the lighter ones after, as the artist comes back to more conscious awareness. The state of "no-mind" familiar to Eastern thought is largely foreign to the modern West (van Gogh was *out* of his mind, not in no-mind), for no-mind is a state of detachment or wholeness, and this indicates that the healing takes place *before* the work begins. This material does not reflect the *search* for unity; it is, rather, an artistic expression of psychic unity *previously attained*. To invert John Fowles, you create from what you have, not from what you lack.

Second, there is no "self-expression" here. It is not a particular person or healing journey being depicted. If there is a twin-brothers' tension here, it is fairly muted. The *unity* is what is being expressed, and that is seen as being universal. As already noted, traditional artists, and Western artists prior to the Renaissance, typically did not sign their work. It is all anonymous because it bears the "mark of God," so to speak—a theme pursued by the great French philosopher and mystic Simone Weil (1947/1952). Weil's idea of creative work was what she called *decreation*—you decreate yourself in order to create the world. It would be more accurate to say that you don't create the work, but rather that you step out of the way and let it happen. In this way, it is significant that so much Oriental art and poetry is about nature, about the physical world, not about the Self and its dilemmas.[11]

Third, there is no schismogenic or Manichaean structure here. The work is spontaneous and regarded as finished. It is also part of a craft tradition—that is, the idea is to stay *within* a genre, not to have to invent a new one constantly. And as with craft, all of this is part of daily life: pouring tea, carving wood, cooking persimmons—all activities are considered worthy of craftsmanship. You don't have a special place called a "gallery" to which beauty is assigned for storage and display, nor do you have a special heroic category in society reserved for creative people (the Balinese are an excellent example of a society permeated by art, rather than having art and artists regarded as exceptional). As Coomaraswamy (1934/1956) once put it, "The artist is not a special kind of person; rather, each person is a special kind of artist."[12] This necessarily means the absence of an addictive or schismogenic structure. This kind of art is continuous with life; it doesn't attempt to "outdo" life by means of psychic acrobatics.

All of this falls into category III, it seems to me, but it is hardly child art. Creativity III, in fact, can be subdivided into two categories: III(a), child art; and III(b), which is the art of an adult who is training himself or herself to be *childlike*—open, immediate, and spontaneous. The difference here is what the Zen master Shunryu Suzuki labeled as Zen mind versus beginner's mind. The early Mozart was possessed of beginner's mind. He began composing at age 5. When he finally became aware of his conflicts, he switched from III(a) to II. This is not surprising; what else would one expect? It is just that the Eastern pattern, or premodern one, is so different. The goal is not to go unconscious, or be a 3-year-old at a Montessori school, but to pull back enough "yang" energy so that yin and yang can balance out. It is spontaneity of a different sort.

To complicate things further, it seems to me that Creativity II can also be subdivided into two categories:

II(a). This is what I have described thus far as Creativity II: The healing of the split takes place by playing the struggle out in the work itself. The "exorcism" is, in other words, indirect, or unconscious.

II(b). This represents a slight shift away from II(a), in that the exorcism is direct. One stays fully conscious of the neurotic dramas that have led one to the particular artistic or creative issue at hand, and one goes directly for the liberation from those dramas, through therapy or one's own internal work. In other words, one moves into one's fears. This releases the energy that is tied up in obsessional patterns, which is then available for creative work, and that starts to come out in a more free-flowing way.

The major difference between II(a) and II(b), then, is that II(b) is on the road to Creativity III, so to speak (Creativity III begins when one is finally done with obsessions), whereas II(a) is not. In fact, in II(a) the artist fears the loss of obsessions, because he or she believes that this would mean the end of his or her career. "Life" and "obsession" are seen as being pretty much identical; the heroic ego whispers in the ear of this person, "Lose me and you'll never create again." And the voice is sincere, because it honestly cannot conceive of a different form of creativity.

The fact that our categories have now developed subcategories, and that these may even overlap, is possibly an important clue to where our culture is going. Creativity II may be our (Western) path to Creativity III, at least in its II(b) form; it is not all II(a), not all a dead end, and this suggests that within the evolution of Western creativity itself lies a tendency toward genuine cultural liberation. This is no small point: The way in which our private and cultural neurotic configuration is framed, or dealt with, may actually be the key in the lock. Those who choose to work through their fears and repressions in the service of creative work may (if they do it before they die) break through to a liberating kind of creativity, and in so doing recode the culture along nonschismogenic lines. This is an earthshaking possibility.

If we look around at the artistic and literary scene today, especially in the United States, we do find some radical departures from the II(a) model, if only in an attempt to express a unitary type of consciousness. This may be premature; Western culture may have to push through II(b) before it can experiment with III(b) in a truly unselfconscious way. However, the alternative attempts are important, nonetheless. Wallace Stevens' work displays obvious "decreative" tendencies in the field of poetry; Henry Moore's work does the same in the area of sculpture. Postmodern minimalist music is clearly in the Creativity III category. This music, as exemplified by composers such as Philip Glass, Steve Reich, and Terry Riley, has so completely eliminated the tension-and-resolution structure typical of Western music since the late Middle Ages that the new form has a curious similarity to Gregorian chant. Reich has stated in public interviews that the study of yoga, Cabala, African and Balinese music, and classical breathing exercises, all of which are aspects of traditional cultures, has had a tremendous impact on his work.[13]

It is not clear what all this means, especially because it can be argued that it represents a retrogression, an attempt to return to an earlier cultural period. For various reasons, I think that unlikely; we should also keep in mind that a major part of the Renaissance involved a revival of antiquity, or what the English potter Bernard Leach (1945) called *revitalization*, the going backward in order to go forward. The modern potter, said Leach, takes Sung (12th-century Chinese) pottery as a model; not for imitation, as an end in itself, but as a way of revitalizing contemporary techniques. It seems obvious that the limits of Creativity II have been reached, and that beyond the tendencies I have described as Creativity II(b), we are searching for completely different modes of cultural and creative expression, in the arts as well as the sciences. As in the case of Creativity II(b), this is a hopeful sign; it suggests that there are somatic forces at work in our culture that are antischismogenic; that are working, perhaps unconsciously, to reverse what appears to me, in a general way, to be a destructive trajectory. We are engaged in turning a corner as significant as that which was turned in Western Europe roughly 4 centuries ago. We can still listen to Gregorian chant of course but most of us don't do it very often. In 2 centuries Mozart may be in the same category and the tension-and-resolution structure of music may be puzzling to our ears.

Beyond the form that creativity will take during the next historical epoch is the question of the human personality structure, the energetic experience that will underlie it and the nature of Western culture as a whole. Who can say what these will be? There is obviously no way to know. However, the following lines from Richards's (1973) book *The Crossing Point* sound what to me is the most hopeful and at the same time most realistic note possible. She wrote:

> Eventually the soul asks to be born again into a world of the same order as itself—a second coming into innocence not through a glass darkly but face to face in consciousness. . . . We pass through cruel ordeals on the way. Estrangement coldness despair. Death.
>
> By going through the experience faithfully we may come through on the other side of the crossing point and find that our faithfulness has borne a new quality into the world. (pp. 63-64)

A new quality . . . a new history . . . a creativity that can be shared by everyone. Lets hope it is still possible.

NOTES

1. On "leaping" see, for example, Bly's (1972) essay "Spanish Leaping."
2. On this especially see Jaques (1970) and Alvarez (1973).
3. Besdine (1968) identified a whole number of individuals for whom overmothering seems to have been an important factor in their creativity. The list includes Michelangelo, Poe, Dylan Thomas, Proust, van Gogh, Goethe, Einstein, Shakespeare, Freud, Balzac, and Sartre.
4. See Menaker (1985), May (1975). Similar studies that see creativity only in terms of the conflict model include classics such as Koestler (1964), Berdyaev (1914/1955). See also the more recent work by Rothenberg (1979). It seems to me that Freud must be credited, at so early a date, with seeing that an alternative to Creativity II was at least conceivable.
5. Quotations from Kung Hsian are taken from translations of texts that were displayed as part of the exhibition at the Metropolitan Museum of Art during 1986-1987.
6. I am very grateful to Michael Crisp for this very imaginative and I think accurate interpretation.
7. The splitting of the Great Mother is discussed by Neumann (1949/1979, pp. 96-97). The terminology *Great Mother Representative* is my own; Neumann's own phrase, which strikes me as being a loaded one, is *destructive male consort.*
8. Miró died in 1984; this quotation appeared in several obituaries that ran in a number of North American newspapers.
9. According to Hildesheimer (1983, p. 375), Mozart believed someone had given him aqua tofana, a slow-working arsenic poison common enough in the 18th century. Shaffer's play *Amadeus* is built around the possibility that Salieri was the villain, and it is certainly curious that Salieri denied poisoning Mozart on his (Salieri's) deathbed (Haldane, 1960, p. 129). An inquest on Mozart's death held in London in May 1983 concluded that he could have been poisoned, not by Salieri, but by a married woman with whom he was having an affair. (This was reported on the BBC.) Dr. Peter J. Davies argued against the possibility of poisoning in a two-part article published in the British journal *Musical Times* in 1984; see also Henahan (1984). The issue will probably never be resolved.
10. See Chang Chung-yuan, 1970, page facing Plate 4. Mu ch'i's drawing is reproduced on the front cover of this work, as well as on the front cover of Shin'ichi Hisamatsu, 1971.
11. Matson (1980) discusses Weil in *Short Lives*, pp. 375-388. There is, of course a large literature on Simone Weil, including studies by Simone Pétrement and John Hellman, among others. T. S. Eliot (1941) had already approached the theme of personality versus nonpersonality in creative work in his essay "Tradition and the Individual Talent."

12. I have substituted the word "person" for "man," which appears in the original.

13. On minimal art, see Battcock (1968). (Philip Glass is perhaps best known for his opera *Einstein on the Beach* and for composing the soundtrack for Godfrey Reggio's films *Koyaanisqatsi* (1983) and *Powaqqatsi* (1987). Terry Riley's most famous work (Steve Reich worked on it as well) is probably "In C"; for an interesting interview with Riley see Pareles (1982). Reich discussed his sources and his own musical development in an interview and performance at the Exploratorium, San Francisco, December 15, 1982; see also the excellent article by Marshall (1982), and the interview with Reich in Parabola.

REFERENCES

Alvarez, A. (1973). *The savage god.* New York: Bantam.

Bateson, G. (1958). *Naven* (2nd ed.). Stanford, CA: Stanford University Press.

Bateson, G. (1973). *Steps to an ecology of mind.* London: Paladin.

Battcock, G. (Ed.). (1968). *Minimal art: A critical anthology.* New York: E.P. Dutton.

Berdyaev, N. (1955). *The meaning of the creative act* (D.A. Lowrie, trans.). London: Gollancz. (Original work published 1914)

Besdine, M. (1968). The Jocasta complex, mothering and genius. *The Psychoanalytic Review, 55,* 259-277, 574-600.

Bly, R. (1972, Spring). Spanish leaping. *The Seventies I,* 16-21.

Chang, C-Y. (1970). *Creativity and Taoism.* New York: Harper & Row.

Coomaraswamy, A. (1956). Meister Eckhart's view of art. In *The transformation of nature in art* (2nd ed., p. 64). New York: Dover. (Original work published 1934)

Eliot, T.S. (1941). Tradition and the individual talent. In *Points of view* (pp. 23-24). London: Faber & Faber.

Erikson, E.H. (1962). *Young man Luther.* New York: Norton.

Fowles, J. (1969). *The Aristos* (rev. ed.). London: Pan Books.

Freud, S. (1964). *Leonardo da Vinci and a memory of his childhood* (A. Tyson, trans.). New York, Norton.

Haldane, C. (1960). *Mozart.* New York: Oxford University Press.

Henahan, D. (1984, November 11). Rest in peace, Salieri, no one killed Mozart. *The New York Times,* Sec. H.

Hildesheimer, W. (1983). *Mozart* (M. Faber, trans.). London: Dent.

Hisamatsu, S. (1971). *Zen and the fine arts* (G. Tokiwa, trans.). Tokyo: Kodansha International.

Jaques, E. (1970). *Work, creativity, and social justice*. London: Heinemann.

Koestler, A. (1964). *The act of creation*. London: Hutchinson.

Leach, B. (1945). *A potter's book* (2nd ed.). London: Faber & Faber.

Lord, J. (1965). *A Giacometti portrait*. New York: Museum of Modern Art.

Lord, J. (1985). *Giacometti, a biography*. New York: Farrar, Strauss and Giroux.

Lubin, A.J. (1972). *Stanger on the earth*. New York: Holt, Rinehart & Winston.

Marshall, I. (1982, December). *Stagebill* (San Francisco), 2(4).

Matson, K. (1980). *Short lives: Portraits in creativity and self-destruction*. New York: Morrow.

May, R. (1975). *The courage to create*. New York: Norton.

Mellers, W. (1967). *Caliban reborn: Renewal in twentieth century music*. New York: Harper & Row.

Menaker, E. (1985). The concept of will in the thinking of Otto Rank and its consequences for clinical practice. *The Psychoanalytic Review, 72*, 254-264.

Neumann, E. (1979). *The origins and history of consciousness* (R.F.C. Hull, trans.). Princeton, NJ: Princeton University Press. (Original work published 1949)

Parales, J. (1982, September 24). Terry Riley moves from minimalist music to improvisation. *The New York Times*, p. C9.

Richards, M.C. (1973). *The crossing point*. Middletown, CT: Wesleyan University Press.

Rothenberg, A. (1979). *The emerging goddess*. Chicago: The University of Chicago Press.

Shaffer, P. (1980). *Amadeus*. New York: Harper & Row.

Stevenson, R.L. (1981). *Dr. Jekyll and Mr. Hyde*. New York: Bantam. (Original work published 1886).

Variations: A conversation with Steve Reich. (1980, May). *Parabola, 8*(2), 6072.

Weil, S. (1952). *Gravity and grace* (E. Crawford, trans.). London: Routledge & Kegan Paul. (Original work published 1947)

4

Creativity, Romanticism, and the Rise of Consumerism

Tony Stigliano

Take a newspaper.
Take some scissors.
Choose an article of the length
    you wish your poem to have.
Cut out the article.
Then cut out carefully each of the words in
    the article and put them in a bag.
Shake gently.
Then pull out each cutting one after the
    other.
Copy them down conscientiously
    in the order in which they left the bag.
The poem will resemble you.
And you will be a writer of infinite
    originality
and of charming sensitivity, although
    incomprehensible to the masses.
    —Tristan Tzara (1920)

Finally, the myth that creativity is largely a matter of the expression of something deep inside each individual and simply needs a kind of therapeutic unblocking of civilized constraint for richness to flow. The

truth is that in our century the great artistic exponents of the interior life, such as Proust, Rilke and Joyce, have achieved their effects through deployment of an encyclopaedic knowledge of outer forms, by which they were able metaphorically to suggest and conjure nuances of feeling and perception.
—Anthony O'Hear (1993)

INTRODUCTION

I argue in this chapter that our contemporary understanding of creativity emerged as part of a fundamental shift in the understanding of consciousness at the end of the 18th century. Specifically, "creativity" was conceived of as a faculty, or even as a "mental force," by early 19th-century critics, artists, their audiences and the new institution of the art market as an explanation for innovation and originality. Moreover, and, perhaps more importantly, "creativity" became a criterion for making value judgements within a new social milieu of consumerism by a newly powerful economic class—the bourgeoisie. Creativity became at once a legitimation for the preeminence of a new configuration of power, and the basis for revising the way consciousness was understood.

Up to the 18th century in Europe, the work of artists was judged and explained in terms of "mimesis" or "similarity" to an object or person. This understanding was replaced by an understanding of art as the "creative expression" of an authentic "inner" subjectivity. As such, creativity took on the significance it has today (Gimpel, 1991). With the rise of modernity, or, more specifically, with the rise of the individual as the constituting foundation of knowledge, ethics, and politics, creativity became the expression of individual freedom and legitimacy. The individual's rights and interests became the purpose of governments. The health of individual consciousness became the purpose of new medical and psychological institutions. The demand for new, redemptive experiences that transcended the new society produced a subjective basis for art and the institutions that supported it.

This shift was, in part, the result of a political and economic transformation in Europe from a feudal system to a liberal democratic polity. Under feudal social and economic relations, artists were the employees of an aristocracy who wanted to surround themselves with celebratory decorations, or pedagogical icons that would reflect their power and status. Domination by a system of production based on the private ownership of property split art and craftsmanship and transformed both into commodities in a class society. Artists produced items whose worth was determined by demand based on desire; that is, fashion, rather than need.

The reasons for this sea change may be found in the controversies surrounding the basis for legitimacy of the revolutionary governments of France and the United States. After the French and American Revolutions, the new societies needed an ostensibly new basis for establishing its political hierarchy. The difference between this bourgeois order and earlier systems lay in the kind of justification required. The aristocracy had claimed "divine right" or "natural law" as the basis for their sovereignty, but the authority of the bourgeoisie was based on self-determination by self-interested consensus.

A society of sovereign individuals bound by a social contract and market relations had as one effect a transformation of the way art was judged and conceived. The *ancien-regime* of the 18th century appreciated and supported an art that was "astonishingly mimetic"; art was judged for its imitation of styles (Murphy, 1993, p. 43). In the early 19th century, mimesis as a criterion and as a function for art was rejected by a new consumer society in which creativity, the unprecedented expression of subjective truth, had become a significant criterion for artistic value and for market price.

For most artists and their art buying audiences at the *fin-de-siecle*, political self-determination was quickly mapped onto aesthetic judgement. For the Romantics, only that which was subjectively "self-determined" was "dynamic" and "creative." Indeed, in many respects, these three terms coalesced in Romanticism. Romantic art, like Romantic politics, aimed at *self-determination* through total revolution. In the work of poets like Schiller, the creation of art and the creation of a redemptive, liberated social order were tantamount to being the same thing. "The function of the artist, like that of the politician, was no longer to *re-present* a variety of characters and forms that were in the world, but to *express* what was unique and singular" (Murphy, 1993, p. 45).

In addition to these profound changes in social and political organization (which should not be taken to have been complete; the forces of the *ancien-regime* would persist until the collapse of the European empires in 1918), a new kind of society began to emerge in early years of the 19th century: a consumer society. Pleasure, experience, and novelty became the basis for a way of life in which style, fashion, and possessions expressed an inner self. This inner self was autonomous, remote from everyday experience and understood as imaginative, authentic and hedonistic (Campbell, 1989). This self also transcended ordinary morality and found its articulation in pure (that is, free of moral or social obligations or responsibilities) aestheticism. The "purity" of this aestheticism was incoherent, however. Class distinctions expressed themselves in judgements of Taste. Class is the condition of consumerism and creativity that is explicitly elitist, while being simultaneously politically radical.

"Newness," "originality," and "creativity" were embodied in the formation of an elite artistic/revolutionary institution: the *avant garde*. Originally a military term that referred to shock troops willing to take severe losses in order to breach an enemy position, the avant garde became the paradigms of creative innovators, willing to risk all for an aesthetic breakthrough by "making themselves" or "finding themselves." At the same time, the avant garde's revolutionary rhetoric provided a new social class with a hedonistic, Romantic ethic of consumerism.

My thesis is that a discourse with creativity/originality as its central principles was constructed, elaborated, and deconstructed in the context of the crises and reactions produced by industrialization and the emergence of bourgeois democracy. Creativity was central to a new social and economic rhetoric. This rhetoric, however, was framed as a psychological process. Creativity became central to a way of speaking about the authentic core of human beings.

The products of creativity were more than merely "new"—creative art was redemptive; that is, transformative on the social level as politically revolutionary, and on the individual level as the liberation of consciousness. Creativity takes on a quasi-religious character as part of an ideological mystification covering over the domination of taste by market and class. *Prima facie*, this seems counterintuitive. How could something like creativity, which is described as being so "private," simultaneously be the product of apparently impersonal social forces? The answer, in part, is that "the private self" is a constituent of this construction of "creativity" by ideology (viz., Romanticism), and its supporting market force (viz., consumerism).

The private self, a transcendent identity that is purportedly beyond the materiality of every day life, is an embodied political construction. It allows the individual to believe that she or he is "beyond" good and evil while permitting society to become the subject of rational administration and market forces. In turn, literature, art, and other creative expressions were used to criticize these forces. My reading of German and English Romantic literature indicates that there is a dialectical relationship between the retreat of the artist from everyday life into an inner world and the expansion of market forces, and cultural power (manifested in the writings and stances of critics, theater producers, art dealers, and other middlemen).

This "journey to the interior," as Heller (1968) called it, resolves aesthetic hedonism and utilitarian calculation through the near-deification of subjectivity and the loss of objectivity in art (what T. S. Eliot called *objective correlations*). As Wolff (1984) pointed out, the individual, creative artist emerges with two crucial changes in society:

> the first was the rise of individualism concomitant with the development of industrial capitalism. The second was the actual separation of the artist from any clear social group or class and from any secure form of patronage, as the older system of patronage was overtaken by the dealer-critic system, which left the artist in a precarious position in the market. (Wolff, 1981, p. 11)

This position was justified as proof of the artist's avant-garde status. As such, he could, by dint of his marginality, become fashionable because the language of Romanticism defined the authentic artist as this individualized, authentic, nonconformist.

Romanticism thereby synthesized market and transcendent self by legitimizing consumerism as a way of life. The Romantics scorned both science and religion, bourgeois self-interest, and traditional community. Instead of public interest or political and social morality, the Romantics dedicated themselves "to the idiosyncratic celebration of personality" (Grana, 1967, p. 45). This celebration, however, was not for just any personality; artistic genius was called an inexplicable gift of nature that should be allowed to overturn norms and standards in favor of a brave new world. As Grana said: "artistic and literary creation became something formidable, awesome surrounded by an aura of trance and revelation" (p. 52). It is exactly this revolutionary stance of constant change in favor of the "new" and the "innovative" that is inscribed in consumerism as a discourse, and as practice.

We can summarize the rhetoric of Romanticism by listing the following ideals (Grana, 1967, pp. 67-68):

1. self-expression, the realization of oneself through creative expression, was the most important endeavor in one's life;
2. the freedom of self-expression;
3. creativity is an unexplainable act of "genius;"
4. every event and person is unique and singular;
5. cosmic self-assertion, the artist is a demi-god, he is the carrier of truth and meaning and special freedom should be granted to him;
6. social alienation;
7. the hostility of society to sensitivity;
8. a horror of daily life.

These general parameters do not appear to be a position consistent with the ideology of an aggressive capitalist society. However, as the literature of the 19th century indicates, people, even those who most benefited from the new order, were uneasy with its impact on cities, nature, and individuals. Nostalgia for simpler ways of life, for peace and quiet, for the provincial life marked by moral discriminations became central to Romantic poetry and novels:

> The Romantic looks inwards, not outwards. In politics, to nationalism, national self-determination, isolationism, nativism; . . . in art, to self-exploration. The Romantic artist opens up the inner continent for discovery. The Romantic artist is introspective, spiritually "withdrawn from the world," solitary. In this state, the Romantic explores feeling states, passions, dreams, moods, hallucinations. . . . At its most banal, this becomes nothing more than a plunge into the chaos of the psyche, or else an ethnological warming over of the legends, folk music and myths of the nation. At its best, it is an attempt to generate out of such "inner contents," a law of one's own. (Murphy, 1993, p. 45)

Romanticism thus enabled the new class to own profit-making property, conceive of themselves as creative innovators or even artists, and to understand market relations, not as avaricious, but as value and meaning making. It did this by subordinating the public sphere of political, cultural, and intellectual debate to subjective introspection, consumerist interests, and authentic expressivity.

In the next few sections, I sketch out a historical interpretation of creativity. Creativity, I argue, requires the construction of a new kind of self using categories (especially "Will," "Autonomy," and "Imagination") derived from Cartesian psychology and Kantian moral theory, and made amenable to the institutions and relations of the market and the new bourgeois state. In order to have a subjectivity that can replace community as the basis of meaning, the formal, isolated, autonomous selves of Descartes and Kant had to be realized as political and economical entities. The free market and the elected legislature presumes the existence of persons who are private, self-sufficient and free; such an idealization is legitimized, structured, and given content in the poetry, art, and criticism of Romanticism. This position was first elucidated and exemplified in the priority of action over reason and contemplation in the work of Hamann, his followers Jacobi, Herder, and others in, or sympathetic to, the irrationalist wing of Romanticism (Berlin, 1993).

Simultaneously, the Romantic interpretation of the self flourished in the new consumer-oriented social order with its valorization of autonomy concretized by pleasure, possession, and originality. Romanticism's newly formed "subjectivity" was most influentially expressed as an art that was "authentic" and "creative" and, as such, "new" and "antitraditional." It was, according to Shiff (1986), art understood as discovery, rather than that of crafting or making.

Ostensibly, the cult of originality had a significant liberatory effect on society; the hypocrisy and alienation of a market driven social order was criticized; cultural critique became a legitimate endeavor; the political transformation of society took on concrete expression in both reformist and revolutionary movements. However, Romanticism's insistence on the foundation of subjectivity and free choice articulated and legitimized a consumer-oriented market. Consumerism was a compelling way of life given an individualist, nonrational (or irrational) interpretation of the self and community.

CONSUMERISM AND ROMANTICISM

With the growing secularization of European society, art provided a religiously skeptical, materialistic, but morally troubled bourgeoisie with an aesthetic that functioned as a religious and moral system of beliefs, standards, and practices. Salient to this aesthetic was the idea that by sheer imagination, individual traumas, and social problems could be transformed: Art was not only religion made palatable to an antitraditional psychology and society, it also formed the basis for revolutionary utopian politics.

Romanticism incoherently disdains the calculated self-interest of a market economy while it provides the market with the hedonistic consumers it requires. Market economies have been largely thought to be justified and articulated by a Protestant ethic of thrift, self-denial, and hard work. Wealth is a sign of divine favor that was not meant to be enjoyed. The Protestant ethic is an ethic of productivity, not consumption. Romanticism is the denial of all the above: It celebrates spontaneity, self-indulgence, pleasure and an antisocial stance.

According to Campbell (1989), the ideologies of Romanticism and consumerism have identical roots. This point was also made by Weber (1965) who called Romanticism a species of "inner-worldly asceticism" in which the individual is under obligation to his/her "god," to do his bidding; "that is, to 'realize' his 'true self,' a process similar to the 'perpetual internalization of the divine' which Weber associates with asceticism" (Campbell, 1989, p. 269).

This "inner asceticism," Romanticism, with its insistence on the uniqueness, self-sufficiency and creativity of the individual was the centerpiece of the aesthetic ideology (and psychology) of consumerism. This Romantic self aestheticizes the world by projecting its meaning onto institutions and relationships. Creativity transcended the mundanity of life, either as a potential for all, or as the mark of an elite (radical and conservative Romanticism, respectively). The idea of creativity justified the aestheticizing projection of individual subjectivity by valorizing original and new expression that repudiated the past (except as nostalgia), and posited the future (as hedonic or ecstatic fantasy).

With the establishment of the ideology that the individual was the sealed, self-sustained vessel of rights, values, meaning, and truth, the individual and his or her experience becomes the sole foundation for political and epistemological order. For the defining thinkers of modernity, Descartes, Hume, and Kant—all knowledge begins with individual experience; moral judgement and action are only possible with an individual moral self or agent. Social institutions and other formations are reducible to individual actions and choices, such as Adam Smith's "invisible hand," which became the basis for Hegel's "cunning of Reason." Moreover, the individual's freedom, passions, and interests are the basis for realizing virtue, order, and value. Although Romanticism appears to criticize some aspects of modernity, its scientific rationalism, for example, it is still a modern ideology.

The free, transparent, self-contained individual described here is also the ideal subject who acts and chooses in a market system. Such individual virtues were "inalienable" and resided in an interior that transcended political institutions and was, in fact, the legitimation of those institutions. Such a valorizing and meaning-giving entity will choose objects and a world conducive to her own inner truth. For Romanticism, these are constitutive of a world of novel aesthetic experiences. The market responded in perfect harmony with this sensitive, self-conscious, inner-worldly sensibility. Max Weber's "inner ascetic" is consistent with "outer aestheticism."

Creativity, as a self-evident expression of that interior world, legitimized the power of this interior by proclaiming and celebrating the source of its transcendence; namely, the "unconscious." In turn, this universal ("metaphysical" in Kant's usage) source provided the basis by which art was judged and priced. Creativity as an aesthetic theory provided critics with judgements that justified the value of art because of its subjective authenticity, and originality. At the same time, these judgements sorted out works for public consumption as commodities. Such judgements became the discourse of the art market which, in turn, became the discourse of consumerism.

"Romantic literature glorified strong passions, unique emotions, and special deeds. It despised normalcy, foresight, concern with customary affairs, and attention to feasible goals" (Grana, 1967, p. 68). What the Romantics sought was the emergence of a new aristocracy based on a capacity to produce and consume original works that broke with what they took to be mechanical, derivative products. In the face of the new factory system, its proletariat, and a mass society, Romanticism's aesthetic ideology distinguished between repetitious, but productive labor and gratuitous, but pleasurable creativity. "Romanticism set the terms of the contemporary traditions of creativity in that it celebrated either the heroic or the intimate, the impulses that put man that side of work day reality by entirely overriding it, or this side of it by withdrawal into a purely personal world" (p. 168).

Romantic ideology's heroes were great warriors, gangsters, athletes, or heiresses who are "really themselves" (W. H. Auden, 1957. pp. 255-256; cited in Grana, 1967, p. 169). Hero worship and idealizations of traditional communities with their myths became part of the Romantic discourse for the same reason: Heroes and myths represented authenticity. The ethic of authenticity, which found a home in the elite of the creative artists, the avant garde, legitimized the bourgeosie's hedonism and its withdrawal from the secular, demythologized world that they created, and which supported their consumerism.

Creativity as an aesthetic judgement and as a personal trait was central to a hedonic ethic subscribed to by artist, critic, and audience (the art-buying bourgeoisie). It was a relationship fraught with paradox, for instrumentalism and calculation (it was the bourgeoisie who purchased the art) made this ideology possible by requiring it as a cover. What made this complex relationship possible was the emergence of consumerism as a spontaneous, creative act, as purely pleasurable and in the present.

We may see this process in the construction of ideal types like Baudelaire's Dandy, who despised any mention of what one does for a living. The Dandy is supported financially, but work or money are too indelicate and distasteful for the sensibilities of this ideal Romanticist. We may also observe this nexus of poetry and market relations manifests itself in contemporary consumer attitudes, and the advertising that articulates those attitudes. According to Romantic thought, mass-produced goods are neither "individual" nor "creative." However, if the goods are separated from profit and mass production by imbuing the work with the signifiers of individualized pleasure and it is assessed by the appropriate institutions as "fashion"—a concept that, with consumerism, first appeared around 1800 (Campbell, 1987)—the goods can be understood as individual, creative, or innovative. Behind the fashion and creativity, factories, sweat shops, and class struggles were easily hidden. If this seems paradoxical or counterintuitive, I invite you to examine any high-fashion advertisement. Designer labeled goods are as mass-produced as anything else, yet the illusion of individuality is preserved by use of a Romantic rhetoric of pleasure, fantasy, spontaneity, and arationalism.

This, one might respond, should not be the case with the arts, however. Surely a Picasso or a Van Gogh, to take two well-known commodities, is not mass-produced. How, then, could these be considered in the same way as designer jeans or perfume? They can be; for one example, consider Danto's (1992) discussion of the impact of the recent claim that the "The Polish Rider" is not by Rembrandt:

> To be a Rembrandt is to claim pride of place in the greatest collections and to command the close aesthetic attention of artistic pilgrims. . . . Whereas to be merely by the Master of "The Polish Rider" gives the work claim only on experts in the minor artists of the seventeenth century in Holland. . . . There is the further consequence of reevaluation in the crassest meaning of the term: were "The Polish Rider" to come onto the market as genuinely by Rembrandt, it might just break the hundred-million dollar mark the art world has been waiting for. But the reclassification of a piece of furniture as a work of art would have similar institutional and financial repercussions for the object. . . . And the work, now art, is in candidacy for interpretations comically inappropriate for mere beds and vessels. (pp. 21-22)

What may count as art, or, better, "great art" produced by "creative artists" depends more on how art is marketed or institutionalized in museums or art galleries than on any claim about its "internal" worth. This echoes Campbell's (1989) thesis about the connection between consumption and Romanticism: "autonomous, imaginative pleasure-seeking [is] the force largely responsible for the dynamic form taken by modern consumerism" (p. 99). The production of works of art for pleasure remains the mask for the mass production of consumable items. Creativity is the justification for the high price tags.

THE EMERGENCE OF THE CREATIVE SUBJECT AND ITS MARKET

One important criticism of this argument is that creativity was and is an aesthetic judgement considered significant prior to the emergence of a consumer society (ca. 1800 in Western Europe), most notably in the Renaissance. Something called "genius" did have significance for patrons who paid for art. The genius may have been considered a skilled craftsperson or designer as much as an artist, however. Hauser argued that:

> The fundamentally new conception of [Renaissance] art is the discovery of the concept of genius, and the idea that the work of art is the creation of an autocratic personality, that this personality transcends tradition, theory and rules, even the work itself, is richer and deeper than the work and impossible to express adequately in any objective form. . . . The idea of genius as a gift of God, as an inborn and uniquely individual creative force, the doctrine of the personal and exceptional law which the genius is not only permitted to but must follow, the justification of the individuality and willfulness of the artist of genius—this whole trend of thought first arises in Renaissance society. (Hauser, 1968, p. 61; cited in Wolff, 1981, p. 26)

The Renaissance "genius" has some important semblance to the Romantic idealization of the "creative artist." Nevertheless, Wellek (1955), for example, pointed out that imaginative fervor was always balanced by judgement and design. He also noted that Inspiration was a catchphrase of Renaissance thinkers and had little significance. The Renaissance never lost its rationalistic check. Artistic production and consumption were subservient to civic humanism and public interest. Art as an escape from the gravity of public life into the authentic depths of the human psyche is not a Renaissance understanding.

Creativity as the authentic and authenticating ground for human being becomes culturally significant only with the emergence of an individualist self and a market society bound to the quest for what Heller (1968) called "its ultimate realization and freedom in its own proper medium: *the pure inwardness of human subjectivity*" (p. 113). This understanding of subjectivity is at the heart of Romanticism, market economics, and the self-contained individual embodied in the artist-hero.

In Europe this site starts to open up immediately after the French Revolution reaching its zenith in the 1840s and 1850s; the connection between originality, creativity, and freedom was taken as a given by the artists supported by the revolutionary bourgeoisie in the formation of new categories of the heroic individual. In this discursive setting, society was rejected as an abstraction, but art was idealized as the expression of freedom. As Bourdieu (1993) argued:

> Intellectual and artistic life has progressively freed itself from aristocratic and ecclesiastical tutelage as well as from its aesthetic and ethical demands. This process is correlated with the constant growth of a public of potential consumers, of increasing social diversity, which guarantee the producers of symbolic goods, minimal conditions of economic independence and, also, a competing principle of legitimacy. It is also

correlated with the constitution of an ever-growing, ever more diversified corps of producers and merchants of symbolic goods, who tend to reject all constraints apart from technical imperatives and credentials. Finally, it is correlated with the multiplication and diversification of agencies of consecration placed in a situation of competition for cultural legitimacy: not only academics and salons, but also institutions for diffusion, such as publishers and theatrical impresarios, whose selective operations are invested with a truly cultural legitimacy even if they are subordinated to economic and social constraints. (p. 112)

The emergence of an art market obsessed with the new combined with an ideological stance skeptical of standards as a constraint on authentic creativity formed the basis for what has been described as a "culture industry" (Horkheimer & Adorno, 1982, pp. 120-167). The "inward journey" is consistent with the frenzy for fame and money. This demand for the marketability of art contributed, among other things, to the introduction of industrial methods into artistic production. Charles Dickens used such methods—serialized stories—in order to expand his audience. Art was tacked on to the new processes of industrialization as the consumerist ethic.

Bourdieu's description of art as symbolic capital captures the dialectic relation of market and creativity. A painting or a poem is an article of merchandise *and* a "unique" product (in fact that quality made it marketable) of an artist (and his or her critical circle, art gallery, and audience). The critic, the theatrical director, and other taste makers could and did determine the marketability of artists' products. Artists produced freely, and could thrive so long as their work was not derivative according to the judgement of critics and art dealers. "Symbolic goods are a two-faced reality, a commodity and a symbolic object" (Bourdieu, 1993, p. 113). Consumerism, the art market, and the aestheticization of the public world by the inner subjective ended the role of the aristocratic collector and the emergence of the market with its systematic capacity to reduce meaning to information (i.e., price) became the determinator of art as symbolic capital. Rather than being subjected to the refined taste of the nobleman, the successful artist had to produce art as an investment and as a consumable object of pleasure.

The invention of culture as a "higher" reality provided an Olympian height from which the artist could express his or her disdain for mass society, but it was just that culture, hungry for the haute couture, that gave artistic work its market value. Constitutive of this "reality" was the "ideology of free, disinterested 'creation' founded on the spontaneity of innate inspiration" (Bourdieu, 1993, p. 114). Such an ideology rejects bourgeois materialism by distinguishing the artist as "creative"; however, such a distinction insures the function of the art as an expression of dominant (class-determined) taste.

Nonetheless, "like any other product [the literary work] had to be marketed in such a way as to insure a return on the investment. . . . 'Spiritual rates shift in the same fashion as industrial rates'" (Grana, 1967, p. 33). The social emancipation of artists also meant that the rates for originality and creativity was the only objective for writing, painting or composing. This led, perhaps, to the production of new artistic forms, but it also led to institutionalized forms of artistic display. Museums, concert halls and other places for the display of art were built. The formation of a public art market and the desire of the bourgeoisie to legitimize itself and its values (which included its social and economic position) complemented one another. Because of the public nature of art, combined with Taste as a class distinction, these new institutional arrangements produced the necessity for "expert" opinion based on "educated Taste," or connossieurship.

The new significance of the art critic (e.g., Ruskin, Poe, Baudelaire), in consort with the art dealer and the connossieur, cannot be underestimated in the construction of creativity. Because the old style patronage system was gone, artists competed with each other in an art market dominated by the critics and the dealers. Art became the "new" and "unique" expression of the owner's aesthetic judgement and, therefore, cultural and political legitimacy.

Romanticism, with its emphasis on authenticity and expressive individualism, resisted the commercialization and popularization of art while, ironically, transforming it into a commodity. This movement also articulated a revolutionary understanding of the purpose of art by internalizing art and apotheosizing the artist as a kind of hero/martyr/saint. Romanticism's interiorization of artistic expression constructed the idea of creativity as exclusive, private and "beyond good and evil." Art became a new quasi-religious transcendence, but a transcendence which was simultaneously mired in the crass materialism of a social and economic class that saw culture and nature in terms of property and profit.

According to this ideology, creativity was an act of sheer freedom; on the other hand, it was economically dependent on being a market commodity. The more independent one was from the materialism of commerce, the more one was dependent on the taste of the owners of that commerce. In order to resolve this paradox, Romanticism invented the "interior" that is free of the crassness and commodification of the "exterior." Walter Benjamin commented:

> For the private person, living space becomes, for the first time [around the time of the July Revolution], antithetical to the place of work. The former

is constituted by the interior; the office is its complement. The private person who squares his accounts with reality in his office demands that the interior be maintained in his illusions. This need is all the more pressing since he has no intention of extending his commercial considerations into social ones. In shaping his private environment he represses both. From this spring the phantasmagorias of the interior. For the private individual the private environment represents the universe. The interior is the retreat of art. The collector is a true inmate of the interior. He makes the transfiguration of things his business. To him falls the Sisyphean task of obliterating the commodity-like character of things through his ownership of them. (Benjamin, 1978, pp. 154-155)

Benjamin's analysis of the relationship of art to some "interior," either a physical space (a museum, an art gallery, or a private collection) and/or a personal space locates and circumscribes the cultural distinctions involved ("inner"—expressive; "outer"—assertive) in the ideological response and complement to the encompassing advance of technology. The "inner world," ascetic and semidivine provides the subject with the fantasy of a freedom that is apolitical and transcendent.

An example of this understanding of the "inner world" can be found in various 19th-century writers. However, it is constitutive of 20th-century artists as well. We can see it, for example in the writings of contemporary artists like Robert Motherwell, who says that "in this [bourgeois] world modern artists form a kind of *spiritual underground*" (Motherwell, 1944, p. 11). The artist is withdrawn from the world into the creative haven of an underground. In 1951, Motherwell expanded this point: "Abstract art represents the particular acceptances and rejections of men living under the conditions of modern times. . . . It is a fundamentally romantic response to modern life—rebellious, individualistic, unconventional, sensitive, irritable." He goes on to say that this "attitude arose from a feeling of being ill at ease in the universe, so to speak—the collapse of religion, of the old close-knit community and family may have something to do with the origins of the feeling" (p. 24). Such views summarize the thinking and work of the previous century's artists as well.

CREATIVITY AND REDEMPTION

These distinctions and the cultural conditions that made them possible were constituted in Romanticism's transformation of the person as a free, autonomous "interior" subject and the society as an oppressive, mechanistic "exterior" requiring the redemption of Beauty. This new ontology entailed two significant distinctions.

The first distinction, already discussed at length, is the grounding of moral, cognitive, and aesthetic judgement in an inner, transcendent self. This idea is dependent on the idea of the magisterial self, an identity above and beyond the moral and political. The self becomes solipsistic and self-legitimizing. We can see such a socially shattering understanding in the apotheosis of the "unconscious" mind as accountable to no one but its inner authority.

The second distinction, which provided a justification for utopianism, was that art could "heal" humanity by restoring it to its putative natural wholeness still found in the inner, subjective worlds of "primitives," children, and artists. Romanticists of both conservative and radical stripes saw humanity divided against itself. Art, they believed, especially poetry, would provide the conciliation of the alienated fragments "man" had become under industrialization and the rationalization of everyday life. Borrowing from Rousseau, Romanticists believed that in some unsullied interior, the creative force could be set free to redeem humanity. It was in this context that "creativity" acquired its political significance as the authentic core of the authoritative self that could heal society by an act of subjective will. Such an act expressed in a work of art, if it were "really" creative, would leap beyond the rational calculus and dualities of bourgeois life.

Merely a political revolution, Schiller (1967) argued in his *On the Aesthetic Education of Man*, would never work on its own to transform the dehumanization of humanity. "The removal of [the dehumanizing spirit of society] requires a total revolution: a revolution which transforms the whole of human character by attacking the sub-political roots of social interaction" (Yack, 1986, p. 9). The aim of any such revolution would be the redemption of humanity through the transformation of human action from mechanical movement to creative action. This was possible because the authoritative self was a priori free and spontaneous once free of the impersonal causal forces of society and history.

"Subjectivity or self-consciousness is the salient problem of Romanticism" (Bloom, 1970, p. 1). Subjectivity for the early Romantics was, however, not merely a theoretical issue; it was the necessary condition for social transformation. "Art," said Theophile Thore in 1855, "changes only through strong convictions, convictions strong enough to change society at the same time" (quoted in Kossuth, 1991, p. 129). The Romantic hope was that of freedom; the imagination's freedom which, although redemptive, also destroyed the social self.

"The high cost of Romantic internalization, that is, of finding paradise within a renovated man, shows itself in the arena of self-consciousness" (Bloom, 1970, p.6). Wordsworth's and Blake's poetry was meant to heal the breaks within "man" and "man" and nature, if not between "man" and "man." The stage in which this quest was played was the self. The healing function of art, for Wordsworth (1974), is "when the poetry shows the power of the mind over outward sense" (p. 9).

The creative "inner" source of redemption that would overcome the mechanical "outer" man can be found in an influential essay by Martin Luther published in 1520. He argued that the inner man was to be preferred because it could remain pure and free. The only objective thing the soul needs, according to Luther, is the word of God. By the 19th century, the "word of God" is no longer important, but the individualistic emphasis on self as what needs liberation and transcendence is stronger than ever. "Faith," said Schleiermacher in 1830, "is neither knowledge or action; it is a trend of feeling, or a trend of the undividable self-consciousness" (p. 3). Hence, the possibility for an undivided, "truly" human person is deeply intertwined with the rejection of the material world, and in the Protestant Reformation's internalization of the divine. In the great democratic revolutions of 1776 and 1789, the internal, "private" world of the pursuit of happiness becomes the foundation for a new political and social order. This order was based on the rational control of nature and the liberation of private, property owning individuals constituted by passions and interests (Hirschman, 1981). As the possibilities of political change waned and industrialization mobilized society into a class structure, the arts became what Freud would come to call a kind of "forepleasure," an "incitement premium" or "narcissistic fantasy" (Bloom, 1970, p. 3).

For Romanticism, the magisterial self became the last great chance for some "essence" or "eternal truth" to survive capitalism; the world where, in Marx's terms, "all that is solid melts into air" (Marx & Engels, 1964, p. 12). The free self that lives only in interior spaces is likened by Van den Berg (1970) to a "haunted house" that contains everything of value (p. 63). As Rilke (1938) said in reference to the Mona Lisa, she "contains within herself all that is human" (p. 218). Such an ideology, translated into Western society's cultural horizons, makes Freudian psychology possible because the *fons et origo* of human existence, the hidden self, could be discovered without reference to a social world. The basis of health, an unfragmented self, could be found in the libido: "ultimately man must begin to love in order not to get ill" (Freud, 1914, pp. 151-152). Art thus redeems us, keeps us healthy, and permits us to resist a world of hypocrisy and faithlessness. Creativity enables art to do this because it springs from what is most authentic in us: "By the 1880s the function of art [in America] as quasi-religious uplift was beginning to modulate into a still more secular form, that of art as therapy, personal or social" (Hughes, 1993, p. 178).

Creativity as a concept and as an ideal reflects an inner self, proudly alienated from a despised world. At the same time, the world may be transformed or redeemed by means of a creative act. The inner self's expression of its authenticity could revolutionize and heal society. The basis for this revolutionary stance lies in the imagination, which, as Kant argued, is free from empirical and rational constraints. This unencumbered freedom, expressed as an original and authentic creation, became a value central to the art market. The creators and owners of the "new money" found the redemptive and transcendent values of art impossible to resist in the world they created. In this world, the dealer and the critic became the important actors along with the artist. Initially, they, in turn, were dependent on a discriminating audience. However, that audience's sense of Taste was based largely on what the critics and dealers had to tell them. The desire for owning what Taste called "great (viz., creative and original) art" became a matter of determining what the most innovative art was, rather than the best according to a standard based on skill or imagination. Romantics certainly did not intend the complete overtaking of art by its market and the cooptation of art as fashion by a pleasure seeking mass audience, but they did create the conditions for its cooptation.

The free (self-contained and transparent) personality was the epitome of the transcendent freedom of a deep self expressed in the truly creative work of art. In Schiller's (1993) words, "What makes him man is precisely this: that he does not stop short at what mere nature made of him but has the ability to transform the work of need into a work of free choice, and to elevate the physical into moral necessity" (*Aesthetic education*, Letter Three, p. 90). From Kant (among others), the Romantics had absorbed the idea that external forces (heteronomy) were enslavers of humanity. Only when the will was grounded in an inner moral law (autonomy) could humans be free. Kant (1964) said:

> that nature affords us an opportunity for perceiving the inner finality in the relation of our mental powers engaged in the estimate of certain of its [nature's] products, and, indeed, such a finality as arising form a supersensible basis is to be pronounced necessary and of universal validity, is a property of nature which cannot belong to it as its end. For otherwise the judgement that would be determined by reference to such an end would found upon heteronomy, instead of founding upon autonomy and being free, as befits a judgement of taste. (p. 220)

Kant went on to connect the beautiful with the moral good that was made possible by its detachment from nature and history. The Romantics identified freedom with this detachment.

Morality, according to Schiller (1967), makes humanity human, but it is not the basis of authentic humanity. Freedom has to be realized for all humanity through art:

> that I . . . put beauty before [moral] freedom, can, I believe, be justified on principle, not merely excused as my own inclination. I hope to convince you that this subject is far less alien to the needs of our age than to its taste, and, moreover, that if man is ever to solve the political problem in practice he will have to take the aesthetic way, because it is only through beauty that man makes his way to freedom. (*Aesthetic education*, Letter Two, pp. 89-90)

Creativity was, thus, the redemptive path away from a commodified society, yet in the condition of a society dominated by market relations and the private ownership of the means of production, art also became a commodity, a symbolic good. Creativity became both the source of free art and the justification for high prices and the transformation of the artist into a star.

Romanticism also became the inadvertent cover for this blatant consumerist construction. The Romantics believed that the aesthetic experience produced by the creative genius would overcome the servility and fragmentation of industrialized, urban society. This assessment of a "fragmented humanity" was based on the understanding that understood modern humanity as a unity (e.g., Marx's "species-being," or, Hegel's "unhappy consciousness") divided against itself. Where this split could be observed was in the yearning for wholeness that was answered by art either as a model for the unity of worker and the fruits of his labor, or as one who transcended materialism for "higher" reality. Ironically, the evocation of these ideas of fulfillment and unity in advertising and in popular expression and, later, in certain forms of psychotherapy, deflected social questions to the issues of an interior world (where we "really" live).

Alienation, or variations thereof, was the diagnosis of society by Romanticism. This condition was generally defined as the loss of control over what should be one's own, the loss of one's "essentially" creative nature, to an object which shows up having authority over one's subjectivity. This analysis of subject (knower, agent, creator) and object is theorized by Fichte and Hegel as stages on the way to freedom understood as a unified consciousness which has sublated (*aufgehoben*) the object into itself. How this is possible is the key problem facing Romanticism in its critique of modern life.

"The fragmentary character of modern culture appears to be an obstacle to the realization of human freedom in the external world" (Yack, 1986, p. 159). Free and unified individuals would be made possible by aesthetic experience, however. All dichotomies would be overcome and a self-conscious "establishment of internal and external harmony, a fully human community" would arise (pp. 181-182). For the Romantics, creativity was more than the producer of tasteful and profitable innovations, it was the path to genuine freedom; the unity of opposites, the overcoming of difference and contradiction.

The fundamental task of art in this redemptive/revolutionary posture was to heal the split between subject and object:

> the obliteration of the object in a subjectivity which expands to incorporate it ('in our life alone does nature live') is the negation of desire, because desire depends on the existence of an object that can be desired precisely insofar as it is outside the subject, radically other. (Belsey, 1986, p. 68)

Subjectivity can only exist if it is different from something, a world, or an object, something to which we give meaning, and yet is beyond our control, and, hence, we desire it. William Wordsworth's *The Prelude* both sustains and eliminates difference; desire is therefore contained as "a reciprocity between subject and object which 'consecrates' the mind until it breaks free of its objects" (Belsey, 1986, p. 73). The end of Wordsworth's poem is the reconciliation of the nostalgic adult with the birth of a new, redeemed world that he can see with the eyes of a child.

In his *Biographia Literaria*, Coleridge (1907) proposed a theory of the imagination in which the knowing subject and its object are identified in an "I AM" that is an eternal act of creation. This is an ideal synthesis in which the other, the different, the desire, and the desired is transformed into a symbol. Only in the work of Freud, roughly a century later, would Coleridge's and Wordsworth's understanding of a divided subjectivity containing both a self-I and an object-I find theoretical expression.

Thus, the Romantic solution to a paradoxical self that was both free and unfree was to deconstruct the Cartesian unified *cogito*. Descartes' invention of a unified, secular mind divided the mind between a reason capable of certainty and a will that could choose to be governed by reason or not. When the society that emerged from the wreckage of monarchy and church in the French Revolution and its aftermath was one driven by perpetually unsatisfied desire. Historically, the inner world of the self as its own meaning and its own object of desire became paramount in the quest for a new unity. The free act of a creative artist could make this unity attainable.

Romanticism had established a kind of delicate balance between the domination of the art world by the marketplace and the ideals of the French Revolution. With the rise of Napoleonic despotism, however, and the failures of the various revolutions (particularly the 1848 Revolution), the possibility for total redemption became more and more a matter of private, internal concerns for those who managed to realize their own desires as commercial interests. Romantic ideals did remain potent for radical critics like Marx or Bakunin, who sought the goals of total revolution among the "workers" whom they regarded as the creative subject of history.

The shift of bourgeois society from being a "revolutionary" (vis-à-vis feudalism) class to a class pursuing its own commercial interests came to understand art as a private, introspective form of expression. Nonetheless, among the more progressive elements of the property-owning classes, the idea that such personal interests would improve the world was articulated as early as David Hume's writings: "The milder views of gratitude, honor, friendship, generosity, are frequently able, among princes as well as private persons, to counterbalance these selfish considerations" (cited in Hirschman, 1981, p. 48). In both revolutionary circles, the subject (whether individual artist-hero or heroic proletariat) was the source of change that was the key to redemption and fulfillment. Only a free, creative subject could produce the needed changes however they were conceived.

Bourgeois tastes became paramount in a world dominated by money rather than noble rank and privilege. Art transcended that world of money and commerce not by positing a transcendent world but by positing a kind of inner transcendence, an unconscious mind. Bellah's (1985) complaint in his *Habits of the Heart* is that the public world of moral and ethical concerns have been overwhelmed by this kind of "inner" expressivity. What may have been a source for social change has now become a kind of perpetual quest for personal fulfillment devoid of larger concerns. Under such a purely consumerist ethic, creativity is understood separately from any aesthetic judgment or political action. Creativity was originally supposed to expressed a deeper or higher reality. At the same time, the possibility for critical judgement was based on the existence of a deeper subject that, in principle was outside of the realm of observation and universal standards. With the expansion of a hedonistic consumerism in this century, judgement began to be more a matter of persuasion and rhetoric. Creativity became more a matter of either technique or simply arbitrary fashion.

The shift from art as a reflection of reality—realism—to irrealism in the course of the 19th century, led to an abstractionism whose meaning was wholly constituted by the private emotional expressions of artists, reflected a deepening of the importance of the unconscious mind as a source of creativity. The roots of this dynamic can be found in early 19th-century Romantic understandings of art. Art became for the Romantics a conviction that the "spontaneous overflow of powerful feelings" expressed the perceptions and emotions of a person "possessed of more than usual organic sensibility" (Wordsworth, 1974, p. 126). In the 1840s, Romanticism was still within a realist framework. But, the artist, according to Ruskin:

> induces in the spectator's mind the faithful conception of any natural objects whatever; the second, to guide the spectator's mind to those objects most worthy of contemplation, and to inform him of the thoughts and feelings with which these were regarded by the artist himself. (Ruskin, 1840, pp. 133-139, cited in Belsey, 1980, p. 8)

The Romantics, out of their desire for a redemptive transformation of humans and society, thus set out on a journey to what Schiller, for example, thought were the roots of mind and society. They ended up with a dubious distinction between the world as they felt it to be and the world which they rejected. The creative imagination became one of devising ways of expressing inner feelings in a way which would be commodified in a world they could not, and would not, change.

The "journey to the interior" (Heller, 1968) was one of valorizing the unconscious as the only place in which the creative imagination could be set free. What was produced by Romantic poets, especially their poetic descendants in this century, was comprehensible only to a smaller and smaller audience. Not that they thought this was a bad thing; Charles Baudelaire, like many Romantics, reviled the idea of democracy (Hughes, 1993). Nonetheless, such private meanings became all the more marketable just because of the craving of the society for the redemptive and therapeutic pleasures claimed for the New.

The avant garde became the source of critique, consumerism, and redemption. However, it was a consumerism that was not meant merely to meet human needs. What one consumed helped establish one's social and political identity. Moreover, it was not just any identity, it was a healed self. Isolated from the social and public worlds taken for granted by early American democrats and English radicals incredulous of, or bored with, tradition, life reduced to fashion and fad, the bourgeoisie of the 19th and 20th centuries craved redemption. The new would be liberating and healing; the creative would be a form of secular grace, therapeutic and hopeful. Bersani (1990) discussed the failure of redemptive art in these terms:

> The culture of redemption might be thought of as the creation of what Nietzsche called the theoretical man—who Nietzsche claimed first appeared in the West in the person of Socrates—the man who attributes to thought the power to "correct" existence. . . . The redemptive aesthetic asks us to consider art as a correction of life, but the *corrective virtue of works of art depends on a misreading of art as philosophy*. . . . A

redemptive aesthetic based on the negation of life (in Nietzschean terms, on a nihilism that invents a "true world" as an alternative to an inferior and depreciated world of mere appearance) must also negate art. (p. 2)

Creativity emerged from a time of social breakdown, but also social hope. Rationality had been captured by technology and industry; science had removed the magic from the world. Everyday life had become a technical problem with no moral or aesthetic guidelines. Religion was not available as a source of identity or possible actions. Art and creativity, for some at least, became the substitute for these guidelines.

SUMMARY

The future is behind us.
—Nina Goncharova (1913)

In this chapter, I have argued that "creativity" as a value, a criterion and a characterization of the artistic process is a historical phenomenon made possible by a complex social and cultural context. Creativity as a determination of artistic value, and as a defining characteristic of authenticity made possible by the social hegemony of consumerism. This, in turn, was expressed as Romantic rhetoric. This rhetoric consisted in an apparent rejection of the material world in favor of an interior world untouched by the industrialization of work and life. According to Shiff (1986), critics like Emile Brenard, writing in 1910, "decided that works came into being not by controlled design, but as a result of vicissitudes of unconscious process" (p. 223). Technique, skill and talent were, according to this ideology, to be hidden from the viewer.

The art work could not hint at imitation, or craft; it had to be pure discovery. As R. G. Collingwood said in 1938, "expression is an activity of which there can be no technique" (Collingwood, 1938, p. 111; cited in Shiff, 1986, p. 224). Collingwood sought to deny that in genuine art existing discourses and practices have any determining role in its production, although Collingwood was aware of the "circumstances" that facilitate expression. However, "every word [i.e., every objectified artistic expression] as it actually occurs in discourse, occurs once and once only" (Collingwood, 1938, pp. 245-249; Shiff's insertion). "Artistic language does not await its use in repetition; man 'creates' language as he 'goes along.' Every expression is original, every making is a finding" (Shiff, 1986, p. 225).

This cultural discourse was first enunciated with more theological, but similar, emphasis on the "true," that is, inner, Individual at the beginning of the 19th century by Coleridge and Wordsworth in England, and Schiller and Schelling in Germany. It was later picked up by the French in the writings of Baudelaire. I have argued here that this discourse became the dominant understanding of art in conjunction with the emergence of a new social order, one dominated by the market place. Originality and creativity were determining criteria imposed by critics that justified a safe artistic investment. "Without appearing importunate, artists can impose even trivial forms of their self-expression on the public's attention; in the modern mass market especially, such public exposure seems to further professional careers" (Shiff, 1986, p. 226).

A market dominated society, I argue, became the arbiter of art, ontologically and aesthetically. The judgement of creativity shielded both artist and audience from this reality. Indeed, market and bourgeoisie were denounced in the name of creativity. Agents, conscious and otherwise, of the marketplace, critics, art dealers, theater impressarios, and the connoisseur determined whether a work was art. They did this by tracing it back to an unconscious, spontaneous, or even "divine" origin. What made the synthesis of apparently opposed social types, the bohemian artist and the capitalist speculator, possible by consumerism. The late 18th and early 19th centuries saw the emergence of a consumerist society. "Where once material possessions were prized for their durability, they were now increasingly prized for their fashionability" (McKendrick, Brewer, & Plumb, 1985, p. 1). This was not a trivial shift, but rather required the transformation of an entire culture from the broadest areas of commerce and politics to such apparently trivial practices as shaving, dog breeding, children's literature, and popular hobbies. "Appetite for the new and different, for fresh experience and novel excitements, for the getting and spending of money, for aggressive consumption lies at the heart of successful bourgeois society" (p. 316).

I have drawn a connection between this new confident, modern society and Romanticism with its insistence on originality; "fresh experience" requires new art. The stable crafts with their reliable, repetitious production of planned artifacts were of little value in such a world. One may be skilled in technique, but without "inspiration" that can only come from one's the authentic depths there could be no art.

Those who were so inspired became the avant garde who combined artistic originality and capitalist aggression. Creativity, fashion, and originality were all personified in this new institution. The avant garde's rhetoric and actions became the paradigms for not only determining the artist's self-understanding, but the rhetoric of consumerism itself. I have attempted to show that the erasure of technique that Collingwood saw as central to the artist was also central to the ideology of the bourgeoisie. The factory system, urban sprawl, poverty, and mass society were also erased.

By the early part of the 20th century, the avant garde were proclaiming the "death of art." Poetry, for Tristan Tzara, was merely a matter of pulling lines cut from newspapers from a paperbag (Krauss, 1990). The Romantic idealization of the artist as embodying the best possible, or being the "avant garde" of an aesthetic/political revolution has been called into question:

> Today, revolts restricted to the aesthetic are welcomed by the middle class as a solace; they revive the aroma of the exciting times when hostility and misunderstanding between artists and the public were considered dangerous. . . . In this [contemporary] parody of vanguardism, which revives the academic idea of art as a separate "realm," art can make revolutionary strides without causing a ripple in the streets or in the mind of a collector. (Rosenberg, 1968, pp. 90-91)

This may indicate a new shift in the nature and understanding of art and creativity; market forces, not critical judgment, may have become the determinators of aesthetic value and creativity.

Such an argument is highly suggestive for other researchers in the field. Certainly, there is a great deal here that needs to be examined. Many connections and inferences I have drawn are based on work already done in European cultural history. The relationship between creativity, irrationality, and totalitarianism can be found in the work of Walter Benjamin and Isaiah Berlin. The interconnected emergence of consumerism and creativity, and extreme forms of individualism and Romanticism have been clearly adumbrated by other scholars. What does this all mean for psychologists and other social scientists studying the phenomenon of creativity for art, business, or other endeavors?

Whatever it is that we are calling creativity, we can no longer be innocent of the historical circumstances in which the term is used, understood or ascribed. Its existence as a psychological or social category is dependent on whether or not a given social order values the new or the novel in itself. Certain postmodern artists and critics would consider the judgement of creative or original problematical to say the least. Regardless of the kind of research one does, the historical/cultural context cannot be ignored. Work done by social and behavioral scientists on creativity must, therefore, include the research of cultural and intellectual history. If this context is not included, what may appear to be objective knowledge will obscure complex ideological and political relationships between individuals, social institutions, and practices.

REFERENCES

Auden, W. H. (1957). *The dyer's hand.* Garden City, NY: Doubleday.

Bellah, R. (1985). *Habits of the heart.* Berkeley: University of California Press.

Belsey, C. (1986). *Critical practice.* New York: Methuen.

Benjamin, W. (1978). Paris, capital of the nineteenth century. In P. Demetz (Ed.) & E. Jephcott (Trans.), *Reflections: Essays, aphorisms and autobiographical writings* (pp. 146-162). New York: Schocken Books.

Berlin, I. (1993). The magus of the north. *The New York Review of Books, 40*(17), 64-71.

Bersani, L. (1990). *The culture of redemption.* Cambridge, MA: Harvard University Press.

Bloom, H. (Ed.). (1970). *Romanticism and consciousness.* New York: W. W. Norton.

Bourdieu, P. (1993). *The field of cultural production.* New York: Columbia University Press.

Campbell, C. (1989) *The romantic ethic and the spirit of modern consumerism.* New York: Basil Blackwell.

Coleridge, S. T. (1907). *Biographia literaria.* J. Shawcross (ed.). London: Allen and Unwin.

Danto, A. C. (1992). *Beyond the Brillo box: The visual arts in post-historical perspective.* New York: Farrar, Straus & Giroux.

Freud, S. (1914). Zur einfuehring des Narzissmus [On narcissism]. *Gesammelte Werke, X,* 79-91.

Gimpel, J. (1991). *Against art and artists.* Edinburgh: Polygon.

Grana, C. (1967). *Modernity and its discontents.* New York: Harper & Row.

Hauser, A. (1968). *The social history of art, Vol. 2.* London: Routledge.

Heller, E. (1968). *The artist's journey to the interior.* New York: Vintage Books.

Hirschman, A. O. (1981). *The passion and the interests: Political arguments for capitalism before its triumph.* Princeton, NJ: Princeton University Press.

Horkheimer, M., & Adorno, T. W. (1982). *Dialectic of enlightenment.* New York: Continuum.

Hughes, R. (1993). *Culture of complaint.* New York: Oxford University Press.

Kant, I. (1964). *Critique of judgement.* (G. Meredith, trans.). New York: Oxford University Press.

Kossuth, J. (1991). *Art after philosophy and after: Collected writings, 1966-1990.* Cambridge, MA: MIT Press.

Krauss, R. E. (1990). *Passages in modern sculpture*. Cambridge, MA: MIT Press.

Marx, K., & Engels, F. (1964). *The communist manifesto*. New York: International Publications.

McKendrick, N., Brewer, J., & Plumb, J. H. (1985). *The birth of a consumer society: The commercialization of eighteenth-century England*. Bloomington: Indiana University Press.

Motherwell, R. (1944). The modern painter's world. *Dyn, 1*(6), 8-14.

Motherwell, R. (Ed.). (1951). *The Dada painters and poets*. New York: n.p.

Murphy, P. (1993). Romantic modernism and the Greek polis. *Thesis Eleven, 34*, 42-66.

Rilke, R. M. (1938). *Von der Landschaft* [On landscape]. *Ausgewaehlte Werke, II*, 221-236.

Rosenberg, H. (1968). Collective, ideological, combative. In T. B. Hess & J. Ashbery (Eds.), *Avant-garde art* (pp. 90-110). New York: Collier.

Schiller, F. (1967). *On the aesthetic education of man* (L. A. Willoughby & E. M. Wilkinson, trans.). New York: Oxford University Press.

Schiller, F. (1993). On the aesthetic education of man. In. W. Hinderer & D.O. Dahlstrom (Trans.), *Essays* (pp. 86-179). New York: Continuum.

Schleiermacher, F. (1830). *Der christliche Glaube* [Christian belief]. Berlin: Göschen.

Shiff, R. (1986) *Cezanne and the end of Impressionism: A study of the theory, technique, and critical evaluation of modern art*. Chicago: University of Chicago Press.

Van den Berg, R, (1970). The subject and his landscape. In H. Bloom (Ed.), *Romanticism and consciousness* (pp. 57-65). New York: W. W. Norton. 57-65.

Weber, M. (1965). *The sociology of religion* (E. Fuchoff, trans.). London: Methuen.

Wellek, R. (1955). *A history of modern criticism* (Vol. II). New Haven, CT: Yale University Press.

Wolff, J. (1981). *The social production of art*. New York: New York University Press.

Wordsworth, W. (1974). *Prose works* (W. J. B. Owen & J. W. Smyser, eds.). Oxford, UK: Oxford University Press.

Yack, B. (1986). *The longing for total revolution*. Princeton, NJ: Princeton University Press.

PART THREE

LANGUAGE AND THE REDISCOVERY OF THE ORDINARY

5

Knowledge Creating as Dialogic Accomplishment: A Constructionist Perspective

Frank J. Barrett

Language is a change-creating force and therefore to be feared and used,
if at all, with great care, not unlike fire.
—Lakoff (1990, p. 13)

We have become accustomed in this culture to viewing knowledge creation as something that is an individual contribution. Recently, postmodern critiques have challenged the accepted centrality of the individual subject. Even the notion of individual authorship of ideas and books has been undermined (Derrida, 1978). I would like to review some of the constructionist challenges to the primacy of individual subjectivity and discuss the implications for the way we understand the knowledge creation process. I propose the view that knowledge creation is an inherently social-dialogical process, that the basis of human nature does not lie within the private recesses of individual mind, but lies within dialogical interaction. The view here is that innovation is not an event that occurs in one particular moment, nor is it seen the expression of some inner essence. I propose that activities such as thinking and creativity are dialogical processes that occur within the context of relationships. Further, the ongoing relational activity of everyday life is an immensely creative process that shapes and is shaped by the linguistic and symbolic forms at our disposal.

After briefly revisiting the foundationalist claims of the modernist tradition, I review some of the philosophical challenges to the rationalist/modernist view of knowledge from the perspective of hermeneutic theory, ordinary language philosophy, speech act theory, and the work of Soviet philosophers Lev Vygotsky and Mikhal Bakhtin. Taken together these perspectives claim that what we have taken to be the property of the individual organism—mind, thinking, cognition—are rooted in social processes. The theme that ties together these streams of inquiry from various disciplines is the power of language to create, maintain, and transform the conventions by which we constitute our lives. The implication of this relational perspective is that interaction and dialogue shape and transform not only how we talk about experiences, but indeed how we actually have experiences. Toward this end, I cite a short real-life illustration to suggest how the natural, improvisational nature of everyday conversation both constrains and liberates the repertoire of possible actions that may proceed. It appreciates, in Weick's (1989) terms, how small events, including simple utterances, have far-reaching consequences.

The modernist project, beginning with the Enlightenment philosophers (Locke, Descartes, Hume), holds that it is possible to develop an objective knowledge and a universal moral order. Grounded in a dualistic assumption that separates mind from world, inner from outer, the belief is that the real world exists out there, independent of any observer. This view holds that meaning making is an internal, mental activity: the mind acts as a mirror that registers sense impressions. Language, in this paradigm, acts as a conveyer of reality. Words are capable of capturing features of the world and transmitting meaning to a listener or reader, who then is able to grasp these features. Rorty (1979) called this the *picture theory of words*. Thus, for example, I can use the word "book" to convey information about a particular object and I can be confident that others will apprehend the meaning I intend. This is sometimes referred to as the *correspondence theory* of truth: meaning is achieved because the word "book" corresponds to a particular referent.

This "correspondence" view of knowledge has been challenged from a number of different perspectives. Whereas the traditional, enlightenment view holds that knowledge is the result of pure, accurate observation, the constructionist perspective holds that it is not possible to perceive an object or event without some predicate, some preunderstanding. Heidegger (1927/1962) named these mental predicates *anticipating forestructures* that guide what we notice, how we translate meaning, indeed how we construct our experiences. In this view the mind is not a mirror that reflects the sensory data it sees. Rather, there is no perception without the prior existence of meaningful precepts that construct how we make sense of data. We are always already anticipating, projecting forms of meaning. Thus if I were to witness 2 men standing on a beach waving their arms in the air, how am I to construe this situation? We might assume it is a greeting of sorts—perhaps they are trying to get someone's attention. Or perhaps they are choreographing a dance. If we hear them scream "Help!" we might conclude that something harmful has happened. If we hear them singing "om" we might revise our account of their activity still further. We would continue to make interpretive moves to construe and label this activity depending on the cultural forms of meaning that are available to us.

There is no objectively intrinsic meaning tied to the aforementioned men's gestures. Interpretive moves are made possible because of the prejudice and bias that we bring to an encounter. Following Gadamer (1976), Heidegger's student, every act of perception involves interpretation. These interpretive biases are the constructs and language forms we inherit from prior social experiences. In that it is the forms of language at our disposal that trigger us to project one interpretation rather than another, Gadamer challenged the rationalist separation between mind and world. The subject's biases do not get in the way of understanding, but *bring forth meaning* by anticipation, expectation, and projection. This interpretation is a *retrospective* form of sense making: perception and understanding involve retrospectively fitting data into familiar patterns of understanding. Further, these biases are culturally embedded, so that *there is no direct access to reality unmediated by language and preconceptions.* In the earlier example of the two men, would it be possible to perceive them practicing tai chi with one another if no such word was in our vocabulary? Without such a word (and its family resemblances), we might propose various interpretations to construe their activity (could they be be in an actual fight?). Each interpretation would carry certain action implications. For example, if we construe that they are signaling for aid, we might be drawn to act differently than if we construe that they are practicing a martial art. The point is that we meet the world with forms of language already in use and it is these forms that determine what we notice, how we interpret, and how we coordinate action with one another. Without this culturally inherited language, there would be no means by which to make the world intelligible. Gadamer (1976) put it succinctly:

> It is not so much our judgements as it is our prejudice that constitute our being . . . the historicity of our existence entails that prejudices, in the literal sense of the word, constitute the initial directedness of our whole ability to experience. Prejudices and biases are our openness to the world. They are simply conditions whereby we experience something—whereby what we encounter says something to us. (p. 9)

This is why every generation, every culture, will interpret a situation in a different way with no means of determining which is the accurate interpretation, which interpretation is closer to the nature of the external world. The meaning is not in the words themselves, but emerges in the interaction between various language users. The open, indeterminate meaning of utterances is humorously depicted in Jerzy Kozinski's novel *Being There*, in which the hapless character, Chance the Gardner, utters simple, inane statements like: "In a garden, growth has its season. There are spring and summer, but there are also fall and winter. And then spring and summer again." From this utterance journalists, economists, and political statesmen take literal statements as metaphors and then construct profound insights into political dynamics and economic cycles. Audiences respond according to how they interpret the gardener's utterance within their normal discourse patterns. It is fruitless to try and determine which metaphorical interpretation of his words is correct. Each interpretation triggers diverse streams of action. An economist cites this utterance in support of Keynsian policies while a political statesman cites it to attack socialist policies. The grounds for establishing accuracy are not to be found in the nature of the world itself or in the structures of inner consciousness; rather, the determination of meaning is dependent on the social conventions, the background set of interpretive assumptions that attune the perceiver/reader/listener to notice certain features and ignore others. This constructionist perspective suggests that meaning is created not when the mind registers sense impressions, but when a linguistic form triggers an interpretation.

Following Wittgenstein and the ordinary language philosophers, meaning is not to be achieved by isolating the correspondence between word and object free of context. Rather, the meaning of words depends on its context within sets of language games. In this view, the word achieves meaning because of its usage within a systematic pattern of activities. This is why the very same word can have different meanings depending on its placement within a wider network of activity. The signifier "automobile" has no inherent relationship to the concept "automobile" but to utter the word may be useful if I want to get a friend to go for a drive with me. To a mother whose son was killed by a drunk driver, "automobile" signifies a potential weapon. To a nature conservationist, it signifies a threat to the environment. The meaning of the word changes depending on its use within the activities and language patterns that different discourse communities engage in. Consider that the !Kung tribe in Africa, which migrates in groups of 30 or 40 people and until recently were isolated from the outside world, had no word for "stranger" or "acquaintance." There was no need for a language that could coordinate behavior appropriate to civil inattention or compliant politeness between strangers in Western culture that Goffman so well documented. Ordinary language philosophy then proposes that it is no longer useful to think of words as pictures, but instead to think of words as tools that allow members of a culture to coordinate ongoing relations with one another.

What makes the achievement of meaning possible is the tacit commitment participants share when engaging in the exchange of utterances. What this suggests is that people have at their disposal a range of vocabulary that expands or contracts the repertoire of possible actions and responses that may follow. Each relational scenario is an ongoing negotiation process and the available expressions are like steering devices that lay out the future path of interaction: Each utterance commits one to a limited number of inferences and probable consequences, depending on the context that the utterance itself helps to shape. Consider the following example: Imagine an organizational meeting in which a number of project teams meet to offer program initiatives and proposals to the division vice-president. On hearing one of the proposals, the executive has a range of responses available. He might say that he feels "ecstatic" about the proposal. This might seem to be an excessively affirmative response. However, such an expression might be appropriate if this particular group has had trouble cooperating with one another in taking collective initiative, and the manager's strong affirmation follows months of impatience. Such an utterance has implications for the future—it may open the door for other groups to follow the same model, for example. On the other hand, perhaps he chooses a more reserved response. He sees potential in the idea, but it is not yet what he hoped for—he calls the idea "promising." Perhaps he says he is "disappointed" in the proposal and offers a mild rebuke that serves to create some distance between him and the idea, or perhaps he expresses feelings of aversion or hostility towards the group. If he were to express "disgust," it would create unambivalent distance between him and the others. Following this response, it is unlikely that he wants to meet them for drinks after the meeting to discuss other ideas or for social exchange. *Each utterance navigates the course of future responses available to all parties: there are a limited number of moves available following each of these statements.* Each utterance contributes to fashioning a latitude of action that shapes evolving relational scenarios. Certain expressions would probably be out of place. If the executive finds the proposal "deeply moving," he might be accused of being too emotional or inauthentic. If he responds that the proposal moves him to dance wildly, he may be suspected of being out of his wits. In other cultures and historical settings, such expressions might be imaginable. This interaction, like all relational exchanges, is a fragile, delicate process. If he finds the idea "very stimulating," for example, it does not leave him the option of rejecting the idea outright and disbanding the team. As he improvises various responses, his words outrun him, like a train carrying its own tracks. Commitments are being forged, relationships are being formed, futures are being negotiated based on the choice of expressions available.

In fact, speech act theorists argue that tacit rules of relational commitments are what keeps the interaction going. We set guideposts and limits on one another's responses as our interactions proceed. This unstated background set of possibilities seems to be so obvious as to be unarguable and goes largely unnoticed unless there is a breakdown in expectations. By virtue of our participation in a society and a tradition that produces patterns of regularities in the use of language and genres of speech, we make certain validity claims when we speak and listen; thus even simple exchanges are forms of unstated promises. If you ask me if there is gas in the car you intend to drive, and I respond affirmatively, I have some explaining to do if in fact there is none. Habermas (1979) recognized the importance of commitment in his discussion of the validity claims of an utterance:

> The essential presupposition for the success of an illocutionary act consists in the speaker's entering into a specific *engagement*, so that the hearer can rely on him. An utterance can count as a promise, assertion, request, question, or avowal, if and only if the speaker makes an offer that he is ready to make good insofar as it is accepted by the hearer. The speaker must engage himself, that is, indicate that in certain situations he will draw certain consequences for action. (p. 61)

Speech act theorists contend that every language act has certain consequences for the participants, leading to other immediate acts and commitments to further action (see Winograd & Flores, 1986). Making a statement is the equivalent of making a promise to act in an appropriate way in the future. It is our continual mutual recognition of shared rules of relating and commitment that allows us to coordinate our relationship. When this tacit promise is broken, we then need to dialogue about these agreements if we are to continue relating.

These commitments appear even more precarious when we consider the fluidity of words. One central notion of constructionist thought is the indeterminancy of meaning. Following Wittgenstein, it is not the meaning of words that determines how they are used; rather, it is the way words are used within the dynamic ensemble of social relations that determines meaning. Words develop new meanings through novel applications that lie within patterns of practices. Utterances are continuously extended beyond the boundaries of their existing applications, altering the fabric of interpretive assumptions. Wittgenstein compared this dynamic to the growth of an expanding town: Like the construction of new houses and new roads, language is constructed as we go along.

This undermines the notion of the self-contained, autonomous individual as the origin of action. It is testimony to the dialogic basis of our lives—through our language we exert an enormous amount of influence over one another. We collectively co-create the symbolic conditions that we then experience as constraints (and facilitations) in our daily activities. Russian philosophers Lev Vygotsky and M. Bakhtin wrote extensively on the dialogic basis of understanding and the role of language as a creative tool that at once is both the product of relationships and defines the boundaries of relational activity. They offer some clues as to how this tacit background of preunderstanding emerges. Vygotsky (1981) discussed how what we normally take to be "mind" is constructed from the "outside in," through social processes. He introduced the *intermental* as a unit of analysis to illustrate the process by which relational activity is internalized as cognition:

> Any function in the child's development appears twice, or on two planes.
> First it appears on the social plane and then on the psychological plane.
> First it appears between people as an interpsychological category, and
> then within the child as an intrapsychological category. (p. 163)

What first appears on the social plane as a negotiated event between people later becomes internalized as "collaboration with oneself." His classic example of the infant reaching for an object illustrates the mediational role of the other in the formation of knowledge:

> At first the indicatory gesture is simply an unsuccessful grasping movement directed at an object and designating a forthcoming action. The child tries to grasp an object that is too far away. The child's hands, reaching toward the object, stop and hover in midair. . . . Here we have a child's movements that do nothing more than objectively indicate an object. When the mother comes to the aid of the child and comprehends the movement as an indicator, the situation changes in an essential way. The indicatory gesture becomes a gesture for others. In response to the child's unsuccessful grasping movement, a response emerges not on the part of the object, but on the part of another human. Thus other people introduce the primary sense into this unsuccessful grasping movement. And only afterword, owing to the fact they already have connected the unsuccessful grasping movement with the whole objective situation, do children themselves begin to use the movement as an indication. The functions of a movement itself have undergone a change here: from a

movement directed toward an object it has become a movement directed toward another human being. This grasping is converted into an indication . . . this movement does not become a gesture for oneself except by first being an indication, that is, functioning objectively as an indication and gesture for others, being comprehended and understood by surrounding people as an indicator. Thus the child is the last to become conscious of the gesture. (pp. 160-161)

The infant's reach *sends a message* to another person who then begins the process of designating for the child the relationship between the child's desire, the spontaneous reaching, and the external object, so that eventually the child integrates the sense of this gesture and is able to consciously and deliberately ask for something. As Vygotsky put it, "the child is the last to know the significance of the sign" (p. 161). Only after the adult's interpretation does the infant begin to understand the grasping gesture not as a gesture toward the object but as an action directed toward others. After infancy, language assumes the mediating role. When the child points at the object, the adult begins to propose words: "Ball? Would you like the ball?" the child learns that uttering these particular words replaces pointing as the navigating tool that stimulates others to respond and thus achieve her desired results. Vygotsky emphasized that the process of knowing involves the mediation of other people and words are the tools through which we accomplish things.

The Vygotskian view suggests that many of the activities we associate with individual psychology are relational accomplishments. Consider this example cited by Tharp and Gallimore in Wertsch (1991) that proposes expanding the boundaries of the analysis from the intramental to the intermental:

A 6-year-old child has lost a toy and asks her father for help. The father asks where she last saw the toy; the child says "I can't remember." He asks a series of questions—did you have it in your room? Outside? Next door? To each question, the child answers "no." When he says "in the car?", she says, "I think so" and goes to retrieve the toy. (p. 14)

In this example, Wertsch asked, "Who did the remembering?" Was it the 6-year-old girl? Was it the father? Wertsch suggested the Vygotskian perspective that the memory event was jointly shared, that it developed in the context of the conversation between them. Through the linguistic tools at their disposal, they lead each other through various possibilities until they arrive at a satisfactory conclusion. There is no sense in which any of their acts is predetermined; nor are they totally free to say or do anything as a response to the other's queries. They are making it up as they go along, providing clues and guides for one another. The questioning, the probing, the listening, the wondering—these responses that occur within the contexts of relational exchanges—trigger the retrieval of the lost object. Consider a similar point made by Bateson (1972), that what we take to be mind includes the person's dialogical, mediated relationship with the environment:

> Suppose I am a blind man, and I use a stick. I go tap, tap, tap. Where do I start? IS my mental system bounded at the handle of the stick? IS it bounded by my skin? Does it start halfway up the stick? Does it start at the tip of the stick? But these are nonsense questions. The stick is a pathway along which transformations of difference are being transmitted. The way to delineate the system is to draw the limiting line in such a way that you do not cut any of these pathways in ways which leave things inexplicable. (p. 459)

What Vygotskian perspective suggests is that much of what we take to be individual psychology—thinking, memory, etc.—are in fact improvised joint activities.

Following Shotter's (1993) review of Vygotsky's intermental approach, words are prosthetic devices, instruments through which we navigate through the world. Our queries, our responses, our wonderings—are like extensions of our senses that reveal information. Just as the blind man no longer feels the cane as separate from him, but experiences the features of the terrain itself, in asking and telling things, we actively discover and experience features of the world, usually unaware of the linguistic tools we are deploying.

Even in the simplest exchanges these linguistic prosthetic devices lead us to information that facilitates our successful relating. In successful exchanges we embody the words, dwell in them as extensions of our selves. Words serve to reveal our intention, stir and arouse others, reveal features of others' character, outline the boundaries of moral action.

Following the work of Bakhtin, every interaction is a relationship between two individuals in appearance only. Because every word has meaning due to its position within a language game, a single word is never a single word. One word may carry a whole perspective that reverberates with a myriad of possible meanings. Every gesture, every utterance is linked to previous utterances within given spheres of discourse. From this perspective, all language is dialogical (Bakhtin, 1986) in that every utterance carries traces of meaning from other utterances spoken in other social contexts. "Every utterance must be regarded as primarily a response to preceding utterances of the given sphere. . . . Each utterance refutes, affirms, supplements, and relies upon the others, presupposes them to be known, and somehow takes them into account" (p. 91).

So, for example, to refer to an organizational member as a "subordinate" triggers traces of other utterances consistent within a hierarchical context in which members cite words like "managers," "chain of command," "performance measures," etc. Bakhtin referred to this as the process of *ventriloquation*—the speaker before me now is carrying over traces of other voices and social structures that are not present. So, in a sense, when we utter an expression we are continually citing or indexing others whether we intend to or not. Bakhtin wrote that "the word in language is half someone else's . . . the word does not exist in a neutral and impersonal language (it is not after all out of a dictionary that the speaker gets his words); but rather, it exists in other people's mouths, in other people's contexts, serving other people's intentions" (p. 60). Every utterance that a speaker (or writer) makes carries overtones of other voices, from other social roles embedded in social patterns and structures.

Bakhtin (1986) called these typical expressions *speech genres*, common ways of talking that are relatively stable, yet "boundless because the various possibilities of human activity are inexhaustible" (p. 60). So for example, when a medical student learns terms, diagnoses, treatments, she is joining a community of professionals who employ similar interpretive repertories that guide what they notice and talk about in relation to the human body. The typical expressions and discourse rules of the community dictate what is deemed reliable knowledge. Most physicians would not consider an "intuitive sense" of the patient's health problem as constituting valid diagnosis. Rather, the physician lives in a community that regards the citing of hard scientific data backed by statistically sound studies as legitimate claims that warrant one particular treatment over another. An apprentice in homeopathic medicine adopts different linguistic practices with different implications for action that join her to quite a different interpretive community. Each utterance employs at least one, and often several repertories of speech genres. Thus, a doctor may speak to an intern in a way that invokes expressions typical of a medical discourse community, but also may utter deferential phrases that invoke a discourse of gentleness and intimacy that typify the way he speaks to his teenage daughter.

Every utterance is always spoken from the position of some *voice* that invokes a social position. The speaker's position conjures some social language that "shapes what the speaker's individual voice can say" (Bakhtin, 1986, p. 59). Therefore, a father would not speak in a militaristic phrases to his 1-year-old infant; nor would he employ baby talk in his exchanges with his colleagues. Likewise, when a student greets her instructor as "Professor Cooper," she is invoking a language that typifies certain kind of deferential learning relationships and places a tacit limit on what kind of exchanges are likely between the two, unless one of the parties invokes a different kind of speech. When a Naval officer speaks in military command language, it does not leave a junior officer the option of responding in informal, friendly style, something that would be feasible at the officer's club on a weekend night. These traces of words shape and limit how interaction proceeds. As a speaker, when I utter a statement that employs a given speech genre, I begin to influence the kind of response that may proceed from the other.

The co-shaping of utterances involves real or imagined others, through what Bakhtin called *addressivity*. As one produces utterances, one shapes them in anticipation of the other's response. I shape my words anticipating how you, the audience might respond, how you place my utterance within patterns of discourse and genres of speech you have engaged. We edit and shape our utterances not only for a face-to-face other, but also generalized others who may not be physically present. We fashion utterances that summon other forms of expression that shape not only what we say, but how our words are interpreted.

In addition, we cannot separate these reverberations of meaning from the dynamic ensemble of power relations; a very important point that I can only only briefly touch on here. Words that appear as natural descriptions of essence belie the dynamic by which they attained such status. Groups develop speech genres and typical patterns that privilege some categories to the exclusion of others such that these descriptions appear natural and normal rather than the expression of social construction. We then begin to think that certain characteristics are "natural" in essence and forget that much of what we take to be normal and natural is an ongoing social creation. Dominant groups grant privilege to preferred definitions, which achieve their primacy by virtue of comparison to related differences:

> We cannot describe something's existence without employing a framework in which that something's presence occurs by virtue of its being seen against an implicit background of something else from which it differs. Indulgent child-rearing is not an essence to be found within Culture X, but rather reflects a relational judgement based on differences with another culture taken as the implied but absent standard. . . . Neither male nor female is a category-in-itself; each is defined by virtue of relational judgements based on treating one group—typically the male— as the standard and the other as the comparison. (Sampson, 1993, p. 90)

From this perspective, knowledge is seen as what a community takes to be normal discourse; in other words, the patterns of normal dialogue in which members engage. Challenging the concept of knowledge as mental representation, Gergen (1985) wrote, "From this perspective, knowledge is not something people possess in their heads, but rather something people *do* together" (p. 270). Normal discourse is:

> the sort of statement that can be agreed to be true by all the participants whom the other participants count as "rational" . . . (what participants agree as a) set of conventions about what counts as relevant contribution, what counts as a question, what counts as having a good argument for that answer or a good criticism of it. (Rorty, 1979, p. 320)

Knowledge from this perspective is the "social justification of belief" (p. 170). We create and maintain knowledge through our interactions—through versions and accounts of events, through tacit promises and commitments that we enter, and by sharing our ways of understanding the world. In short we cocreate the presuppositions and forestructures that make our interpretations preferable. Although our justifications within a given knowledge game are all we have, Rorty (1970) was quick to remind us that this does not belittle the status of what we construe as normality:

> (This) is not to say that human knowledge is less noble or important, or more cut off from the world than we had thought. It is merely to say that nothing counts as justification unless by reference to what we already accept, and that there is no way to get outside our beliefs and our language so as to find some test other than coherence. (p. 178)

The notion that what accounts as justification, is only by reference to what we already accept, is another way of saying that interpretation is retrospective sense making. We relate statements and accounts to other accounts we currently do not question. The implication is that learning and creativity involve changing one's relationship with one's peers.

Although speech genres shape the terms of normal discourse outline what is taken to be normal, they do not fix or predetermine what members must do or say. These patterns can themselves become the targets of practice. Following Rorty (1979), abnormal discourse emerges when consensus no longer exists with regard to rules, assumptions, goals, values, etc. Abnormal discourse is "what happens when someone joins in the discourse who is ignorant of" the conventions "or who sets them aside." Whereas normal discourse produces "the sort of statement which can be agreed to be true by all participants whom the other participants count as 'rational' the product of abnormal discourse can be anything from nonsense to intellectual revolution" (p. 320). Unlike the participants engaging in normal discourse who sound "rational" to the others in the community, a person speaking abnormal discourse sounds "either kooky (if he loses his point) or revolutionary (if he gains it)" (p. 339). When "abnormal" or creative utterances emerge and achieve a legitimacy, participants begin to see the contingent nature of the rules that bounded their previous actions.

AN ILLUSTRATION

A recent event that occurred in a military context helps to illustrate how learning involves changing the patterns of normal discourse, how evolving new linguistic repertories is a creative achievement that implicates new forms of practice, and how challenges to normal discourse rules threaten power relations. In February 1993, a female first year student at the Air Force Academy reported that she was sexually assaulted on the school campus by several men. If the meaning of practices and utterances are cocreated and emerge from background of presuppositions, what background presuppositions may have influenced the way this event was construed? In particular, within a military institution that has created and inherited forestructures of knowledge that privilege males' versions of events and in which masculine practices appear in the everyday conversations that outline normal discourse, how would the institution interpret this event and having done so, how would they fashion a response?

The terms *sexual harassment, sexual assault,* and *date rape* were not commonly accepted versions of events a few decades ago, a testimony to the indeterminancy of meaning and the evolution of new terms of discourse that navigate behavior. There was no wider network of activities, no recognizable language game that marked off appropriate and inappropriate activity between men and women in this way. It is unlikely, for example, that telling a "dirty joke" would summons accusations of sexual harassment in the workplace. It is unlikely that if the exact same events had occurred at a military institution 100 years ago (or even 20 years ago) it would be reported on the front page of *The New York Times,* as this story was.

However, we are witnessing a change in the background presuppositions that make certain claims arguable. No doubt the terms sexual harassment and sexual assault were uttered and interpreted against a changing background of meaning in regard to what kind of behavior between men and women is considered valid. No doubt when the woman filed the complaint, her phrases reverberated with traces that invoked the Clarence Thomas-Anita Hill hearings and the 1991 Navy Tailhook convention. Like all utterances, this was more than a single woman uttering a single phrase.

Following the patterns of normal discourse, how would the Air Force Academy address it? Would the woman's complaint be interpreted as a valid claim? A manipulative attempt to seek revenge because she was having trouble making the grade at this tough institution? Or perhaps some would imply that the woman should have known better than be alone with a group of men, that she somehow created this incident herself—an interpretation widely put forth by male Naval officers after females were assaulted and harassed at the Tailhook convention. Would an investigation ensue? If so would the men "close ranks" and portray one another as innocent victims? Would it be framed as a misdemeanor, a criminal violation, or as an infringment of the military honor code similar to cheating on an exam? When General Bradley Hosmer, the school's superintendent, heard about these charges, did they reverberate with stories of failed leadership, such as the consequences that befell many of the Navy leaders who dismissed the complaints of Lieutenant Paula Coughlin and other women who were assaulted at the Navy's Tailhook convention? Or perhaps he had heard stories that women have been hesitant to publicly raise accusations toward male perpetrators because of fear of being seen as willing participants, or for fear that their careers would be jeopardized by men in power (see Enloe, 1989).

In fact, what is interesting about this case for our purposes was the response that General Bradley C. Hosmer, the school's superintendent, improvised: He deliberately created an alternate speech genre, a context in which the normal rules of discourse were suspended. Within 2 weeks of the assault, the superintendent held a meeting in the campus auditorium with the school's 518 female cadets. He ordered all men, including his aides, to leave. *The New York Times* reported:

> Then he removed his insignia of rank and promised the women confidentiality in exchange for the "ground truth" about sexual harassment on the campus. For nearly four emotionally charged hours, the women poured out their fears and grievances in response to Hosmer's questions on how many had experienced sexual assault or other forms of harassment, or knew someone who had. ("Air Force Confronts," 1994, p. 1A)

Following Vygotsky's view of the intermental, when the women reported their experiences of harassment, who did the remembering? This was a jointly shared improvisation in which the various parties led each other through the terrain, providing prosthetic guides—questioning, responding, probing—that triggered linguistic repertories and various versions of events heretofore inadmissible. Symbolic gestures such as removing the rank insignia, dismissing all other men from the conversation probably signaled to the women that a different conversation was invited. *Even before the general heard a single utterance from the women, a change was already occurring.* He was creating a context in which he would hear the women's claims as valid and the women could presumably tell their stories without fear of reprisal.

He proceeded "as if" the women had something meaningful to say. The general sought to undo the confines of military-command speech genre that might limit how the women would discuss their versions of experiences. They could discuss their experiences without having to file formal grievances—the official policy for dealing with such incidents. He altered the social positions of the interlocutors, making it possible for the women to speak, and for him to interpret, from different locales. He created conditions that legitimized the emergence of what Rorty (1979) called *abnormal discourse*, allowing women to speak outside the normal rules in which seemingly neutral descriptions of events are embedded in a discourse that favors males' versions.

Following the notion of addressivity, perhaps the women's anticipation that their audience would interpret their claims as valid altered what they said, and perhaps the general was not the only one who triggered and cocreated the stories and versions of events. Perhaps the women themselves, hearing one another's stories, provided prosthetic guides for one another, or triggered buried memories, or began to construe taken-for-granted incidents in different terms. Perhaps they themselves had not previously regarded certain gestures and jokes as inappropriate, but now interpreted such events in different terms—terms made available by new conversations.

What Hosmer heard was that men and women generate two very different versions of the same events: Whereas 50% of the women said they experienced or knew of sexual harassment cases, only 9% of the men did. Following Gadamer's (1976) point, meaning making involves projecting an interpretation of events based on familiar linguistic forms. At the Academy, what looked like flirting and common friendly behavior from one perspective was construed as inappropriate sexual advance from another. The superintendent concluded, "It was common knowledge among the females and virtually unknown to the males, whose perception was that sexual harassment didn't exist here." Hosmer, a former inspector general, reported that he was "stunned and disappointed" by the pervasiveness of women's versions of mistreatment (Air Force Confronts, 1994, p. 1A).

Given the divergent interpretations of normality, if the Air Force leaders were to follow through with their commitment to hear the women's stories as valid, then they would have to alter the formative context, to symbolically redefine the presuppositional background that interprets the taken-for-granted routines and practices. The actions they took seem to be an effort to alter the way men and women construe gender relations. In addition to assigning 14 full-time investigators to examine all complaints and actively pursuing and prosecuting the male perpetrators, they began a reeducation program:

- 4,000 cadets were divided into focus groups of 8 to 12 men and women to discuss sexual harassment and the ethics of leadership.
- a new course was created, entitled "Gender, Race, and Human Dignity".
- recalling the failure of the Navy's senior officers to respond to sexual harassment, the Air Force initiated a training program for the faculty to recognize sexual harassment.
- when first-year students arrive on campus, they will witness skits performed by upper-class students depicting date rape.

Each of these new practices are efforts to rename motives, intentions, gestures, and relational scenarios between men and women. In short, they are an attempt to redefine previously taken-for-granted gestures and propose an alternate version of events that they hope will reshape the commitments and engagement that, as Habermas (1979) pointed out earlier, make relating and shared meaning possible. When old gestures are tied to new terms that support a new range of activities, an important social innovation is occurring. Following Rorty's (1979) argument, learning involves changing one's relationships with one's peers. Perhaps a new language and interpretive repertories will insinuate themselves into everyday conversations, perhaps men will be more clandestine in making jokes and informal references, or perhaps they will confront one another about the inappropriateness of certain gestures. Perhaps women will encourage one another not to ignore unwanted advances. And perhaps a new desexualized language will emerge to navigate relations between men and women at the Academy. Maybe the presuppositions that members project will alter so for example, what was formerly defined as friendly flirting may now appear as a different object. Or maybe none of these things will happen. Perhaps the males' sexist language and practices will simply go underground temporarily, only to re-emerge in the future, testimony to the resilience of normal discourse embedded within power relations. Like the child whose toy was just beyond his grasp in Vygotsky's vignette, perhaps many of the military officers are at the very boundary of their knowledge of the world of gender relations and are developing a new language to mediate the distance.

What this example illustrates is the formative and creative potential of language. We see here that the interpretive assumptions that guide what we know as normal are the product of past patterns of linguistic practice. Changing these formative contexts and presuppositions involves changing the norms of discourse. Change begins when members of a discourse community engage in debating alternative ways of doing things and remove routines and normal practices from exemption. By making it legitimate to talk about the taken-for-granted character of gender relations, the superintendent created an opportunity to recognize, revisit, and challenge these practices.

CONCLUSION

In this chapter, I have reviewed the intellectual challenges to the modernist project that has dominated our approach to knowledge since the Enlightenment. I reviewed a few of the contributions of hermeneutic theory, ordinary language philosophy, speech act theory, and the work of Soviet philosophers Lev Vygotsky and Mikhal Bakhtin. Taken together, these contributions invite us to consider how the taken-for-granted world comes to be seen as real. More importantly, however, the constructionist perspective, in proposing that knowledge is a relationally embedded activity, allows us to see how our daily lives are shaped by dialogic interaction and the immensely creative power of language to configure and fashion our activities.

Two participants in a conversation are never only two participants. They proceed using the elements at hand, the linguistic forms available, discovering the information that their relating creates as they proceed. The utterances that they cocreate are the prosthetic devices that lead to some action possibilities rather than others. The social-cultural horizon, the social structures that they experience as reality, are themselves an ongoing accomplishment of social practice. The forms and categories by which they discover and know the world, the materials by which they improvise their way through situations and coordinate actions, are created through dialogic processes that these structures make possible. By their conversations they create the social reality that they experience as the taken-for-granted, horizon of preunderstanding. And their experiences of the taken-for-granted horizon determine how they proceed in their conversations.

One of the implications that flows from taking a relational perspective on knowledge is that we notice the ongoing relations of everyday life are immensely creative processes that yield subtle and

remarkable innovations. Humans are capable of responding to
unprecedented challenges, and of fashioning a fresh alternative to well-
ingrained routines. Like bricoleurs, we are able to create fresh possibilities
out of the social-cultural materials at hand. These materials are themselves
ongoing human creations, at once altering our actions and being altered by
them. By looking at the relational basis of knowledge, we can appreciate
how language allows us to improvise, to create as we go along, to coordinate
interdependent action, to respond to novel demands. In this light, we need to
appreciate the recursive dynamics that underlie the improvisation and
ongoing creativity of ordinary life, how we create the artificial conditions—
the linguistic and symbolic materials—that determine the actions which may
proceed. And it is these actions that generate the guiding symbolic materials
which we experience as constraints (and facilitations).

REFERENCES

Air Force confronts its own Tailhook. (1994, May 1). *The New York Times*,
    p. 1A.
Bakhtin, M. (1986). *Speech genres and other late essays*. Austin:
    University of Texas Press.
Bateson, G. (1972). *Steps to an ecology of mind*. New York: Bantam.
Derrida, J. (1978). *Writing and difference*. London: Routledge & Kegan
    Paul.
Enloe, C. (1989). *Bananas, beaches, and bases*. Berkeley: University of
    California Press.
Gadamer, H. (1976). *Philosophical hermeneutics*. Berkeley: University of
    Berkeley Press.
Gergen, K. J. (1985). The social constructionist movement in modern
    psychology." *American Psychologist, 40*, 266-275.
Habermas, J. (1979). *Communication and the evolution of society*. Boston:
    Beacon Press.
Heidegger, M. (1962). *Being and time*. New York: Harper & Row. (Original
    work published 1927)
Kozinski, J. (1980). *Being there*. New York, Bantam.
Lakoff, R. (1990). *Talking power*. New York: Basic Books.
Rorty, R. (1970). *Philosophy and the mirror of nature*. Princeton: Princeton
    University Press.
Rorty, R. (1979). *Contingency, irony, and solidarity*. Cambridge:
    Cambridge University Press.

Sampson, E. (1993). *Celebrating the other*. Boulder, CO: Westview Press.

Shotter, J. (1993). *Conversational realities*. London: Sage.

Vygotsky, L. (1981). The genesis of higher mental functions. In J. Wertsch (Ed.), *The concept of activity in Soviet psychology*. Armonk, NY: M.E. Sharpe.

Weick, K. (1989). Organized improvisation: 20 years of organizing. *Communication Studies, 40*, 241-248.

Wertsch, J. (1991). *Voices of the mind: A socio-cultural approach*. Hemel Hempstead: Harvester Press.

Winograd, T., & Flores, F. (1986) *Understanding computers and cognition*. Reading, MA: Addison-Wesley.

6

*Ordinary Creativity**

Mary Catherine Bateson

The conventions we have developed for labeling a few individuals and activities as creative, contrasting them with others, often depend on originality or on later recognition. These conventions leave unrecognized the creativity of the ordinary, which may remain invisible or may involve multiple small moments of discovery that are only original for the individual involved. This deprives us of a range of models for the creative process. More seriously, it may blind us to the way in which small acts of ordinary creativity weave and reweave the fabric that makes social life possible.

Ordinary creativity plays an essential role in education. Educators have recognized that when a child learns by discovery or reinvention those things which are already well known and could be conveyed by instruction, this kind of creativity makes other kinds of creativity possible. Piaget (1973) said, "To understand is to discover, or reconstruct by rediscovery, and such conditions must be complied with if in the future individuals are to be formed who are capable of production and creativity and not simply repetition" (p. 20).

*Some of the ideas in this chapter were developed in an unpublished paper for a Wenner-Gren conference on ritual in 1973. A draft of this paper was discussed at a seminar on "Disciplined Rhetorics of Inquiry" at George Washington University in April 1994, and benefited from comments made there.

Learning and adaptation in adult life also depend on discovery and new construction (Bateson, 1994). Ordinary creativity is pervasive and often unremarked. In fact, survival or adaptation in contemporary society demands a steady increase in the capacity of individuals for ordinary creativity by confronting them, day by day and year by year, with more and more situations for which there are no adequate models. Here I am particularly interested in interactions for which there are differences in the preparation of the participants, and the way in which improvised responses to such situations set the stage for learning. Sometimes too ordinary creativity transcends the need of an immediate situation and becomes a model for the future, achieving a degree of elegance or effectiveness that leads to further imitation.

How does one know what to say or do in an unfamiliar situation, and how is putting together a way to respond similar to the work of an artist? Here I move back and forth between events of very short duration—gestures, sentences—and events of much longer duration—the decisions and arrangements of a lifetime that underlie the emergence of new structures and forms in society, and the atrophy of others.

In my earlier work on lives, using the concept of composition to examine the analogy between individual lives and artistic products, I focused on the lives of a group of women, because women are currently affected by massive demographic and social change (Bateson, 1989). The art forms that most nearly reflect the ways in which these women go about composing their lives are improvisational art forms, depending primarily on new combinations of familiar elements, combining rehearsal and spontaneity.

My initial interest was in improvisation as a way for individuals to bridge discontinuity. For both men and women, life involves adaptation to discontinuities, but women's lives are especially notable for biological discontinuities and vulnerable to extra discontinuities introduced by their husbands' careers. Composing a life involves bridging these discontinuities in various ways—balancing, echoing, contrasting—as a composer of music changes tempo or adds themes from movement to movement and at the same time arrives at a sense of unity in the total composition. In addition, within any given time period a women is likely to be balancing multiple tasks and responsibilities rather than focusing on a single goal. The effort to harmonize these, including many elements simultaneously in a single composition, is also a creative one, requiring innovative solutions that are better described by analogy with a creative process than by the anxiety-provoking metaphor of "juggling."

A third meaning of composing a life emerges from the study of first-person narratives and autobiographies. People, whether or not they set pen to paper, have theories of their own lives, interpretations that provide the context for ongoing decisions. Such narratives typically combine cultural constructions of the life cycle and of social roles with a process of selection and organization that is also creative. A life feels right and meaningful only after a creative process of interpretation, implicit or explicit. Perception and memory involve the construction of mental images related to previous images and experiences, and performances influence subsequent performances when they are reviewed or reinterpreted after the fact and seem to have been pleasing or effective. Retrospective research on lives must both allow for this element in recollection—and include it in the understanding of creativity. There seems to be a link between the processes of reimagining past and future and the capacity to make new compositions in the present, for learning through a lifetime depends on an interpretative process, selectively recognizing and emphasizing the similarities between experiences that make it possible to transfer learning.

When I began thinking about bridging discontinuities, my focus was on individuals, but an individual composing that work of art called a life is never working in isolation, for there are both social and individual dimensions to creativity. On the one hand, most of what we work with is socially given, through tradition and the behavior of others; on the other, the work is always subject to the responses of others who applaud or jeer or, in a thousand different ways, offer their own performances that set the context for ours. Many performances are necessarily joint, including the "performances" of work and family life and governance. More recently I have been interested in studying improvisation in societies like our own where rapid change or diversity mean that individuals must improvise performances shared with others from different backgrounds who arrive with different repertoires and conventions. In some situations it may be necessary to defy convention, but more often the need is for innovation generated within the framework of learned rules.

The improvisational art forms include jazz, improvisational theater, and a wide range of oral performances from sermons to story telling and the kind of epic recitation that has been shown to underlie the Homeric epics (Lord, 1960; Parry, 1932). These improvisational artforms involve a cycle in which elements are disassembled and recombined, often building in interactions or responses to audiences, sometimes in ways that carry lasting authority.

The most compelling examples of behaviors that are both creative and rule-governed are linguistic. In effect, the generation of ordinary speech involves a kind of creativity in which utterances are novel but at the same time grammatical, conforming to rules that constitute the linguistic competence of the individual. The vast majority of human utterances are spoken for the first time (Chomsky, 1965). All natural languages contain within themselves elements sufficient to express insights that are radically new.

Noam Chomsky shifted the interest of most linguists from the study of performance (actual utterances) to the study of the competence that underlies them, yet the study of events involving more than one person always involves performance—that which is actually spoken or enacted in real time that can be heard or seen or perceived by the other, becoming part of a shared sequence (Bateson, 1975). As societies become more diverse and mobile, it is necessary to sustain joint performances with others who have increasingly disparate competencies, differences that connect to issues of class and locale and social role. In fact, whenever two or more individuals are in interaction, although many forms and rules may be shared, there is always some difference between their competencies. In linguistics, individuals, even siblings growing up in the same household, are said to speak different idiolects, and the same principle applies to other aspects of behavior. Two kinds of improvisation are actually taking place: individual behavior and ways to coordinate that behavior. Both levels are rule-governed and involve improvisation and learning. Often such collaborations provide contexts where one participant learns from the other, either by imitating a sequence or by deconstructing it for reassembly in other forms. Indeed, participants often learn from their own performances. Sometimes, whole improvised collaborations become part of the competencies of participants. Occasionally they become part of the repertoire of a community, and may be recycled almost unchanged.

The question of ordinary creativity can be illuminated by comparing the norm of improvisation with the relatively rare situations in which behavioral sequences are highly specified, closely duplicating previous performances, and with the processes by which these too are created. Rigidly scripted performances occur on stage or in the course of some religious rituals, sequences where the smallest gesture may be specified in advance, but it is interesting that actors sometimes say that each performance is new—and both actors and ritual performers may learn techniques for achieving that freshness. Therapists have fixed phrasings that they recycle in familiar situations, and yet they must modify them to fit particular needs; talented therapists often improvise dramatically. Teachers reuse notes and examples, but incorporate new findings and make them topical. Nurses explaining procedures to be followed by the discharged patient, candidates giving stump speeches and answering and reanswering familiar questions, and the representatives of agencies and organizations, from McDonald's to the IRS—all of these rely on repetitive performances that increasingly are deliberately rehearsed for desired interactions with the public. However, instances where repetition completely replaces creativity are exceptional; more commonly, an individual interpolates stretches of previously rehearsed behavior, or riffs, in longer sequences. Even segments that have been used before generally must have some flexibility to be effective when other participants are involved.

In many cases, the rehearsed performance is new for the one who sees or hears it—audience, patient, customer—so even if both speak essentially the same language, there is disparity in the competence of participants in the joint performance—for one it is novel, for the other routine: One participant speaks or acts in a way that is original, generated on the spot, whereas the other repeats performances from elsewhere.

New performances, new ways of coping and responding, are being generated all the time. Most often new performances are generated without any awareness of originality or creativity, *nonce forms* that, once used, fade into the past. There are other situations into which, consciously or unconsciously, one is aware that only a new performance will fit. In times of rapid change, more and more of behavior may be experienced as improvisational, as new social forms and roles are invented, new constellations put together to meet new social requirements. In a society undergoing rapid change, individuals are at different stages in learning the new forms. In a multicultural society, individuals arrive with different scripts and must improvise their integration. The stakes vary, from play to survival.

A SERIES OF EXAMPLES

To explore the analogies between different kinds of creative improvisation in situations where cultural rules do not specify behavior, I offer a series of examples. The first, an interaction between two people who do not share a common cultural code, contains features we will discover in the others. The narrative was written by a George Mason University student in creative writing, Chessalay Blanchard, for a course I taught on women's life histories, and is used with her permission.

Chessalay described a series of interactions she had had as a 17 year old with the grandmother, illiterate and speaking almost no English, of a Mexican immigrant family living next door. The grandmother, in her 70s, had come to live with a son who had prospered and adjusted to the United States, but had chosen to settle in an outbuilding that gave her privacy and duplicated the simple conditions to which she was accustomed, having neither plumbing nor electricity.

> One day, I came looking for my brother. As I walked around the corner of the house, there was Miaba, stripped to the waist and bathing under a makeshift shower on the side of her little shack. I stopped, quite startled and embarrassed by my intrusion into her private ritual. She saw me and motioned for me to come over. Gingerly, I walked nearer, until I realized that her ablutions were spiritual and that she was using something other than soap.
>
> I am sure that my fear and uncertainty showed on my face, for Miaba smiled and took my hand. Gently, she led me to the barrel under the lean-to. She unbuttoned my light summer blouse and pushed it off my arms. There were jars everywhere, all holding liquids with distinct colors and odors. I could see by this point that she had painted herself with these liquids. She began pointing to different jars and making motions, trying to explain the meanings they concealed. Slowly, she dipped a finger in the reddish jar and pointed to my belly. She folded her arms as if holding a baby. As I watched in complete fascination, she painted circles on my abdomen. Another jar held a thick, blue mud. This she put on my temples and forehead, with the admonition, "No go crazy." The green went on my breasts, perhaps for health or maybe good milk.
>
> She continued until the upper half of my body was covered with paint and I realized that our colors matched. I tried to communicate this, holding our matching arms together. She smiled, nodded.

The relationship between the old woman and the young girl continued, based on small gifts and skills learned through imitation, almost entirely nonverbal, until 3 years later when Miaba's grandson, the playmate of Chessalay's brother, died tragically. Miaba took to her bed, refusing to speak or eat, and Chessalay agreed to stay with her while the family went to the church. She found her lying in a state of despair and withdrawal. Chessalay ran back next door to her own house and found an old set of tempera paints:

> I lifted her, quilt and all, and carried her out into the sun . . . and I began to paint our faces black, smearing the thick mess everywhere. I continued until we were covered, and I held her like a baby while she shook with her grief. Some time went by, and she rose. She returned with a picture of [her grandson] and some matches. I picked up the towel she pointed to and began to wipe the paint off as she searched through my childhood art supply bag. When I looked up, she was holding the jar of white paint. Slowly, she rinsed off all the black and replaced it with white. We turned into crazy white ghosts as she lit a match and put the flame to the picture. When it had dissolved into ashes, she spoke one word: "Peace."

This story offers a kind of paradigm for the social creativity needed in our changing society. The context is created by an acculturated Mexican family that have friendly relations with their Anglo neighbors, supporting the emerging friendship and neighborliness between the children of the two families, including the boy who is later killed. The history includes the grandmother's establishment of a modus vivendi in the new environment and the family's tolerance of her preference. In the first scene, the annointing, Chessalay is exposed to a ritual whose detailed meaning she can only guess, and annointed with substances she cannot identify. Not knowing the script, she is largely passive, figuring it out as she goes along. "I began to understand her gift then," she says, "to know that she was favoring me with lost magic." Belly, breasts—clearly the ritual was related to womanhood. When the story appears in print I hope that one of my colleagues will be able to give me further details of the ethnographic background, for the old woman's actions were surely adapted from cultural scripts, including one for relations between an older and a younger woman. Reaching out to Chessalay across the gap of language and culture, finding the gestures to reassure her, represents a real act of creativity on Miaba's part, a step forward in her translation of her identity in the new environment.

In the second scene, the mourning, we cannot know from the description whether Miaba's withdrawal was culturally appropriate, but we can be sure that Chessalay's behavior was not, for whatever substances Miaba used in the annointing, they were not grade school tempera paints, although black and white painted faces do evoke the images of the Mexican Day of the Dead. Chessalay's behavior in the mourning scene may have been as strange to Miaba as Miaba's behavior was to Chessalay in the annointing. However, just as Chessalay accepted Miaba's behavior then, now Miaba accepts Chessalay's improvisation as an attempt to communicate and to create a new shared ritual that will offer catharsis. Chessalay models her improvisation on the previous performance, which she has deconstructed into constituent elements, and this makes it recognizable and evokes the earlier context. Again, we cannot know Miaba's thoughts, but we can know that she rouses herself and participates in the improvised ritual, adding steps that are probably familiar to her, and that the friendship continues.

Miaba and Chessalay together sustained joint performances without a common script or a common system of meaning. The possibility of improvising such joint performances depends partly on biological commonalities: Belly and breasts, a common femaleness, death and grieving—all of these, although elaborated differently in different cultures, provide a shared frame of reference. It may not be coincidental that disasters often evoke empathetic behavior, for shared humanity is a starting point when ordinary behavioral routines are no longer appropriate. Something not dissimilar to the exchanges between Miaba and Chessalay happens again and again whenever close ties are established between individuals who do not share a common code. The Chessalay/Miaba sequence is reminiscent of interactions between a parent and a child where joint performances are facilitated by mirroring or imitation and by treating differing behaviors as equivalent, treatment which, in one linguistic phrasing, gives them *emic* status (Pike, 1954).

Just as we often do not regard sentences as novel, people do not regard their improvisations as creative when they are made up of familiar components, for the creativity involved in combining them seems invisible. A story used to be told about the cyberneticist Norbert Wiener sometime in the 1950s, emphasizing the fact that this brilliant man lacked oblivion to the obvious. He was riding in a car driven slowly by a student through narrow streets, when they bumped a child chasing a ball between parked cars. The student pulled over, helped the child up, noting that she had a slightly scraped knee, took her into a corner pharmacy, bought her a bandage and a lollipop, called her mother on the pharmacist's phone, and eventually got back in the car with a sigh of relief. (Today he might call a lawyer, and there might be no neighborhood pharmacy available.) Wiener was still sitting in the car, apparently deep in thought. "You have hit a little girl before with your car?" he said. The student, "My God, no, heaven forbid." "But then how did you know what to do?" In fact, in order to know what to do in a novel situation, the student had to combine a truly vast amount of existing knowledge: law, folk psychology (not all cultures give children sweets to comfort them), first aid, how to use a telephone. Even in completely new situations, response depends on recognizing continuity. At the same time, the way the student combined the familiar elements into a swift, effective, appropriate sequence of behaviors in an unfamiliar situation can be recognized as creative.

In the work I have done with women adapting to changing gender roles (Bateson, 1989), I have argued that although many women are moving in comparable directions (i.e., entering paid work, simplifying housework, etc.), they are arriving at creative solutions by putting familiar elements together in idiosyncratic ways. Among the most difficult problems of combining career and family life is providing for childcare. When my own daughter was born, my husband and I were in the process of purchasing two thirds of a three-family house and enlarging one apartment for ourselves. This left us owners of a smaller apartment in the same building. Instead of using it primarily to produce income, we advertised for a couple with a child slightly older than ours and a mother who did not want to go out to work, with whom we could plan a flexible baby-sitting arrangement as a condition of tenancy. The two apartments were connected by an intercom in our daughter's room. The advantages for us were continuity of convenient childcare for a fixed number of hours per month without a full-time employee living in our household. The advantage for them was that the wife could be with her child, making an attractive apartment accessible and preserving family privacy, without going out to work or dealing with a variety of other families. Our daughter could go to sleep in her own bed and the families, and especially the children, became good friends.

This was a "creative" solution, but, as in the previous examples, it incorporated a number of preexisting elements. When my mother was a child, her mother used to hire women with illegitimate children to work for her, allowing them to bring those children into the house instead of placing them in foster care. When I was a child, during World War II, we shared a house with another family (they were the owners) and I was cared for with their children while my mother and the father of the other family collaborated in war-related work. The solution that worked for me as a professional woman with a child in the 1970s is obviously constructed from the two earlier solutions, with a little technology thrown in.

Other problems that recur in the lives of contemporary women requiring creative solutions include the maintenance of relations with divorced spouses, especially with common children, housekeeping with commuting relationships when husband and wife work in two different cities, the reconstitution of careers when they are disrupted by family moves, and the care of aging parents. Solutions to such problems often resemble the anointment/mourning sequence in that they involve improvisations recycling familiar components over long periods of time.

IMPROVISATION AND LEARNING

The need to improvise is not limited to modern societies or even to public spheres, for everywhere the members of a family are at different developmental stages, improvising and learning from each other. Parental care in particular involves a constant process of learning new patterns of communication with diverse and developing offspring. Each child is different and each changes from month to month. Interactions between an adult and a child also offer frequent examples of two participants in an interaction acting on quite different concepts of its internal structure.

A child sitting in a high chair drops a toy and an adult picks it up. The child drops it again and the sequence repeats itself—and the child crows with delight. Suddenly a delightful game—we'll call it "pass-and-drop"—has come into being and simple rules of play have emerged. Two participants following quite different understandings have become joint performers in an improvisation, one that can serve as a model for others of increasing complexity, such as a "game" of peek-a-boo between a mother and an infant. Building the game or the performance starts with repetition, including repetition from performer to performer in the form of imitation.

There is a great deal going on in such interactions; shared gaze and multiple simultaneous articulations and motions of the face and body, some of them echoed or imitated, often moving toward a high degree of rhythmic coordination between voice and gesture and between mother and child. For both, behaviors in emerging games rapidly become conventionalized: hands over face, cry of "peek-a-boo," laughter. As contexts for repetition are developed, behaviors can be seen to have possible alternates, such as cushion over face or face behind table, cry of "Boo!" or "I see you," different tones of laughter. Some of the adult vocalizations are recognizable as English and can be analyzed into smaller structural elements (see Bateson, 1975). There would be a limited set of possible sequences, "rounds" in a game of peek-a-boo, and these would in turn be subsumed in a larger peek-a-boo encounter, with a structure of its own—say, gradually increasing boredom in the adult (this and its manifestations also cultural). This would in turn fit into the sequence of the family's day, and so on.

Peek-a-boo is a good deal more complex than pass-and-drop, yet it is possible to play it with an infant well before she or he can speak, moving within multiple layers of structure and evoking a patterned response. The adult brings some previous learning about such play (which is itself conventionalized) but is also feeling the way and improvising, learning to play with this particular infant, something that human parents often need to be taught by their offspring. Games never repeat exactly, for parent and child have jointly constructed a shared context within which each will improvise. Clearly, both parent and child find the interaction "meaningful," but it is not easy to define that word for each, although part of that meaningfulness involves pleasure, even delight, and a deepening of relationship. This is a very ordinary kind of creativity, shaping and sustaining the contexts within which children master extensive and complex systems of cultural and linguistic rules. The infant who crows with delight at an unfolding game of peek-a-boo may become a master bridge player—and here too will find space for devising new strategies.

Such exchanges are not simple. A full description of any interaction, such as has been attempted from time to time by linguists or anthropologists (see G. Bateson, 1971; Pittinger, Hockett, & Danehy,

1960), with rows and rows of symbols recording the details of behavior, comes out looking like a symphonic score. The layers of details necessarily reflect very different kinds and levels of competence, and analysis reveals unexpected degrees of both convention and variation. What is significant, however, is that we can look at such an encounter both as an example of joint creativity and as a possible step in the child's eventual mastery of the total system. The diagram records what the observer can see—often by intensive analysis of films and tapes—but because of different kinds of competence it cannot show what is happening *in common*—the interpersonal event—in this specific encounter between mother and child. At the transitions, however, both often share the same punctuation. Transition points, whether in a game or in the life cycle, are also the most likely sites for innovation.

Infants apparently respond holistically, so that even though an adult may be speaking in words, probably this segmentation is initially meaningless and the infant's experience is a continuum with various rhythmic properties and discontinuities. When these ultimately become a basis for segmentation, we might say that structure emerges from the differentiation of larger sequences through a growing awareness of recurrence and episode structure. The basic movement would be from large units (limited by memory and attention spans) to their fission or segmentation, and thence to new combinations—analogous to the move in inductive methods of second language learning from memorizing sentences to dissecting them to constructing new ones. The large units are not used primarily to refer or to inform but to serve that most basic function of communication that is referred to as phatic, the establishment and maintenance of a common channel, conveying the message "we are in touch" (Malinowski, 1968). One reason for looking at the creation of similar kinds of messages, often those of ritual, in the context of social creativity in a pluralistic society is precisely the need to provide this phatic function.

In learning to speak, it often appears to adults that a child speaks first single words, then two words at a time, and finally longer, more varied sentences. However, looking at them from a different angle, we see that those single words are actually sentences; they are short, for reasons of limited attention and memory, but they are used in interaction like sentences and in response to sentences, and they have intonation. (Note that "Hungry?" or "Foiled!" or "Hello" are all sentences which happen to consist of single words.)

A 1-year-old child says, for instance, /gogi/, a sentence roughly equivalent to "I share with you the experience of meeting a dog." Most mothers respond to it as a slightly different sentence by saying, for instance,

"Yes, that's a doggie." Note that here too we can see a shared performance without a fully shared code. Sentences like /gogi/ proceed by several months the discovery of naming that occurs after children begin constructing sentences consisting of at least two words, and therefore have a basis for discovering words as distinct from sentences. The child's /gogi/, as a sentence, cannot be said to have the reference *Canis familiaris* but rather the occasion of seeing a dog in common with another person—it doesn't refer to the dog; it is what you say when a dog comes into view, just as "Good Morning" does not describe the morning, and "It's raining" is what we say to each other when we are both hit by wet drops. The sighting of a dog is, among other things, an occasion for communion. Because the communion is successful, a great deal of specific incomprehension can be bridged.

A game like peek-a-boo can be seen both as an improvised joint performance and as a lesson in segmentation, as it demonstrates the repetition and variation of set sequences and substitution classes. A precondition for trying to initiate the game or trying to refer to it is the recognition that it can be segmented off from the rest of the day's experience and identified as play. Taking turns establishes the kind of sequential structure that will recur as conversation. Such games are training in the skills of ordinary creativity, and involve devices important in the arts as well—expectation, suspense and surprise, the manipulation of transitions and segmentation in the presence of alternates, and choice and intention. Somehow children need to discover both that long sequences can be repeated (consider their fascination for hearing the same story again and again) and that they can be deconstructed and reassembled in creating a new order.

The learning involved in moving from the unitary interpretation of an event to a sequence is a kind of analysis, breaking it down into the smallest components whose meaning is not deducible from their structure. Such fission in my interpretation of a sequence may bring me closer to other participants, as I become aware of the steps in what I had first seen as a single event. It may also be mistaken, for other meanings may be present in the sequence as a whole that are lost in analysis.

IMPROVISATION AND RECONCILIATION

Fundamental to the question of social creativity in American society today is the day-to-day challenge not only of getting along with neighbors with different cultural backgrounds but of developing and affirming a sense of shared meaning. Anxiety about whether this is even possible underlies much of the debate about multiculturalism (see, e.g., Schlesinger, 1991). "Getting along" is of course both pragmatic and aesthetic, for some actions can generate unifying meaning even when codes are not fully shared, like the profound sense of commonality created by participation in the March on Washington, or the communion created by Chessalay and Miaba.

In meeting others with different backgrounds, it is often necessary to react to great stretches of behavior we do not know how to segment or interpret. Sometimes it is necessary to perform such sequences, as in a conversation in a foreign country where I have a phrase-book knowledge of the language—I can rattle off whole sentences without knowing the grammar to analyze them but my listener may attend word for word.

Although speakers do not assemble their sentences like beads on a string, they are differentiated and sequenced in performance. Human interactions occur in time and the question of segmentation is always raised by the fact of sequence. The issue of sequence is also raised by difference. Chessalay can turn the unfamiliar actions of Miaba into a step-by-step narration without having the vocabulary to label them as part of a ceremonial whose structure she does not know. In an interaction between participants who do not share the same code, whatever pattern is experienced in common occurs in time. One might argue that the higher the degree of novelty the more the experience of the interlocutor is shaped by sequence; however, sharing in the interaction also depends on some agreement not to attend too closely to the details, to accept very rough approximations. Listening to an unfamiliar dialect of a known language can be facilitated by, as someone once said to me, "throwing your ear out of focus." The management of perception to blur inappropriate elements and to fuse unaccountable segments into larger wholes has the potential of creating needed commonality, but can also allow the projection of negative assumptions.

Before we call an action beautiful, before we give it authority in our lives, it is necessary to recapture some of the necessity and unity that precede analysis. The dancer performs an extraordinarily intricate sequence of muscular movements—one leap. The human speaker strings the muscular adjustments of articulation, sounds, parts of words, words—one utterance, a declaration, a report—a single speech act. The painter works stroke by stroke and the eye moves back and forth over the surface of a painting, sending its messages to the brain in sequenced impulses—yet we respond to a unified work of art, and it is often to this fused product of composition that we attach the term creativity. Indeed, the work of art and the leap are often evaluated on the extent that they are unified, as one of our basic aesthetic criteria, however vaguely stated.

I believe that a number of conventions provide a sense of commonality by drawing strangers into interactions whose rhythms are shared, providing the context for the performance and production of shared social forms. It is striking that in American society today dance forms allow a wide range of improvisational skill and experience rather than consisting of precisely rehearsed steps. Physical cues that channel movement through space and time provide a certain orchestration, and shared responses to highlighted events make everyone a participant in a common history; thus, we discuss the events on the sports page and stand in line as neighbors. On the other hand, many of the conventions of courtesy that used to orchestrate interactions between individuals with disparate backgrounds and purposes have atrophied. There is a continuing need to create new ones.

Not all improvisations are transient in their effects. The mourning sequence is especially interesting because in it a novel improvised behavior had the effect of a ritual, a sort of timeless authority, even though it was designed on the spur of the moment. When John F. Kennedy was assassinated, Jacqueline Kennedy set out to design a ritual, drawing on the forms that followed the Lincoln assassination and incorporating others. When my mother returned to Bali in the 1970s, some 30 years after she had originally done field work there, she told a story of how a Rajah had improvised a novel ritual to restore a sacred spring that had been desecrated. The procedure for purification involved sending messengers to sacred springs all over Bali to bring back small samples of water that were then mingled and poured into the desecrated spring, along with prayers, chants, incense, and other markers of sacred activity. The improvised ritual was accepted as valid. If the need were to arise again it might be repeated in toto.

Many cherished rituals that play significant roles in sustaining relationships or communities originate in improvisations. For example, a couple become engaged on an evening when they go to a particular restaurant and play particular music, and thereafter repeat the same sequence on their anniversary. The segments of an original improvisation are now fused into a fixed sequence that is part of the competence of both participants. She knows what dress to put on, he knows what flowers to bring. Something new has been created: A series of actions are repeated and given a unitary meaning. The Christian eucharist, we are told, is just such a reenactment. The ordinary can become extraordinary. Thus, ritual often contains very long stretches that have been fused into a unitary structure for most participants. There seem to be two interlocking rhythms; a rhythm of fission or analysis, where complex behavior is broken into its component parts, and sometimes a rhythm of fusion, where they are built into a new whole in ritual and the arts. A certain creativity is involved in putting together each new sequence, but often we pick out and recognize as creative those sequences that are most aesthetically and emotionally effective.

There are a number of ways whereby a sequence is fused so that it acquires meaning as a whole, as in the formation of an idiom. The phrase "that man in the white house" would once have had no more significance than the six words that compose it. However, first "white house" acquired an idiomatic meaning and became "White House," and during the Roosevelt administration the entire phrase was used by his opponents to refer to FDR—expressing a certain unity of point of view. The same words, the same phrases, but changes in meaning (triggering changes in intonation). Clearly for every transition in meaning there must be some encounters between individuals who do not share the same system. In fact, one must assume that there are slight differences of this kind between individuals at all times and that fission and fusion, analysis and composition, learning and creation are constantly taking place. Words and actions framed to meet the needs of the moment can be crystallized into a new unit by associated emotion providing an increment of significance, but significance can also be lost through repetition. When a sequence has aesthetic qualities that make it seem necessary this promotes fusion.

Consider the following case: I sneeze, you say "God bless you" (a fused conventional response that does not, for most users, mean that God should confer a blessing), and I reply, to your surprise, "He always does,"—or, indeed, "She always does." The disconcerting feature of these replies is that I respond to your phrase as if you were speaking in words (or morphemes), not sentences. The familiarity of "God bless you" involves both a loss and a gain of meaning. It has lost for most speakers the ordinary meanings of God and blessing, but it has been fused into an expected social courtesy. Such a shift of familiar ways of attaching meaning to the elements of a text can make changes in interpretive systems very disconcerting. In different ways, both religious fundamentalism and deconstructionism involve such changes.

Sometimes the creation of fused sequences involves a deliberate loss of awareness of the point of segmentation, or social facilitation of that loss. Here there are odd symmetries between the processes of religious ritual and those of the arts, both of which involve intense repetition in their evolution and use, and the processes of ordinary creativity, which are interwoven with the routines of every day. It is striking that improvisational artists, like athletes working together on a team, must devote a great deal of time to practice, even while keeping their performances fluid. Practice or the process whereby a series of motions is integrated into one smooth motion are ways of achieving fusion, so the dancer's leap, whatever its components, is seen as single. The poet works and reworks his lines, so that in the finished product the end does affect the beginning. In religious ritual, sequences are not only fused but repeated again and again with multiple shifts of meaning through the successive repetitions of generations. Neither poetry nor ritual is adequately experienced on a once-through basis, because the first line must be encountered again in the light of the last, and although dramatic and climactic structures occur in both, sequence and segmentation are blurred by the continual looping back. Oddly, art and religion both tend to get caught in paradoxes of valuing and devaluing spontaneity and escape from form. Contemporary American culture tends to regard spontaneity—which is to say improvisation—as an index of sincerity.

Continual small modifications occur in the composition of poetry and the evolution of ritual, as multitudes of tiny changes are made to enhance the "rightness" (or the truth) of a passage by enhancing the internal relationships. Often the usual distribution of linguistic forms is distorted as various types of partial repetition and echoing images are introduced. These processes give a poem or the verbal form of a ritual qualities of unity and necessity. Watching someone go about a familiar daily task, it is possible to see the smoothing effect of habit expressed as grace.

There is a complementarity between ritual fusion and aesthetic fusion, for art involves the purposeful introduction of regularities and patterns, creating a pressure toward fusion on a formal level, so that someone reading a poem or observing a painting for the first time is led to respond to it as a whole, which in turn results in an intensity of experience. At the same time, artists deliberately violate the expectations they have created in their audiences. A twist in the plot gives new meaning to what came before. We are in the habit in this society of thinking of ritual as alienating, as the antithesis of creativity, yet it also illustrates important issues in bridging alienation and in the creation of patterns for acting and interacting without complete sharing of codes.

I think we could list a very great number of pressures for fission in contemporary society, pressures on individuals to construct behaviors and messages new for them step by step, again and again. Some obvious examples would be learning a new technology from a manual or cooking by following a recipe step by step or bathing a baby by the rules in a textbook. Some applications of "systems analysis" fall precisely into this trap, as when an architect complains to me that the "systems analysis boys" in his office want him to break the design process down into steps, each of which he can justify separately, instead of moving toward a total aesthetic conception of a building. We can also find pressures toward fission in many areas of technology, where activity once performed "because that's the way we have always done it" must be justified step by step.

Modern reforms in the Catholic Church have tended toward fission in ritual. These range from the introduction of possible variants (thereby designating segmentation points) and single word shifts (which imply that the meaning of a ritual is a composite of its word meanings) to a new emphasis on intelligibility. One of the complaints that was often made about the new translation of the liturgy when it was first adopted by the Catholic Church was that individual words "stick out"—and gather doubts. I remember a conversation I had in the 1960s with a nun who was explaining how long it had taken her to get beyond the separate words and phrases of the English offices so as to make a single act of worship. "It doesn't flow any more," she said. Thirty years later the new forms have settled into a familiar unity, and Miaba, in spite of her lack of knowledge of English, has learned the word "Peace" as a meaningful exchange.

There is a relationship between this unity and the sense of authority in ritual, for an unsegmentable statement is much less subject to contradiction and query than a segmentable one, yet some individuals move and speak in a way that carries authority. If one analyzes "The Lord is One" as four words subject to rearrangement according to the grammar of the language, the statement coexists with a family of related sentences: "Is the Lord one?" "The Lord is not one." "The Lord is six." "Moloch is one," just as the statement "It will snow tomorrow," coined on the spot, coexists with the related sentence "It won't snow tomorrow," etc. I would contend however that the Shema is a unit and reciting it a unitary act of commitment, like the recitation of such other sentences as "There is no God but Allah and Muhammad is His Prophet." The same religious experience (Rappaport, 1979) that gives statements this unquestioned quality can be analyzed further as fusing them, making them nonreferential and unsegmentable and therefore not subject to verification. Colliding systems of meaning, however, propose segmentation, whereas unfamiliar contexts require improvisation.

The language of a ritual or a poem is only referential to a minor degree. Each refers to a subject matter or a theology and each expresses the speaker and implies some effect on the hearer, but, in a more important sense, poetry is always about poetry, whereas ritual is always about communion. Poetic language is concerned primarily with the quality of the message itself: "A poem should not mean but be" (MacLeish, 1933, p. 122). Religious ritual on the other hand is phatic, communication concerned with the state of the channel. "A sacrament effects what it signifies" (Denziger, 1965), when what it most profoundly signifies is the existence of a relationship. If we say that the ritual jointly constructed and performed by Chessalay and Miaba is sacramental—that it effects what it signifies—we need to explore what that might mean outside of a shared theology or semiotics. In effect, their actions do not share a common reference but they do establish a shared occasion. This example of the creation of a shared performance without a common code is paradigmatic of ways of bridging cultural diversity. It seems probable that in our own society the arts—not perhaps the "high arts," which are currently functioning in a highly individualistic mode, but popular art—might play the reconciling role once played by public rituals.

The study of social creativity involves looking at the ebb and flow of fusion and fission that allows not only learning and the invention of new forms but also the reassurance and reinterpretation of old ones, mixed in with practice and play, allowing the creation of deep and shared convictions. We must examine these activities and see how they vary, what supports them in human society and in what ways they are flexible. We need to compare works of art produced in a blaze of emotion with others shaped in conscious artistry and still others made by craftsmen faithfully producing a slight permutation of a cultural style, or to compare the writings of mystics about their own moments of illumination with the ways in which they have tried to institutionalize their insights for others.

Examining the way in which an adult and a child can create a shared game opens up the discussion of what can be achieved by holding on to that game and repeating it and what can be achieved by learning to vary it and introduce further complexity. Examining the way in which it is possible to adjust the circumstances of life into new configurations and to transfer learning opens up the search for meaning in a different way. In both cases, and in the intermediate forms discussed earlier, we are dealing with the ordinary creativity of the ways that individuals weave new meaning in their lives and relationships.

In considering the possibility that the arts might provide a needed kind of commonality, I am reminded of an early movie by Steven Spielberg, *Close Encounters of the Third Kind.* In this fantasy about the arrival of extraterrestrials, communication is established by a process of imitation, variation, and elaboration of a simple musical theme—very much like the process that establishes play between an adult and a preverbal child. The back-and-forth exchange of a sequence of notes blossoms into a burst of common music that is extraordinarily moving with its implication of communion.

REFERENCES

Bateson, G. et al. (1971). Natural history of an interview [University of Chicago Microfilm Collection of MSS]. *Cultural Anthropology, 15,* 95-98.

Bateson, M. C. (1975). Linguistic models in the study of joint performances. In M. D. Kinkade, K. L. Hale, & O. Werner (Eds.), *Linguistics and anthropology: In honor of C.F. Voegelin* (pp. 53-66). Lisse: The Peter de Ridder Press.

Bateson, M. C. (1975). Mother-infant exchanges: The epigenesis of conversational interaction. In D. Aaronson & R. W. Rieber (Eds.), *Developmental psycholinguistics and communication disorders* (pp. 101-113). New York: Annals of the New York Academy of Sciences.

Bateson, M.C. (1989). *Composing a life*. New York: Atlantic Monthly Press.

Bateson, M.C. (1994). *Peripheral visions: Learning along the way*. New York: HarperCollins.

Chomsky, N. (1965). *Aspects of the theory of syntax*. Cambridge, MA: MIT Press.

Denziger, H. (Ed.). (1965). *Enchiridion symbolorum: Definitionum et rationum de rebus civii et morum* (33rd ed., nos. 1606, 1639). Freiburg: Herder.

Lord, A. B. (1960). *The singer of tales*. Cambridge, MA: Harvard University Press.

MacLeish, A. (1933). Ars poetica. In *Poems, 1924-1933* (p. 122). Boston: Houghton-Mifflin

Malinowski, B. (1968). The problem of meaning in primitive languages. In C. K. Ogden & I. A. Richards (Eds.), *The meaning of meaning* (pp. 296-336). New York: Harcourt, Brace & World.

Parry, M. (1932). Studies in the epic technique of verse making: Homer and Homeric style. *Harvard Studies in Classical Philology, 43*, 1-50.

Piaget, J. (1973). *To understand is to invent: The future of education*. New York: Grossman.

Pike, K. (1954). *Language in relation to a unified theory of the structure of human behavior*. New York: Humanities Press.

Pittenger, R. E., Hockett, C. F., & Danehy, R. E. (1960). *The first five minutes: A sample of microscopic interview analysis*. Ithaca, NY: Martineau Press.

Rappaport, R. (1979). The obvious aspects of ritual. In *Ecology, meaning, and religion*. Richmond, CA: North Atlantic Books.

Schlesinger, A., Jr. (1991). *The disuniting of America: Reflections on a multicultural society*. Knoxville, TN: Whittle Direct Books.

PART FOUR

CREATIVITY AT WORK

7

The Social Construction
of Creative Lives*

Carol A. Mockros
Mihaly Csikszentmihályi

INTRODUCTION

Researchers who study creativity often concede that cultural norms and practices influence the development and expression of creativity. Nevertheless, the degree to which such forces influence expressions of ability and creativity is generally underestimated. For the most part, attention is focused on how cognitive factors or other individual characteristics such as personality, values, problem-finding orientation, and motivation contribute to the appearance of creativity and eminence. Such an orientation only peripherally addresses how historical, social, and cultural environments impact various life experiences and expressions of creativity.

Recently theorists have begun to recognize the importance of looking at creativity in terms of interacting multiple systems (e.g., Albert, 1990; Csikszentmihályi, 1988, 1990; Feldman & Goldsmith, 1986; Gruber, 1980, 1981, 1982; Gruber & Davis, 1988; Simonton, 1988; Tannenbaum, 1987; Walters & Gardner, 1986). The systems in question are comprised of individuals, fields, and domains, as well as the social and cultural forces

*The Creativity in Later Life research project referred to in this chapter was supported by the Spencer Foundation.

that impact these subsystems. Systems theory offers a framework by which multiple forces and complex processes involved in attaining high levels of creativity and eminence may be analyzed. According to systems theory, discussed in greater detail elsewhere (e.g., Csikszentmihályi, 1988, 1990) creativity should be viewed as a part of a complex dynamic system of feedback in which novel ideas and acts may result in creativity only in the context of an interaction with a symbolic system inherited from previous generations, and with a social system qualified to evaluate and accept the novelty. In this model, creativity is not an attribute of individuals, but of social systems making judgments about individuals.

Most theorists agree that people are considered creative if they have been recognized by experts as having contributed something of original value to the culture. Over a century ago Galton (1869) suggested that eminence is partially determined by others who are expert and experienced enough to appreciate and judge the performances or results. Hence, before any novelty can be considered creative, appropriately qualified judges must assess the ideas and products as likely to produce a lasting impact on the domain. In this way, accomplishments become recognized as valuable and innovative after they have received social recognition either from the larger society, or from a specialized field. The field is responsible for acknowledging and legitimizing the efforts of *potentially* creative individuals as well as deciding what ideas get incorporated into the domain. Although the field provides the context for activity in the domain, the domain itself, comprised of the structured or organized body of knowledge, exists independently of people and serves to transmit information to individuals. For instance, the domain of music contains the various notations systems, styles of compositions, and past musical masterpieces. A creative musician is one who, working within the symbolic system of music, produces a new composition that the field (other musicians, conductors, critics, recording executives, etc.) deems worthy of adding to the domain. The more a person's work changes the existing domain, the more that person will be considered creative.

Although fields are necessary to insure that poor ideas and products are not too easily assimilated into domains, they may also constrain growth and development by being too conservative. In any case, the complexity and diversity of eminent and creative adult lives suggests the need for a more thorough understanding of how social relationships, institutions, and cultures provide a context for stimulating and judging creative efforts.

This chapter examines how individuals develop through an interaction with social institutions, norms, and rules. In addition, it considers some of the ways fields and domains determine progress via historical, educational, professional, and cultural systems and practices that impact which ideas and knowledge are deemed relevant and valued. We intend to present several basic theoretical assumptions that influence the expression of creativity. In particular, we focus on how social and cultural norms and practices contribute to the apparent absence of eminent and creative women in virtually every field. Examples and documentation based on narrative data gathered from a study of creativity in later life are used to illustrate how socializing mechanisms and personal priorities and values contribute to expectations, choices, decisions, personal perceptions, and attitudes regarding career related abilities, goals and aspirations. These, in turn, ultimately determine how far and how high a potentially eminent life will go. The ideas that follow have implications for theories of creativity by indicating how social and cultural norms and practices influence the expression of creativity for both men and women.

CREATIVITY IN LATER LIFE PROJECT

The strength and full impact of a creative piece of work is often not recognized by the field until after the creator is dead; as a result, samples of living geniuses are hard to come by. On the other hand, studying contemporary geniuses allows us to gain relatively equivalent information on all individuals that would not be possible using exclusively biographic information of historical figures. As a result, 6 years ago, with the assistance of the Spencer Foundation, we began a research study to learn more about creative lives, and about the current attitudes and work habits of individuals who, at a stage of life when most people are preparing for retirement, are vigorously involved in important new activities. The project, called "Creativity in Later Life," involved interviewing persons over 60 years of age who have made significant contributions to a domain.

Sample

The selection of individuals to interview was based on three general criteria: (a) Subjects are at least 60 years old; (b) there is consensus among experts in the field who recognize the subjects work as original and having significantly impacted the domain; (c) the population of subjects is distributed across gender, general area of expertise, and geographical/cultural background. The four main areas of expertise are Natural Science, Social Science, Arts and Humanities, and Business, Media, and Politics. These domain categories are not mutually exclusive, as some individuals will have worked within several disciplines. The goal of the original study was to interview 100 individuals. Thus far, 91 interviews have been completed.

The process of selecting our interviewees involved several stages. Names were acquired through (a) published records of prestigious awards such as Nobel Laureates and Pulitzer prize winners, (b) recommendations of other experts in the field, and (c) sources such as books and articles that recognize the significant work of various individuals. Following the acquisition of a group of 10-20 names, short biographies were gathered and read by the research team to determine the relative eminence of individuals. Based on this information, the research team made judgments about which subjects to pursue. At this stage potential subjects received a brief letter and consent form explaining the nature of the project and requesting their participation in the study. If subjects responded affirmatively, subjects were contacted and an interview date was arranged. If subjects did not respond to the initial request, a follow-up letter was sent. When possible, subjects who had not responded to the follow up letter were contacted by phone. At this point, if we were unsuccessful at making contact, no further attempts were made to acquire their participation.

Among those who were kind enough to participate in our interviews were several Nobel-Prize-winning scientists such as Linus Pauling, Rosylyn Yallow, John Bardeen, Hans Bethe, Jerome Karle, and Manfred Eigen; Pulitzer Prize winners such as C. V. Woodward; the eminent German poetess Hilde Domin and the Italian writer Grazia Livi; and the innovative CEOs of Motorola (Robert Galvin) and Citibank (John Reed).

The sample on which we are drawing for this chapter consists of 12 women and 17 men. For purposes of identification, the sample has the following characteristics:

Women (12)

F1. Psychologist, author. Created an influential theory of personality development.

F2. Social scientist. Pioneered the study of aging. Past president, Gerontological Society; recipient Kleemeier Award, Brookdale Award.

F3. Sociologist, educator, author. Recipient Lentz peace prize, National Woman of Conscience Award.

F4. Mathematician, computer expert, politician. Executive Board, Association of Women in Science. First woman elected a fellow of the American Nuclear Society.

F5. Astronomer. Past director Association University Research in Astronomy; past president Committee on Galaxies, International Astronomical Union.

F6. Chemist. Recipient Lifetime Achievement Award Women in Science and Engineering; past president, American Crystallographic Association.

F7. Historian. Writer of screenplays. Past president, American Historical Association.

F8. Visual artist. Winner of many prizes, works in the permanent collections of the Library of Congress, Denver Art Museum, Museum of Contemporary Art.

F9. Sculptor. Widely exhibited sculptor, facilitator of intellectual and cultural exchanges.

F10. Editor of one of the most distinguished European newspapers.

F11. Ceramicist. Work exhibited in the New York Museum of Modern Art and elsewhere. Owner-manager of mass-produced quality ceramic factory.

F12. Physicist, Medical researcher. Winner of Nobel Prize.

Males (17)

M1. Physicist. Winner of two Nobel Prizes.

M2. Historian. Winner of Pulitzer Prize.

M3. Physicist. Winner of Nobel Prize.

M4. Physicist, author. Winner Einstein and Niels Bohr Prizes.

M5. Physicist, author. Recipient Max Planck Medal and National Medal of Science.

M6. Lawyer, author, sociologist.

M7. Historian, author. Winner National Book Award.

M8. Psychologist. Former Cabinet member.

M9. Physicist, historian of science, author. Recipient R.A. Millikan medal.

M10. Physicist, literary author. Fellow of the Royal Society and the National Academy of Sciences.

M11. Historian, educator, author. Past president American Historical Association and American Philosophical Society.

M12. Pediatrician, activist, author, U.S. Presidential candidate.

M13. Biologist, educator, ecological activist, politician. Recipient Newcomb Cleveland prize, First Humanist International Prize.

M14. Medical researcher, author, philanthropist. Decorated Legion of Honor, Robert Koch medal, Presidential medal of Freedom.

M15. Chemist, activist. Winner of two Nobel Prizes.

M16. Economist, educator. Recipient of Distinguished scholarship in Humanities; Corecipient of International Peace Research Award.

M17. Chemist. Winner of Nobel Prize.

Interviews

The primary method of data collection was a semistructured interview. The semistructured interview format allowed for some flexibility and variability with regard to responses. The interviews were videotaped and lasted approximately 2 hours. The interview protocol was designed to address several broad issues concerning the creativity of eminent older adults. It consisted of four primary groups of questions. These included *Career and life priorities*, related to interests, obstacles, and goals; *relationships with other people*, which inquired about the nature of various social interactions with mentors, colleagues, and family; *working habits and insights*, which attempted to elicit information about how individuals come up with and solve problems; and *attentional structures and dynamics*, which involved how and on what individuals spend time. A sample of the specific questions in each of the four categories include: Of the things you have done in your life, of what are you most proud? Has there been a specific person or persons in your life who have influenced or stimulated your thinking and attitudes about your work? Can you describe your working methods? If we would have spoken to you 30 years ago, what different views of the world and yourself would you have had? Supplementary sources of information on the eminent adults included published books and articles containing autobiographical and biographical information on the subjects.

CREATIVE WOMEN

Some important differences concerning how social and cultural influences impact creativity emerged as soon as we began to compose lists of potential interviewees. When the study was initially proposed, we intended to interview equal numbers of eminent men and women. In soliciting names for participants we perused anthologies of people who have made major accomplishments, and won distinguished prizes (e.g., Nobel Laureates, Pulitzer Prizes) as well as inquired with experts within each field. It quickly became clear, however, that we were going to have great difficulty locating eminent and creative women. Moreover, the women who consented to be interviewed were not comparable to many of the men in terms of their renown or apparent creativity. Indeed, a brief glance at history, science, or literature texts reveals that few eminent women are listed as having made major contributions to a domain. Even in disciplines that are traditionally associated with women such as teaching and cooking it is unusual to find female principals, superintendents, or head chefs. Although all sorts of reasons have been offered to explain why this should be so, little attention has been paid to understanding the effects of this state of affairs on the development of future cohorts of creative men and women.

A combination of explanations may explain why it is difficult to locate highly creative older women. The lack of eminent women may be due to the fact that their abilities haven't been appropriately recognized by educational and professional institutions, or that they haven't had adequate opportunities to develop their ability, or that they are not encouraged to develop the skills and abilities necessary to achieve eminence in a domain, or that they have different definitions and expectations of success, or perhaps their mental orientation differs from that of the people who are in charge of dispensing recognition? Each of these reasons may be rooted in sociocultural limitations inherent in the ways we socialize young children into the world and young adults into a field, as well as how we promote adult achievement in later life.

Social norms and values determine whether a person will become eminent. Expectations influence whether talent is noticed, appreciated, and nurtured. The remainder of the chapter illustrates how cultural expectations influence the development of creative identities, and account for the differential between the number of eminent men and women represented in various fields.

THE INTERACTION BETWEEN SELF-CONSTRUCTIONS AND SOCIAL SYSTEMS

High levels of self-confidence have been found to help eminent individuals to seek out opportunities for continuing advancement in a field. Creative achievement depends on a combination of important personal qualities including skills, ego strength, a sense of purpose, and the ability to mobilize and productively orchestrate aspects of one's life. These skills are necessary to sustain a committed, enduring career. In addition, a strong willingness to take risks coupled with high degrees of self-motivation and discipline are also characteristic of highly eminent and creative individuals (Albert, 1990; DeGroot, 1965; Getzels & Csikszentmihályi, 1976; Gruber,

1986). Cox (1926) found that intelligence in the standard "IQ" sense did not appear to be the hallmark of future achievement as much as perseverance in work and confidence in one's abilities. In any case, self-motivation and confidence are considered essential to the development of creativity and eminence.

But where do motivation and confidence come from? And how are they are developed within an individual? It appears that there is a dialectical relationship between the development of the creative person and the social influences that determine which abilities are valued and reinforced. Through direct and indirect feedback from parents, teachers, peers, colleagues, authority figures, and media sources, some people are encouraged and validated for their ability. These fortunate individuals often notice their own abilities because they have been noticed, labeled, or validated by others. Future demonstrations of ability become subsequently affected by increasing the availability of opportunities and networks of relevant people. Conversely, obstacles, impediments, restrictions, or the lack of opportunities and positive external affirmation for one's interests and abilities will generally produce negative attitudes about one's self-concept and competence. In light of this, it follows that the development of self and ability are fundamentally social processes determined by cultural norms, values, and expectations. Hence, attempts to understand the development of confidence and eminence in adulthood requires a deeper understanding of the ways competent behavior, definitions of success, and pedagogical strategies are influenced by other people throughout the life span.

THE EARLY SOCIALIZATION OF CREATIVE AND EMINENT INDIVIDUALS

The systems model suggests that the key issues that will determine whether a young person will have a chance to develop in a creative direction—in addition to innate ability. Exceptional development rests on whether: (a) there is a domain appropriate to a child's talent available in the culture (i.e., if the culture is ignorant of mathematics, a math-talented child cannot become a creative mathematician); (b) the domain is accessible (caste, gender, social class, or ethnic origin may prevent some children from being exposed to a given domain); (c) the society supports involvement in the particular domain; and (d) the child is perceived by the representatives of the field as suitable for training in the domain.

The field operates through processes of social selection and social interaction. Selection mechanisms determine the values and abilities people are allowed and expected to cultivate, as well as the opportunities available for developing these abilities. Social interactions involve the communication of expectations, attitudes, strategies, and direction as well as the provision of guidance and support, to develop. It is through both social selection and social interactions that young children receive the opportunities and the affirmation that contributes to the development of early ability and talent. Numerous biographical studies have revealed that individuals who have made great accomplishments received critical supports as key stages in their early development (Albert & Runco, 1987; Bloom, 1985; Cox, 1926; Feldman & Goldsmith, 1986; Goertzel & Goertzel, 1962; Gruber, 1986; Holloway, 1986; Kanigel, 1986; Ochse, 1990; Roe, 1953; Simonton, 1983, 1986, 1988; Zuckerman, 1977).

For young talented children, the commitment of parents, teachers and other adults is crucial to the development of self-concept and confidence. In particular, talent in the child may be of less importance than parental encouragement. Adults responsible for the early development of creative individuals devote a great deal of time and energy to their children's development (Bloom, 1985; Cox, 1926; Csikszentmihályi, Rathunde, & Whalen, 1993; Goertzel & Goertzel, 1962; MacKinnon, 1978; Ochse, 1990; Pariser, 1991; Roe, 1953; Simonton, 1988; Zuckerman, 1977). They often help children develop habits of practice, discipline, and attention to detail and both implicitly and explicitly transmit values such as commitment, critical thinking, learning, and achievement. In addition, adults organize, stimulate, and facilitate the learning process via the provision of academic opportunities to work with appropriate teachers and mentors during early childhood. Parents themselves often have personal interests and drive toward intellectual and creative achievement. In this way they serve as models of the work ethic and are likely to emphasize the importance of doing one's best.

Although parents are generally thought to be the primary influences on children's development, other relatives and teachers contribute to developing abilities and aspirations by encouraging and supporting talent. Teachers often identify and recognize the ability and interests of talented young people and may subsequently nurture or encourage the development of these abilities by talking to the child and his or her parents about it. They also provide the child with materials, exercises, or experiences that facilitate the development of talent. In any case, families and early teachers are instrumental for providing opportunities and experiences that introduce talented youth to the field. Likewise, they support and encourage talent development by affirming ability and interests during early childhood. This early social support and encouragement contributes to the development of self-confidence and subsequent independence.

The Differential Socialization of Boys and Girls

The literature on the social influences leading to gender differences with respect to aspirations and achievements among the gifted and talented is extensive. Only a cursory discussion of these differences will be given here. Research has looked at factors that influence academic success and productivity as well as career decisions among gifted and talented youth (Astin, 1974; Bloom, 1985; Fox, 1977; Hollinger, 1985, 1986; Holloway, 1986; Kerr, 1985; Solano, 1983; Tomlinson-Keasey & Burton, 1992). Most of this research focuses on the attitudes, aspirations, and achievements of young boys and girls in mathematics and science. The findings show that during elementary school by most measures girls tend to be intellectually equal or superior to boys. Over time, however, girls' achievements progressively fall off as compared to boys. As girls mature, their talent and giftedness become sources of conflict, whereas for young boys the cultivation and expression of ability is a source of pride and generally enhances their overall image of themselves. This may be due to the fact that girls are not encouraged to develop their interests, talent, and abilities. A critical component of attaining eminence in this culture involves the development of a specified identity that allows a person to differentiate oneself from others, and develop independence and autonomy in one's field of endeavor.

Research has found that boys generally evaluate themselves more positively when they identify themselves as being more competitive, autonomous, and independent. Girls, on the other hand, root self-concepts more in dependency, and relational competencies and values. As a result, competition and independence may have more favorable effect on men's identity development than women's. Our culture partly defines creativity and eminence with characteristics and qualities that are appropriate for males and somewhat inappropriate for females. Cultivating and expressing independence and competitiveness may be difficult for women because it interferes with priorities and attitudes toward work.

Studies have found that parents and teachers respond differently to achievement and intellectual competence in boys and girls (Helson, 1990; Hollinger, 1985, 1986; Holloway, 1986; Solano, 1983). In general, given similar external accomplishments or scholastic achievements, the ability of boys is recognized as superior to that of girls. In addition, young boys are affirmed for their progress and ability, whereas the accomplishments of girls are either ignored or discouraged by significant adults. Likewise, boys' early academic and artistic choices tend to be more readily supported by parents and teachers. In addition, parents and teachers generally select a particular child in which they invest their time and energy. They locate educational opportunities that will serve the child identified as best suited to take advantage of the opportunities. The chosen child receives intense socialization in the field. In general, girls are less likely to be the chosen child by parents or teachers. In this way, the processes of socializing girls involves an increasing negation of intellectual and creative goals that may interfere with the development of their identities. Although this assumption has not been adequately studied, much of the literature suggests that young girls actively choose to forgo academic success and intellectual achievements when social and personal values and expectations of behavior conflict with the development of a positive (feminine) sense of self.

As young children, both the men and women in our sample of eminent individuals received recognition and encouragement from adults. Virtually all eminent people discuss the importance of someone else who believed in what they were doing and encouraged them at some time in their lives. In this way, young people invariably benefit from the encouragement of an adult. Nonetheless, as young boys, the men were more often the chosen child in the families:

> I was not considered very bright. My brother was older than I and I never felt I was treated quite as well. I was a girl, and I think this had a profound impact on the way we were treated. I came from this very intellectual family and everybody was supposed to be at least a university professor if not a medical doctor. I was not considered the gifted child in the family. So maybe being a second class citizen took the seriousness out of my ambitions. [F11]

> I had a sister who was smarter than I in school. She was younger and she pushed me. The relationship between my sister and I was not totally smooth because I did better than she in academic life and her subsequent career has not been as happy as mine. She said she was not pleased with the fact that I left her behind. [M7]

The majority of the men received support and encouragement as children from a parent or family member:

> Both my parents were valedictorians of their classes. So, I had very strong parental model and example of accomplishment and ambition which pervaded my childhood. My parents never put overt pressure on me to do anything I did not want to do, but I think it's also true that they expected superior performance from me and they got it. I think breaking the parental bond for me was very difficult because they were very kind to me and certainly did all that they could to facilitate my life [M7]

My father was the dean of the medical school and very busy. Still, he encouraged me by frequently giving me extra math problems to do. [M1]

They left me complete freedom to do my stuff which was science. And neither of them was a scientist but they understood what it was about. [M10]

My mother was very strong and had a lot of courage. She would always tell me, "understand this, even the angels cannot do any better than their best." [M11]

My parents always supported me, although sometimes they were not in agreement. They thought it was important I get in touch with what I wanted to do. They supported my scientific interests by buying books or giving me money for instruments even though they themselves were not very interested in science. My mother had a strong influence on me, not in science, she didn't understand much about science, but in art and music. She loved me very much. I didn't have a lot of worries as a child. [M5]

Typically in the evening the family would be sitting around the living room, everybody with his book or homework . . . my father was very interested in science . . . but he was limited in how he could get around because he had a family to support. . . . One of his motto's was that "there is nothing that cannot be done better" . . . (they gave) encouragement of being behind me . . . ". . . That a boy! Go after it." [M4]

I had an aunt and uncle who were intellectuals. My uncle kept an eye on me and encouraged me to move in intellectual directions. So I was lucky that way. My father wanted me to become a radio repairman. But, my uncle made it clear that I should go to college. [M13]

Many people, including various neighbors encouraged me and helped me accomplish what I wanted accomplish, which was to learn more about chemistry. [M15]

Although most of the women were not overtly discouraged, they rarely received the affirmation or encouragement for their early interests, performance, and achievements comparable to that received by the men. Here are some typical accounts:

I joined the *Amateur Astronomers*, which was an adult organization in Washington and (father) would come to meetings with me. I think he thought it was improper for a young girl to go off. . . . My father thought I should become a mathematician—do something more practical—he was afraid I would never be able to make a living as an astronomer. . . . Maybe my mother would have liked me to have been more social. I really preferred to read and to study and was not really interested in an active social life. [F5]

My father was a lawyer and then a judge. . . . I don't think my mother had a particular direction she wanted me to go. I think my father wanted me to be a probation officer or something like that, to be helpful to a judge. . . . He liked me, but he had very sexist ideas about the professions, and he didn't quite approve of my being a psychologist. [F1]

My parents wanted me to be a school teacher. [F12]

I wanted to be a chemist and that threw my parents. My mother thought I would be a teacher and my father thought I would be a lawyer. . . . They didn't really know what my interest in chemistry would lead to. [F6]

My father was a mechanical engineer. I remember when I was interested in going into mechanical engineering and he told me—and that was the only time he ever said anything to me one way or another about what to do—and he said, "Well, if you are a women going into mechanical engineering you will end up filing blue prints. Don't do that." [F4]

My family was very middle class and bourgeois and always doing the right things. No one in my family considered for one second that I would be anything except a wild girl. Everybody always thought I was imaginative and wild, but they did not encourage it. They were absolutely upset, terrified and horrified that I wanted to study theater. It was like being a street walker to them. I think they wanted me to be quietly married off somewhere. [F9]

Adults outside the family often perpetrated the same differential treatment of boys and girls. Young girls received considerably less encouragement and affirmation from teachers than the men did as boys.

I skipped from grade 3 to grade 7 and took High School algebra at age 10. In seventh grade I worked closely with a mathematics teacher at the University High School. My early intellectual interests in math and later academic success are due to this teacher's interest and encouragement. [M1]

I always scored well on exams in school. I got a scholarship to high school, and had excellent excellent teachers who helped me get a scholarship to Oxford. [M16]

I was told right from the beginning that I would have to work harder, twice as hard as anybody else (due to antisemitism). But my teachers thought I was bright enough and it would be worthwhile. [M13]

When I came upon obstacles I don't think I took them very seriously. I just felt that the people who presented obstacles did not understand that I really wanted to be an astronomer. And, I tended to ignore them or dismiss them. . . . In general I think there was just a lack of support. I always met teachers who told me—in college, in graduate school—to . . . go and find something else to study . . . they didn't need astronomers . . . I wouldn't get a job . . . I shouldn't be doing this, and I really just dismissed all that. I just never took it seriously. I just thought they didn't understand. [F5]

I went to the counseling center and a counselor told me that psychology was too mathematical for me. . . . He based that on my college aptitude test. . . . Still, apparently I knew enough to get good grades, but he decided on the basis of my exam that math was too hard for me. [F1]

Many women find out that they haven't got the background for math or science because they copped out early on. Also, I think when children get into high school and there are lots of social activities, and women seem to spend their time watching men do sports. Like cheerleaders. They themselves don't participate in the competitions as much. [F4]

I have not had a formal education. I went to school, but I never attended university. I went to university, but only to occasional lectures. [F10]

I knew my parents were sacrificing to send me to college. So, I thought I'd better get something out of it. In fact, that is the reason I went into math. I felt it was something for which my parents were getting their money's worth. It was hard and I felt I was learning a lot. [F4]

Not surprisingly, such differential reinforcement leads to particular attitudes about one's potential, and often negative consequences for the subsequent professional goals of girls. Again, however, it should be pointed out that despite differential treatment, gifted girls were more like gifted boys than they were like average girls in their interests, abilities, and aspirations. Moreover, eminent women frequently demonstrate a great deal of self-confidence, autonomy, and independence in pursuing their goals. Many describe social influences that helped them develop self-confidence and counteract standard messages and expectations of female achievement and performance. In particular, as is discussed later, women often received considerable support from their husbands. In addition, eminent women mathematicians and scientists talk about having performed well and received attention, encouragement, and affirmation from parents and early teachers:

I was in high school by the time I was 11. That was because we lived in a small town and nobody knew what to do with a bright child so they just kept on pushing me up a grade. [F2]

After I graduated from high school I went on to a university in Detroit and by some quirk in scheduling my chemistry course was with the chemical engineers and I was the only girl. I was good at it, and the teacher soon singled me out as the one who got 100s on the tests. I graduated from college when I was 19. I got my PhD a month after my 22 birthday. [F6]

I was 15 when entering college. [F1]

What distinguishes eminent women from their peers may lie in the fact that they *did* receive encouragement and recognition for their early abilities. The fact remains, however, that the social environment does not consistently reward and encourage intellectual rigor and curiosity in young girls. Cultural norms are generally less antagonistic to developing profitable characteristics for men's success and achievement. As a result, men more frequently encounter relationships that support their intellectual and creative efforts. These social mechanisms not only lead to girls' decreased interest and motivation, but also to a decrease in the opportunities that are available to them during the early stages of their careers. Moreover, unless young girls are exposed to someone who encourages and supports their interests it is unlikely they will persevere given the opposing messages on identity development as well as impending constraints on educational opportunities.

ADULTHOOD AND PROFESSIONAL SOCIALIZATION

The construction of a creative life is a complex developmental process that occurs over the life span (Albert, 1983, 1990; Bloom, 1985; Csikszentmihályi, 1988; Feldman & Goldsmith, 1986; Gruber, 1980, 1981, 1986; Tannenbaum, 1987). Young adulthood is often the time during which one's "purpose" begins to form. At this time, people formulate a personal vision or dream for their life (Erikson, 1950; Gergen, 1990; James, 1990; Levinson, Darrow, Klein, Levinson, & McKee 1978; Roberts & Newton, 1987; Stewart, 1977; Terman & Oden, 1959). For both men and women, career choices are often defined by interpersonal needs. The dominant issues surrounding identity formation for young men generally center around professional goals, aspirations, and achievements (Levinson et al., 1978; Valliant, 1977). As a result, it is important to understand how people make personal and professional choices when examining this portion of the life span.

Socializing experiences during adulthood also have a profound impact on people by validating or invalidating competencies. For this reason, the mobilization of critical segments of the field is important as young people continue to develop their personal and professional aspirations. For young adults, professional institutions, mentors, and spouses are the chief socializing agents. Just as teachers and parents provide instrumental support, encouragement, and opportunities for talented children, during young adulthood, mentors and spouses function similarly. We turn now to a discussion of the ways young adults are reinforced and socialized into professional communities; in particular, the way the field defines and develops the attitudes, abilities, and people it perceives to be beneficial to the domain.

Mentors

During young adulthood, people generally benefit from relationships that endorse a more highly developed, domain-specific self-concept. At this time, identity development occurs in the context of identifying with role models within the career and work context. At the same time, hierarchical training systems indoctrinate young people into a field. The mentor-apprentice relationship transmits information, knowledge, and skills from one generation to the next. Professional communities have long recognized the value of mentor-apprentice relationships in cultivating ability (Kanigel, 1986; Kram, 1985; Simonton, 1978, 1984; Zey, 1984, Zuckerman, 1977). People who do well in senior positions have often been guided and taught by a mentor.

Not surprisingly, mentor relationships are often one of the most important relationships during young adulthood. A mentor can be a teacher, supporter, guide, protector, and counselor for a young adult as he or she enters the adult world of work. Mentors play a critical role in helping negotiate both personal and professional issues. They contribute to the development of young people by building self-confidence, affirming and encouraging their abilities, and helping them develop a stronger and clearer professional identity. For some, mentors help increase self-confidence by expressing or demonstrating faith in the apprentice, whereas for others mentors specifically and directly communicate positive feedback regarding performance or life circumstances. In this way, mentors effect a fundamental transformation in the way young people perceive themselves, their value, their potential, their careers, and their relationship to the field and domain.

Generally, a less important aspect of the apprenticeship revolves around teaching specific substantive knowledge; rather, the value of the relationship stems from seeing how mentors operate, think, find, and solve problems. In this way, the principal benefits of apprenticeships include exposure to procedures and standards of work as well as inner processes of thought. Thus, although apprenticeships provide the beginner with access to the overt aspects of developing skills through close collaborations with mentors, novices learn dimensions of knowledge that are not formally articulated.

Good mentors offer young students the freedom and expertise needed to cultivate problem-finding abilities. Likewise, they help recognize innovative ideas that may be tested and pursued. In this way they serve as gatekeepers in deciding what ideas and projects are worthy of being pursued as well as those that are inappropriate or not likely to come to fruition. Mentors often provide a safe, secure environment in which novel ideas can be developed, nurtured, and experimented with. In addition, they advance young people in an organization by teaching specific skills or strategies of work and problem solving, providing them with opportunities, sponsoring them, challenging them, and protecting them from negative gossip and feedback. At the same time, mentors use their position and influence to raise the visibility and credibility of the young person while providing insight into effective ways to function within an organization or system. Hence, mentor-apprentice relationships contribute to the development of ability, self-confidence, as well as positions and credibility within the field.

Zuckerman (1977) demonstrated that both apprentices and masters are engaged in a motivated search to find and work with scientists of talent. For the Nobel Laureates, both self-selection and social selection enlarge opportunities for further work that, in turn, opens up additional opportunities. In choosing an apprentice, the mentor makes judgments and assessments about his or her perceived skills in the field. In this way, the promotion of young people is not based on current performance but on perceived potential, which is highly subjective. At the same time, those perceived to be lacking the skills necessary to succeed will be overlooked as useful and valued apprentices.

In selecting apprentices, many senior people look not so much for a good worker as for a replica of themselves. In this way, the selection processes are biased toward people who display characteristics or attitudes similar to those the mentors possessed as young people. Women and minorities in business, for example, are automatically perceived to be less competent in managerial, leadership, and technical skills. As a result, opportunities to be apprenticed to top executives often do not exist.

Among our eminent adults the value and importance of having mentors were often discussed:

> Young people should try to get personal contact with scientists at the university. Talk to them and work with them. That's the way to learn. Not by just taking courses. The apprenticeship is very important in science. [M5]

> When you are young I think personal encounters with others are especially important. [M7]

> People can grow beyond their fears or early low self-estimates of their worth during midlife if they get the affirmation. They may get the

affirmation on their own or with the help of a mentor who brings out what is in them. [M8]

What you need in teachers is to have people you can go to, like friends when you have a problem. Graduate school is tough, people need support; moral support and encouragement from teachers. [F5]

I think having a sponsor helps. Somebody who recognizes your work and pushes you forward. I think the kind of recognition you get with, for example the National Academy depends on having somebody there to push you. It's such a Byzantine system. You have to have somebody who will push for you. [F1]

I think women need to have women who are role models and people who are doing things, not just looking on from the audience, but participating. [F4]

By all means it is important to try to be an apprentice to an artist. Being an apprentice is a very very, very, basic and important element of education. It is important because it is not learning the facts of making art. Working with a person who is creative and you become part of their body. You begin to learn that way. You learn what it is about studio discipline and also being an artist is not just making art. It is keeping books and being a business person. You learn about that. You learn how tough it is to work with dealers and what it means to have shows. [F8]

Men and Women in Mentor Relationships

Although mentors play a significant role in the development of creative individuals during the formative years of their careers, men and women do not have similar experiences with teachers and mentors. In the past, research has suggested that women and men have different needs with respect to mentors (Jeruchim & Shapiro, 1992). Whereas men seek mentors who are useful to their career advancement, women seek mentors who teach them how to live their lives. At the same time, both young men and women establish mentor relationships for different reasons, at different times, and with different expectations. It appears, for example, that women who have received support and basic affirmation for their abilities and competence as children, may have fewer personal, emotional needs as young adults. At the same time, if a young man has not had sufficient early affirmation and has not developed an inner sense of direction and purpose, he may need a mentor who can offer these things rather than (or in addition to) career and professional guidance.

For the most part, however, men and women have different experiences with mentors. Most of our women cannot point to a particular person in the field who influenced them during the early stages of their careers; rather, they indicate that many people influenced their development. For example, in one woman's case numerous undergraduate teachers encouraged her ability and interests and thereby contributed to her self-confidence in the field:

> Almost all of the teachers I had at Vassar were female . . . and they were very good . . . and maybe from them I acquired some of this self-confidence. [F5]

Women also discuss not having been significantly influenced by anyone during the early years of their careers:

> I don't remember modeling myself after anyone, even as a child. I have been asked this often and I have thought about it so it must be true. I can never come up with anybody who influenced me in an overt sense. [F2]

> Well, I didn't really have (an advisor), I mean it was during the war years and it would have been . . . although our ideas were antithetical. So I think technically it was . . . but he wasn't too much interested in the kind of thing I was interested in . . . so I just did my own thing. [F1]

> He (graduate advisor) was a fascinating person to work with but my relationship to him as a graduate student was really not very close. . . . I don't think he had an enormous influence on me professionally. [F5]

> I don't know if I had a role model or not, I don't remember one. [F4]

> I don't think I can find a single person who particularly influenced my style. I can't think of anybody. [F11]

> At the University of Michigan I enjoyed most of the professors but they were a little distant. I don't think that I had any bad experiences. I had indifferent experiences, so (to them) if I survived that was fine. No obstacles were put in my way. I didn't have bad personal relations with others. They were nonexistent in some ways, but if I did my work, it was OK. Most of what kept me going were my own personal interests. [F6]

> I was put into my place by my master. I had to wear waterproof pants and a red kerchief. He took me to nice houses to set ovens to show that my job as an apprentice was not an elegant one. . . . I did not identify with him. I played out my role. [F11]

Many of male respondents, on the other hand, had significant influential teachers and mentors during the early years of their careers. In addition, their mentors were often highly eminent figures in the field such as Niels Bohr, G. H. Hardy, and Richard Feynman.

> He was a critical role model who introduced me to the history of science and technology in China. My relationship with him led to my initial interest and entry into the field. [M16]

My relationship with him (Bohr) was absolutely wonderful. He was somebody who kept his eye on the ball and depended so much on talking with others to clarify issues. If he couldn't talk he was lost . . . and he had a great sense of proportion. [M4]

I had essentially undivided attention from a great mathematician . . . we would go for long walks around the country side in Cambridge and talk about all kinds of things . . . and his style in mathematics was quite influential. . . . I mean that is the way I think and do mathematics. He had what was a kind of meat-grinding approach to mathematics. He would get a hold of a problem and put it through the grinder and just grind it very, very small. Out of it would come a theorem or whatever it was that he was trying to prove. . . . From time to time I would write things to him which led to my first published work, so I have felt very much indebted to him. [M10]

When I went to Columbia, I wasn't admitted. . . . But one of my relatives got me in. . . . I was going to stay at Columbia as a graduate student, a professor of mine called me in one day when I was about to start graduate work. He said, "You're going to Harvard. . . . I've arranged for you to become a graduate student. . . . " I hadn't applied . . . that's how I got to Harvard. He was a very bright man, who was enormously devoted to his work. But on top of that, he was somebody who labored very hard to explain why he was so interested in the work. And you knew damn well that he was somebody who felt that what he was doing was important. It was important for me to understand why he thought it was important. Also, this was a guy with a keen interest in social and political problems. I was a student in his course. What I learned was the importance of data, intellectual discipline, and rigorously dealing with information, but on top of that, being interested in it. That is, having an emotional link to the process. [M13]

When I was young there were several important individuals. . . . They taught me a great deal. In part my views about teaching come from the man I did my dissertation with. He wanted me to be myself, and I suppose I modeled myself partly after him. . . . He himself was a very famous historian and had some very good ideas. He continued to have new notions and ideas as long as he was alive. The place that he kept his ideas alive was in his writing. He was a man who was trying to think things through. [M7]

I had one (mentor) when I was a graduate student. He did me an invaluable service by reading my book manuscript, taking it seriously and helping me improve it. He also influenced me in many ways by his vigor and his example. [M2]

I don't think my curiosity was developed or encouraged until I met him my senior year in college. He was 10 years older in age but he was really light years older than I. He saw more in me than I saw in myself. He gave me a sense of the wider range of possibilities. I felt very marginal and unconnected although visible and active. He gave me a sense of possibility and I feel very fortunate for that. Also the combination of challenging me and respecting me was just extraordinary. I think it was he who helped me also appreciate a broader way of thinking. [M6]

My PhD supervisor in experimental physics was P.W. Bridgman, who is very well-known and really the father of operationalism. One of my very dear professors, for whom I was a teaching fellow, and later became a colleague was Philipp Frank. I was lucky that as a graduate student I was allowed to sit in on a shop club of people like Norbert Weiner, Giorgio de Santillana, Bridgman and Frank, and others. They would have discussions and internal fights. I was allowed to help out with the group. And although I was the secretary, I was almost treated as an equal. [M9]

In 1933 I heard the Institute for Advanced Study was opening at Princeton with Einstein and other notables. I had a couple of years of graduate work but I didn't have a PhD, so I decided to go to graduate school at Princeton. I was at Princeton for two years. At Princeton I worked under Eugene Wigner. He was one of the pioneers in the field who taught the first generation. He had much broader interests. I was Wigner's second student. [M1]

In any case, mentor relationships not only cultivate self-confidence and ability, but also influence choices, opportunities, and experiences relevant for career advancement. It may be that a lack of eminent women in different fields is a result of social selection mechanisms that reduce women's access to professional mentors early in their career. This point is illustrated well by two women:

At some level I think the system is kind of a self-fulfilling prophecy. The people that you give the opportunities tend to develop. [F5]

The management is still almost all male and they talk to each other. A lot of the news about what opportunities are available at the laboratory does not even filter down. I think all of the people making the decisions and policies and doing the hiring are men. Their friends are men and they talk to men. [F4]

Among the eminent adults, several individuals articulate how the field tends to discriminate against women during the early stages of their career:

Yes, I'm sure for a long time I was not taken seriously because I was a woman, but I was really so naive that I didn't know or didn't even know enough to think about it. [F5]

Professionally people who have succeeded see themselves as the model for how to succeed. That is, if you are the chairman of the department and male and attended a particular type of college and post doc, you see this as a program for success. Consciously or unconsciously you think this is the recipe for success. If someone comes in with a different kind of background, it is hard to believe he or she will be as successful. . . . Being female is a slight disadvantage because women look different, and talk in a softer voice. . . . I think people look upon people who are most similar to them as potentially most successful. If you are a minority or foreign, I think you are perceived as having less potential to be successful. [F5]

Differences between men and women are built in from the biology and all of the socialization. It takes a special kind of support and fortitude for women to deal with that. And there are an awful lot of casualties. There is a lot of wasted talent, and probably more often with women because you have to have very subtle and longstanding encouragements to rise in a field. [F2]

Women's letters of recommendation often talk about whether they're attractive or not attractive, or whether they get along with people, while men's discuss their ability and achievements. [F5]

The little children used to say, "Auntie . . . are you an uncle or an auntie?" because I had those pants on and they had never seen a women in pants. I had to carry the pots on a big plank to the other side of the road. The little children used to throw things at me. [F11]

It was completely out of the ordinary for a young lady from a good family to go there. This was a slumy sort of place. It was not where young ladies made pottery. [F11]

In another instance, when asked about female students one eminent male physicist talked about how his professional association with a female graduate student was limited because fellow colleagues and students often gossiped about their relationship when they saw them together:

I can recall, to my shame, that I had to look . . . and here I was on the Princeton campus, as if I were not always going around in her company because there were colleagues there that were rather old-fashioned. [M4]

Although men in positions of authority are often reluctant to work with young women, some women are able to work well with male mentors. Nevertheless, these relationships may lack the emotional and social support for issues that are salient and significant to women's identity development and needs:

It might be possible that a supportive male could fill that role, but I am not sure he would want to. Also, I don't know many women or young girls who would feel comfortable with that. What young people need is to have people like friends they can go to when they have a problem. [F5]

At the same time, young women rarely have the opportunity to work with eminent women because very few women are in senior positions. In addition, if a woman is able to find a female mentor, she is likely to have less power than a male mentor. Women also tend to be overextended as they struggle to balance family and career commitments. Because of this, eminent women may simply not have the time or energy to invest in the careers of young people. Not only are distinguished women scarce, they may often find themselves overwhelmed by young people who need support and counsel:

> I am often the first women in the department and I make it my business to get to know all of the young women. There have been episodes where after a few months I really felt that the emotional drain was almost more than I could bear. These women really had no one else to talk to so they told me all their troubles. . . . At this particular place women just came out of the woodwork, from all departments, because there were just so few women around. Yet here were a group of brilliant men, and every time they hired a faculty member they did not see the need for hiring a women. Had they seen the need, given approximately equal professional scientific qualifications and the fact that you had to support your women students, being female would have been an important requirement. But having men making the decisions and doing the hiring meant that having someone support women graduate students never became an important part of the job description. [F5]

> There are still very few women here. There are some divisions that do not have any women. We would have women come in as post docs and they would be there a very short time. While they were there they would often be the only woman in their department and they would not see other women during the day. [F4]

In any case, whether a result of different expectations or ideas of men and women's competence or the result of social biases and constraints on the development of ability, by and large, women have less access to mentors than do men.

Spouses as Social Influences

In addition to mentors, spouses play a significant role in helping creative achievement during adulthood. Unfortunately, until now little research has explored how spouses influence the professional lives of eminent individuals. Research has generally focused on the social support provided by parents and teachers. Spouses, however, can be very helpful both at early and later, more prominent, stages of one's career. They can provide encouragement, emotional and financial support, and a peaceful home environment conducive to full concentration on professional goals. The literature also shows that spouses function differently for men and women with regard to the developing aspirations, goals, and achievements.

Wives, for example, play a supportive role more consistently for the husbands' goals and aspirations (Droege, 1982; Furst, 1983; Mockros, 1993; Roberts & Newton, 1987; Terman & Oden, 1959). When there is a conflict between husbands' and wives' goals, it is almost always the wife who makes the sacrifice (Droege, 1982; Furst, 1983). According to Levinson, Darrow, Klein, Levinson, and McKee (1978) the "special woman" in a man's life is the one connected to his "dream." Her significance lies in part in her ability to help facilitate the achievement of his dream. Our interviews corroborate previous research regarding gender differences between husbands and wives of eminent individuals. As is the case with mentors, men and women do not receive the same type of support from a spouse. Men rarely talk about having made a decision to move or not move because of family obligations; they make decisions that are best for their own career. Moreover, their families subsequently support these decisions. For the men wives generally provide emotional support and encouragement:

I am married to a college classmate of mine. We have been married 50 years. I couldn't have done what I have done if she hadn't been the type of person that she is. She is understanding, cooperative, long suffering, loyal, and terribly terribly good. I remember several of my colleagues at various institutions have said, "John you can do what you do because you have the kind of wife that you have." She never said "Well I want more of your time, or I want . . . or we should do this . . . we should do this, we should . . . don't bother with that . . . why do you have to write that?" That is what some fellows are faced with. I never faced that. She never raised a question about anything like that. She was a librarian at the law school here and would send me my expenses as I needed them. I stayed and I broke the back of that book up there. In my view she had as much to do with making me as I did. And therefore there is nothing too good for her. And whatever benefits we have derived from what I have done, she shares in them equally. I could not possibly have done what I have done, as large or as small, without her and the kind of sensitivity, and understanding, cooperation and loyalty that she has provided. I don't mind talking about it to all of the world. [M11]

My wife was very helpful. She was interested in what I was doing. She was not a scholar herself but she was sympathetic and supportive. She gave me emotional support. She was somebody to rely on. And she would often go on these trips with me and take notes. I enjoyed having her along. [M2]

My wife has very much influenced my life and made me happy. Before I was married, I never was very happy. I had happy times, moments, weeks, but since I got married I am more or less continually happy. It is just her being there. We talk a lot over meals and we take long walks together. She has made my life settled, happy, and easy. [M3]

Oh, she's terrific. She has good sense, good judgment. She has often been left with the problem of looking after things. That has been a lot of responsibility. She has also backed me up and tried to get me to steer in a good direction. She generally has good judgment about people and who I should devote time to and who I shouldn't. . . . She supports me. Right now, for example, I don't have a grant from the National Science Foundation, but I still have a secretary and I can't let her work for nothing so I pay her, expecting that someday I may get some money back. My wife goes along with that. [M4]

I found a wonderful wife. We had a wonderful, harmonic marriage, and raised a family, with great children. There was rarely any conflict. That's very important because conflicts really take away from your work because you worry about them. Your mind wanders and you can't think about your scientific problem if you are worrying about your personal problems and whether your wife will run away with somebody else. In a good marriage both sides know what the other is interested in, and they know it is important to leave time for it. I guess I was very lucky in this regard. [M5]

I've been privileged to have a wife who has not had a job. That's meant that part of her life has been involved with mine. She has enjoyed academic ethnography and when we visited colleges she has gone to classes, and enjoyed meeting people and making reports. We have enjoyed being a team, in fact one of the books that gives me pleasure is the diaries we kept when we were in Japan. [M6]

I had very great luck in my family. My wife always agreed that it was worthwhile having me do what I wanted to do when it came to writing books and she went to great lengths to allow me to do so. Having a good wife is important. A wife who is supportive in the immediate family setting. I am sure that is absolutely important. It is like having bad health, it can disrupt you terribly. [M7]

I've been married 57 years. I have a very strong family orientation. I have two daughters, who are now in mid-life, and their children, four grandchildren. We're a very close unit and that is important to me. I think it's an important counterbalance, particularly to an active professional life or being successful. [M8]

As a hobby I was editing a journal I founded. In fact my wife figures in this because she was an editor then and knew about editing. The two of us adopted this journal as a family hobby. . . . I stopped by and the woman in charge of this group was very interested, not so in much in me as in my wife. I think she had a lot in common with my wife, so she invited me to come the following year. [M9]

When my wife and I came here we decided we would try to implement it. . . . The major method developed for the work (for which he won the Nobel Prize) came from my wife. I had a lot of input from her. It was the practical aspect she offered. She was very helpful in something called *bridging*. On the one hand you have ideal theoretical mathematics and on the other hand you have the real world of finite and approximate data that you get. The particular scheme we were working with was very complex. She had a real talent for finding criteria that would enable us to find a pathway to the solution. She has a marvelous talent for solving complex structures. Through the '60s, for all intents and purposes she did practically all of the major structures. [M17]

By contrast, the literature suggests that husbands are more of an obstacle to the fulfillment of an achievement-oriented career woman's dream (Roberts & Newton, 1987). Although our eminent women were not thwarted by their husbands, the majority still built their careers around their husbands' plans. They describe how they went to (or stayed at) a particular university or geographical location in order not to interfere with their husband's career:

This wasn't a very congenial place for me. . . . I mean I would have been happy at the University of California, but then I got married and so. . . . [F1]

Of course I stayed because my husband was fixed. He was in the world of business. . . . For example, I never took a year off and went to the think tank although I was invited. He couldn't leave his business career . . . and in that sense we were stabilized with his career. . . . I didn't go on the job market or respond to job change because I was not geographically mobile. [F2]

I'll tell you another obstacle and though it did not remain an obstacle, it was during the early years of our marriage. My husband was already very famous when we met. I was 10 years younger. I got tired of going to conferences with him because he was surrounded by people and I would be standing there in limbo without anything to do. The way I dealt with that was simply to create other spaces, and choose activities so that I wasn't left standing on the periphery of his circle. [F3]

I met my future husband and we decided to get married. That's why I came back to the lab. I really came back because of that. I didn't think commuting would make a very stable marriage. [F4]

Well, the first obstacle would have been to find a professional position after getting the PhD. As we already mentioned during lunch, it was difficult for both a husband and wife to get a good position in the same city. [F6]

Given the time in history, it is not surprising that the husband's career tended to take precedence over the wife's. Most women did not express bitterness about these decisions, rather they felt fortunate to have had a successful career and a husband who supported their career interests. As we probed to find out how women's husbands were supportive, it quickly became clear that "support" is defined relative to one's own cohort rather than current social norms and expectations of a "supportive" husband. People's identities are tied to their assessment and comparison of themselves in relation to their peers. At this time in history, the husbands' attitudes and behavior toward their wives' careers was indeed very unusual. The women often describe how their husband "allowed" them to work after they had made adequate arrangements for the care of the children and the household. In addition, they often supported their efforts to balance family and career responsibilities:

> My husband said, "I want you to be content and I want the kids to be properly cared for and I know you share that, and so I don't have to worry about that. After that do as you like. I mean if you want to be away half of a day from the house, or all day, fix it up." [F2]

> He was very supportive when we had children. Still, although in some sense, he helped enormously, much of the burden fell on me. I still was the person who had to shop and cook and get the kids to school. He still took my career very seriously. He took care of the kids when I went off observing. He encouraged me to go to meetings when I was invited and it just seemed impossible to leave. [F5]

> I had awful good backing in my husband. He has always been supportive. It was very difficult in the beginning. Mostly, there were just so many things pushing against me and if he hadn't kept telling me to keep working, I probably would have given up. When my son was born they wanted me to quit because they had no policy for when you have children. At that time all of the women's magazines were talking about latch-key children and that you should stay home with your children. . . . I just couldn't take all of that. My husband was the one who really encouraged me. He said, "you let the house go . . . you wouldn't be happy," so he went out and hired someone. Even my sister was saying she would take my son if I didn't want him. My husband was very very supportive all of the time. [F4]

Indeed, most women had the primary responsibility for the children and running of the home. No husband made a radical personal career sacrifice or attended to the child care and household responsibilities.

Compared to their female peers, however, the women in our sample regarded themselves as extremely fortunate to have had a husband who not only allowed them to work, but also conveyed interest and encouragement to them regarding their career. The biographies of eminent women such as Marie Curie, Margaret Mead, and Georgia O'Keefe confirm the narratives of our women regarding their husband's provision of psychological support as well as professional encouragement, inspiration, and help for his talented and ambitious wife. These data suggest that eminent women often receive the affirmation and assistance from a husband that many men receive from a professional mentor (Kerr, 1985; Mockros, 1993; Roberts & Newton, 1987). Husbands frequently encourage their wives' careers, help them make valuable connections to other professionals in the field, as well as in some cases collaborate with them:

> He encouraged me all along. He had a PhD a few years before I did and he just knew my work was very important to me. He encouraged me all along the way. He was very supportive of my work. For a number of years I really did not know another astronomer. It was he that I talked to every night. He never annoyed me with his work but I must have annoyed him nightly with my work. . . . Probably the greatest role he played was in encouraging and listening in a professional sense. Also, I really knew no astronomers and scientists so the physicists that I got connected with were those I knew through my husband. So, very early in my career a lot of the connections came from him. [F5]

> I think my husband is the brightest man who ever lived, as far as mathematics go. He and I worked together a lot. He did the mathematical analyses and I did the programming. We worked together. We complement one another. I am someone who could check his ideas and see what was not quite right. He is someone who is probably not quite as detailed as I was. I check things many times. He is more likely to think of things out in left field and I am more of the detail person. [F4]

> Of course, my husband was my teacher. I learned a lot from him regarding the whole field and how to go into it as a professional. That is partly because he was one of the founders of the field. Although we didn't collaborate I learned a lot from our conversations. Since we are in the same field there has been a very rich interaction between us. [F3]

Although for the most part husbands rarely made radical career sacrifices for their wives, a few women talked about how their husbands made some provisions for their careers. These included either taking a position at a place that would also be beneficial for the wife's' career or having a marital relationship in which the husband and wife each had personal and professional freedom and led a relatively independent life.

Several women were separated from their husband for months at a time while they each pursued career opportunities and interests. Some also thought that marrying relatively late in life was significant in determining the course of their career and subsequent success. In any case, even though many creative women did prioritize their children and family above career advancement, few had marital relationships that would be considered conventional for the time. Even by today's standards, the attitudes and support of their husband was considered beneficial for a woman's career:

My husband and I and the kids spent a year at the University of California—San Diego, where the Burbidges were a very important influence. It was 16 years after my PhD. I had four children and I was really ready to get back into astronomy. My husband had received a National Science Foundation Senior Post-Doctoral fellowship and decided to go to La Jolla because he knew I could do astronomy there. [F5]

My husband was most anxious I carry on my career and realized there were only so many hours in the day. [F6]

My husband is not here. He teaches at Toronto. We often talk on the phone in the morning before work. Then, on the weekends we are always together. [F7]

We are both artists. We went to graduate school together. He has been extremely supportive. For the last 15 or 20 years now we spend a great deal of time separated. We have a place in Massachusetts, and I have a loft in New York. We decided a long time ago that the best way to maintain our relationship, both personal and professional, was to have separate lives and interconnect when we felt like it. So sometimes I go up for a weekend. He lives in Massachusetts and I live in New York. I have a free life which is supported by his. He also has a free life. We just feel we have been able to maintain that and get along. We have what I would call a perfect marriage. I spend summers up there because I love the garden. When I am there he goes out West to go fishing. So, we have never been with each other all that much. It works out because I don't really think that at a certain stage, at least for a woman, it would have been possible for me to do what I have done without living by myself and pursuing my work by working every day and following my own schedule. I spent years as a mother and a wife and those years were very formative and important. When my daughter went to college, though, I began to really live as an individual. It is not something everybody can do. Most men would not have put up with me for a minute. [F8]

I think my husband and I give each other a lot of space. In the winter time he is at Harvard and I am here. Originally when we built the addition onto the house including his study and my studio, my husband wanted to make them connecting so we could talk to each other during the day. I didn't think I wanted do that because although I loved seeing him, I didn't when I was working. We will see each other in the evening. I am quite sure he likes to see me, but he wants to be left alone when he works. So we have separate buildings and we go to our separate places. I think it is important to be left alone. In the summertime when our lives are much closer together, we have separate cabins. In one cabin my husband does his writing and in one cabin I do my work. So we see each other in the morning and sometimes in the late afternoon we meet for a sandwich. It works perfectly well. But I am fortunate. I guess we are both a little fortunate since we both understand the need to be left alone when one is thinking through things and really enveloped by the work. [F9]

I wasn't married and I did not have children for many years. I can't imagine being able to have a career like this with a family. I know today my younger female colleagues are very tired. It is very hard. I married very late. Looking back, when I started it was my ambition to be very good. But, I realize today I lived like a nun for the first 10 years of my career. In privacy and seclusion. [F10]

It should also be pointed out that for some women husbands provide the financial support that allows them to pursue their creative interests without the pressure of having to support the family. This allows them relatively more flexibility and freedom to take risks in their professional endeavors because the family does not depend on their salaries:

I had a situation in which I didn't have to be accountable for an idea, or something rested on it. I did not have a big investment in becoming successful or having to make money and I think I was reflecting my husband's attitudes. He would say, "Do what you want to do," and nothing hung on it. [F2]

It is interesting that in advising young people about their futures and careers, no men specifically refer to the importance of their wives, but as one woman pointed out:

The advice . . . to a young woman, and probably a young man as well, is to marry the right person, because if you don't marry the right person it will not work, and that's a shame, that's a tragedy. You have to make decisions really early in life if you get married very early and the decision you make about who you will marry is going to influence an enormous amount of your later life. [F5]

Hence, although both men and women's careers benefit from the encouragement of a spouse, given the overt and covert educational and social barriers women face regarding academic and professional success, establishing eminence for a woman may be more contingent on whether she has a supportive spouse.

Colleague Interaction and Collaboration

Professional socialization does not end with entry into the field. For many adults, the field continues to be significant to the development of eminence. The importance of interacting with colleagues has often been overlooked in the literature. Nonetheless, colleague interaction and collaboration undoubtedly influences productivity and eminence by facilitating both problem finding and problem solving. Given that no one is an expert in all aspects of a domain, it is important to read about and discuss the ways one's own work may be informed by others in the field. Numerous eminent individuals stress the importance of actively maintaining professional networks and relationships with colleagues. Interestingly, many creative individuals discuss the necessity of being intellectually autonomous and independent, yet most are also eloquent about the professional environments facilitating the expression of their creativity:

> It is only by interacting with other people that you get anything interesting done. . . . I was in an advantageous position of being familiar with both of them (two eminent colleagues) and I got to know and work with each of them. [M10]

> Usually ideas grow slowly, they're like flowers that have to be tended by reading, and talking with people . . . if you don't kick things around with people you are out of it. Nobody, I always say, can be anybody without others around. [M4]

> I was able to do creative work collaborating with other people. Most of my work is collaborative. That's how you find out how to do something which hasn't been done before. Collaboration is extremely important. First of all, it prevents you from making mistakes because another guy can correct you. In addition, there is a division of labor. One person may be better in mathematics, while the other may be better in other things. In this way, we complement each other. . . . I, myself, have collaborated on several important papers. My collaborator was certainly a better mathematician than I, but I think I had a better overview of the problem. And this is how we can help each other. [M5]

> A colleague of mine and I were working very closely together and the arguments went back and forth. . . . This is an instance in which he had a very different expertise than I and I have a certain background that he does not have. This is a case in which two quite different fields of research are brought together, not to be compared but so that parts of one can be integrated with parts of the other. [M17]

> Traveling, lecturing, and consulting does take me away from my work but it also keeps me in touch with the professional community. I get a certain stimulus from listening to other people and thinking about what they say. [M7]

By that time my colleague . . . had joined us and was working on something. . . . I phoned him and told him that it looks like the problem is solvable. He agreed and then the deck was clear. You see, there was so much in the literature that said this was not solvable. I ran it off to him to see if he could see something that I couldn't. He said no. Now that was encouragement. [M18]

As you interact with the scientific community you get ideas that are very interesting. You can have them in your head for years until you get the opportunity to do it. [M18]

I often learned from contemporary historians with whom I work and lived. Colleagueship is important because of the values derived from them. . . . I have numerous colleagues I talk to and I show my work to. I ask for criticism and receive good suggestions. The recent changes and conclusions for the different editions of my book come largely from criticisms. I think that the worst mistake a historian can make is to be indifferent to or contemptuous of what is new. There is nothing permanent in history, it is always changing. [M2]

I think one needs colleagues. But they can be invisible colleagues, they don't have to be here. They can be the books one reads. They can be people that one knows about but doesn't necessarily know, face-to-face. I've always looked for colleagues and I found them in different ages, and fields. They thought they depended on me but I also depended on them. One does need a network of people to be connected with, and it's better if they're living, and if you have commensal times together, but it's not essential. [M6]

Out of it came this contact with Campbell and after a long conference we hit it off very well. He introduced me to some people in Switzerland that might want to hear about my work in science. The amazing thing was that you could really try out your ideas with this very rich and wonderful group of people. I used this group to formulate my ideas and to set them forth. There was no audience anywhere else at that time. [M9]

I knew one very fine executive. He was the head of a great corporation. He told me he was an inventor and was very interested in new technology. He said he wanted to work for NASA. At the time I was on pretty good terms with the President. I called him and before you knew it he was in charge of what was then the beginning of the space shuttle. [M8]

Bell Labs has a pretty outstanding group. The theorists talked among themselves and it was a very exciting time to be there. There was great enthusiasm for quantum theory. [M1]

Again, women do not report similar experiences with regard to collaboration and the influence of colleagues. By and large, they discuss having been relatively more isolated than the men:

I didn't have a job in the department until I was 55 years old. We came here in '45, so I have been on the outside all those years. I was never really part of anything. I just did my own thing. I taught courses, but I didn't have tenure. I didn't have a position in the university. I wasn't integrated into the department. . . . I didn't have a lot of colleagues. I haven't had a lot of students and the closest I ever came to the mainstream was serving on a committee. I've just hung on by my fingernails. [F1]

There are still very few women here. There are some divisions that still do not have any women. I don't know why the number of women participating in the group has dropped. I don't know if it is because women are so busy with their careers and homes and they don't have time. We had women come in as post docs who would only be there a very short time. While they were there they would often be the only woman in their department and they would not see any other women during the day. [F4]

For a number of years I did not know another astronomer or scientist. . . . I still work in a very personal way and I make all of the decisions myself. I do all of the observing myself. It takes me a long time and I think it is because I don't have graduate students and colleagues working with me . . . so it is hard. [F5]

There are a lot of connections, career-type connections I didn't have when the children were little because I had two main things, the children and my writing. . . . I wasn't much part of the university community at that point. So, granted, in terms of career context, the children may have been a drawback. [F7]

I can't say that I belonged to a group of artists or anything. [F11]

After I got involved in the structure field I was a bit apprehensive since I was outside of the biochemical community. I had nobody to talk to. I mean, the National Institute of Health is 35 miles away. . . . It has worked out OK, but . . . [F6]

Regarding early career development and mentors, some women discuss overt discrimination in connection with colleagues and rules within professional institutions. Needless to say, peers and colleagues are central to professional development throughout adulthood. As a result, women's relative lack of peer interaction inhibits productivity and the development of their careers.

Colleague Affirmation and Approval

Aside from professional collaboration with others, people are also frequently influenced by unsolicited feedback, including affirmation and criticism from either the field or the larger society. Aging and intellectual functioning are related to the social interaction. Competent social and intellectual behavior is either discouraged or encouraged by social institutions leading to individual's internalization of these expectations. Such a socialization process produces conditions and attitudes that result in a self-fulfilling depreciation of abilities and functioning (Bengston & Kuyper, 1973; Labouvie-Vief, 1985). If negative expectations and the lack of encouragement and affirmation for one's abilities has a negative effect, it follows that positive experiences or the encouragement of others—particularly colleagues in the field—are likely to promote self-confidence and subsequent professional development. In this way, during later adulthood one's sense of self, ability, and competence are generally enhanced by the affirmation of colleagues and the admiration of students and younger people in the field.

Based on her research, Amabile (1983, 1990) claims that external evaluation plays a negative role in creative production. Likewise, her work implies that the absence of such evaluation from the consciousness will invariably have a positive impact on one's creativity and work. Moreover, public recognition and fame is constantly discussed among critics and artists as one of the greatest possible threats to the artist's creativity and continued growth. Once artists earn a reputation and begin to sell their work, there is pressure to continue to produce work that "sells." In this way, the marketability of the work can become an inherent part (and sometimes destructive element) of the artistic process. At the same time, external evaluations, affirmation, and praise for ideas and work often leads to continued work in that area, but also to the assimilation of valued work into the larger domain. In this way there appears to be a more complex relationship between the value of intrinsic and extrinsic reward systems for creativity and eminence.

As noted earlier, the field plays a critical role in the recognition and assimilation of ideas into the domain. Our research suggests that highly eminent and creative individuals are often able to take advantage of the opportunities that come their way.

> I really have a lot of ability in management. At the age of 29, I was totally unaware of it. When the war broke out I was thrown into a management position in the Federal Communications Commission. Almost immediately I received very high praise for my management skills. I was totally surprised because I had no image of myself in that way. [M8]

> A professor at the University of Wisconsin who later became a professor at Harvard. It was through his influence that I got an appointment at the Society of Fellows at Harvard after I got my PhD. [M1]

One of the biggest influences came when I was 34. I worked with men in their 50s and 60s who had held quite high responsibilities all their life. They were a remarkable group. After the war I met these individuals who lived with a sense of responsibility about what went on in the world. That had a big impact on me. They displayed a sense of social responsibility that was inspiring. They had strong good characters and a largeness of view with a deep sense of responsibility. So it's a little later than one normally thinks of having influences, but it was one of those influences that can have a big impact on you. [M8]

In another case, although one of the women scientists did not have a significant mentor during graduate school, 16 years after completing her PhD she had the opportunity to work with an older, well-established female colleague with similar interests. This relationship was particularly meaningful to her.

It was really a very remarkable year for me because, apart from actually working with (her), and doing the work that I was interested in, I really learned that she was interested in my ideas. I think it was the first time I was in a position where someone took me seriously as an astronomer. [F5]

In addition to the direct influence of older colleagues, people discuss the relevance of peer feedback and affirmation for their work. Overall, among our group of eminent individuals men were more frequently affirmed for their work and accepted by professional institutions.

Of course the feedback is very strong in both (science and writing) . . . after you have published a book it is out in the world you get a tremendous enrichment of contacts. . . . The most enjoyable part of doing science or writing is the response. Telling your friends about it and being involved with people. People either saying it is good or it isn't, or else just talking about the problems. . . . When I am writing I write for a particular person or a particular audience, not just to create something for myself. [M10]

The success of the book earned me respect among colleagues as well as served to open doors for me professionally. Although my reputation was "defamed" by another prominent colleague in the field, I am proud of the fact that the book has remained popular. [M12]

I think I have earned my way into the National Academy of Sciences five times over . . . but every time my name was proposed I was turned down because I had offended various big shots, by treading on their toes in the work I had done. Obviously I was disappointed. Most objective people agree that I have earned it . . . but somewhere along the road I decided I didn't really care if I was a member. What I have instead is people who say to me "you know I read your book and it changed my life." That's good too. [M13]

I have accepted and welcomed criticism. It is important to not be indifferent to criticism and new information. [M2]

For the most part, previous research has found that women receive less positive affirmation from the field for their interests and abilities. Professional institutions reward women less than men for comparable achievements. Women receive less pay for performing similar tasks and are promoted and honored less than men for similar accomplishments.

There are only 10% women in Research and Development. Most of them are in the lower positions such as scientific assistants. The management is still all male and they talk to each other. A lot of the news about what opportunities are available at the laboratory does not filter down. Two times I went to talk to the management because the pay of women was significantly less than the pay of men. They made some adjustments. But they did not admit there was a problem. They never announced to the employees that they were making this adjustment. So, a lot of women still did not know if they were making the same pay as the men. All of the managers are male and they don't pass the information down. Women are very unsure of where they stand and want some kind of feedback. They are just not told or rewarded like the men. I talked with a young woman who received an absolutely stellar evaluation from her boss, yet she did not get a raise. The evaluation process is very difficult for everyone, but it is especially hard for women because they are always talking to men. These women don't know where they stand. They don't know if there is going to be a cut back so they are very insecure. The young men may get together on the golf course and be told, "Hey you are doing a great job. I like what you are doing." Somehow a lot of women do not get any sense of how they are doing. [F4]

The biggest barrier was trying to find a place where both my husband and I could work. [F6]

I had what was called a research development award. There was a provision in that the university was supposed to make a place for me. So, one year I sent back my contract. It took 18 months before I got a reply. They wrote back and said something about not having anything against women. I wrote back and . . . within a week I was a member of the department This was about 1970. [F1]

I felt very frustrated. . . . That was a time when I felt there was no where to go and decided I should get out and let someone else in. As a woman I did not feel I was going to get promoted because upper management was all male. [F4]

Many eminent men and women find ways to continue working in spite of the conflict their work may evoke. Some choose to pursue less contested problems whereas others choose to persevere in their current endeavors even if doing so embroils them in controversy. It does seem, however, that conflict, controversy, and competition may be more abrasive to women. It may also be that women may have more difficulty "detaching" themselves emotionally form work. As a result, they may have trouble receiving criticism about their work. Pursuing creative ideas often results in critical feedback from the field. Unless gifted men and women have the self-confidence and assurance to persevere in spite of such feedback, it is unlikely that they will be able to withstand such scrutiny. One eminent female scientist noted that controversy from the field often caused her to switch problems in order to avoid a highly visible and challenged position, and the competitive aggressive atmosphere connected with it. Because she has multiple ideas and projects of interest, she prefers to direct her research to another problem rather than wasting energy in professional debates:

> I really found it very unpleasant. I just didn't like to be in that environment. So I decided to find a problem to study that no one would bother me with and work on it by myself for a couple of years. Hopefully people would be very interested in what came out of it. . . . There is really both a public and a private controversy. I really found the private part of it very unpleasant. . . . Getting calls and letters from people saying "I know you are wrong and you shouldn't be doing this. I know what the answer is" . . . I don't know, maybe I am a coward. That just made my life unpleasant. Part of the reason I was doing astronomy was because it had always been pleasant. So rather than continue to compete in this unpleasant environment, I would do something else. . . . Lately, in retrospect, I am sorry I have done that because there was still so much more to be learned and some of it has now been learned by just the people who made my life unpleasant . . . I almost feel these people robbed me of the pleasure of continuing the problem. It was just unpleasant. [F5]

Men, on the other hand, more easily disregard negative feedback. Likewise, they are more comfortable when confronted with professional conflict. None of the men, for example, ever considered changing their professional position or problem due to controversy engendered by work. Instead, they asserted the opposite:

> I talked to a professor of organic chemistry. He decided the next course for me and I asked him whether I should take it this semester or later and he said I could take the course later on if wanted to and if I lasted. I never forgot that conversation because it was a serious source of unhappiness for me. I had gone through a number of struggles including working for a

while between a previous master's degree. I had saved up enough money to get to Michigan. After I struggled for many years hoping I would finally find a niche for myself I was not pleased with this statement. It didn't effect my work. If anything I was more determined than ever to succeed. But I thought it was the perfect example of how one should not deal with students. [M17]

Trust (your) intuition, don't necessarily listen to others, peer pressure or other kinds of influences that have a counterbearing influence. . . . Overcoming obstacles that have to do with people seeing things differently is just a matter of persisting and finding ways and means around the obstacles. [M14]

I always follow my own path. I always have. [M13]

In any case, social selection and affirmation contribute to a greater differential in the career paths of men and women during adulthood. Invariably, attitudes and responses from the field are interpreted and constructed based on earlier experiences. Hence, the Matthew effect (Merton, 1968) applies to the emergence of eminence and creativity during later life as well.

CONCLUSION

This chapter examines some of the ways societal expectations and influences impact the careers of eminent individuals during their lives. In particular it examines how creativity exists within a social and historical context made up of multiple interacting systems including an individual, field, domain, and culture. The following conclusions are based on preliminary analyses of the interviews:

1. Social support systems and interactions are critical throughout the life span for the emergence of creativity. Interactions with others often determine the provision of relevant academic and professional opportunities. The value of the social support received depends on the particular needs of the individual. For some, emotional support is crucial, whereas for others professional connections or intellectual affirmation are vital for advancement in the field.

2. The nature of the social support will vary depending on one's specific developmental stage. During childhood, parents or teachers recognize, encourage, and affirm a talented young person's interests and ability. In addition, they provide materials and opportunities that facilitate the development of interests.

3. During adulthood relevant interactions are with people in the field such as teachers, mentors, or colleagues. Mentors serve as teachers, sponsors, friends, counselors, and role models. They advance young people by teaching specific skills and relevant problem finding and solving strategies. They also provide opportunities and challenge and encourage interests and abilities, and build self-confidence and protection from negative feedback.

4. Colleagues provide critical and affirmative feedback for work. In addition, they render professional recognition in the form of awards, exposure, and promotions within the field.

5. Spouses are a significant source of support for both eminent men and women. For men, wives offer emotional support, general encouragement and professional sacrifices. For women, husbands often provide professional opportunities and intellectual affirmation for career interests and ambitions.

6. The field interacts with characteristics of individuals and the needs of the domain to provide opportunities that contribute to the advancement of creative individuals. The field's perceptions of an individual's ability and potential to succeed influence the emergence of eminence by determining if an individual's contribution will be accepted into the domain.

7. There is a dialectic between interpersonal relationships and identity formation. Both are influenced by experiences, opportunities, aspirations, and achievements. Talent development is influenced by the provision of opportunities and positive experiences as well as restrictions from, or negative experiences with, educational and professional social systems.

8. Early educational opportunities and the availability of later professional experiences vary between groups of individuals. For the most part, people within a field consider students and colleagues most similar to themselves as more likely to be successful.

9. Men and women have different experiences and exposure to academic and professional communities. Although men in our culture tend to strive for personal and professional independence and autonomy, on the whole they are generally less socially isolated than eminent women during adulthood.

10. During childhood, parents and teachers affirm and promote the abilities of talented girls less frequently than talented boys. During young adulthood women have fewer relationships with mentors. During later stages of their careers women have less social interaction with colleagues and receive less social affirmation for their work.

In conclusion, recent theories have expanded previous models of creativity that tended to ignore the social context. Nevertheless, current theories lack an adequate treatment of the ways social and cultural systems transmit values, provide opportunities, encourage interests, and develop competencies and self-confidence that contribute to eminent careers. Understanding creativity and how interpersonal relationships and social norms influence the development of eminence requires a more comprehensive view of the social system's contribution to early career choices and achievements. In light of the fact that cultures impose particular expectations and reinforce attitudes that shape people's perceptions of themselves and others, different populations are selectively rewarded and discouraged from intellectual and creative endeavors.

For instance, women's chances of emerging as eminent and creative in a field are reduced because women do not have equal access to the people responsible for acknowledging their contributions. Moreover, although this chapter has not addressed the issue of discrimination faced by minorities, there is some evidence to suggest that the Jewish and African American interviewees also faced comparable limitations and barriers to professional development. Studies of creative women and minorities will do well to attend to the role of the historical context, the availability of social support systems, and differential familial and cultural expectations surrounding their lives. Definitions of creativity need to incorporate multiple definitions of success and competence which are influenced by personal and social directives that lead to lives characterized by eminence. Future inquiry might reveal that adult creativity and eminence are as much a function of the interaction between social responses to early biological determinants such as sex and race as they are a function of the motivational and intellectual characteristics on which previous theories have been based.

REFERENCES

Albert, R. S. (1983). Family positions and the attainment of eminence: A study of special family positions and special family experiences. In R. J. Albert (Ed.), Genius and eminence: *The social psychology of creativity and exceptional achievement* (pp. 141-154). Oxford, Pergamon.

Albert, R. S. (1990). Identity, experience and career choice among exceptionally gifted and eminent. In R. Albert and M. Runco (Eds.), *Theories of creativity* (pp. 13-34). Newbury Park, CA: Sage.

Albert, R. S., & Runco, M. A. (1987). The possible personality dispositions of scientists and nonscientists. In D. N. Jackson & J. P. Rushton (Eds.), *Scientific excellence: Origins and assessment* (pp. 67-97). Newbury Park, CA: Sage.

Amabile, T. (1983). *The social psychology of creativity.* New York: Harcourt.

Amabile, T. (1990). Within you, without you: The social psychology of creativity and beyond. In R. Albert & M. Runco (Eds.), *Theories of creativity* (pp. 61-91). Newbury Park, CA: Sage.

Astin, H. (1974). Sex differences in mathematical and scientific precocity. In J. Stanley, D. Keating, & L. Fox (Eds.), *Mathematical talent: Discovery, description, and development* (pp. 70-86). Baltimore: Johns Hopkins University Press.

Bengston, V. L. (1973). *The social psychology of aging.* New York: Bobbs-Merrill.

Bengston, V., & Kuypers, J. (1971). Generational difference and the developmental stake. *Aging and Human Development, 2*(1), 249-260.

Bloom, B. S. (1985). *Developing talent in young people.* New York: Ballantine.

Cox, C. (1926). *The early mental traits of three hundred geniuses.* Stanford, CA: Stanford University Press.

Csikszentmihályi, M. (1988). Society, culture and person: A systems view of creativity. In R. J. Sternberg (Ed.), *The nature of creativity: Contemporary psychological perspectives* (pp. 325-339). Cambridge, England: Cambridge University Press.

Csikszentmihályi, M. (1990). The domain of creativity. In M. A. Runco & R. S. Albert (Eds.), *Theories of creativity* (pp. 325-339). Newbury Park, CA: Sage.

Csikszentmihályi, M., Rathunde, K., & Whalen, S. (1993). *Talented teenagers: A longitudinal study of development.* Cambridge, England: Cambridge University Press.

DeGroot, A. D. (1965). *Thought and choice in class.* The Hague: Mouton.

Droege, R. (1982). *A psychosocial study of the formation of the middle adult life structure in women.* Unpublished doctoral dissertation, California School of Professional Psychology, Berkeley, CA.

Erikson, E. (1950). *Childhood and society.* New York: Norton.

Feldman, D., & Goldsmith, L. (1986). *Nature's gambit: Child prodigies and the development of human potential.* New York: Basic Books.

Fox, L. (1977). Sex differences: Implications for program planning for the academically gifted. In J. Stanley, W. George, & C. Solano (Eds.), *The gifted and the creative: A fifty year perspective* (pp. 113-138). Baltimore: Johns Hopkins University Press.

Furst, K. (1983) *Origins and evolution of women's dreams in early adulthood. Unpublished doctoral dissertation.* California School of Professional Psychology, Berkeley, CA.

Galton, F. (1869). *Hereditary genius.* New York: Appleton.

Gergen, M. (1990). Finished at 40: Women's development within the patriarchy. *Psychology of Women Quarterly, 14,* 471-493.

Getzels, J., & Csikszentmihályi, M. (1976). *The creative vision.* New York: Wiley.

Goertzel, V., & Goertzel, M. (1962). *Cradles of eminence.* Boston: Little, Brown.

Gruber, H. (1980). And the bush was not consumed: The evolving systems approach to creative work. In S. Modgil & C. Modgil (Eds.) *Toward a theory of psychological development* (pp. 269-299). Windsor, England: NFER Press.

Gruber, H. (1981). *Darwin on man: A psychological study of scientific thinking.* Chicago: University of Chicago Press.

Gruber, H. (1982). On the hypothesized relation between giftedness and creativity. In D. H. Feldman (Ed.), *Developmental approaches to giftedness and creativity* (pp. 7-29). San Francisco: Jossey-Bass.

Gruber, H. (1986). The self-construction of the extraordinary. In R. J. Sternberg & J. Davidson (Eds.), *Conceptions of giftedness* (pp. 247-263). Cambridge, England: Cambridge University Press.

Gruber, H., & Davis, S. (1988). Inching our way up Mount Olympus: The evolving-systems approach to creative thinking. In R. J. Sternberg (Ed.), *The nature of creativity: Contemporary psychological perspectives* (pp. 243-270). Cambridge, England: Cambridge University Press.

Helson, R. (1990). Creativity in women: Outer and inner views over time. In M. Runco & R. Albert (Eds.), *Theories of creativity* (p. 46-60). Newbury Park, CA: Sage.

Hollinger, C. (1985). Multidimensional determinants of traditional and nontraditional career aspirations for mathematically talented female adolescents. *Journal for the Education of the Gifted, 5*(4), 245-265.

Hollinger, C. (1986). Career aspirations as a function of Holland Personality type among mathematically talented female adolescents. *Journal for the Education of the Gifted, 9*(2), 133-145.

Holloway, S. (1986). The relationship of mother's beliefs to children's mathematics achievement: Some effects of sex differences. *Merrill-Palmer Quarterly, 32*(3), 231-250.

James, J. (1990). Employment patterns and midlife well-being. In H. W. Grossman & N. L. Chester (Eds.), *The experience of meaning of work in women's lives* (pp. 103-120). Hillsdale, NJ: Lawrence Erlbaum Associates.

Jeruchim, J., & Shapiro, P. (1992). *Women, mentors and success*. New York: Fawcett Columbine.

Kanigel, R. (1986). *Apprentice to genius: The making of a scientific dynasty*. New York: Macmillan.

Kerr, B. (1985). *Smart girls, gifted women*. Columbus: Ohio Publishing Company.

Kram, K. (1985). *Mentoring at work*. Glenview, IL: Scott, Foresman.

Labouvie-Vief, G. (1985). Intelligence and cognition. In J. E. Birren & K. W. Schaie (Eds.), *Handbook of the psychology of aging* (2nd ed., pp. 500-530).

Levinson, D. (1980). Toward a conception of the adult life course. In N. Smelser & E. Erikson (Eds.), *Themes of work and love in adulthood* (pp. 265-289). Cambridge, MA: Harvard University Press.

Levinson, D., Darrow, C., Klein, E., Levinson, M., & McKee, B. (1978). *The seasons of a man's life*. New York: Knopf.

MacKinnon, D. W. (1978). *In search of human effectiveness*. New York: Creative Education Foundation.

Merton, R. K. (1968). The Matthew effect in science. *Science, 159*, 56-63.

Mockros, C. (1993, February). *The mentor-apprentice relationship: Interpersonal influences on creative and eminent adults*. Paper presented at the Esther Katz Rosen Symposium, Lawrence, KS.

Ochse, R. (1990). *Before the gates of excellence: The determinants of creative genius*. Cambridge, England: Cambridge University Press.

Pariser, D. (1991). Normal and unusual aspects of juvenile artistic development in Klee, Lautrec, and Picasso. *Creativity Research Journal, 4*(1), 51-65.

Roberts, P., & Newton, P. (1987). Levinsonian studies of women's adult development. *Psychology and Aging, 2*(2), 154-163.

Roe, A. (1953). *The making of a scientist*. New York: Dodd Mead.

Simonton, D. (1983). Intergenerational transfer of individual differences in hereditary monarchs: Genes, role-modeling, cohort, or sociocultural effects? *Journal of Personality and Social Psychology, 44*, 354-364.

Simonton, D. (1984). Artistic creativity and interpersonal relationships across and within generations. *Journal of Personality and Social Psychology, 46*, 1273-1286.

Simonton, D. (1986). Biographical typicality, eminence, and achievement style. *Journal of Creative Behavior, 20*, 14-22.

Simonton, D. (1988). Creativity, leadership, and chance. In R. J. Sternberg (Ed.), *The nature of creativity* (pp. 125-147). Cambridge, England: Cambridge University Press.

Simonton, D. K. (1978). The eminent genius in history: The critical role of creative development. *The Gifted Child Quarterly, 22,* 187-200.

Solano, C. (1983). Self-concept in mathematically gifted adolescents. *The Journal of General Psychology, 108,* 33-42.

Stewart, W. (1977). *A psychosocial study of the formation of the early adult life structure in women.* Unpublished doctoral dissertation, Columbia University, New York.

Tannenbaum, A. (1987) Giftedness: A psychosocial approach. In R. Sternberg & J. Davidson (Eds.), *Conceptions of giftedness* (pp. 21-52). New York: Cambridge University Press.

Terman. L., & Oden, M. (1959). The gifted child grows up. *Genetic studies of genius* (Vol. V). Stanford, CA: Stanford University Press.

Tomlinson-Keasey, C., & Burton, E. (1992). Gifted women's lives: Aspirations, achievements and personal adjustment. In J. Carlsohn (Ed.), *Cognition and educational practice: An international perspective* (pp. 151-176). Greenwich, CT: JAI Press.

Valliant, G. E. (1977). *Adaptation to life.* Boston: Little, Brown.

Walters, J., & Gardner, H. (1986). The crystallizing experience: Discovering an intellectual gift. In R. J. Sternberg & J. Davidson (Eds.), *Conceptions of giftedness* (pp. 306-331). Cambridge, England: Cambridge University Press.

Zey, M. (1984). *The mentor connection.* Homewood, IL: Dow Jones-Irwin.

Zuckerman, H. (1977). *Scientific elite: Nobel laureates in the United States.* New York: The Free Press.

8

Reconstructing Genius

James Ogilvy

Scene: the living room of our commune back in the early 1970s, a dozen of us gawking at a slide show of pictures from one of the first trips into China after Nixon's ping-pong diplomacy opened up the People's Republic. John Kao, a Chinese American who made the journey, is showing living color shots of teeming masses, happy comrades doing T'ai Chi in the public square before bicycling off to work in the morning. But the image that sticks most with me is that of a wall-sized dragon composed of tens of thousands of multicolored feathers pasted into place by dozens of Chinese "artists." Collectivist art that avoids the decadence of bourgeois subjectivism. Shades of socialist realism! Yes, it looks very like a dragon. But is this art? All those artisans had, in effect, painted by the numbers. Each and every one followed directions for which color feather was to go just where. Is this social creativity? Surely the act of creation was social. And the dragon is an artifact. But if this is the model for social creativity, I'll take mine solo, thanks.

Harvard psychologist Howard Gardner (1989) wrote a book about art education in China in which he contrasted the collectivist ideals of Chinese education, and their emphasis on the one correct way to do things, against the more individualist, libertarian approach to education in the United States. In his concluding remarks, he wrote:

In China, education is considered a race. Students should begin as early as possible and should proceed as quickly as possible along the track which is known and available to all. The education system is judged successful when many individuals have made it to the finish line as soon as possible. In America, we recognize the race too, but we feel that the students should have a chance to wander or meander much more, even if in the end not all of them make it to the finish line. As a result of their wandering, some of the participants may have more to offer by the conclusion of the race.

The advantage of the Chinese way is that more of your students become proficient and make it to the goal line. The disadvantage is that they may have less to say or to show once they get there. The disadvantage of the American way is that many students never make it to the end or even get close. The advantage is that some who do go "all the way" have very interesting and original things to say when they get there. (p. 250)

Second Scene: It's now 1993. A bunch of us are gathered at a Global Business Network conference in London. GBN is a company that some of us created in 1988 to assist large organizations think about the future by formulating alternative scenarios. Our principle technology is the scenario workshop, a collective endeavor in which we elicit from a group of people enough information about their hopes and fears so that we can together create several futures in which today's decisions might play out. In this particular workshop, Brian Eno—student of art history, rock musician, producer of U2's latest albums—is talking about the difference between genius and "scenius." He's making the point that we in the individualistic West may need to modify our mythology about creativity springing only from the tortured soul of the individual genius. Just because the Japanese are less individualistic than we are, it doesn't follow that they can't be creative. Maybe we need to decouple our concepts of creativity and individualistic genius.

Eno's is a radical idea to many of us in the West, where an individualist approach to creativity prevails. This attitude is nowhere less abashedly canonized than by Harold Bloom (1994) in his magisterial book, *The Western Canon*: "Social energies exist in every age, but they cannot compose plays, poems, and narratives. The power to originate is an individual gift, present in all eras but evidently greatly encouraged by particular contexts" (p. 46).

Individualism may have its limits. Robert Reich may be right about America's need for myths that valorize *team creativity*. Most of our American mythology is so individualistic, so heroic, so libertarian as to plunge us into anarchy and narcissism. But if the alternative is painting by the numbers, then what happens to freedom, innovation, and the brute irreverence that has always been so near and dear to the entrepreneurial spirit at the heart of the American economy, to say nothing of the Oedipal struggle that artists have always fought to escape the anxiety of influence.[1]

Here's the rub, the dilemma, the contradiction on which our concept of creativity founders: On the one hand, creativity calls for a break with the elders, innovation, something new under the sun, something that must erupt from the soul of the isolated individual because it is precisely this isolation that allows liberation from *that which has been*, the established, the traditional, the old. But on the other hand, we in the West may have taken this individualism thing a little too far. We have valorized Horatio Alger and Thoreauvian civil disobedience to such an extent that we've got people doing any damn thing in the name of rebellion, then expecting it to be honored as innovation. You can't run a company—or a school, or a family, or a community—if everyone feels entitled, even encouraged, to do any damn thing any damn time any damn place. Not all graffiti is art!

I want to tackle this dilemma on two levels: first in theoretical terms, then in very practical terms. First I want to sort out some conceptual relationships, and then I want to tell some stories that show how the concepts play out. The concepts in question include subjectivity, freedom, personality, and creativity. So first I will address what is good and bad about social creativity in theory, and then I'll turn to what is good and bad about social creativity in practice. At the end I'll join theory and practice in some reflections on the outer fringes of social creativity.

SOCIAL CREATIVITY IN THEORY

We owe a debt to the deconstructionists. I know, I know: "How do you identify a member of the deconstructionist Mafia? He'll make you an offer you can't understand." The deconstructionists are nearly unintelligible. No normal human being can read Derrida *and* root for the Chicago Bears. You've got to have devoted a large part of your life to reading Kant, Hegel, Husserl, Nietzsche, Freud, and Heidegger before you can pick up a volume of Derrida and *get it*. No time for the NFL with a reading list like that!

But for better or worse, I devoted more than a decade to reading my way through *the list*. So for me, Derrida is fun, not an intimidating chore. I actually enjoy reading Foucault and Deleuze and Fredric Jameson. Call me demented if you like, but I find the baroque thickness of their philosophical prose a pleasure. So it is not with the pomposity of someone who has suffered for others' sins and therefore thinks he deserves to impose his salvation on others that I bring you the wisdom of the deconstructionists. No, I have indulged myself in the delights of Derridean play. I have frolicked in the pastures of European intellectual history, and I am here to say (in American) *it ain't all bad.*

Each in a slightly different way, Hegel, Nietzsche, Jung, Foucault, and Derrida have succeeded in decoupling the concept of creativity from the individual ego. This decoupling works in two directions. For Hegel explicitly (and implicitly for the others), the breakthrough lay in showing that subjectivity could inhere is something *larger* than the individual, namely *Geist* as in *Weltgeist*, or "world-historical-spirit." Hegel's idea is easily confused with pantheism, or something like Lovelock's Gaia hypothesis— the idea that everything is somehow alive, a vast system that is internally organized in such a way that, in some sense or other, it can *act* to maintain its equilibrium (Lovelock), or to change and move in some historical direction (Hegel). The hitch in this idea—and the place where many sober secularists find it a little loony—is the identification of a center or ego for this broadly distributed "subject." Where is the *cogito*, the "I think," that could steer this vast beast toward the future? In Washington? On Wall Street? Surely, if the thing (or spirit) is conscious, someone must be in charge, right?

Here's where the other direction of decoupling intentionality from the individual ego becomes helpful. Whereas Hegel elevated intentionality "up" from the individual toward the collective, the others on the list analyzed intentionality "down" toward the intrapersonal. They looked for sources of subjectivity that were *smaller* than the individual self. They deconstructed the unity of the self into a multiplicity of intrapsychic agencies. Nietzsche (1968): "*My hypothesis:* The subject as multiplicity" (p. 20). For Jung (as opposed to the ego psychology of Freud), the self is a teeming pool of often unconscious archetypes vying for their place in the sun of consciousness. For Foucault, the individual is an invention of European intellectual history, an invention whose origin can be dated at the dawn of modernity, and whose demise may be imminent.

And there are others who have picked up the beat, whether or not they read *the list.* Marvin Minsky, MIT's expert on artificial intelligence, argued in *The Society of Mind* that intelligence is not the province of some super-smart homunculus calling the shots from the center of the brain. Intelligence, artificial or real, instead emerges when you get enough stupid little agencies working together to solve problems in ways that, collectively, turn out to be pretty smart. Minsky made individual consciousness sound like an Hegelian emergence of a collective Spirit from the combined acts of so-called individuals.

James Hillman, the link between Jung and Moore's best-seller, *The Care of the Soul*, coined the felicitous phrase *polytheistic psychology* to distinguish the pluralism of Jung's archetypes from the monism of Freud's *monotheistic psychology* based on the singular ego. Hillman sees the self as a society of "selves" who impersonate the gods and goddesses for whom the archetypes are often named, such as Mercury the mercurial (in Rome) or Hermes the hermetic (in Greece).

This second direction for decoupling intentionality from the individual ego comes to the aid of the first: If sober secularists doubt the existence of some transcendent ego pulling the strings, like the wizard of Oz, from some central control room for World Historical Spirit, so be it. Let them have their doubts. Subjective intention *without* an ego is how intentionality works anyway, even in ordinary, person-sized individuals. The second, deconstructionist direction of decoupling helps us see how a self can *look* as if it's being run by a single controller, even though what we discover when we get that self onto the analytic couch is a whole community of little spirits and agencies duking it out with one another in the none-too-unified cauldron of consciousness. Ego? It's an illusion. And not just in the sense that Buddhists believe. It isn't so much that we each *have* or *are* an ego that we can transcend in order to escape the wheel of karma. Rather, we never had one in the first place. "Ego" is a concept, an invention, the product of a kind of conspiracy-theory-of-the-self. We see all of those actions that a self performs, and we become convinced that there is some unified conspiracy *behind* the actions, some unified *intender*, some ghost in the machine. But as Nietzsche (1887/1956) wrote some time ago, "No such agent exists; there is no 'being' behind the doing, acting, becoming; the 'doer' has simply been added to the deed by the imagination —the doing is everything" (p. 178f).

Whether you relocate subjectivity "down" into the sub-personalities of an individual person, or "up" toward the spirit of the times (Zeitgeist), in either case the unity of a controlling ego is, as Napoleon said of God, an unnecessary hypothesis. No, Virginia, you don't need Santa Claus to explain Christmas. You don't need God to account for the world. You don't need an ego to account for subjective, intentional action, whether in the history of spirit or in the biography of an individual. And, finally, *you don't need individual genius to account for creativity*. The distributed scene, if it's the right kind of "scenius," can provide all we need to account for creativity.

I know this all sounds oh so nihilistic—no Santa Claus, no God, no ego, nothing? But here's where Nietzsche (1968) helps us again. He distinguished two kinds of nihilism: a nihilism of weakness and a nihilism of strength. The first, if I may paraphrase, said, "God is dead. O woe. We are doomed." The second says, "God is dead. Daddy's gone. Now we can play."[2] This second, active, lyric nihilism animates the lighter mood of the deconstructionist movement (although there are shades of the first in figures like Foucault and Paul de Man). And it is this second, active, dancing nihilism that can animate social creativity precisely to the extent that it liberates us from the looming presence of God or the Superego telling us what we *ought* to be doing rather than playing. This is the debt we owe to the deconstructionists.

This, then, is the good news, the glad tidings of deconstructionism. Where is the theoretical bad news? Well, in the resistance to theory altogether (see de Man, 1986). To the extent that deconstruction disabuses us of all attempts to impute unity where there is none—whether we're talking about attempts to make sense of the universe by imagining it as God's creation, or attempts to make sense of a text by involking the authority of the author (see Said, 1975), or attempts to make sense of someone's actions by involving a singular actor called the ego—in each case the corrosive power of deconstruction works to press our noses in the mess of phenomena that are not unified by some explanatory noumemon *behind* phenomenal appearances. But this is just the job that theory is supposed to perform—to tell us what is *really* going on, despite what untutored opinion *thought* was going on. Thus, you may have *thought* that the sun was falling below the horizon, but astronomy tells us that the sun is stationary, and the *appearance* of the sun's falling is really to be explained by the twisting of the earth on its axis. You may have *thought* that you were going to work in the morning of your own will, but Marxist *theory* will inform you that your so-called "will" is but the pawn of imperialists, and that you have been alienated from your true self by a false consciousness imposed by the workings of global capital . . . and so on. We use theory to get beneath the multiplicity of surface phenomena to find the unifying noumena that function as theoretical explainers of what we see with our untutored senses.

The bad news about deconstruction is that it robs us of those unifying explainers that are the workhorses of theory. And what do we have left? A kind of literary philosophy that lacks the power of proof (see Rorty, 1982, for a critique of philosophy as science, and a defense of "literary philosophy"). How intellectually unsatisfying! No wonder so many academics are waking up to the danger of deconstructionism: They see that this new "theory" is not so much an advance in the theoretical foundations of literary criticism, but instead a revolt of the palace guard in the citadel of academia. These people called deconstructionists are blowing the whistle on one kind of intellectual game; they are saying, in effect, the ladder of abstraction that ascended from the multiplicity of phenomena to the unity of abstract ideas leads nowhere. The mental map that placed form over matter, mind over body, and theory over practice—that vast Judeo-Christian-through-the-Enlightenment conceit that we could find The One over the many—is all illusion. Just a map. A construct that functioned to keep the intellectuals in power. Take away that map and you take away a large part of the prestige of academic intellectuals. Bad news for the academy, but not necessarily for artists who never functioned that easily in the academy anyway.

SOCIAL CREATIVITY IN PRACTICE

Now I want to turn from theory to practice—and none too soon, given the resistance to theory inherent in deconstructionism. Let's see if we can get at social creativity not so much by descending from the heaven of a theory of creativity or a theory of socialism, but instead by ascending from the practice of living, breathing practitioners. In order to keep this concrete rather than abstract, I must exploit my own experience in making the move from academic theoretician to practicing corporate consultant. I want to talk about the differences between life as a solitary professor of philosophy and life as a member of a network of people trying to create a better future. I've been to both extremes, done the solo trip and the team effort, and I'm here to say that social creativity is not to be confused with group sex any more than solitary creativity is masturbation. But social creativity has its problems, even if Brian Eno is right about the need to move from genius to scenius.

As in the first section on theory, in this section on practice I want to follow the same good news/bad news format. I'll begin with four very practical advantages of social creativity, then address some very practical disadvantages. Those reflections on the practical disadvantages of social creativity set up the concluding section on ways to overcome the challenges of social creativity.

So what's so good about social creativity? First of all, it's fun. Working and playing with a bunch of people you like can be a lot more amusing than banging the keys in the solitude of one's study. Not that writing can't be enjoyable. I'm relishing this very solitary day of writing. But I get a lot more laughs out of working with my colleagues than I do in the privacy of my loft.

Second, social creativity brings more resources to bear on a given creation than any single individual can master. Whether or not the whole is greater or less than the sum of its parts, it's certainly greater than any one part. Different members of a team bring different resources to a team. We know different things. We have different strengths. We can make up for one another's weaknesses. In both quantity and quality of contributions to a task, a team has more to offer than any individual.

Third, if Koestler (1964) was correct to argue that creativity often springs from the unexpected juxtaposition of realms of thought not often combined, then how much more likely is it that creativity will be found where different people with different realms of expertise find themselves thinking together. Koestler's insights into the Janus-faced logic of creativity argue persuasively against the organization of the modern research university with its departmental walls among different specialties. Indeed, if one were to try to invent an organization whose structure precluded the kind of creativity that Koestler described, one could hardly do better than the modern university. The scenario workshop, whose participants are selected precisely for the diversity of their realms of expertise, offers a far richer medium for the cultivation of creative ideas in a social setting.

Fourth, teams can provide multiple sanity checks. It's no accident that in the tradition of European geniuses, there's a high degree of correlation between madness and creativity. Look at the tradition of mad or at least manic geniuses: Beethoven, Van Gogh, Wittgenstein. The tradition of genius glamorizes madness as the route to creativity, as if you had to be slightly off kilter in order to get free of the established way of doing things. Maybe you have to be mad to get in contact with some other-worldly wellspring of creativity. How romantic!

This mythology of the mad genius has something to it: Weirdness is, almost by definition, nonconformist. And if the creative is, also by definition, out of the ordinary, then weirdness might provide a route to creativity. But my oh my what a license to self-indulgence! What an attractive rationale for being careless about the concerns of others! "Sorry for upsetting the entire applecart. I was just trying to be 'creative.'" It may be tough to be a genius without seeming to be a little weird; but the converse does not hold. It's easy to be weird without being a genius.

Why is this point important to our understanding of creativity? Because the weird-genius model runs the danger of decadence; it is antisocial to the point of being sociopathic. Granted, society can, over the long run, benefit from publishing the ravings of sociopaths like Ezra Pound or Jean Genet. But just as evolutionary biology teaches us that most mutations perish because they don't improve the adaptability of a species, so social history teaches us that most deviations from the law don't improve society. Yes, civil disobedience is sometimes necessary; but no, not every punk is a Thoreau.

Social creativity has this advantage over the mad-genius model: A team is less likely to be delusional than an individual. Simply by matching wits with one another, the members of a team have the advantage over an individual in that they reassure themselves that they are not losing touch with the rest of humanity. Consequently, the creations of a team are more likely to be of service, or at least of interest, to the rest of humanity. This, therefore, is a fourth advantage of social creativity: It is more likely to be sane.

What are some of the disadvantages of social creativity, practically speaking? One thinks of old saws like, "A camel is a horse designed by a committee" or "Too many chefs spoil the broth." Clearly, there are coordination costs. Say, for example, you're working on a project that calls for different people to contribute different skills in sequence. The report has to get to the client next Tuesday. Tom writes his section on Thursday, Mary adds hers on Friday, and Edward the editor has to have both their contributions in front of him on Monday if he is to work his magic before Tuesday. Tom cannot wait around for inspiration to strike, or he'll never make the hand-off to Mary in time for her to add her section before Monday.

This all-too-familiar dynamic of teamwork calls for *management*, and the "management of creativity" strikes many of us as an oxymoron. This is why we romanticize the renegade, the outlaw, the lone ranger who can break away from the pack and solve the problem on his own. Forget about going through channels! Forget about entrusting our security to the massed might of the CIA or the British secret service. Leave it to Bond, James Bond, 007. We in the West like our individualistic heroes. In the East it's a little different. But does that mean that the Japanese cannot be creative? That they can only copy or, at best, make incremental improvements but no breakthroughs?

Look at the linkages between different concepts and practices: The genius myth goes together with the valorization of the individual over the collective. It also fits with the Christian concept of creation as *creatio ex nihilo*—creation from nothing. The God of Abraham didn't pick up where some earlier God left off. He started from scratch. So, likewise, the solitary genius is not supposed to settle for mere modifications on the work of prior masters. The solitary genius—on the American model that praises the garage inventor over the corporate functionary—would rather do it all by himself. See the linkages: individual heroics, Christian monotheism, creation *ex nihilo*. Conversely, Oriental culture's emphasis on conforming to social norms fits with Hindu polytheism and an approach to creativity that does not start from scratch but works by incremental improvements and line extensions that respect the value of what has gone before.

The trouble with the Oriental model—and this is the downside of social creativity—is that sometimes you need a break with the past, a breakthrough to a novel future. Sometimes respect for the tradition and social norms will lead to a groupthink that cannot see its way clear of shared delusion.

HOW TO

Granting the fact that both the individual and social models of creativity have their good and bad sides, both theoretically and practically, how is one (or some, or all) to know when one or the other is most appropriate? To leave this question up to the individual, or to the group, is to foreordain the answer, and thus to beg the question.

I can think of two criteria that could be used by either the individual or the group. First, and fairly obvious: Does the challenge at hand call for a minor modification or for a major transformation? If things are going pretty well and you just want to make them better, then look to an in- house team to come up with incremental improvements. If the system is going critical and anomalies suggest fundamental disorder, then you may want to call out for a renegade consultant to take an entirely fresh look.

Second, is a solo performance possible in the particular arena at hand, or are we looking at a situation where only an ensemble can get the job done? It's hard to perform symphonies or make movies all alone. Movie-making is a paradigm case of social creativity. Sure, there is a place for individual genius, but at the end of the day, if the ensemble doesn't work well together, even geniuses can look pretty bad.

Assuming that in a given situation, the application of these two criteria suggest the need for social rather than solo creativity, how do both the theoretical and practical considerations apply in any given situation? Here at the end I want to reflect on the question: What is necessary for social creativity to be possible? And here I have to say that, despite the transcendental philosophical formulation of the question,[3] my answers are based much more on practice than on theory. In making the transition from academia to consulting, I've noticed that there is much less teamwork in academia, where we used to practice the art of maximizing minimal differences. A graduate seminar in philosophy is not an arena where you build on the ideas of others. It is instead an arena where you build up your own reputation by destroying the arguments of others. It is much more competitive than cooperative.

At Global Business Network, the company with which I've been privileged to work for the past 8 years, there is instead a spirit of generosity such that we each see the benefit of making sure that the others are enjoying themselves as much as possible, not in a self-indulgent sense of taking time off from work, but in a self-actualizing sense that sees the doing of the work as the realization of the self. We do not always succeed in this noble and playful endeavor. But when we do, it has the feeling of a jazz ensemble jamming up a storm. The leadership shifts as one or another takes the lead. We don't work from a fixed score. There is a premium on improvisation, but at the end of a project, the whole thing has to fit together.

What is necessary for jamming to be possible?[4] For one thing, trust. In order to allow yourself or others to take the risk of deviating from the norm, repeating received wisdom, or spouting the party line, you have to trust that what you or someone else is saying is said in a spirit of good will. No one is trying to trick anyone else. Unlike the graduate seminar or board room shoot-out where people are trying to argue each other to the ego death, our meetings usually have the feeling of a good conversation that builds, circles back, allows itself to wander into the unknown, then leaps to new connections. No one is in charge. Everyone (or almost everyone—we all have our slow days) contributes. In the end the product bears the overlapping fingerprints of many hands. But you need to trust the other people in order to place in their hands the infants of your own intellect, the children of your dreams, the progeny of your fondest hopes.

Another requirement: In addition to trust in others, you need enough confidence in yourself that you don't have to keep proving your worth to others. Insecure people can wreck a team. Those who are desperate to prove themselves worthy are way too liable to grab the ball at the wrong times and to take shots they have no hope of making. They are too desperate to prove themselves, and consequently they make fools of themselves. I've come to admire most those who can remain silent the longest until, just at the right moment, they make an economical remark that puts a new spin on everything that has gone on before.

Patience, respect for others, a sense of humor, a reservoir of knowledge and experience, the ability to listen closely to what others have to say—all of these individual and team skills are important in contributing to an ensemble performance. But the one I come back to as most important, or at least most significant to me in my limited experience, is a spirit of generosity. If each member of the team is genuinely committed to giving more than he or she expects to get—if each member of the team is ready to extend the benefit of the doubt to others, always construing their remarks in the best possible light, never becoming defensive or sullen—then the ensemble performance will show each and every one to advantage. It's so simple, really. As simple as love. But I don't want to romanticize what is often an arduous process: long days and nights, the discipline of learned skill, sheer stamina, and a perseverance that does not wander too far afield. These are the ingredients of social creativity, and they are not easy to come by, especially in large groups. The more people you have in a meeting, the more patience, the more close listening, the more conciseness is required. So there is some upper limit to the number of people that can jam. I don't begin to know what that number is, but I think it's somewhere in the neighborhood of 15 to 20. Beyond that, you're no longer an ensemble. Big bands need a conductor and a score, and any deviation from the score is not an improvisation but a mistake.

You don't have to be close friends with everyone on the team, but it sure helps if you are close friends with at least a few. You don't even have to like everyone on the team; chances are, if you've assembled a group diverse enough to bring different talents, knowledge and experience to bear, then some people won't see eye-to-eye with others, which is why patience and respect become all the more important.

Precisely to the extent that you allow others to be *other* and not cookie-cutter clones cut from some corporate cloth, to just that extent you need to challenge your own sense of completeness and self-sufficiency. You cannot be a know-it-all and function well in a team; and the more you think you know, the less well you will listen to others. So this business of teamwork requires more than the warm fuzzies of self-confidence and the love of others. You need to be hard on yourself, and subject yourself to others whom you do not always like.

What does it *feel like* to engage in social creativity? You're not in control. If you already know where the conversation is going, then you're not going to hear anything new. But if you're not in control, you may sometimes feel confused, as if you're hanging on to the conversation by your fingernails. Sometimes you feel more like a predicate than a subject, or maybe like a dangling participle. You have to stay alert or you'll lose it. There is some risk that you will be the victim of the corrosive version of deconstruction and that you will fail to follow, much less contribute to, the stream of collective consciousness. One's peers are sometimes so smart and eloquent. The feeling is very much like that of being one of the dumb agents described in Minsky's (1986) *Society of Mind*, or one of the sub-personalities described in James Hillman's (1971) polytheistic psychology. You are not in Zeus-like mode, claiming to be in charge. Instead, your consciousness is possessed by one of the lesser deities, subjective, idiosyncratic, and characterized by an identifiable personality to be sure, but only one among the several personifications that make up the entire pantheon. You listen for the ways that others contribute, and you ask them to add a riff where you know they can help. You look for places to jump in yourself, but not unless no one else plays the notes you know.

I often play the note of deconstruction, because almost no one knows what those French are talking about, and I listen for the insights of my colleagues, who know far more than I about any number of subjects. Together we try to come up with scenarios of the future that are enough like and enough unlike the past and present that problems can be solved without assuming that we are radically other than we are.

To return to the opening notes on deconstructionist theory, and tie them down to the practice of the scenario development workshop and to the etiquette of online computer conferencing where much of our work in GBN gets done, I want to conclude with some reflections on the issue of *intellectual property*. The work of the solitary genius is very much *his* (and I use the male pronoun intentionally). The works of a scenario workshop are *ours*. Trusting the good will and generosity of others, unanxious about one's own abilities or achievements, one is able to contribute to a social product that is the property of the group, not the individual. This is important if it is the fate of the group that is at stake. If it is the company or the community that is trying to find its path into the future, then it is important that the creation of that future be owned by the whole community, not just a few individuals in charge.

The ownership of ideas is an odd concept in some respects. We have copyright laws to protect the value of intellectual property. Authors should get royalties when their books are translated into foreign languages. Software writers and inventors should reap the rewards of their hard work. But when it comes to fashioning the hopes and fears of a community into strategies for the common good, it seems odd to attribute ownership of ideas to just a few social-engineers-as-saviors. When I first heard the job description of "policy analyst" or "policy maker," it seemed odd to me that a few individuals could presume to set policy for the many. Doesn't the very idea of a policy maker presume a distinction between shepherd and flock?

If we are to take seriously the idea of citizenship in a democracy, then the setting of policy *must* be an act social creativity, not just the steering of a community by a few individuals. But if a community is to take responsibility for its direction, and not merely back into the future by force of happenstance, then there must be a means of setting that direction in a way that calls forth the creative impulses of that community in a coherent and thoughtful way.

Simply voting on options that have been predetermined is a less creative form of choice than the collective shaping and fashioning of the options themselves. The scenario workshop provides a format for the collective shaping and fashioning of alternative futures from which a community can then choose its eventual path. If the choice that is made is a choice of a scenario that was not *given* to the community but *created* by the community, then the community will more likely assume *ownership* of that choice.

These dynamics of collective creation, choice, and eventual ownership are nowhere more evident than in the case of education and school reform. Despite all the years of educational research and experimentation, school reform in the United States has virtually stalled over the dilemma created by the conflict between calls for broad, sweeping reform of the entire system on the one hand, and the greater efficacy of highly decentralized, site-based management on the other.

One way out of this dilemma of educational reform would be to conduct scenario workshops on the future of each community across the land. This tool of social creativity can be applied everywhere, thus satisfying the need for something "broad and sweeping." But the very nature of the tool is such that its practical application calls forth the uniqueness and creativity of each community. It is a tool that invites each community to come up with its own solutions, thereby inciting a sense of ownership. That sense of intellectual ownership will in turn overcome the not-invented-here syndrome which inhibits the spread of bright ideas in other attempts at broad, sweeping reform. If a community thinks collectively about its future, it cannot help but discover the importance of its children, the citizens who will populate that future. So if a community thinks collectively about the course it wishes to set, the very nature of the assignment is bound to lead to acts of social creativity directed at school reform. No one can do it alone. As an African proverb has it, "It takes a whole village to raise a child."

In summary, the first section explored the theoretical good news and bad news about the deconstruction of solo creativity. The second section turned to more practical aspects, again covering both the advantages and disadvantages of social creativity. Finally, this concluding section has explored the application of these ideas, both theoretical and practical, to the particular case of scenario workshops on the future of education. The point of this chapter has not been to argue that individual creativity is wrong, but rather to open up the possibility that some of our ideas about the ontology of individuality might be wrong, and that the delights and benefits of creativity we previously ascribed to individual persons alone might *also* be practiced by groups to great advantage.

NOTES

1. Cf. Bloom's (1994) arguments in his book, *The Anxiety of Influence*, that "strong" poets are those who survive the Oedipal struggle with their greatest predecessors.
2. See, for example, Book One, Section One, "Nihilism," pp. 9-39.

3. Kant's so-called "transcendental" method of doing philosophy started from the question, What is necessary (in the way of theoretical presuppositions) in order that knowledge should be possible?

4. Here I refer ahead, not back, to a book called *Jamming* by John Kao (1996) who showed the slides of China mentioned in the first paragraph of this chapter in the early 1970s when he was a student at Yale. He is now a professor at Harvard Business School, where he teaches courses on entrepreneurship and creativity. He is also a member of Global Business Network.

REFERENCES

Bloom, H. (1994). *The western canon.* New York: Harcourt Brace.

de Man, P. (1986). *The resistance to theory.* Minneapolis: The University of Minnesota Press.

Gardner, H. (1989). *To open minds: Chinese clues to the dilemma of contemporary education.* New York: Basic Books.

Hillman, J. (1971). Psychology: Monotheistic or polytheistic. *Spring,* 197ff.

Kao, J. (1996). *Jamming.* New York: HarperCollins.

Koestler, A. (1964) *The act of creation.* London: Hutchinson.

Minsky, M. (1986). *The society of mind.* New York: Simon & Schuster.

Nietzsche, F. W. (1956). *The genealogy of morals* (F. Golffing, trans.). Garden City, NY: Doubleday. (Original work published 1887)

Nietzsche, F. W. (1968). The will to power. (W. Kaufmann, trans.). New York: Vintage.

Rorty, R. (1982). *The consequences of pragmatism.* Minneapolis: University of Minnesota Press.

Said, E. (1975). *Beginnings.* Baltimore: The Johns Hopkins University Press.

PART FIVE

CULTURE AND PERSONALITY

9

Creativity Need Not Be Social

Mark A. Runco

One of the most popular emphases in contemporary creativity research is social. No doubt this research has contributed a great deal to our understanding of certain expressions of creativity. It is quite objective, which allows reliable and convincing investigations to be conducted and reported, and it is practical, with numerous suggestions for encouraging creativity. Still, the social view of creativity gives a somewhat biased view of what it takes to be creative. It can even be quite misleading.

One reason for this is that social research tends to focus on creative actions and products that can be shared and observed. This maximizes agreement among judges, which of course translates directly into highly reliable data and trustworthy findings. It is fairly easy to agree when discussing the end results of the creative process, in part because there is some product to examine and re-examine. However, taken to the extreme the social view emphasizes observable exchanges and products at the expense of critical intrapersonal processes. In actuality, it is the social factors that are not necessary for creativity. Intrapersonal contributions are absolutely necessary; without them no potentially creative behavior or product would be available for social approval.

Clearly, it is only the extreme social view that is misleading, but movement in that direction is apparent in the research on domains

(Csikszentmihályi, 1990), in empirical work relying on consensual assessments (e.g., Amabile, 1990; Hennessey, 1994; MacKinnon, 1962), and in case studies that rely on unambiguous cases (e.g., Gardner, 1993a; Wallace & Gruber, 1989). Granted, those doing this kind of research do not explicitly state that the individual is unimportant; in fact, those using the concept of domains include "the individual" in their tripartite scheme (the third component being "the field"). Similarly, consensual assessments are typically used to quantify individual traits, and case studies are by definition concerned with individual cases. Yet in many systems theories the efforts of the individual mean nothing without social recognition. And which individual cases are studied?—Picasso, Einstein, and others who are unambiguously creative in the sense of wide agreement. A dependence on social judgment is, then, implied by these three approaches.

Not only is the problem merely implied; several examples can be cited to show that the emphasis on unambiguous cases is actually taking research away from studies of potential. In one, Lindauer (1992) suggested:

> the age-old works of contemporary artists may be difficult to evaluate until after they have died, that is, until sufficient time has passed for some reconsideration. Contemporary critics may be highly critical of the older works of contemporary artists if their evaluations are biased in favor of the late-life characteristics of artists from previous generations. (p. 17)

Along the same lines, Gardner (1993b) proposed in an amusing and yet serious fashion that those of us with ambiguous or everyday creativity can take heart by the fact that important judgments about our work will be offered only after we are dead. In the third example, which happens to be a review of Gardner's (1993a) work, Plucker (in press) wrote:

> Although I agree that biological investigations may eventually lead to insight into creativity, I question the intensity of this impact. For example, the possible implications of a neurobiological basis to creativity and, more generally, to behavior are obvious. *But how would this affect the acceptance of creative products, a process which can take decades if not centuries?* The importance of the biology-behavior link should be kept in proper perspective. (emphasis added)

This seems to suggest that neurobiological processes may be less important than other contributing factors because they do not directly influence "acceptance."

A final example of the social emphasis is from Shalley's (1991) definition of creativity as dependent on ability, intrinsic motivation, and cognitive activity. She suggested:

> An individual must engage in certain *cognitive activities* for creative
> responses to emerge. . . . Creativity involves search through large spaces
> of possibilities where individuals actually are attempting to reach new
> knowledge states. The cognitive activities that are necessary in order to be
> creative are problem definition, environmental scanning, data gathering,
> unconscious mental activity on the problem, insight to the problem
> solution, evaluation of the solution, and finally, implementation of the
> solution. (p. 180; emphasis in original)

This is a comprehensive list and useful when thinking about underlying
mechanisms, but it does include the problematic *implementation* (see also
Treffinger, Tallman, & Isaksen, 1994). The thesis of this chapter is that work
can be creative even if it is not implemented, recognized, and accepted.
Similarly, various contributing factors should be considered if they affect the
originality of an individual's thinking, even if they do not affect the
implementation, acceptance, impact, or social recognition of that thinking.

This chapter examines the problems that arise from the social
emphases in creativity research. The most general of these was already
described as an inappropriate emphasis. The more specific problem follows
from the theory that creativity is dependent on social recognition; this
detracts from other important topics of study (e.g., intrapersonal and
subjective processes). A second specific problem reflects the relativity of
social recognition. Social recognition may seem quite objective, but, in fact,
it is dependent on context, which is itself quite varied and slippery. There are
many difficulties involved in social judgment, and these suggest that we may
not want to rely on such data. Even when stable and reliable, what does
social judgment predict? In a word, it is predictive only of impact, and that
might be but certainly is not always creative. This last point is important
because it leads to a redefinition of creativity, with impact being distinct
from the other *components* of creativity (e.g., problem generation, insight).

This chapter does not dismiss the social view, nor does it clump
together all social research. As I stated earlier in this chapter, social research
does contribute to our understanding of why some creative individuals earn
reputations, achieve eminence, and have an impact on society, or at least
within their field. If the interest is in this kind of eminence, then certainly
creative efforts that are made social should be studied. This does not mean,
however, that personal creative processes should be disregarded or even
relegated. Most likely, all creative efforts that eventually lead to repute or
eminence were initially very personal, and, therefore, if we study only the
social components, we may very well miss the critical early stages of the
process. Moreover, if we ignore the personal contributions to creative
activity, we will not be able to understand *potential*, nor what is coming to

be known as *everyday creativity* (Cropley, 1990; Richards, 1990). I would like to think that the research on creativity will at some point allow us to maximize the potential of individuals who might otherwise not achieve much. To do that, we have to admit that they have potential—even if they have not yet produced a recognized creative product. Stein (1985) seemed to feel the same when he wrote, "Data collected on persons with already acknowledged creativity may not be good predictors of the creativity of others *who have yet to make their contributions*" (p. 418).

THE ARGUMENTS FOR SOCIAL EMPHASES

Csikszentmihályi (1990) described how certain achievements—deemed creative at one point in time—were unappreciated earlier, the difference being in the judgments offered by the experts working in the particular *field*. In Csikszentmihályi's words, "Creativity is not an attribute of individuals but of social systems making judgments about individuals" (p. 198).

This explains why an individual might earn a reputation at one point but lose it later, or why other individuals (e.g., Rembrandt) may be unappreciated in their own time but highly regarded some years later. But surely this is a matter of *reputation*. What the individual actually did is in many ways independent of the judgments of others. As Einstein worked in that famous patent office, his thought experiments were not controlled by the reactions of anyone else working in the field. They certainly were grounded in earlier work, but social reactions came into play only when Einstein discussed, wrote, and published his ideas. Any temporal variation in reputation is, then, a function of changes in the judgments and not the creative act. Reputations change, but these can and should be kept distinct from personal efforts and creative potentials.

I am suggesting that the creative *process* can be delineated such that the sharing and implementation of ideas and insights is distinct from the discovery or generation of those ideas and insights. Although stage theories are often unrealistic (Runco, 1994b), in the present instance I think we can we actually separate steps on the basis of temporal and functional order. An individual can create, and after that may implement the creation, and that implementation might or might not be recognized as creative. In this light, the first of the steps can occur without the other two. This delineation will help us to avoid the assumption that the third step is necessary, and that, in turn, should insure that research is not directed solely toward unambiguous cases and away from individuals with great potential, including children.

The second step in the process, describing the possible implementation of an idea or insight, is also unnecessary, although unlike *impact*, at least it allows for everyday and less-than-eminent creations (see Treffinger et al., 1994). This last step has also been described as a kind of *expression* (Dudek, 1974; Taylor, 1963) or *persuasion* (Simonton, in press). Persuasion is an interesting descriptor, and it has the advantage of fitting into the typical alliterative scheme for describing the creativity literature (i.e., person, process, product, press). It may also connote an active effort, however, with the individual actively attempting to convince others of the value of his or her product or idea. For this reason I continue to use the terms *implementation* and *impact*. Other stage models have *verification* as a last step (Hadamard, 1954; Wallas, 1926), but this is not problematic because that is not social, which is the criterion I am suggesting we avoid. Importantly, the most realistic of the stage models allow for recursive feedback, from verification to incubation, and so on. This might help to account for social influence on the initial and personal processes, when there is, in fact, influence.

The systems view should alert us to the second problem, namely, that of the relativity of judgments (Csikszentmihályi, 1990; Runco & Chand, 1994). Judgments are far from stable; they vary enormously. So why trust them? One reason is given in Stein's (1963) definition of creativity as *social transaction*. In his words:

> For purposes of empirical research our definition of creativity is as follows: creativity is that process which results in a novel work that is accepted as tenable or useful or satisfying by a groups at some point in time. By this definition we limit ourselves to the study of individuals who are regarded as creative by "significant others" in their environments. (p. 218)

Note that Stein is explicit about the breadth of the definition: It is for research purposes. This should be underscored because it is one thing to say that certain phenomena are *determined* by social factors (or that they *depend* on social factors) and quite another to say that the only way we can be objective and scientific is to focus on unambiguous features—features about which there is some consensus. Creativity falls into the latter category.

The personal underpinnings of creativity are difficult to study objectively, but this does not mean that they are unimportant. Consider here Skinner's (1974) concessions that his favoring overt behavior was simply an effort to be scientific and was not a reflection of a belief that covert behavior was unimportant. His push for the study of only observable behavior was a reflection of his beliefs about science. He agreed that certain covert processes were important for human behavior, but he felt that we could not be objective enough about them to satisfy the scientific method. We could, on the other hand, be scientific about overt behavior. For Skinner, then, overt behavior was important and amenable to science; covert processes might be important but were unscientific (see also Epstein, in press). This applies to the topic of creativity: We can only be scientific in the traditional sense about socially recognized products and unambiguous cases (Albert, 1975).

No doubt we can be more objective about socially recognized and unambiguous instances of creativity than we can about personal instances, but I would suggest that at this point in creativity research it is better to have an only moderately objective understanding of the actual creative process (i.e., the information processing and intrapsychic dynamics) than to have an entirely objective understanding of only one part of the process. This is particularly true because that one part of the process (the social part) is usually last to occur; thus, without some deterministic confusion the earlier parts cannot be dependent on it. Perhaps we can modify the scientific method to fit the subject matter rather than modifying the subjective matter to fit the method.

While on the topic of the scientific method, recall the assertion earlier in this chapter about keeping the term *creativity* as specific as possible by recognizing its distinctiveness from *reputation*. Creativity can be kept distinct by defining it in terms of novelty and aesthetic appeal rather than social value and impact. Novelty and aesthetic appeal can be defined for individuals; reputation cannot. This distinction makes for good science in the sense of parsimony and in terms of explanatory power. Parsimony is satisfied because this definition is more specific than one that requires the additional impact or reputation component, and power is increased because a wide range of behaviors is kept under the creativity umbrella, including personal, childhood, everyday, and potential creativity.

In some ways the definition suggested here is not so different from that used in the social theories. Typically creativity is defined in terms of originality (or some related concept, like novelty) and fit (or appropriateness, adaptiveness, or value) (Rothenberg & Hausman, 1976; Runco & Charles, 1993). Aesthetic appeal is also widely cited, though not as often as the other two, at least in the psychological research, perhaps because it is related to appropriateness, or perhaps because of the same bias toward objectivity I have been describing throughout this chapter. In any case, social theories define originality and fit in terms of social rather than personal norms and standards. A creative product must be novel for a large audience, and that large audience must recognize its value and fit. The definition I have suggested uses the same criteria as social theories, but they use norms rather than personal standards. More will be said later in this chapter about definitions.

Ironically, the separation of *creativity* and *impact* may actually increase the objectivity of creativity research. This is, in part, because of relativity of the reputation and impact. If that relative part of the concept of creativity is excluded, the remaining parts might be more manageable. Relativity is implied by the rationale for systems theory (Csikszentmihályi, 1990; Gruber, 1988) but is also obvious in empirical work on interpersonal judgments.

Some success has been reported in research utilizing interpersonal judgments, at least in terms of interrater reliabilities (e.g., Amabile, in press; Baer, 1991; Hennessey, 1994). In his work on creativity and art as a function of age, for instance, Lindauer (1993) reported that there was "considerable agreement among experts on the world's greatest masterpieces" (p. 234). The experts in this case were authors of four art compilations. Lindauer went into some detail about the qualifications of these experts. One was, for example, a former Director of the "Old Masters Picture Department" of Christie's (the art auctioneer). Notably, the interjudge agreement was indeed only modest. Of 120 artists in the four sources, only 31 (26%) were in three sources (e.g., van Gogh, Homer, Monet, Degas, Raphael, Pollock, and Whistler). Coincidentally, 31 artists were listed in two sources, and 58 (48%) were listed only once. Lindauer also reported that only 9 of the 31 "artists of the first rank" were also in Lehman's (1953) well-known list of eminent individuals. These so-called "giants of art" were da Vinci, Gainsborough, Hals, Masaccio, Michelangelo, Raphael, Rembrandt, Turner, and Velasquez.

Others investigators have had even clearer difficulties with interrater agreement (Csikszentmihályi & Getzels, 1970; Korn, Davis, & Davis, 1991; Rothenberg, 1986; Rothenberg & Sobel, 1980; Runco, 1989; Runco, McCarthy, & Svensen, 1994; Sobel & Rothenberg, 1980). Korn et al. (1991) complained that even in work with Fellows of the American Psychological Association and Department Chairpersons, assessments can deteriorate into "a popularity contest" (p. 792), and Csikszentmihályi and Getzels (1970) and Rothenberg and Sobel (1980) went so far as to argue that professional raters or judges should not be expected to agree. They suggested that disagreement among experts could be a virtue! The lack of agreement exists because the experts have different perspectives; the reasonable assumption is that a wide set of perspectives is desirable.

Consensual assessments generally rely on expert opinion; but here again there are problems. One reflects a kind of circular argument: Consensual techniques are useful because they use only things about which social judgments will agree. Some time ago Murray (1959) asked, "Who is to judge the judges? And who is to judge the judges of the judges?" To answer this, one must be precise about what it is that one intends to predict. Runco et al. (1994) suggested that experts might be fitting judges only when it is expert performance that is the primary concern. Runco et al. had experts as judges of artwork, and their judgments were compared with ratings from student judges and students' self-ratings. The student judges gave ratings that were associated with the self-ratings, but neither of these were associated with ratings from the professionals. Runco et al. concluded:

> If research is intended to predict future success as a professional artist, it would make sense to rely on judgments given by professional artists. . . . But if the objective is to study *current* performance levels or the present levels of creative *potential*, peer- and self-ratings might be more tenable. (p. 29)

Admittedly, self-ratings may not be objective enough to use by themselves. Self-ratings can be distorted by inaccurate memories, socially desirable responding, or even dishonesty. Roth (1975) was obviously aware of this when he stated, "It is well known that scientists frequently build their original work on the memories of the antecedent contributions of others which are not always clearly in consciousness" (p. 373). Roth looked to Zeitgeist, but also to specific readings and experiences that individual scientists draw from memory. Freud (1920) is an apt example: In his "Note on the Prehistory of the Technique of Analysis," he acknowledged that free association was not an entirely original innovation.[1] Roth (1975) proposed that Freud was influenced by both Ludwig Boerne and Francis Galton. Of course, it is possible that Freud was creative in his application of free association, even if he was not the first to uncover its efficacy. In this sense he might deserve credit for innovation rather than creativity (cf. Rickards & De Cock, in press).[2]

A second possibility is that Freud was creative in the sense that he was drawing on recollections that were integrated into his personal or subjective conceptual structures. This is a convincing argument because human memory does allow individuals to fill in details (Loftus, 1979). Even if Freud drew from his memory when developing free associative techniques, his memory was itself a personal construction rather than exact and literal. That seems to be congruent with the concept of creativity, or at least with *creation*. More will be said later in this chapter about literal constructions, but for now the point is that there are problems (e.g., accurate memories) with intrapersonal judgments.

Runco and Smith (1991) and Simonton (1985) presented empirical findings that do nothing for the validity of self-ratings. They found creators themselves to be very poor judges of which of their ideas or products would be well received. This was true of both nonexperts (Runco & Smith, 1991) and experts (Simonton, 1985). There are a number of reasons why we should not expect creators to be good judges. One was suggested by O'Quin and Derkes (1997) in their review of the research on creativity and humor. In that area production and recognition are quite distinct. Many individuals can recognize a creative and humorous joke but not produce one, and the same may be true for other kinds of creative acts. Perkins (1981) described this as a kind of paradox: Good judges might not be very good creators.

A second explanation involves the well-known *divergent perspectives hypothesis* according to which differences between judges and creators may reflect the different points of view, with creators tending to focus on the product and judges tending to focus on the creator and possibly the context. Creators also have different knowledge bases than judges. They know, for example, what other ideas they have had and might have rejected. This can lead them to underestimate the originality of their work because it is probably much like works and ideas they have had. Judges will not know about these earlier efforts and may see originality where the creator him- or herself did not. Other biases can explained in terms of specific cognitive heuristics (Nisbett & Ross, 1980). The research on heuristics shows that individuals rely on less than optimal decision strategies, at least some of the time. Runco (1994a) used the anchoring and representative heuristics in his description of judgments of originality.

With all this in mind, who can give objective and meaningful judgments? Experts are often used, but they are, after all, human and will thus be biased by the same cognitive subjective tendencies that characterize nonexperts (Nisbett & Ross, 1980). The pessimistic view is that social judgments will never be both objective and useful. Rogers (1970) seemed to hold this view and claimed that "no contemporary mortal can satisfactorily evaluate a creative product at the time it is formed, and this statement is increasingly true the greater the novelty of the creative product" (p. 141). His view was that "the value of the creative product" is in the eyes of the creator, rather than judges, experts, or some audience. Maslow (1971) held a similar view, and he gave an example of a child who discovered something new for him- or herself, something personally original and meaningful but lacking all "social value" (p. 60). Maslow specifically stated that value is not a good criterion for creativity because it always begs the question, "Valuable for whom?"

The biologist Stephen Jay Gould (1991) was critical of judgments offered across historical periods. He referred to these inappropriate judgments as *Whiggist* "in dubious memory of those Whig historians who evaluated predecessors exclusively by their adherence to ideals of Whig politics unknown in their own times" (p. 343). Though directed at a different literature, this argument is relevant. It suggests that we should be very careful with all judgments of creativity. All of them reflect some bias—historical, personal, or otherwise. Hennessey (1994) and Runco and Chand (1994) took a more optimistic route and suggested that there are individual differences in the ability to offer sound judgments. If this is the case, it is just a matter of finding the right judges.

Rubenson and Runco (1995) used psychoeconomic logic to predict that older judges might be the least useful. (Following Simonton [1990], *career age* rather than chronological age is most important.) This prediction assumes possible *depreciations*. According to Rubenson and Runco:

> One important premise is that individuals invest in their own potentials, beliefs, and knowledge bases. An individual might, for example, invest time into the mastery of a field, the comprehension of a technique, or the development of a theory. As a result, there is a definite cost to the individual if his or her theory loses respectability. For this reason, individuals with more of an investment—and these are generally the more experienced individuals—tend to be more rigid in their beliefs and therefore more resistant to change. Less experienced individuals, on the other hand, have smaller investments, and other things being equal, will tend to be more flexible and receptive to new ideas and theories.

Rubenson and Runco (1995) used this idea to define groups that would be optimal for creative achievement. Flexible individuals should be involved in order to explore possibilities and synthesize new ideas, and inflexible individuals should be involved to contribute knowledge and expertise and to motivate change by fighting with other inflexible individuals. Rubenson and Runco (1990) applied this same theory to education, suggesting that teachers be careful not to resist creative ideas of students because of fears of a depreciation of their own knowledge.

The biases mentioned earlier in this chapter are not limited to research on creativity. Many reflect very general human thinking tendencies or cultural values (Kasof, 1995; Raina, 1992). A good example of a cultural bias is the one that has maintained attention on the so-called "mad genius" (Becker, 1978). This idea has led researchers to look to the creativity of exceptional individuals and, in particular, the creativity of those with psychiatric disorders. The representative bias is apparent in that certain individuals, like van Gogh, are easy to remember and easy to retrieve when thinking about creative individuals. The larger cultural bias will probably be apparent if you think for a moment about which famous writers come easily to mind. Which Nobel or Pulitzer Prize winning authors can you name? Now, how many committed suicide or suffered from an affective disorder? Very likely most of those you named had some sort of affective disorder (see Ludwig [1995] for actual data). The problem is that writers are socially recognized only if they say something profound about "the human condition." The cultural bias comes in here because the human condition is surely quite subjective and mostly a matter of interpretation (Kelly, 1955; Langer, Hatem, Joss, & Howell, 1989). Experience may play a role, but it is filtered through knowledge structures and value systems, both of which are highly selective. What is the human condition? It depends on who you ask!

Think again about the specific individuals who win the prizes. Most winners describe a serious human condition—Steinbeck received critical praise for *The Grapes of Wrath*, not *Sweet Thursday*—and who better to describe the human condition as serious than someone who has a depressive interpretation of the world? No wonder so many have found high rates of affective disorders in creative samples (Andreason, 1987; Jamison, 1993; Ludwig, 1995; Richards & Kinney, 1990), and no wonder creative individuals are often seen as exceptionally sensitive (Jamison, 1993; Wallace, 1991). The point is that famous individuals may be known for their affective disorders, in part, because of a bias in the existing reward systems. To be famous, you have to have a serious (i.e., not comical) view of the human condition, and this may be facilitated by the possession of an affective disorder.

In addition to a statement about existing reward systems and cultural values, this bias may be influencing our research on creativity. The creative process is often thought to be a marginal and potentially unhealthy activity (Kaun, 1991). In a sense it is, however, just a problem of restricted range: We are basing theories of creativity (or at least the creative personality) on samples that have been identified as creative through a particular value/reward system. Those individuals who are not depressed write happy fiction, but they do not win any prizes for it, nor earn critical acclaim, and thus they are excluded from studies of eminent creators. There are productive yet happy writers. Perhaps they are creative in the sense of originality of thought and in terms of certain aesthetic factors (e.g., humor), but because of their nonserious world views and products, they do not earn impact and recognition. Does this mean they are not creative?[3]

SUBJECTIVE PROCESSES

In addition to problems of relativity and biased judgment, an exaggerated focus on social emphasis can easily detract from important but personal creative processes. Examples of important subjective processes are easy to find.

In developing his recent ecological theory, Barron (1995) described how *singularity* and *solidarity* can be involved in creative work. He argued that, as individuals, we are essentially alone. One effect is motivational—we exercise our imaginations. We also have myth, art, music, family, and religion for relief, according to Barron.

Smith and van der Meer (1990), Smith and Amnér (1997), and Rothenberg (1991) described other important but subjective creative processes which might be overlooked if emphasis is given to products and social instances of creativity. Smith and van der Meer's work on percept-genesis is remarkably consistent with the notion proposed in the present chapter, and especially with the idea that there are distinct personal and social stages in the creative process. Smith (1981) wrote:

> The process "behind" the percept proceeds from primitive, emotionally charged stages, deeply rooted in early experience, to gradually better-structured and more reality-adapted stages. Thus, from one process stage to the next, the distance from the private sphere increases. The conception of reality is formed by repeated stimulation from the outside (e.g., by perceptual scanning); at the same time the subjectively colored layers of the embryonal percept are peeled off one after the other. The ideal end-product of the PG [percept-genesis] process is an impression of the outside reality which seems independent of the subject and is accepted by such by other observers. (pp. 276-277)

Rothenberg's (1991) theory also emphasizes personal processes, though he views creativity as consciously directed and adaptive.

Just as solidarity can motivate an individual (Barron, 1995), so too can social experience. There are, in fact, several means by which the personal creative process benefits from social experience. The most obvious benefit might involve the feedback, offered via social exchanges, on how to make the idea or product more useful. On a more abstract level, Barron (1964, 1995) described how the self can react to the objective world in creative ways, often motivated by the need to express a concern or idea. He argued, "Of all the common psychological antinomies, the most basic is that arising from the distinction between self and not-self" (Barron, 1964, p. 81). This is consistent with Vygotsky's view that the "creative imagination" is personal yet reacts to social experience (see Ayman-Nolley, 1992). Other parallels include Simonton's (1988) theory of chance configurations, with its intrapsychic and social factors, and Sheldon's (1995) thinking that "to achieve our creative potential we must first overcome our social conditioning and develop a strong and autonomous will" (p. 25). This view of motivation may apply best to the arts: MacKinnon (1962) suggested that artistic creativity requires that "the creator externalizes himself into the public field" (p. 485) (see also Dudek & Cote, 1994).

Conversely, social experience can have a detrimental impact on the creative process. This may be the most common when an individual compromises too easily, giving up what he or she personally found to be meaningful but what others have criticized. This may be why dedication (Therivel, 1993), ego strength (Barron, 1964), and self-confidence (Barron & Harrington, 1981) are typically included in lists of core characteristics for creativity. Indeed, Root-Bernstein, Root-Bernstein, and Granier (1993) recently suggested that courage is critical for scientists to maintain their creativity as they age. However, instead of defending one view, Root-Bernstein et al. felt that courage allows the individual to change topics of study, perhaps repeatedly or regularly, and that this in turn can allow the individual to maintain a youthful approach to research. Clearly, this line of thought is compatible with the psychoeconomic theory mentioned earlier (Rubenson & Runco, 1992, 1995).

The effect of social experience is therefore difficult to predict. It can change in either direction, perhaps being inhibitive, leading to a loss of interest and effort, or it can increase, when the individual is challenged to work harder. For the latter, an individual might use his or her creative skills to cope with an unpleasant experience. Creativity is often viewed as coping, or in the words of Smith and van der Meer (1990), "a high-level defense, or if one prefers not to stretch the concept too far, a coping strategy" (p. 25). Valliant and Valliant (1990) also alluded to creativity as a means to resolve conflict, and Cohen (1989), Flach (1990), and Mraz and Runco (1994) described creativity as adaptability. Whatever the terms—coping, high-level defense, or adaptability—creativity can be elicited by seemingly unpleasant social experiences.

Inhibition can occur with the same definition of creativity (i.e., as adaptability). Consider the creative person who adapts but does so by adjusting his or her behavior such that it fits into a situation that does *not* support originality. The result would be unoriginal behavior. Take the individual who adapts to homelessness (Runco & Chand, 1994). He or she may not like it, but they may adapt to that routine (using creative skills to do so) and eventually find themselves in a rut that might appear to be quite uncreative, at least from the perspective of social recognition. Alternatively, creative persons may *refrain* from adapting and as a direct result appear to be uncreative. Consider individuals who refuse or fail to adapt to a 9-to-5 job. They may be creative in the sense of doing their own thing (freelance work of some sort, or even homelessness), but, again, few observers would consider them creative, particularly with a definition that emphasizes impact and recognition. The point of all this is that it is difficult to conceptualize creativity as adaptiveness; we again have problems of relativity. Creative work may be adaptive, but adaptable for whom? For the individual—in which case certain routine behaviors can be creative—or in terms of larger norms—in which case you must ask about the creativity of the norms.

A related problem is specifically involved in studies of unambiguous cases. Gardner (1993a), for example, found highly eminent individuals to be "self promoters," and Therivel (1993) included "abilities to sell" in his argument about the creative personality. Therivel distinguished between creators and performers, the latter presumably behaving more socially than the former. Promoters might be concerned about what I have called impact or reputation, or what Therivel called *sales*. Creators might, on the other hand, be primarily intrinsically motivated. This is not say that performers are not intrinsically motivated (Alter, 1989) nor that creators are entirely intrinsically motivated (Rubenson & Runco, 1992; Stohs, 1992). It does, however, raise the possibility of different primary motives for social and asocial creativity.[4] An individual who is creative in the social sense might have different motives than an individual who does not have social motives, and the study of the former may tell us little about the latter.

What about the motive implied by *dedication*. As Therivel (1993) suggested, dedication can be very important because individuals who make some impact often must persist with their insights, actually moving beyond the "a-ha" or insight proper; they must communicate their findings or ideas or solutions to some public. They would not do that unless that public could give them reinforcement of some sort, or unless they were highly dedicated to the work itself and impervious to the lack of extrinsic reinforcement. (It is much like the situation described earlier in this chapter in which courage was necessary, but here it is dedication to stick with one topic, style, or approach rather than courage to change topics, styles, or foci.) This, in turn, suggests a paradox: Why would an individual who is impervious to extrinsic pressure share his or her work with the public? Feasibly, the individual might not care about the reactions of critics or other experts but might be sensitive about some larger public (or vice versa). The novelist James Michener (1991) explored these possibilities in his book, *The Novel*. He quoted Ezra Pound as saying, "Work only for your peers. Ignore the general public. They always follow false gods" (p. 351).

Incidentally, the theory about varied motivations leads to an interesting but probably untestable hypothesis: Given that energy and attention is needed for insight, and given that sharing ideas, products, and solutions requires energy, the latter could actually detract from the resources available for further insightful work. Granted, this is a difficult if not impossible hypothesis to test, as is the logical extension that those individuals who bother to share their ideas actually have a lower potential for further creative work than do those unrecognized individuals who do not bother to go public. Not only might there be unrecognized creative genius; those who are not recognized may be the true geniuses!

Modifications of an individual's ideas and creations can either enhance the creativity of the process or sacrifice something in order to make them publicly acceptable. My concern is that creativity will be seen as dependent on social actions, but I admit that social experience can contribute to creative activity. The argument in this chapter is not that social and personal processes are entirely independent, but rather than the social is dependent on the personal, whereas the personal is not always dependent on the social. Though it is arguable whether creative insight cannot occur without being influenced by social experiences and conventions, it can occur without social recognition. Social *recognition* is only necessary for creative impact.

STUDIES OF POTENTIAL

What is sorely needed in creativity research is the study of the actual mechanisms that allow an individual to create (Jay & Perkins, 1996). This may be best accomplished by avoiding the social approach and by studying potential.

For the child, a creative idea or insight may be creative primarily in a literal sense—as the creation or construction of understanding (Maslow, 1968; May, 1975). Recall what was said earlier about Freud and his drawing from memory for the construction of new insights. Consider also the Piagetian view that any new creation (or understanding or insight) is an invention (Piaget, 1976). Again, it is creation in a literal sense, with insights fitting and original, if only for the individual. One could argue that such literal creations or insights have no social value, but as I suggested earlier, social value may not be judged in any reliable fashion anyway. It is too relativistic.

One reason studies of potential are so useful is that process does not need to be inferred from achievement, as it does in studies of unambiguously creative individuals. Moreover, eminent and unambiguously creative individuals might be very difficult to investigate, particularly if eminence is a trustworthy designation only after the individual in question has died (and their work complete). Studies of eminent individuals are nearly always retrospective; but we can study children and everyday instances in the act while the process is still a process. There is no guarantee that potential will be fulfilled in the sense of impact or recognition, but similar tradeoffs are common scientific research. As a matter of fact, this is very similar to the tradeoff between internal and external validity. Even in these terms, studies of everyday creativity have an advantage because they have a kind of generalizability across noneminent individuals and groups, and some findings may apply to the eminent. They also allow research with high internal validity, at least when potentially creative persons are actually brought into the laboratory for controlled and internally valid studies (e.g., Mumford, Reiter-Palmon, & Redmond, 1994; Weisberg & Alba, 1981). The primary attraction of studies of potential is simply their own potential to inform us about how potential is fulfilled or expressed.

IMPLICATIONS AND CONCLUSIONS

This theory of the subjective and personal facets of creativity has several additional implications for research. Two involve problem solving and the definition of *problem*. The third involves brainstorming.

There is a controversy about the relationship between creativity and problem solving. Some view problem solving as a kind of creativity; others view creativity as a kind of problem solving; still others argue that there is some overlap but also some distinctiveness between creativity and problem solving (see Runco, 1994b). This is pertinent because the appreciation of subjective tendencies seems to be the most likely when the independence of creativity from problem solving is recognized. Research in support of that position is supplied by Jausovec (1994) and Metcalfe (1986) on *feelings of warmth* and by Dudek and Cote (1994) on *problem expression*.

Much depends on one's definition of *problem*. A problem may be unnecessary for creativity that is self-expression (Dudek & Cote, 1994) or that which is involved in general well-being or health (Runco, Ebersole, & Mraz, 1990; Runco & Richards, 1997). On the other hand, what is health? Is it problem-free existence? Some would say no; problems are inherent in life, and creativity is tied to health because it allows the individual to cope with the problems that are encountered. In this line of thinking life is filled with problems—recall my discussion of the "serious human condition"— but creativity allows efficient adaptation and thus health. The alternative is that the experience of life is subjective and a matter of interpretation, and for this reason a problem-free existence *is* possible. But isn't "interpretation" a kind of problem solving? In a way, it is. Furthermore, it is construction, which I already tied to creativity (see also Mumford et al., 1994; Runco, 1990-91).

A second important implication of a theory of personal creativity involves the well-known practice of brainstorming. Brainstorming as originally proposed is still used (Osborn, 1953) and has also been modified in the work of Basadur (1994; Runco & Basadur, 1993) and Treffinger et al. (1994). The key premise is to postpone judgment and generate as many ideas as possible. If my argument that personal processes are all-important holds up, it would imply that judgment—at least intrapersonal judgment—cannot and should not be postponed.

The most relevant theoretical refutation of brainstorming is provided by descriptions of a preconscious filter or censor of ideas. Included here is the psychoanalytic view of the creative process (Kris, 1952; Kubie, 1958), as well as the recent work of Simonton (1988) and Runco and Chand (1994). Preconscious processes are by definition subjective, and for this reason they are often overlooked.[5] Contrary to what the individual is asked to do when brainstorming, try to follow a train of thought without some sort of filtering. Short of random thinking, it cannot be done. Empirical evidence against the feasibility of postponing judgment was given by Diehl and Stroebe (1987, 1991), Khandwalla (1993), Mullen, Johnson, and Salas (1991), and Runco (Chand & Runco, 1992; Runco & Okuda, 1991).

The easy rebuttal to this is to suggest that preconscious filters work on a personal level, but brainstorming is a social technique. This makes some sense, though several ideation-enhancement techniques such as explicit instructions (Harrington, 1975; Runco, 1986; Runco & Okuda, 1991) are, for the most part, interpersonal, and they show selections to be beneficial and thus contrary to brainstorming theory. Additionally, there seems to be a fairly robust "productivity loss" in brainstorming groups, and this has been tied specifically to the interactions of the group (Diehl & Stroeb, 1987, 1991; Mullen, Johnson, & Salas, 1991).

The title of this chapter is "Creativity Need Not be Social," and throughout I have tried to avoid the suggestion that creativity *cannot* be social. Social experiences are relevant to judgments about actions and products, and they regularly influence the creative process itself. The problem is that social factors are not vital to the *process*, or at least to the initial stages of the process. Personal processes are vital, for without them, nothing would be created, nor shared, and thus not judged.

Ludwig (1990) seemed to have held a similar view, for he argued:

> While it is common to regard artistic expression as the truest representation of the self, it is a dangerous practice to equate a person with his works other than at the most general and therefore least informational level. Because the qualities or attributes that are responsible

for creative expression may have little to do with the qualities or attributes that make a person who he is, it is logically impermissible to extrapolate from one to the other. The work of art may transcend the individual, and, by the same token, be less than the individual. No matter how thoroughly, for instance, an observer comes to know a Beethoven, Picasso or Tolstoy, he never can predict what each is capable of composing, painting or writing; and, conversely, no matter how familiar he becomes with the *Eroica,* the *Guernica* or *War and Peace,* he has no rational basis for being able to reconstruct the distinctive personalities of the originators of these works. Therefore, any psychological inferences drawn from such works are more apt to reflect the biases of the observer than the inherent attributes of the producers. (p. 517)

Ludwig's view not only supports what I have suggested about biases and problems of a product-focus; it also offers an opportunity to reiterate the concerns about ex post facto research on established reputations.[6] Many studies of unambiguously creative individuals rely on a retrospective approach; but this kind of research insures a retrospective bias. To understand what happens during the creative moment, the moment itself should be experienced.

Before closing I should also be explicit that the theory proposed in this chapter is primarily psychological and not intended as social constructivism. Some metaphysical asides were included such as the notion that there is a reality (or "self") that is influenced by but not dependent on social experience. Although a detailed examination of the social nature of subjectivity would be quite interesting, I must leave that for much more capable metaphysicians. The concern here was truly psychological, with behavioral and methodological rationale and implications. It may be a self that can create and choose whether or not to share the creation; but my point is simply that it is beneficial and parsimonious to separate the personal mechanisms and processes from the social (e.g., impact and recognition).

Several social biases were described in this chapter. Runco (1996) also described biases in creativity research: one toward objectivity; a second toward originality to the exclusion of integration; and a third toward salient but unrepresentative cases. This last bias can be applied directly to the research on unambiguous cases, for they "carry too much weight in decision processes and memory, even though they may unrepresentative of general tendencies and in fact exceptions to the rule" (Runco, 1996, p. 73). The solution to the problem of unrepresentative examples involves the use of appropriate controls, a method for which was proposed by Runco (1993).

Other biases should be made explicit. Some are personal such as Matthew effects (Simonton, 1988), which describe how highly productive individuals gain more and more attention. Is that attention deserved or is it indicative of a tendency to associate originality with a name, and then, as predicted by cognitive dissonance (Festinger, 1962) and confirmatory heuristics (Nisbett & Ross, 1980), to look only for further manifestations of talent? From the opposite angle, there are biases against individuals. I recently co-authored a chapter on developmental trends and had to think hard about whether or not to cite Cyril Burt's work. He proposed a number of reasonable things in his work on creativity (including the idea that the differential rates of development for various indices of divergent thinking supported their discriminant validity [Burt, 1970]), but he is now known primarily for his fraud.

Helson (1990) and Piirto (1991) described what are essential gender biases, and there are a variety of what may be called topical biases in the literature (Richards, 1994; Stein, 1985). Stein, for example, pointed out that researchers in the United States refused to listen to qualified claims about divergent thinking given by Europeans (Haddon & Lytton, 1968) at least 30 years ago. Richards (1994) suggested that psychologists are not open to phenomena that have yet to be objectively explained. This of course fits nicely with my argument, given that it too brings up the question about the need for objectivity. Richards described a published survey in which 55% of the professors of some natural science believed in Psi phenomena ("the processes of information or energy transfer which presently have no explanation using 'physical or biological mechanisms'"), as did 77% of the professors in education and the humanities and the arts, but only 34% of the psychology professors thought Psi phenomena were likely or well-established. Ironically, openness to experience and possibility has been found (by psychologists themselves) to be indicative of creativity (e.g., Davis, 1975). Hence, we might be limiting our own creativity by being biased against nonfactual possibility. This is, of course, another way of talking about a bias against *potential.*

Levinson, Darrow, Klein, Levinson, and McKee (1978) described a bias whereby anxiety about "decline and restriction" in old age will color any effort at studying the elderly (p. ix). More recently, Root-Bernstein et al. (1993) noted how

> young scientists displaying the sort of variegated research pattern predictive of long-term contributions are apparently discriminated against by more narrowly focused scientists who believe that if one has not settled upon a single area of research by the age of 30 or so, one has no future in science. (p. 342)

This bias is apparent in peer reviews, pressures to publish and obtain grants, and in the various suggestions to specialize.[7] It is diametrical to the empirical findings of Root-Bernstein et al. (1993): They found high-impact contributions from scientists who do, in fact, study a variety of topics. A related example of bias was suggested by the prediction from psychoeconomic theory, mentioned earlier, about the flexibility of older scientists (Rubenson & Runco, 1995). A final developmental bias was highlighted by Cohen-Shalev (1986). He suggested that life-span studies will be biased if they take only productivity into account and relegate the style, form, and content of creative work. Empirical support for this view was presented by Lindauer (1992, 1993). There certainly is a large number of potential biases influencing both what we study to how we interpret what we find.

The biggest concern I expressed may have been the one about the social emphasis detracting from the vital personal components of the creative process, such as preconscious filtering (Kris, 1952; Schwebel, 1993), and detracting from important sources of creativity, such as children or individuals of any age with potential (Runco & Charles, 1997). We cannot afford to overlook children or others with creative potential. They are resources, and if we do not recognize them as creative we certainly cannot nurture their natural talents. Moreover, we will never fully develop techniques for recognizing and nurturing not-yet-unambiguous creativity. Creativity may be inherently subjective, and it may be almost entirely subjective, at least in those initial stages. There are objective influences, but it is the individual who must be interested or sensitive enough to select and use them. Hence, although the social factors may determine whether or not the individual will be reinforced for their efforts or earn a reputation, we will never truly understand creativity unless we admit that a critical part of it is entirely personal and subjective.

NOTES

1. Though outside the sciences, it is interesting that Helen Keller suggested something very similar: "I cannot always distinguish my own thoughts from those I read, because what I read becomes the very substance and texture of my mind" (cited in Piechowski, 1993, p. 467).
2. This might imply that innovation is the term that should be used when discussing implemented creativity; but in reality we need terms for creative applications, like Freud's, as well as creativity applied. The problem is not just a matter of distinguishing between creativity (which might not be implemented) and innovation.
3. The related issue concerns the creativity of the research. If biases represent entrenchment, as I am suggesting here, they certainly limit the creativity of research, like a kind of fixity limiting problem solving.

4.   This dichotomy was chosen to fit with the thrust of the present chapter, which is an attempt to isolate the phases of the creative process that are independent of social processes. The motivational issue could, however, lead to additional categories, including that which is required for antisocial creativity (see McLaren [1993] on "the dark side of creativity").

5.   It is of course possible that the preconscious has a logic of its own. This logic might even be objective, at least in its own terms or if we knew the rationale it uses. What we view as subjective (and unreliable or unpredictable) may be quite objective (in the sense of being reliable and predictable) if only examined using the same "logic" of the unconscious.

6.   This argument may remind readers of a second Skinnerian (1974) caveat, namely, that although a focus on overt behaviors insures objectivity, it is always a look backwards at behaviors that have been completed. Explanations of future behaviors are probabilistic, at best.

7.   It is common for reviewers to disagree with one another. If they are to judge submissions for creativity, and if my argument in this chapter is acceptable, a solution involves first recognizing that creativity is not an objective phenomenon, and thus, that the scientific method needs to be modified. As an example of modification, more reviewers (e.g., 10) than is common (3-5) could be consulted, and an actual content or qualitative analysis of referees' comments could be attempted. Such an analysis might not be entirely objective, but it might capture more accurately what is offered.

REFERENCES

Albert, R. S. (1975). Toward a behavioral definition of genius. *American Psychologist, 30*, 141-151.

Alter, J. (1989). Creativity profile of university and conservatory music students. *Creativity Research Journal, 2*, 184-195.

Amabile, T. M. (in press). Within you, without you: The social psychology of creativity. In M. A. Runco & R. S. Albert (Eds.), *Theories of creativity* (rev. ed.). Cresskill, NJ: Hampton Press.

Andreason, N. C. (1987). Creativity and mental illness: Prevalence rates in writers and their first-degree relatives. *American Journal of Psychiatry, 144*, 1288-1292.

Ayman-Nolley, S. (1992). Vygotsky's perspective on the development of imagination and creativity. *Creativity Research Journal, 5*, 77-85.

Baer, J. (1991). Generality of creativity across performance domains. *Creativity Research Journal, 4*, 23-39.

Barron, F. (1964). The relation of ego diffusion to creative perception. In C. W. Taylor (Ed.), *Widening horizons in creativity* (pp. 80-86). New York: Wiley.

Barron, F. (1995). *No rootless flower*. Cresskill, NJ: Hampton.

Barron, F., & Harrington, F. (1981). Creativity, intelligence, and personality. *Annual Reviews of Psychology, 32*, 439-476.

Basadur, M. (1994). Managing creativity in organizations. In M. A. Runco (Ed.), *Problem finding, problem solving, and creativity* (pp. 237-268). Norwood, NJ: Ablex.

Becker, G. (1978). *The mad genius controversy*. Newbury Park, CA: Sage.

Burt, C. (1970). Critical note. In P. E. Vernon (Ed.), *Creativity* (pp. 203-216). New York: Penguin.

Chand, I., & Runco, M. A. (1992). Problem finding skills as components of the creative process. *Personality and Individual Differences, 14*, 155-162.

Cohen, L. M. (1989). A continuum of adaptive creative behaviors. *Creativity Research Journal, 2*, 169-183.

Cohen-Shalev, A. (1986). Artistic creativity across the adult life span: An alternative approach. *Interchange, 17*, 1-16.

Cropley, A. J. (1990). Creativity and mental health in everyday life. *Creativity Research Journal, 3*, 167-178.

Csikszentmihályi, M. (in press). The domain of creativity. In M. A. Runco & R. S. Albert (Eds.), *Theories of creativity* (rev. ed.). Cresskill, NJ: Hampton Press..

Csikszentmihályi, M., & Getzels, J. W. (1970). Concern for discovery: An attitudinal component of creative production. *Journal of Personality, 38*, 91-105.

Davis, G. A. (1975). In frumious pursuit of the creative person. *Journal of Creative Behavior, 9*, 75-87.

Diehl, M., & Stroebe, W. (1987). Productivity loss in brainstorming groups: Toward the solution of the riddle. *Journal of Personality and Social Psychology, 53*, 497-509.

Diehl, M., & Stroebe, W. (1991). Productivity loss in idea-generating groups: Tracking down the blocking effect. *Journal of Personality and Social Psychology, 61*, 392-403.

Dudek, S. Z. (1974). Creativity in young children: Attitude or ability? *Journal of Creative Behavior, 8*, 282-292.

Dudek, S. Z., & Cote, R. (1994). Problem finding revisited. In M. A. Runco (Ed.), *Problem finding, problem solving, and creativity* (pp. 130-150). Norwood, NJ: Ablex.

Epstein, R. (in press). Generativity theory as a theory of creativity. In M. A. Runco & R. S. Albert (Eds.), *Theories of creativity* (rev. ed.). Cresskill, NJ: Hampton Press.

Festinger, L. (1962). Cognitive dissonance. *Scientific American, 207*, 93-102.

Flach, F. (1990). Disorders of the pathways involved in the creative process. *Creativity Research Journal, 3,* 158-165.

Freud, S. (1920). A note on the prehistory of the technique of analysis. In *The standard edition* (vol. 18). London: Hogarth Press.

Gardner, H. (1993a). *Creating minds.* New York: Basic Books.

Gardner, H. (1993b, May). *From youthful talent to creative achievement.* Keynote presentation at the Wallace National Research Symposium on Talent Development, University of Iowa, Iowa City, IA.

Gould, S. J. (1991). *Bully for brontosaurus.* New York: Norton.

Gruber, H. E. (1988). The evolving systems approach to creative work. *Creativity Research Journal, 1,* 27-51.

Hadamard, J. (1954). *The psychology of invention in the mathematical field.* New York: Dover.

Haddon, F. A., & Lytton, H. (1968). Teaching approach and the development of divergent thinking abilities in primary schools. *British Journal of Education Psychology, 38,* 171-180.

Harrington, D. M. (1975). Effects of explicit instructions to be creative on the psychological meaning of divergent thinking test score. *Journal of Personality, 43,* 434-454.

Helson, R. (in press). Creativity in women: Outer and inner views over time. In M. A. Runco & R. S. Albert (Eds.), *Theories of creativity* (rev. ed.). Cresskill, NJ: Hampton Press.

Hennessey, B. A. (1994). The consensual assessment technique. *Creativity Research Journal, 7,* 193-208.

Jamison, K. (1993). *Touched with fire.* New York: Free Press.

Jausovec, N. (1994). Metacognition in creative problem solving. In M. A. Runco (Ed.), *Problem finding, problem solving, and creativity* (pp. 77-94). Norwood, NJ: Ablex.

Jay, E. S., & Perkins, D. N. (1996). Creativity's compass: A review of problem finding. In M. A. Runco (Ed.), *Creativity research handbook* (vol. 1, pp. 253-289). Cresskill, NJ: Hampton Press.

Kasof, J. (1995). Explaining creativity: The attributional perspective. *Creativity Research Journal, 8,* 311-367.

Kaun, D. E. (1991). Writers die young: The impact of work and leisure on longevity. *Journal of Economic Psychology, 12,* 381-399.

Kelly, G. A. (1955). *The psychology of personal constructs: A theory of personality.* New York: Norton.

Khandwalla, P. N. (1993). An exploratory study of divergent thinking through protocol analysis. *Creativity Research Journal, 6,* 241-260.

Korn, J. H., Davis, R., & Davis, S. F. (1991). Historians' and chairpersons' judgments of eminence among psychologists. *American Psychologist, 46,* 789-792.

Kris, E. (1952). *Psychoanalytic explorations in art*. New York: International Universities Press.

Kubie, L. S. (1958). *The neurotic distortion of the creative personality*. Lawrence: University of Kansas Press.

Langer, E., Hatem, M., Joss, J., & Howell, M. (1989). Conditional teaching and mindful learning: The role of uncertainty in education. *Creativity Research Journal, 2*, 139-150.

Lehman, H. C. (1953). *Age and achievement*. Princeton, NJ: Princeton University Press.

Levinson, D. J., Darrow, C. N., Klein, E. B., Levinson, M. H., & McKee, B. (1978). *The seasons of a man's life*. New York: Knopf.

Lindauer, M. (1992). Creativity in aging artists: Contributions from the humanities to the psychology of old age. *Creativity Research Journal, 5*, 211-231.

Lindauer, M. (1993). The span of creativity among long-lived historical artists. *Creativity Research Journal, 6*, 221-239.

Loftus, E. (1979). *Eyewitness testimony*. Cambridge, MA: Harvard University Press.

Ludwig, A. M. (1990). Who is someone? *American Journal of Psychotherapy, 44*, 516-524.

Ludwig, A. M. (1995). *The price of greatness*. New York: Guilford.

MacKinnon, D. W. (1962). The nature and nurture of creative talent. *American Psychologist, 17*, 484-495.

Maslow, A. H. (1968). *Toward a psychology of being* (2nd ed.). New York: Van Nostrand Reinhold.

Maslow, A. (1971). The creative attitude. In A. Maslow (Ed.), *The farther reaches of human nature* (pp. 57-71). New York: Viking.

May, R. (1975). *The courage to create*. Toronto: Bantam.

McLaren, R. (1993). The dark side of creativity. *Creativity Research Journal, 6*, 137-144.

Metcalfe, J. (1986). Feeling of knowing in memory and problem solving. *Journal of Experimental Psychology: Learning, Memory, and Cognition, 12*, 288-294.

Michener, J. A. (1991). *The novel*. New York: Random House.

Mraz, W., & Runco, M. A. (1994). Suicide ideation and creative problem solving. *Suicide and Life-Threatening Behavior, 24*, 38-47.

Mullen, B., Johnson, C., & Salas, E. (1991). Productivity loss in brainstorming groups: A meta-analytic integration. *Psychometrika, 20*, 139-148.

Mumford, M. D., Reiter-Palmon, R., & Redmond, M. R. (1994). Problem construction and cognition: Applying problem representations in ill-defined domains. In M. A. Runco (Ed.), *Problem finding, problem solving, and creativity* (pp. 3-39). Norwood, NJ: Ablex.

Murray, H. A. (1959). Vicissitudes of creativity. In H. H. Anderson (Ed.), *Creativity and its cultivation* (pp. 203-221). New York: Harper.

Nisbett, R., & Ross, L. (1980). *Human inference: Strategies and shortcomings of social judgment*. Englewood Cliffs, NJ: Prentice-Hall.

O'Quin, K., & Derkes, P. (1997). Humor and creativity: A review of the empirical research. In M. A. Runco (Ed.), *Creativity research handbook* (vol. 1, pp. 227-256). Cresskill, NJ: Hampton Press.

Osborn, A. (1953). *Applied imagination*. New York: Scribners.

Perkins, D. (1981). *The mind's best work*. Cambridge, MA: Harvard University Press.

Piaget, J. (1976). *To understand is to invent*. New York: Penguin.

Piechowski, M. (1993). Origins without origins: Exceptional abilities explained away. *Creativity Research Journal, 6*, 465-469.

Piirto, J. (1991). Why are there so few? Creative women: Visual artists, mathematicians, musicians. *Roeper Review, 13*, 142-147.

Plucker, J. A. (in press). Can lightning be caught in a bottle—twice? *Gifted Child Quarterly*.

Raina, M. K. (1992). On creativity insights: The phenomenon of calculated ignorance and credibility. *Creativity Research Journal, 5*, 207-210.

Richards, R. (1990). Everyday creativity, eminent creativity, and health: Afterview of CRJ issues on creativity and health. *Creativity Research Journal, 3*, 300-326.

Richards, R. (1994). On Psi Fi? Acceptable and unacceptable research. *Creativity Research Journal, 7*, 87-90.

Richards, R., & Kinney, D. K. (1990). Mood swings and creativity. *Creativity Research Journal, 3*, 203-218.

Rickards, T., & De Cock, C. (1999). Understanding organizational creativity: Toward a multi-paradigmatic approach. In M. A. Runco (Ed.), *Creativity research handbook* (vol. 2, pp. 235-256). Cresskill, NJ: Hampton Press.

Rogers, C. (1970). Toward a theory of creativity. In P. E. Vernon (Ed.), *Creativity* (pp. 137-151). New York: Penguin.

Root-Bernstein, R. S., Root-Bernstein, M., & Garnier, H. (1993). Identification of scientists making long-term, high-impact contributions, with notes on their methods of working. *Creativity Research Journal, 6*, 320-343.

Roth, N. (1975). Free association and creativity. *Journal of the American Academy of Psychoanalysis, 3*, 373-381.

Rothenberg, A. (1986). Artistic creation as stimulated by superimposed versus combined-composite visual images. *Journal of Personality and Social Psychology, 50*, 370-381.

Rothenberg, A. (1991). Creativity, mental health, and alcoholism. *Creativity Research Journal, 3,* 179-201.

Rothenberg, A., & Hausman, C. (1976). *The creativity question.* Durham, NC: Duke University Press.

Rothenberg, A., & Sobel, R. S. (1980). Creation of literary metaphors stimulated by superimposed versus separated visual images. *Journal of Mental Imagery, 4,* 77-91.

Rubenson, D. L., & Runco, M. A. (1990, October). *Teachers' inflexibility and depreciation of knowledge.* Paper presented at the summit meeting of the International Creativity Institute in Portland, OR.

Rubenson, D. L., & Runco, M. A. (1992). The psychoeconomic approach to creativity. *New Ideas in Psychology, 10,* 131-147.

Rubenson, D. L., & Runco, M. A. (1995). The psychoeconomic view of creative work in groups and organizations. *Creativity and Innovation Management, 4,* 232-241.

Runco, M. A. (1986). Maximal performance on divergent thinking tests by gifted, talented, and nongifted children. *Psychology in the Schools, 23,* 308-315.

Runco, M. A. (1989). The creativity of children's art. *Child Study Journal, 19,* 177-189.

Runco, M. A. (1990-91). Mindfulness and personal control. [Book Review]. *Imagination, Cognition, and Personality, 10,* 107-114.

Runco, M. A. (1993). On reputational paths and case studies. *Creativity Research Journal, 6,* 487-488.

Runco, M. A. (1994a). Cognitive and psychometric issues in creativity research. In S. G. Isaksen, M. C. Murdock, R. L. Firestien, & D. J. Treffinger (Eds.), *Understanding and recognizing creativity* (pp. 331-368). Norwood, NJ: Ablex.

Runco, M. A. (1994b). Conclusions concerning problem finding, problem solving, and creativity. In M. A. Runco (Ed.), *Problem finding, problem solving, and creativity* (pp. 272-292). Norwood, NJ: Ablex.

Runco, M. A. (1996). Objectivity in creativity research. In A. Montuori (Ed.), *Unusual associates: Essays in honor of Frank Barron* (pp. 69-79). Cresskill, NJ: Hampton Press.

Runco, M. A., & Basadur, M. (1993). Assessing ideational and evaluative skills and creative styles and attitudes. *Creativity and Innovation Management, 2,* 166-173.

Runco, M. A., & Chand, I. (1994). Problem finding, evaluative thinking, and creativity. In M. A. Runco (Ed.), *Problem finding, problem solving, and creativity* (pp. 40-76). Norwood, NJ: Ablex.

Runco, M. A., & Charles, R. (1993). Judgments of originality and appropriateness as predictors of creativity. *Personality and Individual Differences, 15,* 537-546.

Runco, M. A., & Charles, R. (1997). Developmental trends in creativity. In M. A. Runco (Ed.), *Creativity research handbook* (vol. 1, pp. 115-152). Cresskill, NJ: Hampton Press.

Runco, M. A., Ebersole, P., & Mraz, W. (1990). Self-actualization and creativity. *Journal of Social Behavior and Personality, 6,* 161-167.

Runco, M. A., McCarthy, K. A., & Svensen, E. (1994). Judgments of the creativity of artwork from students and professional artists. *Journal of Psychology, 128,* 23-31.

Runco, M. A., & Okuda, S. M. (1991). The instructional enhancement of the ideational originality and flexibility scores of divergent thinking tests. *Applied Cognitive Psychology, 5,* 435-441.

Runco, M. A., & Richards, R. (1997). *Eminent creativity, everyday creativity, and health.* Norwood, NJ: Ablex.

Runco, M. A., & Smith, W. R. (1991). Interpersonal and intrapersonal evaluations of creative ideas. *Personality and Individual Differences, 13,* 295-302.

Schwebel, M. (1993). Moral creativity as artistic transformation. *Creativity Research Journal, 6,* 65-82.

Shalley, C. E. (1991). Effects of productivity goals, creativity goals, and personal discretion on individual creativity. *Journal of Applied Psychology, 76,* 179-185.

Sheldon, G. (1995). Creativity and self-determination in personality. *Creativity Research Journal, 8,* 25-36.

Simonton, D. K. (1985). Quality, quantity, and age: The careers of 10 distinguished psychologists. *International Journal of Aging and Human Development, 21,* 241-254.

Simonton, D. K. (1988). *Scientific genius.* New York: Cambridge University Press.

Simonton, D. K. (1990). Creativity in later years: Optimistic prospects for achievement. *Gerontologist, 30,* 626-631.

Simonton, D. K. (in press). History, chemistry, psychology, and genius: An intellectual autobiography of historiometry. In M. A. Runco & R. S. Albert (Eds.), *Theories of creativity* (rev. ed.). Cresskill, NJ: Hampton Press.

Skinner, B. F. (1974). *About behaviorism.* New York: Knopf.

Smith, G. J. W. (1981). Creation and reconstruction. *Psychoanalysis and Contemporary Thought, 4,* 275-286.

Smith, G. J. W., & van der Meer, G. (1990). Creativity in old age. *Creativity Research Journal, 3,* 249-264.

Smith, G. J. W., & Amnér, G. (1997). Creativity and perception. In M. A. Runco (Ed.), *Creativity research handbook* (vol. 1, pp. 67-82). Cresskill, NJ: Hampton Press.

Sobel, R. S., & Rothenberg, A. (1980). Artistic creation as stimulated by superimposed versus separated visual images. *Journal of Personality and Social Psychology, 39*, 953-961.

Stein, M. I. (1963). A transactional approach to creativity. In C. W. Taylor & F. Barron (Eds.), *Scientific creativity: Its recognition and development* (pp. 17-27). New York: Wiley.

Stein, M. I. (1985). Creativity at the crossroads. In S. G. Isaksen (Ed.), *Frontiers of creativity research* (pp. 417-427). Buffalo, NY: Bearly.

Stohs, J. H. (1992). Intrinsic motivation and sustained art activity among male fine and applied artists. *Creativity Research Journal, 5*, 235-252.

Taylor, C. W. (1963). Some possible relations between communication abilities and creative abilities. In C. W. Taylor & F. Barron (Eds.), *Scientific creativity: Its recognition and development* (pp. 365-371). New York: Wiley.

Therival, W. (1993). The challenged personality. *Creativity Research Journal, 6*, 413-424.

Treffinger, D., Tallman, M., & Isaksen, S. G. (1994). Creative problem solving: An overview. In M. A. Runco (Ed.), *Problem finding, problem solving, and creativity* (pp. 223-236). Norwood, NJ: Ablex.

Valliant, G. E., & Valliant, C. O. (1990). Determinants and consequences of creativity in a cohort of gifted women. *Psychology of Women, 14*, 607-616.

Wallace, D. B. (1991). The genesis and microgenesis of sudden insight in the creation of literature. *Creativity Research Journal, 4*, 41-50.

Wallace, D. B., & Gruber, H. E. (1989). *Creative people at work: Twelve cognitive case studies.* New York: Oxford University Press.

Wallas, G. (1926). *The art of thought.* New York: Harcourt Brace Jovanovich.

Weisberg, R. W., & Alba, J. W. (1981). An examination of the alleged role of "fixation" in the solution of several "insight" problems. *Journal of Experimental Psychology: General, 110*, 169-192.

10

The Creative Society: Genius vis-à-vis the Zeitgeist

Dean Keith Simonton

Sigmund Freud, Albert Einstein, Pablo Picasso, Igor Stravinsky, T.S. Eliot, Martha Graham, and Mahatma Gandhi: These are the seven figures that Gardner (1993) chose to examine in his *Creating Minds*. By a detailed study of their lives and thoughts, he hoped to fathom the "anatomy of creativity." An implicit assumption of this fascinating inquiry is that creativity is an event or process that takes place inside an individual's head. Some personalities demonstrate creativity, and others do not, but the locus of a creative idea lies within the confines of a single cranium. Of course, there is absolutely nothing unusual about this assumption; it is shared by most of the researchers who study creativity. Indeed, this postulate is as old as the behavioral sciences. The same supposition is found in Galton's (1869) *Hereditary Genius*, the first empirical study of exceptional creativity (Simonton, 1991b).

Nonetheless, increasingly more psychologists are beginning to realize that this position may not be completely justified. To a very large degree, creativity involves interpersonal and sociocultural processes as well (e.g., Amabile, 1983; Csikszentmihaly, 1990; Harrington, 1990). Therefore, to focus exclusively on the individual as the unit of analysis is to succumb to the error of psychological reductionism. Needless to say, colleagues in the social sciences have been accusing psychologists of this sin for some time. Sociologists and anthropologists, in particular, have frequently suggested that the single personality has little if any causal role in the origination of creative ideas. An excellent example is found in the work of Kroeber (1944), whose *Configurations of Culture Growth* represented a direct attack on Galton's (1869) individualistic theory of genius. Kroeber displayed massive amounts of data showing that eminent creators cluster in a fashion not easily explained on the basis of purely psychological principles. Rather than individual genius, we should speak of Golden and Silver Ages, as well as Dark Ages in which significant creativity altogether vanished from a civilization (see also Schneider, 1937; Sorokin & Merton, 1935). Thus, rather than discuss Gardner's seven minds, we might learn more about the creative process if we scrutinized representative eras of creative greatness. Among the many exemplars of the "creative society" we may cite Classical Greece, Augustine Rome, Gupta India, Tang Dynasty China, Heian Japan, Renaissance Italy, and Spain's Golden Century.

In this chapter I review some of the central empirical findings that document a societal-level perspective on creativity. Afterward, I discuss some of the implications of these findings for the psychological understanding of creativity. Are the psychologist's inquiries still justified or should investigators curious about creativity change careers and become anthropologists or sociologists?

EMPIRICAL FINDINGS

The first serious attempt to explain the "configurations of culture growth" documented by Kroeber (1944) was that of Gray (1958, 1961, 1966). He proposed an *epicyclical model* in which ups and downs in political, social, cultural, and economic development were superimposed on top of each other. Genius then tended to cluster in those times and places where the peaks of the cycles coincided. To his credit, Gray actually tried to prove this theory by gathering data on Greco-Roman and Western civilizations. Unfortunately, both his analysis and his hypothesis suffer from problems too numerable to cite here (see Barber, 1981; Kroeber, 1958; Simonton, 1981; Taagepera & Colby, 1979). Even so, one fundamental premise of Gray's theory has been well documented: The rise and fall in creative activity tends to correspond to fluctuations in systematic forces (see also Kavolis, 1966). Let me provide examples from the realms of politics, ideology, economics, and culture (for more details and discussion, see Simonton, 1984c, 1994).

Politics

Creative personalities may or may not be interested in politics, but they cannot escape its influence, especially when the political world is shaken by violence. The most obvious example is war. Commentators on history have often speculated on the detrimental impact of warfare on creative activities (e.g., Norling, 1970). Although some investigators have found no such relationship (Naroll et al., 1971; Simonton, 1976b), others have identified a significant negative relationship between creativity and war so long as the proper analytical precautions are taken (Price, 1978; Simonton, 1976e, 1980a). The main precautions are twofold. First, we must focus on the output of creative products per year rather than creators per generation. This fine-grain analysis is needed because the impact of war on creative activities is transient. Warfare will temporary suppress creativity, but productivity will return to prewar levels when peace ends the violence (see Simonton, 1983, 1986e). Second, we must carefully distinguish between different types of war. In particular, violent conflicts between nation states exhibit the most consistent and powerful negative influence on creative activity (see, e.g., Simonton, 1980a). World Wars I and II both exemplify the adverse impact of such political circumstances. Contrary to common belief, these conflicts even suppressed the overall production of technological advances.

What about internal violence, such as revolutions, revolts, coups d'etat, assassinations, and the like? Here the picture is more complicated. To begin with, the impact of these home-grown events tends to be delayed but also more long-lasting. That happens because these happenings serve as developmental experiences that act on the growing talent during adolescence and early adulthood (Simonton, 1984b). Thus, their effects will not materialize for about 20 years, but when they do so they will endure for an entire generation. In addition, just as we had to do in the case of international war, we must distinguish different types of intranational conflict because they will have contrary effects (Simonton, 1990).

On the one hand, there are those instances of internal political violence that are symptomatic of severe instability, even anarchy. Included in this category are coups d'etat, military revolts, internecine dynastic conflicts, assassinations, and other events that show that matters are ill among members of the power elite. The political system does not support stable transitions of power or peaceful reconciliation of policy differences. These occasions have a detrimental effect on the development of creative talent in those domains that emphasize the logical and linear presentation of ideas (Simonton, 1975c, 1976f). In concrete terms, 20 years after a civilization area has seen a surfeit of such untoward events, there appears a conspicuous drop in the number of distinguished scientists, philosophers, writers, and composers. The only major domain of creativity not so damaged are the visual arts, such as sculpture and painting.

On the other hand, there exist other violent happenings that directly involve the common people, even the powerless. These are the rebellions, revolts, and revolutions that see the masses marching the streets manning barricades or roaming the countryside carrying pitchforks. Such civil disturbances can have a positive impact on creative development in all principal areas of achievement (Simonton, 1975c, 1976g). That is, two decades after we see such a rampage, we are likely to see an increase in the number of notable creators who grace a particular generation. This effect is especially strong when the civil disturbances are directed against large imperial states that rule over a multiethnic, polyglot citizenry (Simonton, 1975c, 1976d). This is because such empires tend to suppress the cultural diversity of its subject peoples by imposing a more homogeneous, "official" language and mores. It is very difficult if not impossible for suppressed nationalities to exhibit their full creative potential under these circumstances (Kroeber, 1944; Naroll et al., 1971; Toynbee, 1946). This relationship is made explicit in the "Danilevsky law," which claims that "In order for civilization of a potentially creative group to be conceived and developed, the group and its subgroups must be politically independent" (Sorokin, 1947/1969, p. 543). Consequently, many nationalities often attain a high point in their creativity after their liberation from foreign rule.

These examples in no way exhaust the connections that have been observed between the political world and creative expression (see also Kavolis, 1963; Kuo, 1986, 1988). However, these illustrations suffice to show that the creative society appears under a set of distinctive political conditions.

Ideology

An issue sometimes closely connected to politics is the role that the prevailing ideology has on the appearance of significant creativity. By "ideology" we mean all comprehensive belief systems, whether they be religious, philosophical, or political. I say that these two issues are related because the data show that political circumstances can both cause and be a consequence of the ideological systems society's favor at a particular time (Simonton, 1976g). Whatever the specific linkage, the ideology that rules a society also decides the fate of creativity in that society. I offer two illustrations:

1. Pitirim Sorokin (1937-41), a sociologist, proposed an ambitious theory that explicated the history of civilization in terms of *culture mentalities*. These modal personalities are essentially coherent systems of beliefs about the nature of reality, the basis of knowledge, the criteria of ethical decisions, and the place of the individual vis-à-vis society. According to Sorokin, there are two principal but contrary mentalities. On the one hand, the *Sensate* personality believes that reality is fundamentally materialistic, deterministic, and incessantly changing, that we know the world through our sense organs, that the pleasure principle provides the basis for all morality, and that the individual has primacy over the group. On the other hand, the *Ideational* personality maintains that reality is at root spiritual and eternal, with a provision for human free will, that knowledge is acquired through reason or revelation, that abstract and universal moral laws govern ethical behavior, and that the individual is irretrievably embedded in the group. Sorokin argued that the prevailing culture mentality dictated the amount and type of creativity that would appear in a given era. However, the coming and going of these mentalities takes place in massive cyclical movements (see also Klingemann, Mohler, & Weber, 1982). Therefore, creative activity in certain fields should also exhibit a parallel pattern. This is indeed the case (Simonton, 1976c). For instance, scientific endeavors are more active when a Sensate ideology prevails, whereas humanistic endeavors are more prominent under an Ideational zeitgeist. Hence, the number of creators representing certain domains of achievement can shrink to zero if the times are dominated by a hostile ideology.

2. The preceding studies were conducted using data for European civilizations from ancient times to the present day. Nevertheless, comparable results have been found for non-European cultures as well. For example, one inquiry looked at the impact of certain belief systems across over 2,000 years of Japanese history (Simonton, 1992a). One such system is militarism, which subordinates all societal values to the cult of the warrior, as epitomized by the ethos of the samurai. Another system is Confucianism, which advocates a strongly moralistic and hierarchical view of the world, politics, and social relationships. To a large extent again, the quantity and quality of creativity in a given period of Japanese civilization was determined by the fluctuations in these ideologies. Of special interest are the consequences for female talent. Because Confucianism places women at the bottom of the social hierarchy, this belief system discouraged the appearance of eminent Japanese women. In addition, because the machismo cult of militarism inhibits creative activity in those areas where women have the most opportunities for achievement, such as in literature, the net effect of these circumstances is also negative.

These two illustrations do not cover all the ways that ideology can affect the manifestation of creativity. For example, the amount of creative activity displayed by a generation is also encouraged by the very existence of ideological diversity (Simonton, 1976d). In other words, when a society is characterized by multiple belief systems engaged in controversy and debate, each vying for the allegiance of a civilization's denizens, creativity has more latitude for growth. Or as Mao Zedong preached but could not practice: "Letting a hundred flowers blossom and a hundred schools of thought contend is the policy for promoting the progress in the arts and the sciences."

Economics

It is often suggested that economic prosperity provides the foundation for creativity (Davies, 1969; McClelland, 1961; Norling, 1970; Rainoff, 1929). People who live in squalor are certainly not going to have the time or the resources to create enduring monuments. For instance, one economist speculated that "art and literature flourish in a rising economy, but they wither and perish in one that declines" (Davis, 1941, p. 572). Even if the empirical research on this question is not huge by any means, what data have been collected support this conjecture at least partially (e.g., Schmookler, 1966). However, the precise nature of the relationship is very complex. Observe the following three points:

1. Insofar as the economy is sufficient to support technological innovations, those advances can then encourage both economic and population growth, which in turn can stimulate further technological achievements (see, e.g., Simon & Sullivan, 1989; Taagepera, 1976, 1979). The upshot is an upward spiral, even a wild explosion in technological growth—and in environmental exploitation as well. In this dynamic situation it is impossible to separate out cause and effect.

2. The economy often operates as a necessary but not sufficient foundation for societal creativity. The economic system must attain a certain level of productivity and complexity to support more specialized activities (Carneiro, 1970), but beyond a certain point further growth in economic prosperity may not translate into additional output of creators or creative products. The Greeks under the Byzantine Empire enjoyed greater material wealth than those under the hegemony of Athens, but their respective creative contributions to world civilization do not stand comparison. In fact, as a society grows in wealth, its creativity may manifest a curvilinear inverted-U function (Kavolis, 1964). Initial increases in property will see growths in creativity, but after a certain point the economy may expand while creativity decays.

3. Economic declines may have effects that are not simply the inversion of economic expansions. When material conditions improve, people's expectations regarding what constitutes a tolerable standard of living grows proportionately. Therefore, when the economy turns sour, and enters a state of deep recession or depression, these heightened baselines are violated. The political result is often riot, revolt, or revolution (Davies, 1962). From our perspective, however, the most powerful repercussion may be what happens to the creative enterprise. When living standards drastically decline, people feel threatened, as if they are under a state of siege. These threatening conditions then favor a shift in the culture mentality toward a more dogmatic or authoritarian personality (Doty, Peterson, & Winter, 1991; Sales, 1973). This shift has ramifications throughout society concerning which forms of creativity receive encouragement and which are discouraged. The consequence is more intense creative activity in astrology, the occult, and parapsychology, but decreased creative activity in more introspective undertakings, such as psychoanalysis (see Doty et al., 1991; McCann & Stewin, 1984; Padgett & Jorgenson, 1982; Sales, 1973).

Culture

Judging from the findings in the preceding section, it is evident that Karl Marx was not totally off base when he claimed that creative expression reflects the underlying economic conditions of a society (see also Dressler & Robbins, 1975; Martindale, 1976), yet Marx overstated this "reflectionist" position. Creativity within a society is just as much governed by events internal to a creative endeavor. Without acknowledgement of this "internalist" perspective, it is impossible to appreciate fully the creative productivity observed in a given era.

At the beginning of this chapter I mentioned Kroeber's (1944) demonstration of cultural configurations—the clustering of creativity into periods of high activity separated by eras of minimal output. Interestingly, Kroeber's own explanation for this phenomenon was internalist. In essence, creativity cannot emerge from nothing, but instead each generation must build on the accomplishments of the preceding generation. However, eventually a point is reached where the initial cultural pattern underlying the developing tradition becomes exhausted. The society then enters a phase of creative decadence until activity becomes nominal. To illustrate this position, Kroeber quoted from an obscure Roman historian, Velleius Paterculus, who ages ago said that:

> Genius is fostered by emulation, and it is now envy, now admiration, which enkindles imitation, and, in the nature of things, that which is

cultivated with the highest zeal advances to the highest perfection; but it is difficult to continue at the point of perfection, and naturally that which cannot advance must recede. And as in the beginning we are fired with the ambition to overtake those whom we regard as leaders, so when we have despaired of being able to either to surpass or even to equal them, our zeal wanes with our hope; it ceases to follow what it cannot overtake, and abandoning the old field as though pre-empted, it seeks a new one. (p. 19)

This hypothesis has been thoroughly investigated and validated in a series of studies spanning over a decade (e.g., Simonton, 1975a, 1975c, 1978c, 1988b). Using generational time-series analysis (Simonton, 1984b), these inquiries show that the number of creators active in one generation is a positive function of the number in the preceding generation. The result is a distinctive pattern fluctuations highly characteristic of autoregressive time series (cf. Sheldon, 1979, 1980). Of course, these investigations all looked at aggregated data—counts of creators per unit of time—rather than individual-level data, but the same conclusions appear if we switch from the macro to the micro level (e.g., Simonton, 1977a, 1984a, 1992b, 1992c; Walberg, Rasher, & Parkerson, 1980). The growth of a young talent appears encouraged by the availability of role models and mentors who are active in the same discipline where eminence is later achieved in maturity (for further complexities, see Simonton, 1976f, 1977a, 1994).

Actually, the impact of this general level of activity doubled in adulthood. If a talent grows up in an era that broadly nurtures talents of the same type, then that developing talent, on entering maturity, will find himself or herself surrounded by many other talents engaged in like creative activities. This enables the creator to form a great variety of social relationships. Creators can then become collaborators, associates, correspondents, friends, and intimates, or then can become rivals or competitors. Research indicates that creators who are thus embedded in a rich matrix of discipline-defined interactions are stimulated to reach higher levels of creativity than those who are more isolated from their creative world (Simonton, 1984a, 1992b, 1992c). Hence, a golden age consists of individuals who are not just standing on the shoulders of giants. On the contrary, the creators during those momentous periods are rubbing shoulders to decide who can see the farthest from that vantage point.

The imagery closing the last paragraph obviously alludes to Newton's famous remark, "If I have seen farther than other men, it is by standing on the shoulders of Giants." Newton himself stood on the shoulders of such greats as Copernicus, Descartes, and Galileo. Just as important was the relationships he established with a whole host of distinguished contemporaries—names like Jean Bernoulli, Bradley,

DeMoivre, Flamsteed, Gregory, Halley, Hooke, Leibniz, Locke, MacLaurin, Römer, Taylor, Wallis, and Wren. These interactions were sometimes friendly and collaborative, sometimes hostile and competitive, and sometimes even both, but the fact remains that Newton was not an isolate. In this sense, Wordsworth was wrong when he said that Newton was "a mind forever/ Voyaging through strange seas of thought alone." He may have placed himself at the apex of the scientific revolution, but he stood atop a broad pyramid, not a narrow tower.

DISCUSSION

The foregoing overview has omitted many fascinating findings about the creative society. The most important omission stems from the fact that we have focused largely on quantitative changes in aggregate creative activity; yet there exists a vast amount of research showing how qualitative changes occur at the societal level as well. These changes concern such things as the content of philosophical systems (Klingemann et al., 1982; Simonton, 1975c, 1976c, 1976g), the specific nature of scientific discoveries or technological inventions (Simonton, 1975b, 1976e), and the styles that predominate in the arts (Hasenfus, Martindale, & Birnbaum, 1983; Martindale, 1990; Sorokin, 1937-41), whether the creative products be visual (Dressler & Robbins, 1975; Lowe & Lowe, 1982; Martindale, 1986; Simonton, 1977b), literary (Martindale, 1975; Simonton, 1983, 1986e; Winter, 1973), or musical (Cerulo, 1984, 1988, 1989; Martindale & Uemura, 1983; Peterson & Berger, 1975; Simonton, 1980b, 1986a, 1987c). Hence, it is not just the amount of creativity that is at the mercy of societal forces: Even the particular form that creativity takes may be greatly influenced by those same massive forces. So, if we reviewed all of this additional literature it might seem that the individual would assume an ever lesser role as an agent of creativity. Should we then always speak of the zeitgeist rather than genius when discussing the creative landmarks of human civilization? Should all researchers in the area of creativity become sociologists or anthropologists after all?

No! These rhetorical questions take the argument too far. In fact, I want to close this chapter by discussing how the psychologist still is in business despite all the evidence on behalf of the creative society. We must be ever wary of replacing a crude psychological reductionism by an equally ill-advised sociological reductionism. To underline this warning, I wish to turn to five issues that allow us to highlight the importance of the individual as an agent of creativity within the creative society. These concern multiple contributions, aggregate data, cultural norms, individual differences, and psychological processes.

1. *Multiple contributions.* One of the most amazing events in the history of science and technology is the occurrence of multiples. Multiples occur whenever two or more scientists (or inventors) independently come up with the same discovery (or invention)—and often simultaneously, to boot. Examples of this curious event include the creation of the calculus by Newton and Leibniz, the calculation of Neptune's orbit by Adams and Leverrier, the theory of evolution by natural selection by Darwin and Wallace, the discovery of Mendelian genetics by Mendel, Tchermak, DeVries, and Correns, the invention of the telephone by Bell and Gray, and the labeling theory of emotion by James and Lange. Hundreds of these episodes have been documented in the history of science and technology, so we are talking here about a very real phenomenon (Merton, 1961a; Ogburn & Thomas, 1922; Simonton, 1979). The received tradition on these events is that they show how the individual is essentially irrelevant to scientific or technological advance (see Brannigan, 1981; Kroeber, 1917; Lamb & Easton, 1984; Merton, 1961a, 1961b). Instead, at a certain point in history a particular discovery or invention becomes absolutely inevitable; the idea is "in the air" for anyone to pick, regardless of talent or even training. Sociologists and anthropologists have therefore pounced on multiples as positive proof that we do not need to discuss psychological processes to understand creativity. Thus, if this argument true, current attempts to construct cognitive models of scientific creativity, such as the recent work on "discovery programs" (e.g., Langley, Simon, Bradshaw, & Zythow, 1987; Shrager & Langley, 1990), would be absolutely pointless.

This zeitgeist interpretation is widely accepted, even within psychology (Simonton, 1995). Yet there is a catch: It fails to survive empirical scrutiny (Constant, 1978; Patinkin, 1983; Schmookler, 1966). In the first place, the multiples phenomenon primarily reflects the influence of chance events rather than bona fide sociocultural determinism (Price, 1963; Simonton, 1978b, 1986c, 1986d, 1986f; cf. Brannigan & Wanner, 1983a, 1983b). More important, theoretical models that make more allowance for the participation of scientific genius do a better job of explaining the details of the phenomenon (Simonton, 1987b). Specifically, I have shown how the occurrence of multiples can be explicated in terms of my chance-configuration theory of creativity, which outlines an inherently socio-psychological model (Simonton, 1988c). Hence, the traditional attempt to use this phenomenon to bolster sociological reductionism may be doomed. This illustrates the danger of pushing an argument too far, however plausible it may appear from a superficial inspection.

2. *Cultural norms.* I already noted that there are qualitative changes as well as quantitative changes associated with the coming and

going of the creative society. Unfortunately, these two different types of sociocultural fluctuations can become confounded, leading to some false conclusions about the level of creativity displayed by individuals within a time and place. For an illustration, let us return to Sorokin's (1937-41) of cyclical shifts in predominant culture mentalities. Ideational personalities differ from Sensate personalities in more than just the type of creativity they engaged in: Their mentality also determines the attitude they have toward personal versus collective identity in assigning credit for creative acts. If the individual human being is but an ephemeral and puny piece of flesh vis-à-vis the eternity of the faith and the collectivity of the faithful, no motive exists for placing an identifying signature on a manuscript, painting, sculpture, or other creative product. It is for this reason, Sorokin argued, that so few names come down to us from the so-called "Dark Ages" of Western European history. Yet this era was far from dark. It was replete with major innovations in thought, art, architecture, and music, as the illuminated manuscripts, Romanesque cathedrals, and Gregorian chants amply testify. It is only when we wish to list the names of creators that this period may appear deficient; and only a Sensate personality would have such a preoccupation.

I am not saying that no decline in creativity occurred during the Dark Ages. I am only claiming that we must be careful to tease out the relative proportions of quantitative and qualitative changes in the forms that creativity takes. We must take special care not to brand all Ideational cultures as noncreative societies. The creativity may be just as prominent at the individual level, but that creativity, no matter how personal, makes no selfish claims for individuality.

3. *Aggregate data.* The preceding comment raised a methodological issue that can sometimes lead our interpretations astray. Here is another illustration: We must always weigh the fact that many studies of the creative society tabulate large quantities of individuals into categories defined by period and civilization (e.g., Gray, 1958, 1966; Kroeber, 1944; Naroll et al., 1971; Simonton, 1975c, 1988b; Sorokin, 1937-41). In generational time-series analyses, for example, lists of creators are tallied into 20-year periods according to their estimated acme or floruit (Simonton, 1984b). The statistics that result, therefore, describe aggregate data only. Inferences drawn from these data can be extended to the individual level only with considerable caution (Hannan, 1971). For example, one fascinating study of philosophical genius in Chinese civilization found an interesting paradox (Kuo, 1986). Even if intellectual creativity may flourish during troubled times, those traumatic events may not impinge directly on the lives of the most distinguished thinkers of the

era. On the contrary, those phenomenal intellects tend to reside in pockets of relative tranquility (see also Kuo, 1988). This parallels findings for philosophical creativity in Western civilization (Simonton, 1976f). Although the number of important thinkers in a given generation is a positive function of the number in the preceding generation, the differential fame of the philosophers shows an inverse effect. The greatest philosophers often arise when there occurs a momentary lapse in intellectual activity.

There exists another individual-level reality that is often obscured whenever we aggregate the data across so many lives. When a culture or tradition undergoes a fluorescence, it does not always mean that the credit belongs to that social unit alone. Many of the central players in the burst of creativity will have roots in alien cultures or traditions. A classic example is the overrepresentation of Jews among the notable creators of modern Western civilization (Arieti, 1976; Hayes, 1989, Table 4; Veblin, 1919). As a Middle Eastern culture transplanted in a predominantly Christian society, Jews received nurturance from more than one ethnic source. Similarly, first- and second-generation immigrants are also conspicuous contributors to the creative resurgence of many societies, again illustrating how no one sociocultural system can claim all the causal applause (e.g., Goertzel, Goertzel, & Goertzel, 1978; Helson & Crutchfield, 1970; Park, 1928). Finally, and at a more restricted level of operation, there is evidence that many key participants in the creative activity of one discipline may owe their intellectual heritage to some other discipline (Hudson & Jacot, 1986; Kuhn, 1970; Simonton, 1984d). As a consequence, we cannot always argue that the development of a creative endeavor is solely determined by some internal impetus. Too often the stimulus comes from outsiders whose contributions could not have been anticipated simply from the maturational logic of the field or culture. Indeed, given the capriciousness by which intellects sometimes switched domains, we are often led to the conclusion that chance events can deflect history along new paths. Maybe the one definite conclusion we can draw from these considerations is that the creative society is one that features highly permeable boundaries so creators of widely varying ethnic or professional backgrounds can engage in fruitful cross-fertilization.

4. *Individual differences.* Let us accept the argument that creative geniuses tend to come and go in grand sociocultural cycles—that they cluster in Golden Ages separated by periods of comparative inactivity. Does that fact imply that the individual is irrelevant? Not at all! For when we place a microscope over these big cultural movements we observe a very interesting reality (cf. Gray, 1958, 1966; Kroeber, 1944; Price, 1963; Simonton, 1988b). During eras of decadence and decay, not only are there fewer creators, there

are also fewer creators of the highest quality. All activity is mediocre. In contrast, when a full-fledged creative society emerges, we not only see more total creators, we also see more all-time greats of human civilization. In noncreative times and places, every creator is obscure, whereas in creative times and places the creators range from the obscure to the illustrious. In Greek philosophy, for example, the same age that produced Aristotle also produced Xenocrates and dozens of other also-rans.

Hence, within a creative society, individual differences in achievement actually expand. The creativity of individuals becomes more heterogeneous rather than more homogeneous, as mediocrity rubs shoulders with true genius. However, notice the paradox here. If creative output is entirely dictated by the sociocultural system, then how can it account for these individual differences? After all, the creators active during a particular high point of cultural activity emerged under the same general sociocultural conditions. Therefore, something else must account for this substantial cross-sectional variation in creative productivity and influence. Furthermore, whatever is entailed by this "something else," it must be characteristic of individuals rather than societies. The individual variation in creative accomplishments ultimately must reflect variation across individuals on the attributes responsible for differential success. Although some of the factors operating here may be sociological in nature—such as socioeconomic class, gender, or ethnicity—other factors may involve cognitive abilities, motivational disposition, and other variables of tremendous intrinsic interest to psychologists. This possibility brings us to the last point.

5. *Psychological variables.* We must never forget the bottom line: Individuals create; societies don't. Beethoven composed the Fifth Symphony, not the Viennese musical tradition; Newton wrote *Principia Mathematica*, not the Scientific Revolution. Moreover, even when we consider a collective masterpiece such as a Gothic cathedral or a Mogul mausoleum, we a still discussing the product of many singular minds—the unnamed artisans whose creativity is no less personal for being anonymous. Hence, a fine-grained analysis of the creative society still mandates scrutiny of what is happening at the psychological level. What are the key variables that guide the creative process in the production of novel ideas? What are the psychological factors that determine individual differences in the magnitude of creative achievement?

The answers to questions like these can originate from three major perspectives, all of which are inherently psychological in nature. First, we can inquire about how cross-sectional variation in psychological variables relates to the quantity and quality of creative work that individuals produce.

The variables that have received the most attention are intelligence, motivation, and various personality traits (e.g., Cattell, 1963; Cox, 1926; Knapp, 1962; Simonton, 1976a, 1991a; Thorndike, 1950). Second, we can examine how the realization of individual creativity develops and grows over the life span. This examination includes both studies of the early developmental experiences that contribute to the emergence of creative talent as well as studies of the adulthood conditions that influence a creator's career path (Goertzel & Goertzel, 1962; Howe, 1982; Simonton, 1978a, 1986b, 1987a). An instance of the former is a variable like birth order (e.g., Ellis, 1926; Galton, 1874; Roe, 1952), whereas an instance of the latter is a variable like personal age (e.g., Hull, Tessner, & Diamond, 1978; Lehman, 1953; Simonton, 1988a; Yuasa, 1974). Both birth order and age are attributes that belong to individuals, not groups. Third and last, we can consider the social psychology of creativity, which focuses on how the social context, interpersonal relationships, and diverse social norms and values affect creative performance. These social factors would articulate with both individual differences and longitudinal changes within single creative personalities (e.g., Goldstein, 1979; Simonton, 1984a, 1992b, 1992c).

So what conclusions can we draw from the review and discussion contained in this chapter? It should be apparent by now that the ever-growing literature on the creative society does not make the psychological study of creativity meaningless. A complete understanding of the phenomenon still requires a detailed appreciation of what is happening within single creators. Psychological processes and variables define the atoms that compose the larger societal mix behind innovative activity. The life and works of Phidias, Lucretius, Kālidāsa, Li Bo, Murasaki, Michelangelo, and Cervantes helped define the Golden Ages of which they were the supreme stars.

At the same time, it should be evident that the findings about the creative society demand that psychologists adopt a wider perspective in their theorizing and data collection. We cannot fully comprehend the etiology of creativity without incorporating what we know about how sociocultural forces impinge on the creative mind and product. The chemical analogy may be a good one: All compounds, no matter how complex, are ultimately made up of elements; However, the properties belonging to those elements are only grasped through the attributes of the compounds they form. In the same way, we cannot capture the significance of a Freud, Einstein, Picasso, Stravinsky, Eliot, Graham, or Gandhi without scrutinizing the zeitgeist and ortgeist of which they are elements.

REFERENCES

Amabile, T. M. (1983). *The social psychology of creativity.* New York: Springer-Verlag.

Arieti, S. (1976). *Creativity: The magic synthesis.* New York: Basic Books.

Barber, R. J. (1981). Comments on the quantitative study of creativity in Western civilization. *American Anthropologist, 83,* 143-144.

Brannigan, A. (1981). *The social basis of scientific discoveries.* Cambridge, England: Cambridge University Press.

Brannigan, A., & Wanner, R. A. (1983a). Historical distributions of multiple discoveries and theories of scientific change. *Social Studies of Science, 13,* 417-435.

Brannigan, A., & Wanner, R. A. (1983b). Multiple discoveries in science: A test of the communication theory. *Canadian Journal of Sociology, 8,* 135-151.

Carneiro, R. L. (1970). Scale analysis, evolutionary sequences, and the rating of cultures. In R. Naroll & R. Cohn (Eds.), *A handbook of method in cultural anthropology* (pp. 834-871). New York: Natural History Press.

Cattell, R. B. (1963). The personality and motivation of the researcher from measurements of contemporaries and from biography. In C. W. Taylor & F. Barron (Eds.), *Scientific creativity: Its recognition and development* (pp. 119-131). New York: Wiley.

Cerulo, K. A. (1984). Social disruption and its effects on music: An empirical analysis. *Social Forces, 62,* 885-904.

Cerulo, K. A. (1988). Analyzing cultural products: A new method of measurement. *Social Science Research, 17,* 317-352.

Cerulo, K. A. (1989). Variations in musical syntax: Patterns of measurement. *Communication Research, 16,* 204-235.

Constant, E. W., II (1978). On the diversity of coevolution of technological multiples: Steam turbines and Pelton water wheels. *Social Studies of Science, 8,* 183-210.

Cox, C. (1926). *The early mental traits of three hundred geniuses.* Stanford, CA: Stanford University Press.

Csikszentmihaly, M. (1990). The domain of creativity. In M. A. Runco & R. S. Albert (Eds.), *Theories of creativity* (pp. 190-212). Newbury Park, CA: Sage.

Davies, E. (1969, November). This is the way Crete went—Not with a bang but a simper. *Psychology Today,* pp. 43-47.

Davies, J. C. (1962). Toward a theory of revolution. *American Sociological Review, 27,* 5-19.

Davis, H. T. (1941). *The analysis of economic time series.* Bloomington, IN: Principia Press.

Doty, R. M., Peterson, B. E., & Winter, D. G. (1991). Threat and authoritarianism in the United States, 1978-1987. *Journal of Personality and Social Psychology, 61,* 629-640.

Dressler, W. W., & Robbins, M. C. (1975). Art styles, social stratification, and cognition: An analysis of Greek vase painting. *American Ethnologist, 2,* 427-434.

Ellis, H. (1926). *A study of British genius* (rev. ed.). Boston: Houghton Mifflin.

Galton, F. (1869). *Hereditary genius: An inquiry into its laws and consequences.* London: Macmillan.

Galton, F. (1874). *English men of science: Their nature and nurture.* London: Macmillan.

Gardner, H. (1993). *Creating minds: An anatomy of creativity seen through the lives of Freud, Einstein, Picasso, Stravinsky, Eliot, Graham, and Gandhi.* New York: Basic Books.

Goertzel, M. G., Goertzel, V., & Goertzel, T. G. (1978). *300 eminent personalities: A psychosocial analysis of the famous.* San Francisco: Jossey-Bass.

Goertzel, V., & Goertzel, M. G. (1962). *Cradles of eminence.* Boston: Little, Brown.

Goldstein, E. (1979). Effect of same-sex and cross-sex role models on the subsequent academic productivity of scholars. *American Psychologist, 34,* 407-410.

Gray, C. E. (1958). An analysis of Graeco-Roman development: The epicyclical evolution of Graeco-Roman civilization. *American Anthropologist, 60,* 13-31.

Gray, C. E. (1961). An epicyclical model for Western civilization. *American Anthropologist, 63,* 1014-1037.

Gray, C. E. (1966). A measurement of creativity in Western civilization. *American Anthropologist, 68,* 1384-1417

Hannan, M. T. (1971). Problems of aggregation. In H. M. Blalock (Ed.), *Causal models in the social sciences* (pp. 473-508). Chicago: Aldine-Atherton.

Harrington, D. M. (1990). The ecology of human creativity: A psychological perspective. In M. A. Runco & R. S. Albert (Eds.), *Theories of creativity* (pp. 143-169). Newbury Park, CA: Sage.

Hasenfus, N., Martindale, C., & Birnbaum, D. (1983). Psychological reality of cross-media artistic styles. Journal of Experimental Psychology: *Human Perception and Performance, 9,* 841-863.

Hayes, J. R. (1989). *The complete problem solver* (2nd ed.). Hillsdale, NJ: Erlbaum.

Helson, R., & Crutchfield, R. S. (1970). Mathematicians: The creative researcher and the average Ph.D. *Journal of Consulting and Clinical Psychology, 34,* 250-257.

Howe, M. J. A. (1982). Biographical evidence and the development of outstanding individuals. *American Psychologist, 37,* 1071-1081.

Hudson, L., & Jacot, B. (1986). The outsider in science. In C. Bagley & G. K. Verma (Eds.), *Personality, cognition and values* (pp. 3-23). London: Macmillan.

Hull, D. L., Tessner, P. D., & Diamond, A. M. (1978). Planck's principle: Do younger scientists accept new scientific ideas with greater alacrity than older scientists? *Science, 202,* 717-723.

Kavolis, V. (1963). Political dynamics and artistic creativity. *Sociology and Social Research, 49,* 412-424.

Kavolis, V. (1964). Economic correlates of artistic creativity. *American Journal of Sociology, 70,* 332-341.

Kavolis, V. (1966). Community dynamics and artistic creativity. *American Sociological Review, 31,* 208-217.

Klingemann, H.-D., Mohler, P. P., & Weber, R. P. (1982). Cultural indicators based on content analysis: A secondary analysis of Sorokin's data on fluctuations of systems of truth. *Quality and Quantity, 16,* 1-18.

Knapp, R. H. (1962). A factor analysis of Thorndike's ratings of eminent men. *Journal of Social Psychology, 56,* 67-71.

Kroeber, A. L. (1917). The superorganic. *American Anthropologist, 19,* 163-214.

Kroeber, A. L. (1944). *Configurations of culture growth.* Berkeley: University of California Press.

Kroeber, A. L. (1958). Gray's epicyclical evolution. *American Anthropologist, 60,* 31-38.

Kuhn, T. S. (1970). *The structure of scientific revolutions* (2nd ed.). Chicago: University of Chicago Press.

Kuo, Y. (1986). The growth and decline of Chinese philosophical genius. *Chinese Journal of Psychology, 28,* 81-91.

Kuo, Y. (1988). The social psychology of Chinese philosophical creativity: A critical synthesis. *Social Epistemology, 2,* 283-295.

Lamb, D., & Easton, S. M. (1984). *Multiple discovery.* England: Avebury.

Langley, P., Simon, H. A., Bradshaw, G. L., & Zythow, J. M. (1987). *Scientific discovery.* Cambridge, MA: MIT Press.

Lehman, H. C. (1953). *Age and achievement.* Princeton, NJ: Princeton University Press.

Lowe, J. W. G., & Lowe, E. D. (1982). Cultural pattern and process: A study of stylistic change in women's dress. *American Anthropologist, 84*, 521-544.

Martindale, C. (1975). *Romantic progression: The psychology of literary history.* Washington, DC: Hemisphere.

Martindale, C. (1976). Primitive mentality and the relationship between art and society. *Scientific Aesthetics, 1*, 5-18.

Martindale, C. (1986). The evolution of Italian painting: A quantitative investigation of trends in style and content from late Gothic to the Rococo period. *Leonardo, 19*, 217-222.

Martindale, C. (1990). *The clockwork muse: The predictability of artistic styles.* New York: Basic Books.

Martindale, C., & Uemura, A. (1983). Stylistic evolution in European music. *Leonardo, 16*, 225-228.

McCann, S. J. H., & Stewin, L. L. (1984). Environmental threat and parapsychological contributions to the psychological literature. *Journal of Social Psychology, 122*, 227-235.

McClelland, D. C. (1961). *The achieving society.* New York: Van Nostrand.

Merton, R. K. (1961a). The role of genius in scientific advance. *New Scientist, 12*, 306-308.

Merton, R. K. (1961b). Singletons and multiples in scientific discovery: A chapter in the sociology of science. *Proceedings of the American Philosophical Society, 105*, 470-486.

Naroll, R., Benjamin, E. C., Fohl, F. K., Fried, M. J., Hildreth, R. E., & Schaefer, J. M. (1971). Creativity: A cross-historical pilot survey. *Journal of Cross-Cultural Psychology, 2*, 181-188.

Norling, B. (1970). *Timeless problems in history.* Notre Dame, IN: Notre Dame Press.

Ogburn, W. K., & Thomas, D. (1922). Are inventions inevitable? A note on social evolution. *Political Science Quarterly, 37*, 83-93.

Padgett, V., & Jorgenson, D. O. (1982). Superstition and economic threat: Germany 1918-1940. *Personality and Social Psychology Bulletin, 8*, 736-741.

Park, R. E. (1928). Human migration and the marginal man. *American Journal of Sociology, 33*, 881-893.

Patinkin, D. (1983). Multiple discoveries and the central message. *American Journal of Sociology, 89*, 306-323.

Peterson, R. A., & Berger, D. G. (1975). Cycles in symbol production: The case of popular music. *American Sociological Review, 40*, 158-173.

Price, D. (1963). *Little science, big science.* New York: Columbia University Press.

Price, D. (1978). Ups and downs in the pulse of science and technology. In J. Gaston (Ed.), *The sociology of science* (pp. 162-171). San Francisco: Jossey-Bass.

Rainoff, T. J. (1929). Wave-like fluctuations of creative productivity in the development of West-European physics in the eighteenth and nineteenth centuries. *Isis, 12,* 287-319.

Roe, A. (1952). *The making of a scientist.* New York: Dodd, Mead.

Sales, S. M. (1973). Threat as a factor in authoritarianism: An analysis of archival data. *Journal of Personality and Social Psychology, 28,* 44-57.

Schmookler, J. (1966). *Invention and economic growth.* Cambridge, MA: Harvard University Press.

Schneider, J. (1937). The cultural situation as a condition for the achievement of fame. *American Sociological Review, 2,* 480-491.

Sheldon, J. C. (1979). Hierarchical cybernets: A model for the dynamics of high-level learning and cultural change. *Cybernetica, 22,* 179-202.

Sheldon, J. C. (1980). A cybernetic theory of physical science professions: The causes of periodic normal and revolutionary science between 1000 and 1870 A.D. *Scientometrics, 2,* 147-167.

Shrager, J., & Langley, P. (Eds.) (1990). *Computational models of scientific discovery and theory formation.* San Mateo, CA: Kaufmann.

Simon, J. L., & Sullivan, R. J. (1989). Population size, knowledge stock, and other determinants of agricultural publication and patenting: England, 1541-1850. *Explorations in Economic History, 26,* 21-44.

Simonton, D. K. (1975a). Interdisciplinary creativity over historical time: A correlational analysis of generational fluctuations. *Social Behavior and Personality, 3,* 181-188.

Simonton, D. K. (1975b). Invention and discovery among the sciences: A p-technique factor analysis. *Journal of Vocational Behavior, 7,* 275-281.

Simonton, D. K. (1975c). Sociocultural context of individual creativity: A transhistorical time-series analysis. *Journal of Personality and Social Psychology, 32,* 1119-1133.

Simonton, D. K. (1976a). Biographical determinants of achieved eminence: A multivariate approach to the Cox data. *Journal of Personality and Social Psychology, 33,* 218-226.

Simonton, D. K. (1976b). The causal relation between war and scientific discovery: An exploratory cross-national analysis. *Journal of Cross-Cultural Psychology, 7,* 133-144.

Simonton, D. K. (1976c). Do Sorokin's data support his theory?: A study of generational fluctuations in philosophical beliefs. *Journal for the Scientific Study of Religion, 15,* 187-198.

Simonton, D. K. (1976d). Ideological diversity and creativity: A reevaluation of a hypothesis. *Social Behavior and Personality, 4*, 203-207.

Simonton, D. K. (1976e). Interdisciplinary and military determinants of scientific productivity: A cross-lagged correlation analysis. *Journal of Vocational Behavior, 9*, 53-62.

Simonton, D. K. (1976f). Philosophical eminence, beliefs, and zeitgeist: An individual-generational analysis. *Journal of Personality and Social Psychology, 34*, 630-640.

Simonton, D. K. (1976g). The sociopolitical context of philosophical beliefs: A transhistorical causal analysis. *Social Forces, 54*, 513-523.

Simonton, D. K. (1977a). Eminence, creativity, and geographic marginality: A recursive structural equation model. *Journal of Personality and Social Psychology, 35*, 805-816.

Simonton, D. K. (1977b). Women's fashions and war: A quantitative comment. *Social Behavior and Personality, 5*, 285-288.

Simonton, D. K. (1978a). The eminent genius in history: The critical role of creative development. *Gifted Child Quarterly, 22*, 187-195.

Simonton, D. K. (1978b). Independent discovery in science and technology: A closer look at the Poisson distribution. *Social Studies of Science, 8*, 521-532.

Simonton, D. K. (1978c). Intergenerational stimulation, reaction, and polarization: A causal analysis of intellectual history. *Social Behavior and Personality, 6*, 247-251.

Simonton, D. K. (1979). Multiple discovery and invention: Zeitgeist, genius, or chance? *Journal of Personality and Social Psychology, 37*, 1603-1616.

Simonton, D. K. (1980a). Techno-scientific activity and war: A yearly time-series analysis, 1500-1903 A.D. *Scientometrics, 2*, 251-255.

Simonton, D. K. (1980b). Thematic fame, melodic originality, and musical zeitgeist: A biographical and transhistorical content analysis. *Journal of Personality and Social Psychology, 38*, 972-983.

Simonton, D. K. (1981). Creativity in Western civilization: Extrinsic and intrinsic causes. *American Anthropologist, 83*, 628-630.

Simonton, D. K. (1983). Dramatic greatness and content: A quantitative study of 81 Athenian and Shakespearean plays. *Empirical Studies of the Arts, 1*, 109-123.

Simonton, D. K. (1984a). Artistic creativity and interpersonal relationships across and within generations. *Journal of Personality and Social Psychology, 46*, 1273-1286.

Simonton, D. K. (1984b). Generational time-series analysis: A paradigm for studying sociocultural influences. In K. Gergen & M. Gergen (Eds.), *Historical social psychology* (pp. 141-155). Hillsdale, NJ: Erlbaum.

Simonton, D. K. (1984c). *Genius, creativity, and leadership: Historiometric inquiries.* Cambridge, MA: Harvard University Press.

Simonton, D. K. (1984d). Is the marginality effect all that marginal? *Social Studies of Science, 14,* 621-622.

Simonton, D. K. (1986a). Aesthetic success in classical music: A computer analysis of 1935 compositions. *Empirical Studies of the Arts, 4,* 1-17.

Simonton, D. K. (1986b). Biographical typicality, eminence, and achievement style. *Journal of Creative Behavior, 20,* 14-22.

Simonton, D. K. (1986c). Multiple discovery: Some Monte Carlo simulations and Gedanken experiments. *Scientometrics, 9,* 269-280.

Simonton, D. K. (1986d). Multiples, Poisson distributions, and chance: An analysis of the Brannigan-Wanner model. *Scientometrics, 9,* 127-137.

Simonton, D. K. (1986e). Popularity, content, and context in 37 Shakespeare plays. *Poetics, 15,* 493-510.

Simonton, D. K. (1986f). Stochastic models of multiple discovery. *Czechoslovak Journal of Physics, B 36,* 138-141.

Simonton, D. K. (1987a). Developmental antecedents of achieved eminence. *Annals of Child Development, 5,* 131-169.

Simonton, D. K. (1987b). Multiples, chance, genius, creativity, and zeitgeist. In D. N. Jackson & J. P. Rushton (Eds.), *Scientific excellence: Origins and assessment* (pp.98-128). Beverly Hills, CA: Sage Publications.

Simonton, D. K. (1987c). Musical aesthetics and creativity in Beethoven: A computer analysis of 105 compositions. *Empirical Studies of the Arts, 5,* 87-104.

Simonton, D. K. (1988a). Age and outstanding achievement: What do we know after a century of research? *Psychological Bulletin, 104,* 251-267.

Simonton, D. K. (1988b). Galtonian genius, Kroeberian configurations, and emulation: A generational time-series analysis of Chinese civilization. *Journal of Personality and Social Psychology, 55,* 230-238.

Simonton, D. K. (1988c). *Scientific genius: A psychology of science.* Cambridge, England: Cambridge University Press.

Simonton, D. K. (1990). Political pathology and societal creativity. *Creativity Research Journal, 3,* 85-99.

Simonton, D. K. (1991a). Personality correlates of exceptional personal influence: A note on Thorndike's (1950) creators and leaders. *Creativity Research Journal, 4,* 67-78.

Simonton, D. K. (1991b). Latent-variable models of posthumous reputation: A quest for Galton's G. *Journal of Personality and Social Psychology, 60*, 607-619.

Simonton, D. K. (1992a). Gender and genius in Japan: Feminine eminence in masculine culture. *Sex Roles, 27*, 101-119.

Simonton, D. K. (1992b). Leaders of American psychology, 1879-1967: Career development, creative output, and professional achievement. *Journal of Personality and Social Psychology, 62*, 5-17.

Simonton, D. K. (1992c). The social context of career success and course for 2,026 scientists and inventors. *Personality and Social Psychology Bulletin, 18*, 452-463.

Simonton, D. K. (1994). *Greatness: Who makes history and why.* New York: Guilford.

Simonton, D. K. (1995). Behavioral laws in histories of psychology: Psychological science, metascience, and the psychology of science. *Psychological Inquiries, 6*, 89-114.

Sorokin, P. A. (1937-41). *Social and cultural dynamics* (4 vols.). New York: American Book.

Sorokin, P. A. (1969). *Society, culture, and personality.* New York: Cooper Square. (Original work published 1947)

Sorokin, P. A., & Merton, R. K. (1935). The course of Arabian intellectual development, 700-1300 A.D. *Isis, 22*, 516-524.

Taagepera, R. (1976). Crisis around 2005 A.D.? A technology-population interaction model. *General Systems, 21*, 137-138.

Taagepera, R. (1979). People, skills, and resources: An interaction model for world population growth. *Technological Forecasting and Social Change, 13*, 13-30.

Taagepera, R., & Colby, B. N. (1979). Growth of Western civilization: Epicyclical or exponential? *American Anthropologist, 81*, 907-912.

Thorndike, E. L. (1950). Traits of personality and their intercorrelations as shown in biography. *Journal of Educational Psychology, 41*, 193-216.

Toynbee, A. J. (1946). *A study of history* (abridged by D. C. Somervell, 2 vols.). New York: Oxford University Press.

Veblen, T. (1919). The intellectual preeminence of Jews in modern Europe. *Political Science Quarterly, 34*, 33-42.

Walberg, H. J., Rasher, S. P., & Parkerson, J. (1980). Childhood and eminence. *Journal of Creative Behavior, 13*, 225-231.

Winter, D. G. (1973). *The power motive.* New York: The Free Press.

Yuasa, M. (1974). The shifting center of scientific activity in the West: From the sixteenth to the twentieth century. In N. Shigeru, D. L. Swain, & Y. Eri (Eds.), *Science and society in modern Japan* (pp. 81-103). Tokyo: University of Tokyo Press.

PART SIX

EVOLUTIONARY PERSPECTIVES ON CREATIVITY

11

Social Roots of Creativity
Vilmos Csányi

Only *systems* can be creative; a new idea, artifact, structure, organism, or molecule can emerge only as a component of a higher system. There are systems whose existence is a continuous manifestation of creativity, and systems and components are nested organizations. Molecules that are themselves complex systems of atoms are the components of the cells, which are organized replicative entities. They can be completely autonomous, but they can also be components of a higher level organism. Organisms are components of ecosystems. The human personality is a complex system in itself: It has individuality and autonomy, but its existence and development can only take place in society. Human societies are one of the major components of the biosphere; there is only one biosphere on this planet, but its incessant creativity, called *evolution*, can be traced back 3.5 billion years.

MODELING SYSTEM CREATIVITY: THE COMPONENT SYSTEMS

Living systems and cultural, technical, and social systems show many common properties that have been discussed in a recent series of papers and books (Csányi, 1980, 1982a, 1982b, 1985, 1987, 1988, 1989a, 1989b, 1989d,

1990, 1991, 1992a, 1992b; Csányi & Kampis, 1985, 1988; Pantzar & Csányi, 1991, 1992). A new intuitive system model was introduced to describe these kinds of entities (for details see Csányi, 1989a; Kampis, 1991). In short all of these systems are *component systems* that are characterized by the nature of their components, by the interactions among their components, and by their organization. One of the most simple of such systems is the living cell, which consists of molecular components and is characterized by a network of chemical and physical interactions among the molecules and the replicative organization of this network. Using the cell as an example, I here show the characteristic features of the component systems.

The components of a cell are molecules, which are made up of atoms regarded as elementary building blocks. The molecules of any cell are in incessant interaction with each other, as the cell is an almost closed network of interrelated reactions. There is, of course, an enormous number of possible molecules, the number of possible chemical reactions among them being even larger, but the particular set of molecules and chemical reactions that represent particular cells being far from random. Organization defines the limits of possible cells. A molecular entity is a living cell only if it is a closed and self-renewing network of molecules and chemical reactions. Such networks are organized for the production of all of its molecular components and are called *replicative networks*; this because production of the components occurs during copying processes. Fidelity of the copying processes is never perfect; therefore, occasionally new components emerge in the cell, which leads to changes in the cell's properties on an evolutionary time scale. This process is called *autogenesis* of the cell (Csányi, 1985, 1989c).

In a similar way, ecosystems or human society can also be considered to be an autogenetic replicative network. Individuals of various species are the components of an ecosystem and they and their interaction represent the replicative network in which the individuals of the species are renewing themselves during regulated reproductive processes. Society is a replicative network of human beings, artifacts, and ideas. In the interactions of everyday life new generations come and old ones pass, new artifacts are made, substituting the discarded ones, and during learning and teaching ideas are also transferred from present generations to the next. At the present time, the replicative networks of societies are in a very active phase of autogenesis. Fidelity of replication is far below that of molecular systems, but the replicative nature of the organization of societies can be clearly recognized (Csányi, 1989a, 1989c, 1992a; Kampis & Csányi, 1987).

THE CREATIVITY OF BIOLOGICAL SYSTEMS

Although there is no accepted definition of a system's creativity, an intuitive approach could be provided by using concepts from biological evolution (Csányi, 1991, 1992c; Kampis & Csányi, 1988). An enormous variety of forms, structures, and behavior patterns has emerged for solving a concrete problem or serving a concrete function during evolution. If, for an example, we look at the forms of beaks in birds, which are tools for catching food, a great variety can be observed. A beak can serve its function if the prey is a tiny insect, a slimy fish or a well-armored creature with four legs. The functional variability represented here by the beak's structure is considered to be the result of creativity in the evolutionary system. Living systems have become increasingly complex during evolution. Not only have new structures emerged for the same function, but the variability of functions themselves has also increased continuously. Energy and material fluxes in the living world flow by the contribution of ever more species fulfilling more and more special functions, supplementing each other in the web of the biosphere.

A living system can be considered as creative, if during its existence it is able to create *new functions* and *new components* to serve these new functions. We also know that new functions and new components emerged during evolution by natural selection. Therefore, creativity in living systems is manifested in selected variability.

The number of chemical elements—the elementary building units of the cell—is around 10 (most of the known chemical elements do not play an important role in the cell), but the number of molecules that can be built from them is immense. The properties of atoms are the same in every cell. Therefore, the differences among the various cells are based on the properties of the particular set of molecular components embodied by the particular cells. Only those sets of molecules that could build up a functionally closed replicative network became cells during evolution. Some cells make new components by genetic mutations in every generation. Only those cells that are able to fulfill some new function which exists on the cellular level of organization can survive among the ones containing new components. They reflect the creativity of the evolutionary system; other variants disappear. This is the process of natural selection.

Some generalizations can be made for the component systems:

1. Any differences in components' structures are regarded as variability.

2. The following is an intuitive definition of system creativity: Creativity is the *variability adjusted to the organization of a system.*

In other words, the measure of creativity is the extent of the functionally fit variability of the components that can exist without altering the identity and survival of the system.

The cell is a class of systems, and its creativity can be defined at different levels of organization. At the level of the elementary building blocks the cells are not creative at all, because their basic set of chemical elements is fixed. At the second level of organization, the level of molecules, there is an enormous variability potential, but only a tiny fraction of it is actually used by the cells because the types of metabolism of the cells are rather uniform. The number of different molecules that fit into this category is not more than around 10,000; therefore, there exists creativity of the cells at this level, but it is low.

At the third, cellular, level of organization, creativity is very high, because there are some 10 million different living species and a couple of hundred different cell types in each, and it is well known that the living species are only a fraction of the total number of species which emerged and disappeared during evolution.

Two questions can be raised: First, what is evolving? Second, where does the creativity of such systems come from? To answer these questions, we look at the problems of the origin of life. Here we have three levels of organization: the primeval "soup" in which protocells are the components, the protocells themselves, and the molecules that are the components of the protocells. Taking these levels of organization in pairs, there is an analogy between the relations of molecules with protocells and protocells with the soup. If protocells are the subject of evolution then molecules were also. But for the latter we have to define molecular lineages, which can be done only in a system framework.

If the evolution of macromolecules has led to the emergence of an organized entity called the cell, then the evolution of the protocells and protocell species also must have led to the emergence of an organized biosphere (proto-Gaia?). What are the relationships of these protospecies to the whole protobiosphere? Is this biosphere a mere set of the cell species, or are there criteria on the basis of which the biosphere appears as a unified whole, as a living system built up from the species as components (Lovelock, 1979)?

For a correct answer to these questions it is necessary to look at classical evolutionary theory. The motor of evolution is Darwinian natural selection, but the theory says almost nothing about the nature and pattern of the selective forces except that they originate from the *environment*.

The environment is the universal *outer* agent that is assumed to be responsible for the creativity of evolutionary changes. The classic metaphor of evolution is turned "upside down" if we realize on the basis of current biological knowledge that the most important parts of the environment of a given species are the *other* living species. It would be foolish to argue against this. If we accept this, however, it immediately becomes clear that we introduce a very special feedback into the model of evolution.

The evolution of a given species is dependent on the selective influence on its environment. However, this statement is true for every species, and therefore the most important power in evolution is *evolution* itself. Every species is changing—adapting continuously—and this process changes the environment and the conditions of selection.

For creativity, the environment—the outer agent of the classic model—becomes an *internal agent* that itself is the subject of the same evolutionary process. Furthermore, the question is not only how a given species was formed by the changing environment, but why and how the environment has changed. This leads to a vicious circle. In the classical paradigm, which is widely accepted in biology, there are no answers to these questions.

If we turn to evolutionary models based on systems science (Csányi, 1989a) the answer is clear: The only source of creativity is the evolving *system* itself. Biological information emerges from "nothing." Its only source is the unfolding process of matter constituted by the molecular structures (Bohm, 1980).

It is of interest that the system-level extension of the evolutionary metaphor has already occurred outside biology. The first notable extension has been formulated by Herbert Spencer (1862), who is quite disliked by biologists. Spencer's general definition of evolution is as follows: "Evolution can be defined as a change from an incoherent homogeneity into a coherent heterogeneity accompanying the dissipation of motion and integration of matter" (p. 16). It is clear from this definition and from the accompanying text that Spencer conceived of evolution not as transformation of certain components of a system during time, but as changes in the whole system.

Creativity is connected to systems features such as unity and autonomy. One perceives living organisms as *unities* that are separated from the background by boundaries. Living unity defines its own boundaries, yet not in the physical but the organizational sense: It is replicative information that determines their limit. The self-maintenance and existence of living entities is realized through their replication. This functionally isolated set of components belongs to the *unity* of the organism. Things which are not endowed with replicative information for a given living individual, do not belong to it as a unity. If unities are replicative wholes then they have a certain degree of *autonomy* (Csányi, 1989a). Only systems having autonomy show creativity because only autonomous units might have selective effects on their components.

The emergence of autonomy is a historical process. Living organisms undergo changes in the amount and type of their components and in their relations and organization. Such changes occur, for example, during ontogenesis. A given zygote can be characterized by its components and component-producing processes; the same is true for a different zygote or a mature organism. This difference in their identity is the basis on which we distinguish them, and gives them individuality. On the other hand, a zygote and the organism that originated from it have a common identity, as they are linked by the *historical process* of the transformation of the organization. This process can be traced via the overlapping existence of the unity, as a nonidentically replicative organization.

The emergence of new properties in the component systems as the expression of creativity was studied in detail earlier (Csányi 1989a; Kampis, 1991). It was found that the emergence of new features of a component system is connected with the so-called *"hidden properties"* of the components, which are inexhaustible in case of the atoms of chemical elements (Bunge, 1963; Csányi, 1989a; 1992a). It can be added that emergence of a new property is also dependent on the organization of the system, because each concrete organization involves only a certain set of the components' properties. Other properties of the components that are not used in the given organization are hidden properties from the point of view of organization.

Change in organization is made possible only by the hidden properties of the components or by introducing entirely new components into the system. Biological evolution is a result of the manifestation of the hidden properties of the atoms in new, ever-higher organizations. Organization depends on the properties of the components, and component status in an organization depends of the organization itself. Organization and components exist only as expressed in each other.

Creativity can be manifested not only in building a large number of components from a few building blocks, but also if the variability is high at the level of the building blocks themselves, which build up different higher components through simple, uniform rules of construction. An example of systems that work with a few elementary building blocks is the cell. Human personality is an example of a system construction that works with a large number of units and with relatively uniform construction rules. Human zygotes, from which a human personality begins, are different in the case of each person (except monozygotic twins). They are different in genes, and mutations, but the human organism is built up with the same set of rules of construction during human development. Adult human individuals show high variability because of the individual differences in the zygotes and because of the pronounced influence of the environment. Human development results in special, unrepeatable individual differences, giving rise to individuality and personality. The essence of such construction is that functional variability emerges because of the action of the agents of the highest level of organization, including the environment.

To make the aforementioned simple, we can give the recipe for creativity of systems: Take a set of elementary building blocks, make components of the system on at least two levels of organization, and then your system will show high creativity in its environment at the third level of organization.

SOCIAL SYSTEMS AS COMPONENT SYSTEMS

Evolutionary emergence in human societies was also investigated earlier (Csányi, 1989a, 1989b, 1990). It was stated that the common ancestor of the apes and humans was already a very intelligent being that lived in highly developed social groups. It had well-evolved communication and cooperative behavior, and most probably already used tools. The social groups of the present day apes, which are similar in many respects to this ancestor, are semiclosed replicative component system in which the components are the individuals and their replication occurs by biological reproduction. The continual renewal of the groups themselves also occurs through the renewals of the components (Csányi, 1989b, 1989c). The apes' groups, as autogenetic replicative systems and as parts of the evolutionary process, are creative systems. Their creativity is based on genetic mutations, and in principle it is biological in nature.

Humans are also a member of the animal world, with our biochemical and physiological characteristics not leaving any doubt as to this. What nevertheless sets us apart from the animals is our behavior, developed and constrained by both environmental and genetic factors, and the characteristics of the human race.

If we examine different cultures, we find that human behavior shows wide variations, but we can also recognize certain general features.

All cultures are based on *language*, and human languages, as different as they may be in their surface structure, represent a well-defined class of the possible communication mechanisms.

Characteristic of all cultures is a hierarchical order of human relations including mechanisms of structuring power and the *kinship* system. Although it is again clear that kinship systems, for example, show large variations across societies, all people living in a society reckon with relatives and classify them in some way, which means that the ability to develop a system of kinship is a *biological trait* of our race.

A third characteristic of cultures is the use of *artifacts*. It is a biological feature of humans that we have an affection for objects of all kinds, and it is hard to imagine an active human being without artifacts. Of course, there are substantial differences between cultures regarding the sophistication and abundance of artifacts produced and used.

The fourth characteristic of human cultures is the use of abstractions, the existence of ideas. These include the thoughts we are thinking, in simple or more complex forms; verbal expressions; and performance, implementation, or expression through the making of artifacts.

These four defining characteristics of human cultures can be traced back to four purely biological features; namely, *linguistic competence* (Brown, 1973), *social affection* (Eibl-Eibesfeldt, 1989), *fondness for objects* (Morris, 1962), and the *ability to follow rules* (Eibl-Eibesfeldt, 1982). Let us consider each of these features in turn, and then look at the social phenomena arising from them.

Linguistic competence is a species specific feature of humans. Animal communication is an analog type of communication and is closed. Each human language possesses a dictionary of symbolic signs interpreted uniformly by those speaking the same language. The signals can be expressed in combinations of different meanings by using definite rules in a great variety; that is, human language is abstract and open. The most important characteristic of the human brain in connection with language is the capability of displacement (Brown, 1973). This term implies that a person is able to reduce a situation perceived through the senses to its components—to analyze it—and in the course of analysis create a new structure from the components. In other words he or she is capable of a kind of linguistic-logical synthesis. With the help of "reconstruction," humans can displace phenomena in space and time, change relationships, create linguistic models of reality, and then operate and analyze them.

Concerning *social affection*, among mammals humans are the most social beings, feeling extraordinary affection for their kin and even being ready to sacrifice their own life for the group. Whatever the culture in question, the individual's life proceeds within the framework of some kind of social group. Even the misanthrope hates *people,* not objects or animals, and social attachment is obvious.

The *fondness for objects* is deeply rooted in all humans, and although the spontaneous and irresistible desire in small children to collect pebbles as a first sign of our fancy for objects may be mentioned, it is not necessary to list special arguments to demonstrate this feature of ours to someone living in the modern world. Throughout our lives we are accompanied by an enormous number of different artifacts. We are constantly occupied by their preparation, their acquisition, exchange, and use.

Rule following behavior is a species specific feature of humans, of which *language* is one of the most manifest forms. However, respecting the rules is not limited to language. The kinship system is, in fact, social affection regulated in a defined way, with family relations being manifested in rules of behavior and in respecting the rules.

The making of artifacts also depends on following rules, activated by the fondness for objects. A tool maker works the natural object in conformity with rules fixed in advance. Animals, too, are able to perform elementary shaping, but they are unable to learn a system of rules no matter how simple it may be. Rule following is also manifested in elaborating ideas: A habit or a technique may be characterized by a description or through a fixed system of given rules, which means that the shaping of an idea, in our mind or in our behavior or in any other way, is reflected, just like the shaping of an object, in the *successive application of certain rules.*

Following rules is the most essential human biological feature. Our nearest relative, the chimpanzee, can be taught to do many things, and with a suitable amount of training he or she may even be taught maneuvers and operations used by people living a simple country life. However, if a few hundred chimpanzees are taught this way and placed in an empty village, a social life characteristic of human communities will never develop, as the colony of chimpanzees is unable to follow complex systems of rules. If hungry, the individuals will acquire food at any price, and they also satisfy their sexual desire immediately and forcefully. A human may die of starvation before touching food in a supermarket if he or she has no money to buy it: That cannot happen with an animal. For humans, obedience to the rules is more important than any other thing. Even if we do break the rules, we do so on the basis of a system of rules considered to be more important.

All human cultures in their essence display systems of rules operated continuously by social affection and the fondness for artifacts. Systems of rules concerning human relations are understood within the cultural group, as well as the rules concerning the preparation, use, exchange, and production of objects, and rules relating to the genesis, values, functioning, and history of the culture. Language is the general communication system that, once again, consists of a system of rules, which intervene in shaping and transmitting the various rules of the culture, and thus reflects its fullness.

INDIVIDUALITY AND THE CREATIVITY OF GROUP—CULTURES

Regarding our behavior's biology, humans belong to social mammals that have permanent, cooperative groups with highly developed group structures. It has been assumed that the appearance of cooperation is in itself a sufficient condition for the emergence of further human characteristics like abstract thinking or language. To contradict this train of thought it is enough to mention that no linguistic ability or conceptual thoughts are necessary for highly developed forms of cooperation existing in some social animals. A pack of wolves or a group of lions can get their prey with a highly organized concerted action. Every member of the hunting troop knows its exact place and function in this action. This kind of cooperation is based on an "action-plan" that, although very flexible, is genetically based. The participants do not need explanations or reconciliation, there are no roles to assign, and no need to set up schedules. All participants have an internal drive for cooperation and everybody fulfills the role that is the consequence of its position in the rank ordering of the group and the actual situation. Therefore, the creativity of such groups is rather limited. The structure of the action-plan is simple and does not change too much during thousands of generations.

These animals living in highly evolved social groups are cooperating, but the result of their cooperation is immediate and the prey is a resource that can easily be distributed on the basis of the rank order. In principle, everybody joins the common action for one's self--interest. There is no group-interest above everybody's own, and the groups are loosely organized. Individuals can leave the groups and try another one occasionally. There is nothing like an object, a possession or a common learned rite that lasts because of the cooperation. There is nothing that can be regarded as a *product* of the group; the participation, therefore, is completely based on individual interests.

The nature of cooperation was entirely different in the early Homo groups that already used tools and primitive language. Cooperation in human groups occurs on the basis of an individual action-plan that is designed well before the action. The participants plan the forthcoming actions, they envisage the proceeding of the actions, and ponder over the different favorable or unfavorable outcomes. There are temporary roles that are discussed and assigned. The basic difference regarding the animals is the individuality of the action-plan to cooperate. Every cooperating animal group proceeds on the basis of a genetic plan, whereas individual plans are the characteristics of the cooperating human groups. Each group designs its own individual action plan on the basis of its learned culture.

Individuality plays an enormous role in evolution (Sterrer, 1992). Individual uniqueness of organisms is the consequence of sexual reproduction; that is, the fact that in a sexually reproducing population no two individuals (except identical twins) are identical in their genotypes, and because of the ontogenetic processes are even less so in their phenotypes. The nervous system of the higher animals is able to modify the behavior of the individual through various learning mechanisms and in this way build a type of neural individuality on the constrained genetic individuality. This enabled animals to react with appropriate behavioral responses to the smallest environmental changes. Emerging individuality, be it genetic or neural, was the *precondition* to the appearance of creativity in living systems, because only the variability of the enormous number of individuals provides the necessary basis for selection to act in producing new life forms.

Among the apes, occasional cooperation has been observed in the chimpanzee. A large portion of the protein need for the chimpanzee is acquired by hunting for monkeys, juvenile pigs, and antelopes (Teleki, 1973). Hunting is an exclusively male adventure and it corresponds exactly to the actions of other social mammals that are based on a genetic action-plan. The chimpanzee group is resting or peacefully foraging fruits when suddenly the males realize the "situation." For example, a young baboon is playing alone in the middle of the chimpanzee group. At that moment the chase starts and every participant knows that the baboon must be encircled, the attention of the baboon's parents must be drawn elsewhere, and then the prey is run over and killed. Every hunter performs the task that is the most plausible in his position and the action is finished in a few minutes.

However developed the cooperation of the chimps seems to be, it is considerably constrained genetically. Because of these constraints chimps can live only in special environments. The individual, learned character of human cooperation provided humans with enormous advantages. We are able to survive in almost any ecological environment on the planet: Humans live in the tropics, in deserts, and even at the poles.

Today it is quite clear why humans have evolved so quickly. The individual action-plan is an entity that in its most primitive form exists as the participants' memory traces, and directs the proceedings of the cooperation. That is, the plan is not given genetically but it is formed by the group itself. Its activity is bound to the very group in which cooperation manifested in the formation of the action-plan. The abstract human language, which is different from any form of animal communication, has evolved precisely as a means to form this individual action-plan. With the help of abstract language, a model of the dynamic of the environment can be built up that is much more effective than those made by the modeling technics of the animal brain (Csányi 1992c). By means of human language, things, phenomena, processes, actors, and actions can be separated into small elements. From these elements new flexible constructs could be built, in which things, space, time, and past and future events occurred or imagined can be evoked in a manner suitable for communication and group process. The action-plan of the human groups is a linguistic structure; although it exists in distributed form in the brains of the group members; it can nevertheless be regarded as an entity above the organization level of the group. This means that a new entity appeared in the evolutionary theater. In fact, if we are considering the important role of individuality in evolution it is clear that new classes of entities appeared whose mere existence started a new level of evolutionary dynamics. These new entities are the group-beings or, using a more widespread term, *group cultures*. These new, variable autonomous unities were subjected to a new cycle of creative process. Group individuality established by human culture allowed an enormous *variability* among the groups to emerge. *Selection* among the variants was the source of creativity in cultural evolution.

There was a heated debate among the students of animal behavioral evolution some years ago concerning whether natural selection acts only on individuals, as it was assumed by the classic Darwinian theory, or among group as well. In *group selection* the competition occurs among groups for the survival and the replication of the group (Alexander & Borgia, 1976).This debate was very interesting because of the fact that a group selection mechanism makes evolution proceed faster than individual selection, and if it really existed it must be accounted for in the theories of the evolution of animal social behavior. A large amount of data was published and there were even some experiments performed, but after a while the general conclusion was that group-selection mechanisms have probably not appeared in any animals except human. It is supposed that human are the only organisms in which aside from individual selection, some role has been played by group-selection process that later accelerated human evolution. Among the conditions for group selection to occur is isolation. If in an animal group new members immigrate in numbers that exceed 4-5% of the number of individuals in the group during a generation time, then group selection mechanisms cease to act. Evolution of the early Homo species has been characterized by isolation of a high degree because of language and culture. We assume that as the group being mentioned earlier started to form, the degree of isolation grew accordingly, and evolution accelerated. That is a system where a positive feedback emerged, and the more it advanced, the greater potential it acquired for further advance.

ACTION—PLANS TURN TO IDEAS

A simple action-plan is a linguistic structure, but action-plans can acquire extreme complexity if they are further organized. They can be divided to small but still meaningful parts, and from these parts new ones can be structured. Using the concept of exact timing, action-plans can acquire very complex organization. To distinguish simple action-plans or descriptions from organized action-systems we introduced the term *idea* (Csányi, 1980).

Ideas can be understood as organized thoughts which are built up from the simplest units that can be considered meaningful, hereinafter referred to as *concepts*, and which lead to the creation of some more complicated thing, idea or behavior. Ideas may be simple habits, techniques, tales, myths, values, and norms, but they may also appear in the form of artifacts as instruments, tools, or items of culture or the arts.

Man-made objects are always expressions of ideas, which means that artifacts can also be interpreted as systems of organized rules of behavior. Let us just consider how many rules are followed when we use an instrument as simple as a key. I have to take the key with me when I leave, I have it on me when I go home. I have to hold it in a given way if I want to open the door, I have to perform well-defined motions in the course of turning it in the lock, and different rules apply as to whether or not I will leave the key in the lock. The notion of the key, the ownership, the lock, the fitting together, and so on are also formulated in complex ideas.However, the making of an artifact itself, for example of the aforementioned key, can be described as a series of fixed rules. In the course of preparing the casting mold, melting the metal, performing the casting, and completing the rest of the work, the producer will obey well-defined rules, with the artifact of use being the result of all these steps.

The ideas of belonging to a group, such as care for the parents, ownership, or freedom are ideas that can also be considered as fixed systems of rules, not as simple sets of rules, but as a complex system of organization between the components of the rules. The idea of parental care, for example, includes all the rules of behavior to be followed by parents in interacting with their children for a given culture. These are partly small techniques of taking care, partly rules of how to decide on interests, but the idea of parental care also includes rules that are commands regarding the relations of subordination between this and other ideas, such as when I may be allowed or obliged to sacrifice my child in the interest of the group or the homeland.

An idea composed of rules for behavior may be considered to be working well if its organization is suitable: It does not imply contradictions, it preferably does not go against biological dispositions, it allows clear-cut decisions in all situations, etc There are also ideas, of course, in which a purely cultural restriction of a biological disposition is expressed; for example, in the case of ideas relating to sexual behavior. In such cases, the idea will be unstable to a certain extent, it will frequently be revaluated, certain component rules will be left out, or new rules will be built in.

It is the *ideas* developed in the group that we have to regard as the most important organizing factor of human group societies. Hunting, fishing and defense against carnivores and other human groups required the development of new ideas. Such ideas cannot be completely independent from each other, however, as the members of a group cannot be expected to behave very differently during the implementation of an idea. It is also clear that the organizing core necessary for the harmonious implementation of ideas must be the group as an autonomous entity. Ideas organize the life of the group, and their harmony must be ensured by the group. Thus, the organizing ideas, fulfilling this harmonizing role, take the form of myths of origin, and legends, religions, values and norms emerge.

The size of Homo groups is generally not too large, consisting on a average of 30-60 people. In a group of this size the acquisition of the same ideas by every group member is possible, which means that the members of the group are not only familiar with their own role in any particular context, but that they are also familiar with the role of others. This fact makes substitutions very easy. According to surveys made, the members of still-existing group societies spend the greater part of their time talking to each other, an activity aimed primarily at continuously sharing and refreshing their experiences as well as at helping the younger members of the group to acquire the set of ideas of the group (Lee, 1969). The group and the ideas belonging to it thus constitute a closed organizing system. Well-organized ideas help ensure the survival and reproduction of the members of the group, whereas the group, on the other hand, provides for the generation-to-generation transmission of the ideas. The group maintaining such a small idea "ecosystem" is a perfect subject for group selection on a higher level of evolution. Biological and ethological group-creating characteristics of humans—the acceptance of a group identity, man's favoring his group mates against outsiders, the protection of the group with ones life—are all in perfect harmony with similar sets of ideas relating to the group.

The harmony between the individual, the group, and the ideas is ideal. Emotional and intellectual stability is ensured for hundreds of generations. This was humanity's "golden age."

Appearance of ideas is only one of the consequences of the evolution of human language that made the effective communication among brain's models possible. The animal's brain, if it belongs to a long-living higher species, is able to construct complex concept superstructures from individual experiences, but because of the very nature of the animal concept units, these superstructures are bound to outer reality, exclusively and finally. They are only the representation of the outer environment, good or bad, but nothing more.

Linguistic concepts can be detached from reality. If the perceptual keys are transformed into words, the referential structures could evoke actions that themselves are words again. Words which could be spoken or written might became keys again. This feature of the linguistic concepts contributes to the creation of a self-generating system of concepts that are only occasionally influenced by reality. The development of linguistic concepts, the ability to form conceptual thoughts in humans, has led to the emergence of a genuinely new brain system. Abstract thinking creates self-organizing concept superstructures that are not only primitive models of reality but *autonomous* entities, units in and of themselves, whose dynamics cannot be appertained solely to the outer environment but to the *relation* of the emerged new system and reality. Self, imagination, fantasy independent of experiences, and their connections and the relations among them are the most important features of this self-created world, which we name *mind*. With the help of his or her mind the individual is not only able to react appropriately to the changes in the immediate environment but can view itself as part of the environment: It can see itself as an acting object, it can analyze its relation to reality in a wide range of the time-space continuum, and project its own position in the past or to the future.

Mind can create a world of fantasy where self plays a relatively subordinated role, but rigorous rules exist concerning the dynamics of other abstract entities, such as the world of mathematics. Worlds can be created in which everything revolves around the self without reflecting the constraints of reality: This is the world of religion. The pure essence of the mind's creative intelligence is personalized in *God*, who is placed above us with unlimited power while we humbly retain only the beautiful concept of the *soul* for ourself.

CREATIVITY OF THE IDEA-SYSTEMS

The behavior of Homo groups at the beginning of cultural evolution may be well described by means of the model of the system of replicative components (Csányi, 1987). The components of the system are the Homo individuals and the few artifacts they are using, together with the experience the group has obtained during its functioning concerning its environment, and which it is able, by means of language, to transmit to coming generations. This system includes an ability to replicate itself in the course of time; that is, the ability to continually renew its components without changing its organization. Individuals who die are substituted by the birth of new group members; objects are renewed through copying, taking care to maintain form and functional similarity. Individual experience is also renewed by means of the cultural inheritance mechanisms of teaching/learning. Such systems are very stable, as has been demonstrated by the first 2 million years of the history of our race. (A more detailed description of the replicative model can be found in Csányi, 1989a.)

It is a significant new phenomenon that the development of huge human masses has rendered the *competition of ideas* possible, something that is unthinkable in group societies. By this means, a new level of the self-organization processes of ideas has emerged. In group societies ideas either served direct practical goals, as procedures or techniques, or helped the group to survive, through myths, legends, or primitive religions. The exchange of ideas between societies was incidental and of low effectiveness. In modern mass societies the number of potential carriers of ideas is enormous, and the acquisition of ideas can also take place outside the framework of the traditional group structure.

The mass media enable certain ideas to make use of carriers who, in an ethological sense, do not comprise a genuine group. The members of different organizations, of a political party, for example, apart from the local groups, its leadership, and a possible party administration, do not know each other personally. Ethological factors can play only a negligible role in the genesis and further evolution of the idea serving the existence of the party. Aside from group cohesion it is increasingly suitably *organized ideas* that unite people.

Variability of the idea entities and their competitions for space in the minds of people have started a new outburst of creation, a new course of evolution. Socialization, early learning, and extremely strong traditions have allowed the ideas of group society to survive. The ideas of mass societies compete for the adult members of the society. This change, decisive for evolution, has brought about a basic alteration in the structures of ideas as well. In the system of concepts comprising an idea, those promoting the acceptance of the given set of ideas and protecting it from rivaling ideas, are also needed. In a group society the myth of origin does not necessarily have to be logical and convincing. As there is only one myth of origin, all members of the society accept it, because it is the one taught by the elders and it would be meaningless to question certain elements of the myth. On the other hand, ideas in mass society are continually exposed to challenges so that, for example, the myths of origin have to be harmonized with the ideas of science and practice as well. We demand logical and generally valid explanations, while wanting the opportunity to choose from alternative answers concerning a given question.

In mass societies, an idea can organize enormously large groups, but only if the concept elements forming the idea include those needed for the longer existence of such large groups. Propaganda and ideology appear as important organizing tools for the perpetuation of ideas. Although ideas function as group-organizing forces, the ethological group-forming traits of humans have not ceased to exist. In all cases where, as a consequence of the functioning of an idea, groups of people appear that allow the ethological factors to work, and ethological organization of these groups will start immediately. Very good examples are offered by the one party systems developed in the Soviet Union and Eastern Europe, where the administration, including the political and central committees due to their small size and closed structure, are, in fact, hierarchical groups organized on an ethological basis. Their activity is only partly controlled by their own ideology, the role of ethological factors being much more important.

Thus, contrary to the mechanisms of ethological group determination, the greatest advantage of a society organized by ideas is the appearance of idea competition that offers a basis for the development of modern science, for example, but also for the creation of welfare societies. A disadvantage of this same phenomenon is one of its other consequences. The individual in the group society also has ideas, in the form of values and norms, that assure an undisturbed coexistence of ideas having different goals. In mass societies the competition of ideas put an end to their concertation. The idea appears as an entity that you can choose, with the individual having to select and accept from a huge array the ideas that determine his or her personality, without their having an idea embracing everything and questioned by no one, an idea that can serve as a basis for selection (Csányi & Kampis, 1988). This is the explanation for the alienation of modern man who loses his self-confidence and values. (It is worth noting here that this is probably an interim period, as global ideas are emerging, such as those of the unity of mankind, global peace, global environment protection, etc., that will certainly reshape the network of organizing ideas, fit for connecting other ideas to them. Of course, that will, again, result in the closing of the world of ideas.)

CREATIVITY AND THE LEVELS OF SOCIAL ORGANIZATIONS

Definition of the levels of organization in society is a rather complex issue. In the following I emphasize viewing social systems as physical entities with the components of humans, artifacts, and memory traces (ideas). The first level of organization is the classes of the components themselves; that is, humans, artifacts, and memory traces. This is where the biological organization of the human body, neurobiological organization of the memory traces, and the descriptions of the structure of the artifacts belongs.

Those processes in which these components are renewed belong at the second level of organization. In the case of humans, this organizational level consist of the family, educational institutions, small groups in the work place, and political and religious institutions, because these are the most influential in forming human personalities. It is recognized, of course, that the separation of those organizations that have more direct influences from those that have only indirect ones is very difficult if not impossible.

In the case of artifacts, social structures concerned with the design and making of artifacts belong to the second level as well. In the case of ideas, organizations concerned with communication, education and artifact making are responsible for the origination and transfer of ideas and these belong to the second level. We note here that our insistence on describing society as a physical system yields here, for example, because the origin and interaction of the ideas occur at every level and every locality of the society, but memory traces, the physical bases of the ideas, are produced only in human brains; therefore, the origination of the idea components are always related to communication, learning, and education—that is, to building up memory traces.

However uncertain the borders of the second level's organizations, it is certain that from human personalities, particular ideas, and appropriate artifacts, higher level structures come into being: factories, companies, institutions of law, politics, and religions, as well as nations, states, and multinational firms.

In surveying these higher structures of society and their components, we can supplement the sources of creativity with the following. In the case of social structures not only the components—that is, humans, artifacts, and ideas—show high variability, but the rules of construction of these structures are also highly variable. The existing social structures therefore show an extreme high structural and functional variability, which is the manifestation of the high creativity of the social system and the cause of the high speed of cultural evolution.

CREATIVE PROCESSES IN THE DEVELOPMENT OF PERSONALITY

In the previous section we sketched the outlines of the evolutionary context of the emergence of group culture. The main point of the argument was the role of group-individuality in this process. However, individuality played a role also at the lower level of organization. Without understanding the nature of the individuality of the group forming Homo itself, a good model of social evolution cannot be built. In the following we turn our attention to the system usually termed *personality*. There are many loose formulations of personality, but the closest to ours is that of Allport (1961) which states that personality is the dynamic organization of those psychophysiological factors that determine the thoughts and behavior of an individual. The replicative model of personality had been developed earlier (Csányi, 1980, 1982a, 1988, 1989a). Replicative systems are characterized by compartmentalization in the formation of subsystems, also replicative in nature, that form a functional network with each other but retain autonomy to a high degree. Human personality can be regarded as such a replicative subsystem of society. Let us start with a rather simplified system model. The human brain is able to produce abstract conceptions in great amounts and is able to communicate a large proportion of these through,the use of language. Therefore, the *concept* will be the basic unit of our dynamical system.

A concept is a functional unit (Csányi, 1988); that smallest piece of thoughts, speech, or behavior which still has a meaning. Actions of everyday life, ideas, and artifacts are produced by the action of organized sets of concepts. Concepts are learned, copied, inferred, and/or recombined. These activities are the very mechanisms of a highly mutable replicative system. Concepts are continuously produced and forgotten, but these processes are not random because the genesis of the concepts are influenced by the very network of the concepts. The concepts of a mature person form a functionally almost closed replicative network. In other words, a new concept can "survive" in the system only if it can be functionally bound to the already existing part of the network and it can join into the overall replication cycles. The consequence of the existence of the replicative network of the concepts is their context dependence. One of the largest problem of the present days' artificial intelligence research is the modeling of the context dependency of the human language and thinking, because every utterance or new thought is understood and accepted not only through the filters of logic and grammar but also through an adjustment to the whole network of concepts of the given personality. The organization of this system is very clearly seen in the cognitive development of children. A still speechless child living in a linguistic environment at the beginning of language acquisition automatically filters out those words and linguistic structures and concepts which do not fit into the already existing concept network. Immediately understood and acquired are those that can be functionally joined into the network. Initiation of the system is occurring by biological motivations and emotional factors. The undeveloped self wants to satisfy its curiosity, hunger, and needs for social contacts. Those linguistic utterances that help him or her are immediately acquired and remembered, and because of their logical and emotional connections become part of a replicative network. The network is replicative and cyclic because the repetition of every word, utterance, or action is replication; the reactivation of the already acquired concepts, reconstruction of the higher concept structures, and, through this, the reinforcement of the functional connections. Animal thinking is based on the processing of the memory of concrete actions. Human thinking, beside this, is able to process the memory traces by the mechanisms of logic and grammar that create such higher structures: ideas which surpass the concrete and manifest in conceptual thoughts (Csányi, 1992d).

Memories can be recalled also by the animal mind, but only on the basis of association. The human mind processes memories by entirely new mechanisms of logic and grammar: The inferences received by this process are new abstract constructions that are unavailable for the animal mind. The rule following behavior is not only a kind of cultural strategy but the very basis of human thinking and the most powerful resource of human creativity.

It is characteristic for the replicative networks that relatively independent compartments are formed in them from the functional connections of components which concerted their replication and to a certain extent are separated from the main network. This feature could explain the human mind's ability to accept ideas that contradict each other. Therefore, the mind is not only a container full of concepts, but has a definite higher organization.

The creativity of the "personal mind" is provided by the replicative nature of the concept system. Replicative systems have multiple sources of creativity, the most important of which is the introduction of new components into the existing network and the functional organization of the "hidden" properties of the already existing components. Organization in a replicative component system is defined by the features of the components, or more exactly those features of the components that make organization possible. This means that the properties of the components and the functional network has been formed from them, mutually define of and conditional on each other. A very frequent act of creation occurs in a system if the properties of certain components that are not participating in the present organization make possible a reorganization process in which "hidden" properties get functional roles. The same thought was expressed by Barron (1963), who wrote that, "At the very heart of the creative process is this ability to shatter the rule of law and regularity of mind" (p. 141). This is the most important feature of the creativity of human language. We use many expressions or concepts during conversations that do not have even an approximate definition. For example, it is meaningful to say, "Something disturbed our work." In this sentence there is no definition of "something," we know only that it disturbed our work but it can be a phenomenon, person, object, feeling, or one of many other things. We could perform quite a long conversation about this "something" without giving a definition, and it is possible that the definition emerges only looking at the whole conversation. Hidden properties play a role not only in the language but also in the social relation systems. When we elect somebody to a certain position new unexpected characteristics might shown up in her or him.

At the end of this short summary I want to underline that the replicative network of the concepts are bound to pure biological mechanisms of motivation, memory processing, and various behavior systems. These are influencing the production and organization of the concept network and give the individual characteristic personality traits and a cognitive style.

The higher level organizations of the ideas built up from concepts existing in individual brains and the fact that such components of the personality can be communicated and learned and have influence in the memory space of an entire group or culture explains both the individuality of persons and their social determination. The social reality around the human individuals provides the personality-forming concepts, but the replicative network that forms in the individuals act as a special filter and results in a characteristic, unique system of personality. The replicative model of personality and culture provide a satisfactory explanation for the creativity of both individual and social levels.

SOCIAL AUTONOMY AND CREATIVITY

In the course of evolution, it is group-society configurations that has defined humans' social existence for the longest time. They also influenced our biological evolution, and we can say that the species-specific characteristics of humans are in an optimal harmony mostly with group society as a superstructure. The texture of the group society is based on kinship relations, and individual development is in harmony with the slow alteration of the social structure. The socialization of the individual born into the group is perfect, with the individual completely accepting the conditions that exist in the society, and, when becoming an adult, the opportunity to climb the social ladder. Values and norms change very slowly, at a pace of generations following one another, if at all.

The harmony of biological factors and a given social structure explains that certain aspects of the group societies have prevailed, and they sometimes even appear in mass societies. In the mass societies before the industrial revolution biological family relationships were a very essential part of the social structure. The relationships that are new, compared to the group societies, appear, in fact, because family relations were no longer capable of organizing the society as a whole. Dependencies based on religion, ownership, and state structure developed, and these can be interpreted as a social extension of family relationships. In a society of relatives, an individual is a member of a network of given dependencies, with his or her existence subject to relationships. The individual is hardly able to change this system of relationships, as is the case with the system of relatives.

Feudal society is a typical example. The liege lord rules over a group that includes many more people than those in his family, but the relationships are nevertheless of family character (for example, vassals get certain protection in exchange for their services), with an important exception; namely, that the shift of generation characteristic on the group society is not followed by a change in the seigniory—vassals do not become liege lords after a time. Feudal relations are quasi-infantilizing of a major part of society, defining forever their place in the social order of ranks. As mass society, due simply to its size, is unable to completely use the early socialization for conserving a given structure, individuals appear who reject the superstructure of the society. However it is only after lengthy development, in fact only during industrial development, that the idea of *social autonomy* emerges. Autonomy results in the appearance of individuals and groups that reject the given family and dependence conditions of the society, and organize themselves around an independent objective or idea. An autonomous individual is able to choose from the different ideologies, ideas, and different social options; the autonomous group, on the other hand, unifies individuals having similar ways of thinking and similar aims in the interest of some common objective or idea. Their social autonomy is the reestablishment of the harmony of groups with an individual group-organizing idea, a creative tool to enhance group variability so necessary to maintain further cultural evolution. The acceptance of autonomous ideas is a refusal of monolithic society-organizing ideologies at the same time.

The acceleration of modern industrial development has been allowed by social autonomy. The society based on family relationships can only change very slowly, with the pace of generation shifts. The appearance of autonomous groups dramatically accelerated the change in social structure; first of all at the field of production, as a special autonomy of production units—enterprises—developed. This has a number of factors: The autonomous entrepreneurs' groups recruit their members with no regard to the social constraints and they recruit those who, due to their personal character, are able to fulfill a given task, to follow a given target, to implement a given idea. If the society shows tolerance toward the autonomous groups the competition of these groups can begin, and the ones unable to achieve their goal will collapse and enable other groups of a new composition to rapidly appear; thus the lifetime of the autonomous groups is usually much shorter than the generation time. Therefore, a certain selection is also taking place which means that their development will also accelerate. The organizers and executives of a given enterprise create a well-defined organization, and this organization will face the given social conditions. If it is successful, it will survive; if it fails it will disintegrate without causing too much harm to its participants. With the participants, as units fit for organization, new autonomous groups and new enterprises may form. A recombination and selection of different organizing ideas is taking place in this way. Of course, not only companies and enterprises, but different social organizations, editorial boards, associations, and parties can function on the basis of autonomy. It is noteworthy here that the autonomous individual who is able to create autonomous groups is the result of a kind of socialization: Modern industrial societies invest significant energy into developing individual autonomy, and the freedom to create autonomous groups in adult life, as well as in their disintegration in case of inadaptability. Jurisdiction and the political system as a whole should be fit for admitting autonomy, but this is only one of the preconditions: the other one is a social-scale production of individuals educated to autonomy. Autonomy cannot simply be introduced in one day.

It can develop, but only in the space of generations because production of the human components occurs in such a time scale.

Kinship societies developed several mechanisms against autonomy in order to conserve the prevailing social structures. The survival self-interest of the higher structures always inhibited the development of autonomy. In modern mass society the isolation of the kinship systems decreased to a great extent and competition of the higher structures appeared—autonomy is the manifestation of this competition. The appearance of autonomy accelerated cultural evolution because it enhanced social creativity by increasing the dynamics of the change of the structures on the third levels of social organization. These changes could lead to the development of a global, interdependent culture as Montuori (1989) predicted which needs "not just adaptation to a putative system, but creation of many systems, through design, learning and the acquisition of evolutionary competence" (p. 47).

ONE COUNTEREXAMPLE: THE DECREASED CREATIVITY OF THE COMMUNIST SYSTEMS

The Russian revolution in 1917 shook up a huge kinship-based society, but the new system did not succeed in introducing the social autonomy indispensable to industrial development. It replaced the family and dependence relationships that had been torn asunder with the new dependencies of Stalinist power. The principle of democratic centralism in the party, for example, clearly demonstrated the tribal power structure. There is no social autonomy allowed at all; its possible animators were oppressed, put to jail, or executed. The milder, new versions of Stalinism, like the social structure developed in Hungary after 1956, are essentially kinship-type societies in which the social existence of the individual is taking place in a complicated kinship and dependence network of relationships covering the whole country (Csányi, 1990). Structures change only in over the span of a generation (about 35 years). Such systems are stable and able to ensure a relative well-being at a certain level. If their isolation is perfect, they can hardly be changed after a generation's time has elapsed, because in the course of the socialization a new generation appears that accepts the system unconditionally. The condition for stability is the absolute closeness of the society. If ideas or objects flow in from outside to the system, it will unavoidably lead to disintegration. Such societies are unable to continuously produce more developed industrial goods on their own, due to the lack of autonomy. At the same time, as a consequence of inflows, new demand appears, causing more and more tension. Concessions made in the course of canalizing those tensions results in further escalation of tensions.

Social structures appearing on the third level of organization of the communist state are characterized by simplicity, uniformity, and total lack of creativity. Social organizations are made to be easily governed and surveyed by one person or a small group. The social institutions adapt only to the need of the persons at the highest level of the social hierarchy, which again decreases creativity. In the time scale of generations this system is slightly creative, because the individuals change at the highest level and the new leaders and new personalities bring new styles and new methods. In the history of the Soviet Union, the eras of Stalin, Hruscsov, Brezsnev, and Gorbacsov signal this kind of creativity.

Such social systems can survive for a long time if they are alone or are completely isolated, but their change is rather slow. Surrounded by liberal states that use autonomy, a special "idea gap" appears in the communist system. After its first couple of years, it develops a complex idea network, a special state ideology that consists of the description and coherent explanations of the social relations in the communist state and its values (including its relations to the free countries). Every other idea that deviates from this centralized ideology is oppressed, and its carriers are punished. Because of the incomplete isolation of the communist state to the incoming ideas, the artifacts and experiences of those few who were permitted to have some travel in the free countries slowly erode the ideology and a loosely organized counter-idea system emerges. This consists of the critics of the state ideology as well as the analysis of the real affairs of the every day life. Because every deviation from the state ideology is repressed, this counter-idea system is never used in public; therefore its formation is rather slow and develops only in the family or in closed circles of friends. After a time, individuals living in a communist state carry a special double idea system. In the public interactions they use the official ideology, in personal interactions they use the counter-ideas. If the self-organization of the counter-idea system is already well-developed, it is suitable for replacing the official ideology, which is prevented only by the state repression. Dramatic change may occur almost in an instant, as it happened first in Hungary, then recently in other Eastern European countries.

Differences in the democratic transformation among these countries are related to the levels of development of their counter-idea systems, which were the most developed in Hungary because,of the liberalism of the Kádár system and in East Germany because of the influence of West Germany having the same language and the same culture. Emergence of this counter-idea system is also a manifestation of social creativity.

REFERENCES

Alexander, E.O., & Borgia, G. (1976). Group selection, altruism and the levels of organization of life. *Annual Review of Ecology and Systematics, 9*, 499-474.

Allport, G.W. (1961). *Pattern and growth in personality.* New York: Holt, Reinhart & Winston.

Barron, F. (1963). The needs for order and disorder as motives in creative action. In C.W. Taylor & Barron, F. (Eds.), *Scientific creativity: Its recognition and development* (pp. 139-152). New York: Wiley.

Bohm, D. (1980). *Wholeness and the implicate order.* London: Routledge & Kegan Paul.

Brown, R. (1973). *A first language: The early stages.* Cambridge, MA: Harvard University Press.

Bunge, M. (1963). *The myth of simplicity.* Englewood Cliffs, NJ: Prentice-Hall.

Csányi, V. (1980). The general theory of evolution. *Acta Biologica Hungarica Academica Scientific, 31*, 409-434.

Csányi, V. (1982a). *General theory of evolution.* Budapest: Publishing House of the Hungarian Academy of Sciences.

Csányi, V. (1982b). General theory of evolution. *Society of General System Research, 6*, 73-95.

Csányi, V. (1985). Autogenesis: Evolution of self-organizing systems. In J.-P. Aubin, D. Saari, & K. Sigmund (Eds.), *Dynamics of macrosystems: Proceedings, Laxenburg, Austria 1984.* (Lecture Notes in Economics and Mathematical Systems No. 257) (pp. 253-267). Berlin: Springer-Verlag.

Csányi, V. (1987). The replicative evolutionary model of animal and human minds. *World Futures: Journal of General Evolution, 24*(3), 174-214.

Csányi, V. (1988). Contribution of the genetical and neural memory to animal intelligence. In H. Jerison & I. Jerison (Eds.), *Intelligence and evolutionary biology* (pp. 299-318). Berlin: Springer-Verlag.

Csányi, V. (1989a). *Evolutionary systems and society: A general theory.* Durham, NC: Duke University Press.

Csányi, V. (1989b). The replicative model of self-organization: A general theory of evolution. In G.J. Dalenoort (Ed.), *The paradigm of self-organization* (pp. 73-76). Berlin: Springer.

Csányi, V. (1989c). Shift from group to idea cohesion is a major step in cultural evolution. *Futura, 8*(1), 36-42.

Csányi, V. (1989d). Origin of complexity and organizational levels during evolution. In D.B. Wake & G. Roth (Eds.), *Complex organizational functions: Integration and evolution in vertebrates* (pp. 349-360). New York: Wiley.

Csányi, V. (1990). Ethology, power, possession: A system theoretical study of the Hungarian transition. *World Futures: Journal of General Evolution, 29,* 107-122.

Csányi, V. (1991). Social creativity. *World Futures: Journal of General Evolution, 31,* 23-31.

Csányi, V. (1992a). Nature and origin of biological and social information. In K. Haefner (Ed.), *Evolution of information processing systems* (pp. 257-281). Berlin: Springer.

Csányi, V. (1992b). Natural sciences and the evolutionary models. *World Futures, 34,* 15-24.

Csányi, V. (1992c). The brain's models and communication. In T.A. Sebeok & J. Umiker-Sebeok (Eds.), *The semiotic web* (pp. 27-43). Berlin: Moyton de Gruyter.

Csányi, V. (1992d). Ethology and the rise of the conceptual thoughts. In J. Deely (Ed.), *Symbolicity* (pp. 479-484). Lanham, MD: University Press of America.

Csányi, V., & Kampis, Gy. (1985). Autogenesis: Evolution of replicative systems. *Journal of Theoretical Biology, 114,* 303-321.

Csányi, V., & Kampis, Gy. (1987). Modeling society: Dynamical replicative systems. *Cybernetics and Systems, 18,* 233-249.

Csányi, V., & Kampis, Gy. (1988). Can we communicate with aliens? In G. Marx (Ed.), *Bioastronomy—The next steps* (pp. 267-272). Norwell, MA: Kluwer.

Eibl-Eibesfeldt, I. (1982). Warfare, man's indoctrinability and group selection. *Zeitschrift für Tierpsychologie, 60,* 177-198.

Eibl-Eibesfeldt, I. (1989). *Human ethology.* New York: de Gruyter.

Kampis, Gy. (1991). *Self-modifying systems in biology and cognitive sciences: A new framework for dynamics, information and complexity.* Oxford: Pergamon Press.

Kampis, Gy., & Csányi, V. (1988). A system approach to the creating process. *IFSR Newsletter, 20,* 2-4.

Lee, R. (1969). Kung bushmen subsistence: An input-output analysis. In P. Vayda (Ed.), *Environment and cultural behavior* (pp. 47-49). Garden City, NY: Natural History Press.

Lovelock, J.E. (1979). *Gaia: A new look at life on earth.* New York: Oxford University Press.

Montuori, A.A. (1989). *Evolutionary competence: Creating the future.* Amsterdam: J.C. Gieben.

Morris, D. (1982). *The biology of art.* London: Knopf.

Pantzar, M., & Csányi, V. (1991). Replicative model of the evolution of the business organization. *Journal of Social and Biological Structures, 14*(2), 149-163.

Pantzar, M., & Csányi, V. (1992). The replicative model of the evolution of business organization. In K. Haefner (Ed.), *Evolution of information processing systems* (pp. 288-307). Berlin: SPringer.

Spencer, H. (1862). *First principles.*

Sterrer, W. (1992). Prometheus and proteus: The creative, unpredictable individual in evolution. *Evolution and Cognition, 1,* 101-129.

Teleki, G. (1973). *The predatory behavior of wild chimpanzees.* Lewisburg, PA: Bucknell University Press.

_____

12

The "Genius Hypothesis": Exploratory Concepts for a Scientific Understanding of Unusual Creativity

Ervin Laszlo

Do unusual acts of creativity occur in the isolation of a closed-system brain, or is that brain—and the correlated mind and consciousness— effectively interacting with other brain-minds in the creative process?

Social and cultural influences on the minds of creative people are undisputed—no person is a Robinson Crusoe, least of all sensitive individuals such as artists, writers, composers, and others of their kind. The question raised here concerns a more immediate and spontaneous interaction than the standard envisaged sociocultural influences: The possibility that the minds of unusually creative people are in spontaneous, direct, although usually not conscious, interaction with other minds *in the creative process itself.*

Subtle interactions beyond the scope of sensory perception have been suggested for millennia: they are an essential part of both Eastern and Western traditional metaphysics and mysticism. In modern times many forms of ESP have been investigated in the laboratory, producing statistically significant results. "Twin pain" and image transference between emotively closely linked individuals even when physically distant is relatively well established. The transactional and transpersonal schools of psychology acknowledge the reality of spontaneous subtle interactions between the emotive and cognitive processes of individuals. Although there is as yet no definitive explanation of the way ideas or images are transferred without sensory contact, there can be little doubt that such transfers do take place.

A basically similar kind of process could also underlie unusual acts of creativity. The creative product could be the product of an interaction, rather than the fully autonomous output of one individual. It may be that unusual, quasimiraculous forms of creativity need to be traced to a confluence of interconnected creative processes, rather than to one self-contained individual. The "genius hypothesis" of interactive creativity could bring the astounding phenomena of genius closer to scientific understanding.

This chapter first reviews the main strands of evidence relevant to the thesis of interactive creativity, and then sketches a conceptual framework capable of providing a researchable and potentially fruitful explanation of the observed facts.

THE PRINCIPAL STRANDS OF EVIDENCE

Cultural creativity—the collective advance of entire populations through the typical creative activity of their members—is one strand of evidence relevant to interactive creativity. In the cultural creativity of a population, not only members of the same population seem to interact (that would be explicable by information transfer through standard means); members of distant populations also appear to be in some form of contact. The fact is that parallel cultural achievements have occurred among populations that are unlikely to have been in any standard form of communication with one another. For example, the control of fire was an invention that occurred in distant populations more or less at the same time. *Homo erectus* tended fires in various locations, such as Zhoukoudien near Beijing, Aragon in the south of France, and Vértesszöllös in Hungary. These far-flung populations could not even have known of each other's existence, yet they appear to have evolved the art of igniting, tending and transporting fires almost simultaneously.

Early cultures also developed tools of striking similarity. The Acheulian hand axe, for example, was a widespread tool of the Stone Age, and it had a typical almond or tear-shaped design carefully chipped into symmetry on both sides. In Europe the axe was made of flint, in the Middle East of chert, and in Africa of quartzite, shale, or diabase. Its basic form was functional, yet the agreement in the details of its execution in virtually all known cultures cannot be readily explained by the coincidental discovery of utilitarian solutions to shared needs—trial and error is unlikely to have produced such similarity in these distant populations.

Other artifacts, too, seem to have leapt across space and time. Giant pyramids were built in ancient Egypt as well as in pre-Colombian America with remarkable agreement in design. Crafts, such as pottery making, took much the same form in all cultures. Even the technique of making fire brought forth implements of the same basic design in different parts of the world. Although each culture added its own embellishments, Aztecs and Etruscans, Zulus and Malays, and classical Indians and ancient Chinese all fashioned their tools and built their monuments as if following a common basic pattern or *archetype*.

Entire cultures have come to flower at the same time, almost or entirely independently of each other. The great breakthroughs of classical Hebrew, Greek, Chinese, and Indian culture occurred in widely scattered regions, yet they occurred practically simultaneously. The major Hebrew prophets flourished in Palestine between 750 and 500 BC; in India the early Upanishads were composed between 660 and 550 B.C. and Siddharta the Buddha lived from 563 to 487 B.C.; Confucius taught in China around 551-479 B.C.; and Socrates lived in Hellenic Greece from 469 to 399 B.C.

Just when the Hellenic philosophers created the basis of Western civilization in Platonic and Aristotelian philosophy, the Chinese philosophers founded the ideational basis of oriental civilization in the Confucian, Taoist, and Legalist doctrines. And when in the Hellas of the post-Peloponnesian wars period Plato founded his Academy and Aristotle his Lyceum and scores of itinerant sophists preached to and advised kings, tyrants, and citizens, in China the similarly restless and inventive "Shih" founded schools, lectured to crowds, established doctrines, and maneuvered among the scheming princes of the late Warring States Period.

"Synchronicities" such as these are not restricted to classical cultures; they have occurred even in modern science. There are documented cases of insight coming practically simultaneously to different investigators who were not aware of each other's work. The most celebrated of these cases concerns the simultaneous and independent discovery of the calculus by Newton and by Leibniz, the likewise simultaneous and independent elaboration of the fundamental mechanisms of biological evolution by Darwin and by Wallace, and the concurrent invention of the telephone by Bell and by Grey.

Insight and discovery could also leap across different branches of the same culture. When Newton used a prism to break down the shafts of light that entered the windows of his Cambridge lodgings, Vermeer and other Flemish artists were exploring the nature of light entering through colored window- and doorpanes. While Maxwell was formulating his electromagnetic theory, according to which light is produced by the reciprocal revolution of electrical and magnetic waves, Turner was painting light as swirling vortices.

In recent years physicists have been exploring many-dimensional spaces in grand unified theories, and simultaneously, and apparently entirely independently, avant-garde artists experiment with visual superposition on their canvases, representing spaces of as many as seven dimensions.

Space and time, light and gravity, mass and energy have all been explored by physicists and by artists, sometimes at the same time, sometimes one preceding the other, but seldom if ever in conscious knowledge of each other. Shlain (1991) explored these "coincidences" in detail and provided stunning illustrations of the power of artists to mirror, and frequently to anticipate, the conceptual breakthroughs occurring in the minds of physicists without knowing anything about physics and the concerns of its investigators.

Researchers of synchronicity found many instances of such "coincidences" (see Combs & Holland, 1990; Jung, 1973; Peat, 1987). Some are easy to dismiss as illusory; others may be due to chance. However, many defy conventional explanation. The phenomenon itself merited the attention of some outstanding thinkers. Hegel formulated his celebrated concept of *Zeitgeist*, the spirit of an age that infuses the minds of its contemporaries, and Jung advanced the concept of the collective unconscious, the sharing of mythic symbols and archetypes in diverse cultures.

Phenomena of cultural synchronicity may indicate interaction between individuals that transcends the known bounds of sensory perception with its limitations of space and time. It is conceivable that some individual acts of creativity would be influenced by such interaction; that some insights would be due not to a spontaneous and largely unexplained stroke of genius, but to the elaboration of an idea or a pattern in two or more minds in interaction. This would be equivalent to a dialogue in the Platonic sense of the term, where it stands for a process of which the results transcend the abilities of the dialogue partners individually. It recalls Plato's view that the Soul "recollects" the key ideas in the course of an insightful dialogue. We would only need to substitute "collection" for "recollection": According to the thesis of interactive creativity, in the course of the creative process persons *collect* (from other creative persons) some elements of their creativity.

Independent evidence suggests that genuine acts of creativity are often based on what the Germans call an *"Einfall"* (meaning a sudden and spontaneous intuition leading to a conceptual or esthetic breakthrough). Individuals of genius, known for repeated *Einfälle*, are regarded as having been born with rare and mysterious gifts: a Mozart, a Michelangelo, or a Shakespeare, to name but a few. This view is reinforced by the phenomenon of child prodigies—children who manifest astonishing capabilities in specific fields, most often in music and mathematics. To call such individuals "gifted" and their achievements "works of genius" is not to explain their abilities but just to label them. How did they come by their unusual accomplishments? Are they the possessors of a fortunate combination of genetic information, or did they receive their gifts from a higher source?

Better explanations than these are possible. We should note first of all that some of the most remarkable *Einfälle* occur in altered states of consciousness. Few artists compose music and poetry or paint and sculpt in an ordinary commonsense frame of mind. There is almost always some element of transport to another plane of consciousness, a deep concentration that approaches a state of trance. In some (relatively rare) cases "these inspired states" are artificially induced—by drugs, music, self-hypnosis or other means. Mostly, however, they come spontaneously to the "gifted" individual. Coleridge composed his celebrated epic poem *Kubla Khan* while lying in what he described as a profound sleep (which was, in fact, induced by laudanum, an opium-based substance he took as medicine); Milton created his *Paradise Lost* as an "unpremeditated song" dictated, he said, by the Muse. Mozart claimed that his compositions came to him during nights when he could not sleep. They came completely, from where he could not fathom. He did not hear the parts one after another, but the whole piece at once. "What a delight this is," he wrote, "I cannot tell. All this inventing, this producing, takes place in a pleasing lively dream" (Owen, 1988).

In the sciences, too, altered states are frequent in processes of innovation and discovery. Although scientific discoveries are paradigms of reason and logic, many of them owe their existence to an unusual states of consciousness in their authors. This is true of mathematical discoveries as well. Evariste Galois, for example, committed to paper his fundamental contributions to higher algebra at the age of 20 in 3 feverish days before meeting an adversary in a duel that he expected to be fatal—and that turned out to be precisely that. Karl Friedrich Gauss sought to discover the proof for the way every number can be represented as the product of primes and, although he made many tries, did not succeed for years. After many failures he could at last write in his diary that he had succeeded but not on account of his painful efforts. Like a sudden flash of lightning, the riddle happened to be solved. Henri Poincaré said with good reason that the elements of a mathematical discovery are harmoniously disposed so that the mind without effort can embrace their totality—divining hidden harmonies and relations.

Exceptional achievements can be given a rational explanation: We can follow up the lead of unusual creativity in altered states. Consider, then, the paradigmatic creative act. A person with a high level of motivation and great powers of concentration focuses on a given task or problem. Another person, likewise highly motivated and concentrated, focuses on the same or a closely similar task. In these conditions the similarity of the states of brain and mind in these individuals allows some level of access to each other's emotive and cognitive processes. This permits a subtle dialogue that can have remarkably creative consequences.

The aforementioned is more than simple conjecture: Significant evidence is now available in support of spontaneous brain-to-brain interactions. Experiments in Italy with the so-called "brain holo-tester" (a computerized electroencephalograph [EEG] device capable of ongoing measurement of the level of synchronization between the left and the right cerebral hemispheres) show that in deep meditation the synchronization of the two hemispheres increases dramatically. More than that, experiments with *two* test subjects measured simultaneously indicate that in deep meditative states the subjects' brain-waves become doubly synchronized: left-right, as well as person-person. As person-person synchronization occurs in the absence of sensory communication, it furnishes evidence that in altered states persons who meditate together influence each other's cerebral processes. Indeed, the transference of images and fantasies among meditating persons is a frequent occurrence. On occasion, the meditators are capable of interacting with each other's fantasies. Space and time seem to make little difference in these phenomena.

A related phenomenon came to light in recent investigations of so-called *telesomatic effects*. Here, one person creates effects on another's body similar to the effects one's own mind would create. Traditionally, telesomatic effects were produced by specially gifted natural healers, who would "send" what they claimed to be subtle forms of energy to their

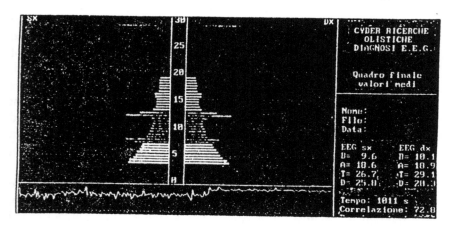

Figure 12.1A. EEG waves of the left and right hemispheres in light meditation (correlation: 78.2%)

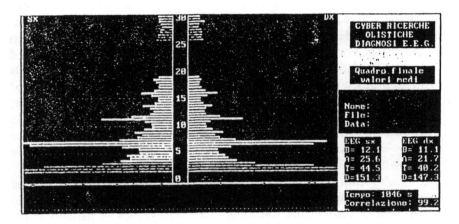

Figure 12.1B. EEG waves of the left and right hemispheres in deep meditation (correlation: 99.2%)

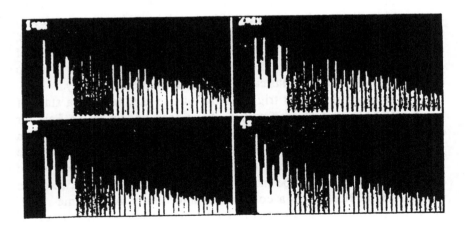

Figure 12.1C. EEG waves of the left and right hemispheres of a woman (top) and a man (bottom) in deep meditation. The four patterns are quasi-identical. From *Cyber*, Milan, No. 40, November 1992.

patients. (The negative variety of telesomatic events came under the heading of voodoo or black magic; they were common in the practice of shamans and witch doctors.) Being largely anecdotal, telesomatic events were of interest mainly to anthropologists; they were dismissed by the scientific and medical community. Now, however, such events have been investigated in controlled experiments where either a sufficient number of trials or a sufficient number of test subjects permit a quantitative evaluation of the results. For example, William Braud and Marilyn Schlitz of the Mind Science Foundation in San Antonio, Texas, carried out hundreds of trials with rigorous controls regarding the impact of the mental imagery of "senders" on the physiology of "receivers". The latter were both distant, and unaware that such imagery was being directed to them. They claim to have established that the mental images of a person can reach another person—effects comparable to those one's own mental processes cause in one's own body (Dossey, 1993).

Another variety of telesomatic experiment makes use of intercessory prayer to achieve telesomatic effects. Following the pioneering experiment of cardiologist Randolph Byrd with groups of patients at the coronary care unit of San Francisco General Hospital, numerous experiments have been made with the healing effect of prayer. Daniel Benor of the Doctor-Healer Network in England undertook a detailed survey of 131 such experiments and found that 56 of the experiments had a probability value (p) of less than .01, and a further 21 had probability values between .02 and .05. Benor also found that of the 155 controlled studies of healing published until 1993—involving subjects as varied as enzymes, yeasts, bacteria, red and white blood cells, cancer cells, plants, and mice as well as humans—67 (or 43%) have had probability values of less than .01, and another 23 (15%) probability values in the range of .02 to .05 (Benor, 1993). Such results cannot be due to simple serendipity.

Telesomatic events triggered by intense meditation—a state of mind not unlike that of deep prayer—have been known in the East for centuries. In 1974 the Maharishi Mahesh Yogi suggested that if but 1% of a population were to meditate regularly, the remaining 99% would also be affected. Subsequent statistical studies showed that this can indeed be the case. There turned out to be more than random correlation between the number of meditators in a community and community crime rates, incidence of traffic fatalities, deaths due to alcoholism, and even levels of pollution (Aron & Aron, 1986).

The evidence regarding a spontaneous transmission of effects between the mind of different individuals, and between the mind of one individual and the body of another, show that separate and possibly distant individuals can affect each other in the absence of information through the sense organs. The synchronization of EEG patterns in noncommunicating test subjects speak to this point.

The same basic kind of mind-mind communication with correlated brain-brain synchronization could underlie acts of unusual creativity as well. As different persons bent on a related creative task enter a state of deep concentration, their brain states are likely to become highly synchronized whether or not they are physically on the same location, and whether they even know of each other. These finely tuned cerebral processes could permit some level and form of interaction. The latter could occur in the absence of any conscious awareness of it. In fact, the absence of conscious awareness is likely to facilitate the interaction. Normal waking consciousness is known to suppress unusual contents of consciousness: It is dominated by the linear logic of the left cerebral hemisphere. The altered state of intense concentration (or meditation) is relatively free of such constraints. It can allow subtle inputs—*Einfälle*—to fertilize and inspire one's creative endeavors.

THE FUNCTIONAL ANALOGY OF NETWORKED COMPUTERS

The aforementioned variety of process, required in a coherent explanation of acts of unusual creativity, can be illustrated with our experience with networked computers. Modern business and professional computing systems, unlike their self-contained predecessors, often consist of distributed work stations linked to each other by internal nets, and linked to data banks, e-mail systems, and a variety of electronic networks by external switched connections. Consequently, the information processed at the typical work station is not limited to operations on its keyboard. An operator can input information both locally, on the work station itself, and through its external linkups. Unless one knows the program or procedure by which an item was created or called up, one would not know whether it was locally produced or downloaded from a potentially distant mainframe.

Information from local and distant sources can be combined and subjected to programmed processing. Doing so furnishes a functional analogy for the kind of local-long-distance information processing that is likely to take place in unusual acts of creativity. The sudden and spontaneous *Einfall* that is often the crucial element in such creativity may originate outside the brain and mind of the creative subject. He or she may receive a vague notion, a contour illuminated in a sudden flash of insight, just sufficient to start off his or her imagination and feed his or her creativity. In addition, creativity could be guided by a sustained though subconscious "dialogue" during which the subject explores first one avenue then another, assisted by flashes of intuition that are often mistaken for guidance by a higher intelligence. (This kind of process occurs also in scientific explorations: The present writer has been fortunate to experience it on a few privileged occasions.)

Interactive creativity is not to be conceived as a dialogue between two similarly bent minds; the thought processes of many individuals may be involved in the process. This, too, can be illustrated with the analogy of networked computers. We need merely to consider what in computer jargon is known as the *bulletin board*.

The electronic bulletin board is a file in a mainframe computer that is accessible not just to one user but to all users who subscribe to it. Programs can be created that allow all subscribers both to read information *into* the board, and to read *out* from the board what other subscribers have inputted. Items are sometimes elaborated by many subscribers together, and those who read out the results receive the final product, without indication as to which part has been contributed by which person. This is a good functional analogue of the kind of information that obtains when not a specific concept or notion "falls in" (becomes the *Einfall*), but a residue or amalgam resulting from the creative acts of many individuals. At the most fundamental level, this kind of *Einfall* amounts to what Jung called *archetypal experience*. Here the collective unconscious (said by Jung, 1962, to be "the psychic expression of the identity of brain structure irrespective of all racial differences") functions as a species-wide bulletin board.

THE PSI-FIELD

The analogy of networked computers cannot be stretched beyond its capacities; it is, and remains, an analogy. In the real world not switched connections and electronic bulletin boards but natural factors ensure person-to-person interconnections, including the synchronization of cerebral processes. Such connections exist not only in the domain of brain and mind, but in a variety of fields of investigation.

In the world of quantum physics, for example, particles exhibit a feature known as *nonlocality*: One particle can interact with an identical particle across space and time (this occurs in the so-called EPR experiment). Particles can also interfere with successively emitted particles as if they were waves—and as if they were still there (in double-slit and in split-beam experiments). In addition, particles seem to be "informed" of each other's quantum state in the electron shells that surround atomic nuclei (in accordance with Pauli's *exclusion principle*), even though they are not connected by any dynamical force.

In the living world, genetic mutations prove to be complexly adapted to changing environments and appear in some way "in-formed" by the milieu, even though the genotype is isolated from the vicissitudes that beset the phenotype. In the world of mind and consciousness, information, as already noted, proves to be transmittable beyond the range of sensory perception, as shown by statistically significant findings in controlled experiments in remote viewing and other forms of thought and image transfer.

This writer has investigated a variety of such findings and come to the conclusion that they have a common thrust: they suggest that phenomena in the natural world are more intimately linked than science has traditionally allowed. A connecting factor appears to be present in all domains of investigation, the physical, the biological as well as the psychological. Indeed, in the absence of such "close connections" we could not expect anything more interesting to have come about in the physical universe than hydrogen and helium; the presence of complex systems such as those required for life would have to be ascribed to an unfathomable stroke of luck—or the will of an omnipotent creator. Likewise, the evolution of biological systems would require explanation in terms of mysterious "building plans" or other metaphysical factors instead of bona fide scientific concepts rooted in the observable characteristics of nature. And many of the most remarkable phenomena of mind and consciousness would have to be relegated to extrascientific domains such as mysticism and parapsychology, or dismissed as simple superstition (Laszlo, 1993, 1996).

In view of these considerations, this writer outlined a concept of the empirically knowable universe of which the principal features may be summarized as follows:

1. The cosmos creates itself in the interaction of basic energy fields. Its "unified interactive dynamics" involves four energy-transmitting and transforming fields (the gravitational, electromagnetic, and the strong and the weak nuclear force fields), and an information-conserving field associated with the so-called quantum vacuum (the "psi-field").

2. The effects of the energy-transmitting and transforming fields are determined by the global strength and local intensity of the fields and vary with distance in space and time. The effects of the information-conserving psi-field depend not on field intensity, but on conserved form. These effects do not diminish in time, and are transmitted quasi-instantaneously in matter-energy dense regions of space. In consequence

they are beyond space and time, both as ordinarily conceived and as they appear in relativity theory.

3. The waveforms conserved in and transmitted by the psi-field are imprints of quanta and supra-quantal matter-energy systems. More precisely, they are Fourier transforms of the 3n-dimensional configuration spaces of quanta, and of macrolevel systems of quanta. In the inverse Fourier transform, the waveforms of the field "in-form" quanta and quantal systems in corresponding configuration spaces. These "psi-effects" are manifest as nonrandom alterations in dynamically underdetermined or nondetermined states. Thus while the energy-transmitting and transforming fields produce dynamic effects on quantal particles and supra-quantal configurations of particles (i.e., on matter-energy systems), the effects of the information-conserving psi-field are nondynamic modifications of otherwise equiprobable trajectories of motion and evolution in such systems (Laszlo, 1995, 1996).

The aforementioned can account for the connections experienced in the sphere of mind and consciousness. Brains (and correlated minds) can interact also through the psi-field. The information transmitted through that field may constitute a nonnegligible component of the flow of information to the cerebral networks. In ordinary waking consciousness the left-hemispheric logic of modern individuals suppresses such commonsensically anomalous information. In altered states, however, psi-field transmitted items can penetrate to consciousness. This may issue in such paranormal phenomena as telepathy and clairvoyance. More importantly for our purposes, it may also issue in the *Einfall* that catalyzes unusual acts of creativity.

The idea of an interconnecting field has been anticipated in the intellectual tradition Aldous Huxley called *Perennial Philosophy*. It also crops up in modern times. The idea expressed by Carl Jung in one of his last letters is particularly pertinent. "We may have to give up thinking in terms of space and time when we deal with the reality of archetypes," Jung wrote in 1961. "It could be that the psyche is an unextended intensity, not a body moving in time. . . . In itself, the psyche would have no dimension in space and time at all" (von Franz, 1992, p. 161). We can, of course, say the same of the psi-field, although this fields claims the status of being a basic element of physical reality.

Spontaneous interconnections among human brain minds are not exceptional processes. They are instances of the close connections that link phenomena in all domains of investigation. The presence of such interconnections in the domain of mind and brain means that human beings are not isolated information-processing systems. They are open to the world not only through the bodily sense organs, but by being embedded in a universal form-conserving and transmitting field. The investigation of the specific properties of this field is one of the great challenges awaiting the contemporary natural sciences. Its sustained pursuit would link the timeless intuitions of Perennial Philosophy with empirically researched and scientifically understood phenomena. It could also conduce to a better understanding of the nature of unusual acts of creativity. These acts may involve a subtle and subconscious, yet entirely crucial, dialogue between two (or perhaps a large number of) intensely focused creative individuals.

REFERENCES

Aron, E., & Aron, A. (1986). *The Maharishi effect: A revolution through meditation*. Walpole, NH: Stillpoint.

Benor, D. (1993). *Healing research: Holistic energy medicine and spiritual healing*. Munich: Helix Verlag.

Combs, A., & Holland, M. (1990). *Synchronicity: Science, myth, and the trickster*. New York: Paragon House.

Dossey, L. (1993). *Healing words: The power of prayer and the practice of medicine*. San Francisco: Harper San Francisco.

Jung, C. G. (1962). Commentary on the secret of the golden flower. In. R. Wilhelm (Ed.), *The secret of the golden flower.* New York: Harcourt, Brace, & World.

Jung, C. G. (1973). *Synchronicity: An acausal connecting principle* (Collected Works, Vol. 8). Princeton, NJ: Princeton University Press.

Laszlo, E. (1993). *The creative cosmos: A unified science of matter, life, and mind.* Edinburgh: Floris Books.

Laszlo, E. (1995). *The interconnected universe*. Singapore and London: World Scientific.

Laszlo, E. (1996). *The whispering pond*. Shattesbury and Rockport: Element Books.

Owen, R. (1988). *Qualitative research: The early years*. Salem, OR: Grayhaven Books.

Peat, F. D. (1987). *Synchronicity: The bridge between matter and mind.* New York: Bantam.

Shlain, L. (1991). *Art and physics: Parallel visions in space, time, and light*. New York: W. W. Morrow.

von Franz, M.-L. (1992). *Psyche and matter*. Boston: Shambhala.

Author Index

Subject Index